EXPERIMENTAL ANALYSIS OF BEHAVIOR

PART 2

Techniques in the Behavioral and Neural Sciences

Volume 6

Series Editor

JOSEPH P. HUSTON

Düsseldorf

ELSEVIER

AMSTERDAM · LONDON · NEW YORK · TOKYO

Experimental Analysis of Behavior

Part 2

Editors

IVER H. IVERSEN

University of North Florida, Jacksonville, FL, U.S.A.

and

KENNON A. LATTAL

West Virginia University, Morgantown, WV, U.S.A.

1991

ELSEVIER

AMSTERDAM · LONDON · NEW YORK · TOKYO

ISBN Volume (Part 1): 0-444-81251-2 (Hardback)   ISBN Set: 0-444-89319-9 (Hardback)
       (Part 2): 0-444-89194-3 (Hardback)   0-444-89320-2 (Paperback)
ISBN Volume (Part 1): 0-444-89160-9 (Paperback) ISSN Series: 0921-0709
       (Part 2): 0-444-89195-1 (Paperback)

This book is printed on acid-free paper

Published by:
Elsevier Science Publishers B.V.
P.O. Box 211
1000 AE Amsterdam
The Netherlands

Sole distributors for the U.S.A. and Canada:
Elsevier Science Publishing Co., Inc.
655 Avenue of the Americas,
New York, NY 10010
U.S.A.

Library of Congress Cataloging in Publication Data

Experimental analysis of behavior / editors, Iver H. Iversen and
  Kennon A. Lattal.
     p. cm. -- (Techniques in the behavioral and neural sciences ;
  v. 6)
    Includes bibliographical references.
    ISBN 0-444-81251-2
    1. Animal psychology. 2. Operant conditioning. 3. Conditioned
  response. 4. Psychology, Experimental. 5. Psychology, Comparative
  6. Psychology. I. Iversen, Iver H., 1948- . II. Lattal,
  Kennon A. III. Series.
    [DNLM: 1. Behavior. 2. Behaviorism. 3. Psychology, Experimental.
  W1 TE197D v. 6 / BF 199 E96]
  QL785.E97   1991
  156--dc20
  DNLM/DLC
  for Library of Congress   91-13086
                                            CIP

Printed in The Netherlands

Dedicated to B.F. Skinner
1904–1990

Preface

The Experimental Analysis of Behavior is a science initiated by B.F. Skinner that studies the behavior of individual organisms under laboratory conditions. A considerable arsenal of control techniques has been developed that enable experimenters to produce a given behavior in an experimental subject and bring it under the control of experimental conditions. For example, behavior is made to operate upon the environment by arranging for a rat to press a lever to produce a small pellet of food. Once established, such operant behavior will conform to experimental conditions and occur reliably in the same pattern day after day. The Experimental Analysis of Behavior is more than a collection of particular types of apparatus and stimuli for precise specification of behavior and environment. Identification of variables that control behavior and development of methods whereby data are analyzed and interpreted also constitute an important part of behavior science. The Experimental Analysis of Behavior is therefore collectively defined as a set of tools to provide specific definitions of responses and stimuli, identification of controlling variables, and methods of analyzing and interpreting results. Behavior is considered lawful in the sense that there are determinants of behavior to be found operating in the subject's environment. In addition, the lawful relations between behavior and the controlling variables, that can be discovered in the laboratory, also can be exploited in non-laboratory environments. Of late, the Experimental Analysis of Behavior has been blending more and more with other areas of the neurosciences, providing basic control and analysis techniques that are useful for various applications of operant conditioning methodology.

This volume is designed to describe representative, effective research techniques in the Experimental Analysis of Behavior. We have selected the most important techniques both for their utility in behavior analysis and for their potential value in expanding the use of behavior analysis methods in the neurosciences. The techniques described in the volume have been derived solely from the study of nonhuman animals. Within the Experimental Analysis of Behavior several important texts have provided theoretical and conceptual discussions. Examples of such books include Honig (1966), Honig and Staddon (1977), Thompson and Zeiler (1986), the series edited by Zeiler and Harzem (e.g., Zeiler and Harzem, 1979), and the series on quantitative analysis edited by Commons and associates (e.g., Commons et al., 1987). To complement these influential texts, the present volume focuses on the practical implementation of the particular procedures and methods of the Experimental Analysis of Behavior in laboratory situations. The volume has only a minimal emphasis on theoretical analyses and is intended as a sourcebook for the practical use of the Experimental Analysis of Behavior.

A complete survey of behavior control techniques cannot possibly be covered in a single volume. The present volume reflects the Experimental Analysis of Behavior as an area, and we have not attempted any unification of its techniques. Chapter topics were selected to present a broad collection of methods. Individual authors have provided expertise regarding techniques based on their particular laboratory experiences. Several relevant general topics of behavior analysis, such as classical conditioning, autoshaping, psychophysics, and adjunctive behavior, are not covered in this volume because they warrant separate detailed coverage.

The methods and procedures of the Experimental Analysis of Behavior have become both detailed and numerous. As a practical consequence thereof the present volume had to be divided into two parts. However, in the preparation of the volume we have emphasized a considerable integration of the different areas covered. The material in Part 1 is thus further extended and elaborated upon in Part 2, and the material in Part 2 presumes knowledge of the basic procedures and methods covered in Part 1. Neither Part 1 nor 2 alone provides sufficient coverage of the Experimental Analysis of Behavior in its current stage of development. We hope that the two parts together will provide the reader with a comprehensive and informative source of the techniques and practices of the Experimental Analysis of Behavior of a science. General descriptions of subjects and their care are provided in Part 1: Chapter 1. Automated recording and equipment control techniques are covered in Part 1: Chapter 1, and specifically for computers in Part 2: Chapter 5. Basic behavior control methods for scheduling of reinforcing and aversive events are described in Part 1: Chapters 2, 3, 4 and 5. Specific procedures related to choice are described in Part 1: Chapter 6, and choice procedures extended to situations involving foraging are presented in Part 2: Chapter 4. Methods of general stimulus control and conditional stimulus control are presented in Part 1: Chapters 7 and 8, respectively. Time as a controlling stimulus is given special coverage in Part 2: Chapter 1. Applications of the techniques of the Experimental Analysis of Behavior to the areas of Behavioral Pharmacology and Behavioral Neurochemistry are described in Part 2: Chapters 2 and 3, respectively. Methods of description, presentation, and interpretation of behavioral data are presented in Part 2: Chapters 6 and 7, with Chapter 7 providing an introduction to basic methods of mathematical description of operant behavior. Part 2 contains an extensive glossary of common terms in the Experimental Analysis of Behavior. Finally, because the volume specifically is directed at research involving nonhuman animals, the official Guidelines for Ethical Conduct in the Care and Use of Animals, from the American Psychological Association, is provided as an Appendix in both Parts of the volume.

We would like to thank the following for having reviewed chapters for the volume: J.L. Arbuckle, N.A. Ator, M.N. Branch, I.S. Burgess, T.S. Critchfield, S.I. Dworkin, D.A. Eckerman, M. Galizio, W.W. Henton, P.N. Hineline, W.K. Honig, P.R. Killeen, L. Lamontagne, S.E.G. Lea, R.L. Mellgren, E.B. Nielsen, W.L. Palya, A.S. Rao, S. Schneider, C.P. Shimp, and J.H. Wearden. In addition, we would like to especially thank Sandra Wood for editorial assistance and Ann Davis for secretarial assistance.

Iver H. Iversen
Jacksonville

Kennon A. Lattal
Morgantown

References

Commons, M.L., Mazur, J.E., Nevin, J.A. and Rachlin, H. (Eds.) (1987) Quantitative Analysis of Behavior, Vol. 5, The Effect of Delay and of Intervening Events on Reinforcement Value. Erlbaum, Hillsdale, N.J.

Honig, W.K. (Ed.) (1966) Operant Behavior: Areas of Research and Application. Appleton-Century-Crofts, New York.

Honig, W.K. and Staddon, J.E.R. (Eds.) (1977) Handbook of Operant Behavior. Prentice-Hall, Englewood Cliffs, NJ.

Thompson, T. and Zeiler, M.D. (Eds.) (1986) Analysis and Integration of Behavioral Units. Erlbaum, Hillsdale, NJ.

Zeiler, M.D. and Harzem, P. (Eds.) (1979) Reinforcement and the Organization of Behaviour. Wiley & Sons, New York.

Foreword

MURRAY SIDMAN

*New England Center for Autism, 33 Turnpike Road,
Southborough, Massachusetts 01772, U.S.A.*

It was in Keller and Schoenfeld's pioneering introductory Psychology lab at Columbia that I first comprehended the feasibility of an experimental analysis of behavior. Still an undergraduate, I had taken introductory lab courses in Physics, Biology, inorganic and organic Chemistry, and Mineralogy, and I was already disillusioned. Except for Mineralogy, in which we did not really do experiments anyway, the laboratory exercises rarely came out the way we had been led to anticipate. Lab sessions were unsuccessful, uninformative, and dull.

And then, in the behavior lab, lo and behold – the experiments worked. Our rat (each pair of students had one) did for us exactly what its cousins had done for B.F. Skinner ten years before. I had failed in the other labs to observe relations that everyone knew existed between physical variables and other events in the external or internal environments, events which nobody doubted were nevertheless strictly determined. Now I was confronted with a living animal, whose behavior was the subject matter of no deterministic science I had ever heard of, who nevertheless was acting in a thoroughly predictable manner when exposed to specified environmental contingencies.

I needed no long waiting periods before data could be calculated and transformed, no 'fudge factors' to cancel out the effects of uncontrolled variables, and no statistics to tease out significant differences. I could see the animal, I could see its behavior, I could observe the behavioral changes while they were happening, and I could often shift the animal's behavior back and forth almost instantaneously just by making small changes in its environment. Here, finally, was the excitement that involvement in science was supposed to generate.

Nearly 45 years later, I still search for, and continue to find lawfulness in the behavior of individuals. New kinds of orderliness continue to emerge in behavior of ever greater complexity, in subjects with more and more extensive behavioral histories, and in environments which control behavior in important ways that we understand much better than we used to. What has come to be called the Experimental Analysis of Behavior remains viable and vibrant. Its solidity and fruitfulness are evident throughout the chapters of this book.

Research methods must, of course, be appropriate to the questions one is asking, and as we ask new questions, we will need new methodological and technical approaches. In Behavior Analysis, formidable methodological issues still remain to be resolved before we will be able to make substantial progress toward the solution of some important behavioral puzzles. The reader will find many such issues discussed in the chapters of this volume. And yet, despite such problems – which are inevitable in any science – the methodology of Behavior Analysis does possess certain features that give it a unique flavor, features that are responsible for much of its progress and underlie the enthusiasm of its investigators and practitioners. Many of those characteristics, too, are shared with other sciences.

For example, the Experimental Analysis of Behavior largely eschews the statistical evaluation of differences between groups of subjects. Instead, it favors direct experimental control over the behavior of individual subjects. Most experimentation in Psychology, and much of today's medical research, first sets up control groups that are not exposed to the experimental variable. The investigator then determines whether other groups that have been exposed to the variable of interest differ significantly – statistically speaking – from the control group. Statistical manipulation is supposed to cancel out the effects of uncontrolled variables.

In contrast, before investigating the effects of a variable, the behavior analyst is likely first to establish a stable behavioral baseline in an individual subject. Then, the effects of the variable being studied will be evaluated by observing whether and by how much the variable causes the individual's behavior to depart from its baseline. The generality of the observed relation between variable and behavior is evaluated not by statistics but by replication – with the same subject, with different subjects, and with the same or different subjects under different experimental conditions. This is control in its best scientific sense; it permits behavior analysts not just to observe differences in central tendency between heterogeneous groups, but to identify the variables and processes which underlie those differences.

In Psychology, except for investigations of the senses in Psychophysics, neither experimental control nor the study of individual subjects has ever been the classical approach. The discovery of controllable behavioral baselines of ever increasing complexity has been a continuing feature of Behavior Analysis, and has enabled behavior analysts to encroach on turf claimed traditionally by various psychological specialties. Behavior analysts have contributed substantially to more different research areas than have investigators in any other behavioral discipline. In other areas in which individual behavior is a datum of interest either as a dependent or independent variable – Pharmacology, Physiology, Neurology, Genetics, Endocrinology, Immunology,

Ecology and others – investigators will find the methods and procedures described in this volume to be sources of potentially fruitful application and collaboration of which they may have been unaware.

An exciting consequence of these extensions of behavior analytic interest into other fields is the emerging recognition that the relations can go in both directions; behavioral variables can influence processes that define the subject matter of those fields. For example, differential reinforcement can sharpen sensory thresholds; reinforcement schedules can modulate drug effects; immunologic reactions can be behaviorally conditioned; programmed instruction can ameliorate genetic and developmental deficiencies; coercive control can stimulate endocrine activity; behavioral units can mediate the evolutionary development both of species and societies. Thus, Behavior Analysis has not only developed its own body of data, principles, and investigative procedures, but has made itself available to other disciplines that want to use behavior as a tool for investigating their own subject matters.

Much of the unique flavor of Behavior Analysis comes from its very definition of behavior. Behavior is not simply what an individual does. It is defined, rather, as a relation between an individual's actions and events in the environment – events subsequent to, concurrent with, and prior to the actions themselves. Thus, the basic units of Behavior Analysis include both acts and their environment. In analyzing behavior, an individual's actions are defined by their consequences, and the environment, in turn, is relevant insofar as it exerts some influence on the individual's actions.

It is the inclusion of the environment in the definition of behavior that has led behavior analysts to investigate stimulus control, the development and maintenance of relational structures in which conduct and the environment are tied together into analytical units. This view of the environment as a necessary element in the definition of behavioral units has stimulated behavior analytic interest in many related fields: for example, Psychophysics, in which controlling properties of the environment are related to the sensory apparatus; Pharmacology, in which defining stimuli arise from chemical and other processes within the internal environment; Neurology and Neurochemistry, in which the central nervous system mediates relations between action and environment; and Cognition, in which knowledge is itself defined as behavioral units that are under the control of relations among environmental elements.

Experimenting with behavior for its own sake, or because one wants to use behavior to measure events in other systems or as a marker to make the presence of hidden events and processes visible, is not easy. Readers unfamiliar with Behavior Analysis can learn much about behavior analytic techniques from this volume. There is, in addition, laboratory lore, which one gains by experience or through collaboration with experienced investigators. For example, every species of subject is characterized by its own set of parameters. And so, although the principle of reinforcement will always be found applicable, the particular reinforcers that will be effective, the kinds of deprivation that will be required, the most efficient amount of reinforcement etc. have to be determined empirically for each species. Every laboratory has to work out a myriad of technical considerations about the experimental space in which the subject's behavior is to be observed, the kinds of behavior to be observed, the techniques and units of measurement, the timing and frequency of experimental observations, the frequency and schedule of reinforcement, and many other details.

But Behavior Analysis is not just a set of techniques and procedures. It is also a set of data and a body of principles derived from the data. As in any experimental science, techniques are not only sharpened by practice but are guided by the general principles of the science. To seek technical proficiency, unaccompanied by a knowledge of the theory and data that have shaped the development of the techniques, is to impose a severe limitation on the possible extensions of one's research.

Behavior is controlled by its consequences; the environment controls relations between behavior and its consequences; the resultant three-term contingencies, of the form 'environment-behavior-consequence', are in turn controlled by higher-order relations among environmental elements. How to characterize these relations, how to measure them, and how to account for their development constitute the domain of the Experimental Analysis of Behavior. The principles of control by reinforcement, and of simple though complex stimulus control, provide a rational background for the development of experimental procedures.

It is important, therefore, that applications of the technology of behavioral analysis go hand in hand with basic Behavior Analysis. The science describes not only techniques but how one goes about studying behavior by using those techniques. Behavior Analysis can be viewed as Psychiatry's and Psychology's basic science, and as a full partner in collaborations with other disciplines. When Behavior Analysis comes – as it must – to be taught as such in the medical curriculum, and as a prerequisite for the doctorate in Psychology, researchers in allied areas, rather than needing this volume, will contribute to its successors.

Yet, although both the experimental and applied sciences of Behavior Analysis have grown and flourished, they remain unknown to many who would find their methods and principles useful, and who could share in the excitement that the kinds of experimentation which characterize the field generate. This volume is therefore timely. With the help of a distinguished group of scientists whose work encompasses most of the current lines of research in the Experimental Analysis of Behavior, Professors Iversen and Lattal have put together an informative and practical volume about its methodology. Its chapters show many examples of the approach, illustrating its successes, its ramifications, and the special kinds of problems it encounters.

More is involved here than just a philosophy of method. The empirical reality is paramount. The very ability of the behavior analyst to create baselines of ongoing behavior in an individual subject is itself a meaningful datum. The existence of techniques for creating whatever behavior one needs to investigate a problem testifies to the power of the analytic method. One might characterize the method as behavioral analysis via behavioral synthesis. By building behavior ourselves, we learn how Nature builds it.

List of Contributors

PART 2

Dr. Marc N. Branch — Department of Psychology, University of Florida, Gainesville, FL 32611, U.S.A.

Dr. James E. Barrett — Department of Psychiatry, Uniformed Services University of the Health Sciences, 4301 Jones Bridge Road, Bethesda, MD 20814, U.S.A.

Dr. A. Charles Catania — Department of Psychology, University of Maryland-Baltimore County, 5401 Wilkens Avenue, Baltimore, MD 21228, U.S.A.

Dr. Edmund Fantino — Psychology Department C-009, University of California, San Diego, La Jolla, CA 92093-0109, U.S.A.

Dr. Lewis R. Gollub — Department of Psychology, University of Maryland at College Park, College Park, MD 20742, U.S.A.

Dr. Iver H. Iversen — Department of Psychology, University of North Florida, Jacksonville, FL 32216, U.S.A.

Dr. Richard L. Shull — Department of Psychology, University of North Carolina-Greensboro, Greensboro, NC 27412, U.S.A.

Dr. Murray Sidman — New England Center for Autism, 33 Turnpike Road, Southborough, MA 01772, U.S.A.

PART 1

Dr. Nancy Almand Ator — Department of Psychiatry and Behavioral Sciences, Division of Behavioral Biology, The Johns Hopkins University School of Medicine, Baltimore, MD 21205, U.S.A.

Dr. Alan Baron	Department of Psychology, University of Wisconsin in Milwaukee, Milwaukee, WI 53201, U.S.A.
Dr. A. Charles Catania	Department of Psychology, University of Maryland-Baltimore County, 5401 Wilkens Avenue, Baltimore, MD 21228, U.S.A.
Dr. Suzanne Gleeson	Department of Psychiatry, Uniformed Services University of the Health Sciences, 4301 Jones Bridge Road, Bethesda, MD 20814, U.S.A.
Dr. J.M. Harrison	Department of Psychology, Boston University, 64 Cunningham Street, Boston, MA 02215, U.S.A.
Dr. Kennon A. Lattal	Department of Psychology, West Virginia University, Morgantown, WV 26506-6040, U.S.A.
Dr. Harry A. Mackay	E.K. Shriver Center, 200 Trapelo Road, Waltham, MA 02254, U.S.A.
Dr. James E. Mazur	Psychology Department, Southern Connecticut State University, New Haven, CT 06515, U.S.A.
Dr. Michael Perone	Department of Psychology, West Virginia University, Morgantown, WV 26506-6040, U.S.A.
Dr. Murray Sidman	New England Center for Autism, 33 Turnpike Road, Southborough, MA 01772, U.S.A.

Contents

PART 2

Chapter 5   Lewis R. Gollub: The use of computers in the control and recording of behavior **155**

PART 1

Experimental analysis of behavior, Part 2
Iversen and Lattal (eds.)
© *1991, Elsevier Science Publishers BV*

CHAPTER 1

Time as a variable in behavior analysis

A. CHARLES CATANIA

Department of Psychology, University of Maryland-Baltimore County, Baltimore, MD 21228, U.S.A.

1. Introduction

Behavior takes place in time and has temporal dimensions. As an independent variable, time is an essential property of the environments within which behavior occurs. As a dependent variable, it includes not only response durations but also, and probably more significantly, the distribution of responses in time. This subject matter is represented by a daunting literature ranging from primarily empirical contributions to strictly theoretical integrations (e.g., Ferster and Skinner, 1957; Schoenfeld, 1970; Richelle and Lejeune, 1980; Gibbon and Allen, 1984; Church, 1988). The present account is necessarily highly selective, illustrating some methodological and substantive concerns by focusing on only a few experimental examples.

2. Multiple causation in temporal control

The first and most crucial issue is that of distinguishing the multiple and often confounded ways in which temporal variables can enter into the control of behavior. The separation of the different contributions to a particular instance of behavior is a problem of behavioral analysis. A good starting place for such an analysis is determining the units that enter into the three-term contingency. In the three-term contingency, a discriminative stimulus (S) sets the occasion on which a response (R) produces some consequence (C).

Consider the fixed-interval (FI) schedule of reinforcement, in which a response produces a reinforcer only after some fixed minimum time has elapsed since some environmental event and in which earlier responses have no scheduled consequences.

As this schedule might be arranged for a pigeon, the discriminative stimulus correlated with the operation of the schedule might be a green light illuminating the response key, the response might be the pigeon's peck on that key, and the reinforcer might be the mixed grain delivered by a food magazine located below the key. In a typical performance, the pigeon responds slowly after the onset of the green light, but its rate of responding increases as time passes; eventually the interval ends and the next peck produces food.

In this case, a specification of the discriminative stimulus must include the temporal dimension of the green light. To the extent that later times after onset produce higher response rates than earlier times by virtue of the correlation of the later times with the peck-food contingency, the pigeon's pecking is discriminated responding under the control of the temporal dimension.

Each stimulus dimension has intrinsic properties, and those of the temporal dimension differ in important ways from those of other stimulus dimensions such as wavelength, intensity and spatial extent. For example, there is no obvious duration receptor, durations are irreversible, and they cannot be varied discontinuously (in the sense that it is not possible to get from 10 to 12 s without passing through 11 s).

Time since the onset of the green light, however, is not the only temporal feature of the FI situation. The pigeon's pecks are spaced in time, and these interresponse times (IRTs) and their interrelations with food deliveries are also part of the FI contingencies (cf. Dews, 1970). The trouble is that this spacing can be influenced by the peck-food contingency in at least two different ways.

One effect of the contingency is to raise the rate or probability of pecking. The relation between rate and mean IRT is necessarily reciprocal (as rate increases, average time between responses must decrease), and this alone will shorten IRTs. This effect of the reinforcer delivery may include its operation on earlier responses as well as on the final response in the interval (Catania, 1971). Thus, responding in a subsequent interval may depend not only on time since onset but also on the delays with which responses at or near that time were followed by reinforcers in prior intervals.

Another effect is that the probability with which a peck produces food varies not only with the time in the interval at which the peck occurs but also with its IRT, i.e., the time since the preceding peck. Given that long IRTs allow more time in which the interval may end than short IRTs, a larger proportion of long than short IRTs will end with a peck that produces food, and this higher probability can be the basis for the differentiation of longer IRTs (Anger, 1956).

These properties of behavior are *molecular*, in that they involve the properties of individual stimuli and responses. But the processes of discrimination and differentiation are *molar*, in that they are aspects of populations of stimuli and responses observed over extended periods of time. Still another level may be added to the complexity created by these interactions by introducing other molar temporal dimensions, such as the overall frequency of food delivery. Such molar variables, however, are likely to be related only remotely or indirectly to temporal discrimination or temporal differentiation.

The distinction between molar and molecular has its origin in other disciplines (especially chemistry and physics). For example, the gas laws that relate pressure, temperature and volume are molar in that they deal with global properties of gases, but they can be related mathematically to molecular events such as collisions between gas molecules. The language of molecular and molar is likely to be invoked in behavior analysis in experimental settings in which attempts are made to relate detailed measures of behavior (such as IRTs) to global ones (such as average rates). But in behavioral usages the two classes of molecular and molar will sometimes be arbitrary. For example, a response sequence might be regarded as molar relative to individual responses within a context concerned with determinants of local response rates, whereas the same sequence might be taken as a molecular unit relative to ratios among response classes within a context concerned with matching of response and reinforcement rates.

3. Procedures in the analysis of temporal control

Whether procedures of temporal control are referred to as instances of temporal *discrimination* or temporal *differentiation* is perhaps merely a matter of convenience. These two terms are distinguished primarily on the basis of whether differential consequences within the three-term contingency are correlated with discriminative stimulus properties or with response properties. The class of responses created by a three-term contingency is called a discriminated operant, and it can be defined jointly by both properties. In the preceding example of the FI schedule, for example, the relevant behavioral class is defined both by the green light and by the key on which the pigeon pecks.

In the case of some temporal procedures, however, the distinction between stimulus and response properties is ambiguous. When two successive responses occur, the second response can be said to be a discriminative response under the control of the time since the preceding response, or the time between the two responses can be taken as a property of responding that has been differentiated. As may be so in this case, some procedural distinctions are behaviorally arbitrary even though they seem otherwise to be convenient.

3.1. *Temporal discriminative stimuli and differentiated responses*

In a temporal discrimination, the three-term contingency may include a temporal stimulus that allows responding throughout some or all of its presentation, or one that allows responding only after it has terminated, or one that is cancelled or reset by a response. In each case, the differentiated dimension of responding may be a temporal one, as in response rates or IRTs, or a nontemporal one, as in the changeover from one response to another (where the changeover is defined by some nontemporal property such as location rather than by such temporal properties as its duration).

These cases do not exhaust the possibilities. A variety of other temporal features of the environment might be added to the above categories. Some distinctions that have been given experimental attention include trace versus delay procedures (e.g., Pavlov, 1927), the presence or absence of exteroceptive stimuli serving as clocks correlated with the passage of time (e.g., Ferster and Skinner, 1957, pp. 266–301), fixed versus variable temporal dimensions, and rates or rhythmic patterns of stimuli rather than unstructured stimulus durations. As for temporal dimensions of responding, these may be interresponse properties such as IRTs (e.g., in differential-reinforcement-of-low-rate or DRL schedules, or differential-reinforcement-of-high-rate or DRH schedules), or they may be intraresponse ones such as response duration, or they may involve combinations of these dimensions in temporal patterns such as rhythms. Interresponse dimensions have usually been favored in operant procedures, probably on the assumption that intraresponse dimensions such as response durations are complexly determined by different contingencies that act on response initiation and response termination (but see Platt et al., 1973, which provides duration data comparable to IRT data). An exhaustive classification is beyond the scope of the present account; given the diversity of possible procedural innovations, it may not even be feasible.

3.1.1. Responding during the temporal stimulus

In an FI schedule, a response is reinforced only after some minimum time has elapsed since the onset of the interval. Earlier responses have no effect on the response-reinforcer contingency at the end of the interval. If FI performance is regarded as an instance of generalization along the temporal dimension, it has the disadvantage that it provides only one side of the temporal generalization gradient because all intervals end with the delivery of the reinforcer; responding cannot continue at times longer than the duration of the FI. Thus, the other side of the gradient can be observed only if some intervals are scheduled in which the reinforcer delivery at the end of the interval is omitted.

This can be arranged in mixed FI FI schedules, in which one of two FI values is scheduled in each interval (in typical mixed schedules, the two components alternate irregularly in the presence of a single stimulus; see Part 1, Ch. 3). If the two intervals are sufficiently different, the rate maintained by the shorter interval may decrease before the rate increases again as the end of the longer one approaches (cf. Catania and Reynolds, 1968, Experiment 5). But responding at intermediate times between the two FI values may be attributed either to the persistence of responding following the time at which the shorter interval ends or to early responding maintained by the longer FI.

This problem can be resolved by arranging a single FI in which the probability that a response will be reinforced at the end of the interval is less than 1.0, as illustrated in Fig. 1 (Catania, 1970). When the first response after 10 s is reinforced with a

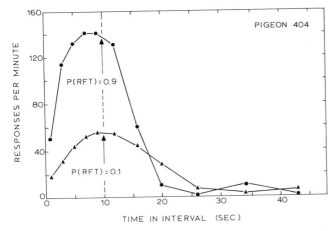

Fig. 1. Responses per min as a function of elapsed time in two variants of an FI 10-s schedule. In one, the first response after 10 s was reinforced with a probability of 0.9, and in the other with a probability of 0.1. In either case, if a reinforcer was not produced at 10 s, the trial ended automatically and independently of responding at 48 s. Successive intervals were separated by a 60-s intertrial interval. (Reproduced from Catania, 1970, with permission of the publisher.)

probability of 0.90, response rate is higher than when it is reinforced with a probability of 0.10, but in both cases rates increase with elapsed time up to about 10 s and decrease thereafter. This arrangement has been referred to as the peak procedure, but that nomenclature may be unfortunate in that it emphasizes the point at which response rate reaches its maximum and thereby draws attention away from other properties of the performance, such as the function that relates response rate to time in the interval and the variable response rates and patterns that contribute to the mean response rates at different times.

The temporal properties of this procedure give it one characteristic that distinguishes it from procedures involving other stimulus dimensions. Each interval includes at most one reinforcer; whenever one is delivered the interval ends. Thus, the procedure does not easily allow the response-reinforcer contingency to be uniformly correlated with a range of temporal values (e.g., responses reinforced throughout the time from 10 to 20 s, but with none reinforced from 0 to 10 s or from 20 to 40 s).

Variable intervals can be scheduled to cover temporal ranges with roughly uniform probabilities of reinforcement. But in such cases each reinforcement prevents the organism from reaching the later times in the interval, so that it is exposed more often to the shorter than to the longer times. Thus, if intervals always end when a reinforcer is delivered, reinforcement probabilities cannot be held constant over a range of durations without making exposure to different portions of the interval nonuniform. For example, if the shortest interval is 5 s, the organism will pass through 0 through 5 s in every interval but it will pass through later times only in intervals longer than the 5-s one.

These limitations could be addressed by procedures in which reinforcement does not reset the interval. Such procedures include not only single-response situations with rate of responding as the primary measure, but also situations involving two or more responses, in which nontemporal dimensions of responding such as the distribution of behavior across the two responses are measured. Because rates can vary continuously, they can sometimes exhibit properties that cannot be studied with topographically discrete measures such as those based on choice of one of two responses (e.g., Hinson and Higa, 1989).

3.1.2. Responding after the temporal stimulus has ended

Situations in which the discriminative response cannot occur until presentation of the temporal stimulus has been completed allow more experimental control over the sequences of temporal stimuli to which the organism is exposed. Probably for that reason, such situations are favored in the design of experiments concerned with temporal psychophysics (Catania, 1970; Church, 1988).

Early procedures involved presentation of one stimulus of variable duration followed by a second stimulus during which the operation of some schedule (usually variable interval or VI) depended on the duration of the first stimulus. In one experiment with pigeons, for example, dark-key periods of 3 to 30 s in 3-s steps were each followed by 30 s of a lit key, but a VI 20-s schedule operated for pecks on the lit key only after the 3-s dark-key duration (Reynolds and Catania, 1962). Response rates on the lit key were highest after the 3-s stimulus and decreased with longer durations. Thus discrimination among the temporal values of the first stimulus was demonstrated by a temporal property of responding rate in the presence of the second stimulus.

More recent procedures have more often used nontemporal response properties. An example is provided in Fig. 2, which shows data from a two-lever temporal discrimination procedure with a squirrel monkey (Catania, 1970; cf. Stubbs, 1968). In successive trials, an intertrial interval (ITI) in darkness was followed by a white noise of variable duration. When the noise ended, a houselight turned on and responses on the levers had consequences that depended on the noise duration. The reinforcer consisted of the illumination of a food cup accompanied with a probability of 0.25 by delivery of food. The following three types of trials occurred with equal probability: after a 1.0-s noise, the third left-lever response was reinforced and produced a 10-s ITI whereas the third right-lever response ended the trial and produced a 30-s ITI; after a 4.0-s noise, the third left-lever response ended the trial and produced a 30-s ITI whereas the third right-lever response was reinforced and produced a 10-s ITI; and after a 2.0-s, 2.5-s or 3.0-s noise, the third response on either lever produced a 10-s ITI. If three responses had not accumulated on either lever within 10 s, the trial ended automatically and was followed by a 30-s ITI. After 1.0-s stimuli, most responses occurred on the left lever; after 4.0-s stimuli, most responses occurred on the right lever; intermediate durations produced intermediate distributions of presses on the two levers.

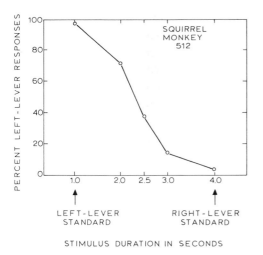

Fig. 2. Temporal discrimination in a squirrel monkey. In a two-lever chamber, left-lever responses were reinforced with food after a 1-s auditory stimulus and right-lever responses were reinforced after a 4-s stimulus. Control by intermediate durations was determined on trials in which lever presses had no scheduled consequences. (Reproduced from Catania, 1970, with permission of the publisher.)

3.1.2.1. Temporal stimuli produced by the organism. The preceding examples involved temporal stimuli produced by the experimenter, but analogous procedures can be arranged when the durations are produced by the organism itself. For example, a pigeon may come to discriminate its own IRTs if the IRTs it produces in the presence of one stimulus determine the schedule that operates in the presence of a subsequent second stimulus (e.g., Reynolds, 1966). Such procedures are relevant to temporal discriminations in which responding occurs during the temporal stimulus, as in FI schedules, because in such procedures the organism's behavior determines the interrelations among IRTs, the times within intervals, and the delays between particular responses and the reinforcers delivered at the end of the interval.

As in the case of experimenter-produced stimuli, the discriminative responses in these procedures can have temporal properties, or they can involve nontemporal dimensions such as choice of one of two responses. For example, if the reinforcement of a pigeon's peck on a left or right side key depends on the duration of a preceding IRT the pigeon has emitted on a center key, the pigeon may come to discriminate this temporal property of its own behavior (cf. Shimp, 1983; Eisler, 1984; Shimp et al., 1989).

There are, however, some constraints on such discriminations. The sequence of center-key IRT followed by side-key response is, in effect, a chain of responses, and therefore the frequencies of the IRTs that serve as discriminative stimuli may be influenced by the consequences arranged for the discriminative responding. In the extreme case, if left-key pecks were reinforced after short center-key IRTs but no right-key pecks were reinforced after longer center-key IRTs, short IRTs might come to predominate the performance to such an extent that the temporal discrimination would be difficult to assess.

Furthermore, although produced by the pigeon's behavior, the IRTs always include correlated exteroceptive stimuli (e.g., the visual stimuli available during production of the IRT on the center key) and these rather than the pigeon's behavior itself may be the basis for the temporal discrimination. If they are similarly correlated with reinforcers, there is no a priori reason why such stimuli should be any less effective as discriminative stimuli than those that are arranged by the experimenter. This is a general problem with the organism's discrimination of its own behavior: exteroceptive stimuli will be correlated with the behavior to the extent that it is public, whereas exteroceptive correlates that might provide the basis for differential reinforcement will be absent to the extent that it is private (cf. Skinner, 1945).

3.1.3. Responding that resets the temporal stimulus

The critical feature that distinguishes the differential reinforcement of IRTs in differential-reinforcement-of-low-rate (DRL) schedules from the varieties of temporal control considered so far is the resetting of timing with each response. The temporal stimulus is typically timed from the preceding response, but it may also be timed from some other event such as a stimulus onset (e.g., as in the differential reinforcement of long latencies: Catania, 1970). As in the cases of Sections 3.1.1 and 3.1.2, many procedural variations are possible, including arrangements for sequences of two or more responses and schedules that operate for particular classes of IRTs (as in schedules that differentially reinforce paced responding, high rates or other temporal patterns). The present account concentrates on the DRL schedule and its derivatives, however, because that schedule is most clearly defined by the differentiation of a temporal dimension of responding (though it must be recalled that an appropriate alternative to this vocabulary is to discuss DRL performance in terms of the organism's discrimination of the time elapsed since the preceding response).

The DRL schedule arranges that a response is reinforced if a minimum time has elapsed since the preceding response. Early responses reset the clock and start the timing anew, much as a coin resets the timing of a parking meter. One consequence is that extinction is unlikely. If short IRTs fail to meet the DRL contingency, no reinforcers are delivered, and responding eventually slows down to the point at which an IRT occurs that is long enough to produce the reinforcer.

In DRL performance, the organism generates a distribution of IRTs some of which produce reinforcing consequences and others of which do not. Much of the interest in DRL performance stems from the frequent finding that the distribution produced by the organism does not correspond closely to the boundaries specified by the reinforcement contingencies (Catania, 1973). Furthermore, the distribution is often bimodal, consisting of a high frequency of short IRTs combined with a population of IRTs at or near the IRT value required by the schedule (e.g., see Fig. 3). Such short IRTs are typically obtained over a substantial range of DRL values.

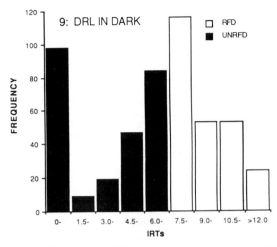

Fig. 3. Distribution of Pigeon 9's interresponse times (IRTs) maintained by a DRL 7.5-s schedule of food reinforcement for pecks on a key in a totally dark chamber over 3 45-min sessions. Filled bars show unreinforced IRTs (UNRFD); unfilled bars show reinforced IRTs (RFD).

3.1.3.1. The three-term contingency and analyses of spaced responding. The tempo-ral property of responding that is differentially reinforced in DRL schedules is the spacing of responses in time. The schedule operates in the context of the three-term contingency, and an examination of the separate stimulus, response and consequence terms can contribute to an analysis of the determinants of DRL performance. For example, consider the short IRTs typically maintained in the DRL performance of the pigeon. As the DRL schedule is usually arranged for the pigeon, these IRTs occur in the presence of a key light, the responses that terminate them are key pecks, and the reinforcer that the pecks produce is food. Each of these three terms – stimulus, response, consequence – can be involved not only in reinforcement contingencies but also in the phenomenon of autoshaping (e.g., Jenkins and Moore, 1973). For exam-ple, if a key light is repeatedly followed by response-independent food, a pigeon even-tually begins to peck the key when it lights (see Part 1, Ch. 2). What happens then if one or more of the terms of the three-term contingency is altered? Could the short IRTs depend on some aspect of stimulus-consequence contingencies rather than re-sponse-consequence contingencies?

The effect of removing the key as a visual stimulus is illustrated in Fig. 3, which shows frequencies of IRTs in 1.5-s class intervals from a pigeon's performance on a DRL 7.5-s schedule; the rightmost class interval shows all IRTs longer than 12 s. Dis-tributions of IRTs are probably most commonly displayed in such form, though they are sometimes also shown in terms of derivative measures such as relative frequencies (proportion of total IRTs that fall in a given class) or as conditional probabilities. The latter are referred to as IRTs per opportunity (IRTs/Op) and are obtained by dividing IRTs in a given class by all IRTs in that or longer classes (see Part 2, Ch. 6). The statistic adjusts for the effect of resetting timing with each response: each shorter IRT elimi-nates an opportunity for the organism to produce a longer one. The temporal effects in the present illustrations are sufficiently large that they do not require transforma-tions to IRTs/Op to demonstrate temporal differentiation.

The performance shown in Fig. 3 began with DRL responding that was established in a standard chamber with a lit key but with the houselight off. The illumination of the key was gradually reduced over roughly 12 h (16 45-min sessions) by increasing a resistance in series with it until the chamber was totally dark. Thereafter, the lamps behind the key were disconnected. The figure shows data after about 60 sessions of DRL in the dark. Standard illumination of the feeder was maintained during rein-forcer deliveries throughout all sessions.

Pecks were accompanied by feedback clicks produced by a relay mounted behind the panel. Presumably the pigeon oriented itself in the chamber on the basis of this auditory feedback in combination with mechanical stimulation (the key moved when pecked but the remainder of the panel did not). Pecks around the key were sampled occasionally by using a carbon paper mask surrounding the key; these pecks de-creased in frequency with continued sessions of dark-key responding, and were in-frequent relative to recorded key pecks by the time the data in Fig. 3 were obtained. It was not possible to estimate the frequency of pecks that ended in mid-air.

The IRT distribution shows a mode at the shortest reinforced class interval of IRTs, 7.5 to 9.0 s, but, like IRT distributions obtained with DRL under normal light-ing conditions, it is bimodal and includes a high frequency of IRTs in the shortest class interval, 0 to 1.5 s. In other words, the short IRTs cannot be attributed to visual stimuli correlated with the peck-food contingency.

In standard environments, the pigeon's key pecks are not only directed at visual stimuli but also at a particularly important class of such stimuli, i.e., the food that often serves as a reinforcing consequence. The analysis therefore can be continued by substituting a different reinforcer for food. The results of this procedure are illus-trated in Fig. 4, which shows a distribution of IRTs obtained after about 11 h (15 45-min sessions) of DRL 3.75 s maintained by water reinforcers delivered by a dipper feeder (see Jenkins and Moore, 1973, for a description of similar apparatus). The dis-tribution is again bimodal, and includes a substantial proportion of IRTs in the shor-test class interval, 0 to 0.75 s. In other words, the short IRTs cannot be attributed to food as a reinforcing consequence.

The survey of the terms of the three-term contingency can be completed by substi-tuting a different response for the pigeon's key peck. In fact, comparisons of pigeons' key pecking and treadle pressing maintained by DRL schedules over a range from DRL 5 s to DRL 60 s show that short IRTs occur with treadle pressing as well as with key-pecking, but usually with a substantially lower relative frequency (Richard-son and Clark, 1976, Figs. 2 and 9). Thus, short IRTs in pigeon DRL performance can be attributed in part to the choice of the key peck as response (cf. Ferster and Skinner, 1957, p. 7: "Such responses are not wholly arbitrary ... In such a bird as

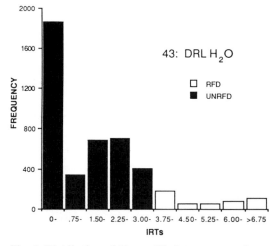

Fig. 4. Distribution of Pigeon 43's interresponse times (IRTs) maintained by a DRL 3.75-s schedule of water reinforcement over 3 45-min sessions. Filled bars show unreinforced IRTs (UNRFD); unfilled bars show reinforced IRTs (RFD).

the pigeon, pecking has a certain genetic unity; it is a characteristic bit of behavior which appears with well-defined topography").

3.1.3.2. Analysis through topographical tagging. The analysis of the response term in the three-term contingency, however, is not exhausted by the substitution of different topographies. Another technique for examining the functional role of the response is that of topographical tagging (Catania, 1971). One of the earliest experimental examples is provided in an experiment concerned with the origins of post-shock bursts in the avoidance responding of rats (Boren, 1961). When the avoidance schedule was broken down into separate avoidance and escape contingencies (cf. Part 1, Ch. 5) so that these component contingencies of the schedule could be arranged on two different levers, virtually all of the post-shock bursts occurred on the escape lever rather on than the avoidance lever. Thus, the procedure allowed avoidance responding to be analyzed into two subclasses. Each of these subclasses was tagged topographically, where the distinguishing topographical feature of each class was the location of the corresponding lever.

An application of topographical tagging to the pigeon's short IRTs in DRL performance is illustrated in Fig. 5. Most DRL pecks contribute to two different IRTs; they are the terminating pecks of one IRT and the initiating pecks of the next (exceptions are the first peck of the session or the first peck after a reinforcer delivery, and a peck terminating an IRT sufficiently long that it produces a reinforcer). The procedure of Fig. 5 separated the functions of IRT initiation and IRT termination by locating them on two different keys.

In a standard two-key chamber, the left key was lit blue and the right key was lit amber throughout each session, except during deliveries of the food reinforcer, when

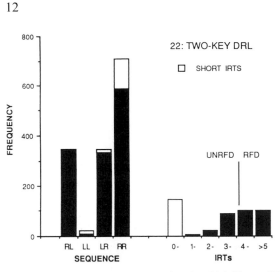

Fig. 5. Data from a two-key procedure in which Pigeon 22's changeovers from the left key to the right key were reinforced according to a DRL 4-s schedule, over 3 40-min sessions. The sequence histogram, on the left, shows the frequencies of different sequences of pecks: right-left (RL), left-left (LL), left-right (LR), and right-right (RR); the unfilled area of each bar shows IRTs of less than 1 s. The filled bars of the IRT histogram, on the right, show the distribution of IRTs from the reinforced class (LR) in 1-s class intervals. The unfilled bar at the 0 to 1-s class interval shows the sum of the unfilled areas from the sequence histogram. The vertical line shows the boundary between unreinforced (UNRFD) and reinforced (RFD) IRTs. In the IRT histogram, almost all of the IRTs in the 0-s to 1-s class interval come from RR response sequences.

the feeder was lit and the keys were dark. A DRL 4-s schedule operated for two-peck sequences that began with a peck on the left key and ended with a peck on the right key; in other words, the sequence of left-key peck followed by right-key peck was reinforced only if the two pecks were separated by at least 4 s. No consequences were arranged for the other possible sequences of pecks (right-right, right-left, left-left) or for left-right sequences that were completed in less than 4 s. A peck that produced a reinforcer was never treated as the initiating peck of a two-peck sequence; a new sequence began with the first peck after the reinforcer delivery.

The figure illustrates one pigeon's performance after about 16 hr of this two-key DRL schedule (25 40-min sessions). The sequence histogram, on the left, shows the frequencies of each of the 4 possible response sequences (changeovers from right to left, RL, are necessarily about equal to changeovers from left to right, LR, because the pigeon cannot go back to one key until it has moved to the other; there are no corresponding constraints on sequences of pecks on a single key, LL and RR). Total right-key pecks (LR plus RR) exceeded total left-key pecks (RL plus LL), probably because right-key pecks were sometimes immediately reinforced whereas left-key pecks were always separated from a subsequent reinforcer by at least 4 s. For each sequence, the unfilled areas show the frequencies with which the two pecks were separated by less than 1 s (short IRTs).

The IRT histogram, on the right, shows the IRT distribution for the reinforced sequence (LR). The mode of that distribution was at the 4 to 5-s class interval (assuming that the rightmost class interval, which included all IRTs greater than 5 s, did not consist exclusively of IRTs between 5 and 6 s). Superimposed on the IRT distribution at the 0 to 1-s class interval, the unfilled bar is the sum of the unfilled areas from the sequence histogram on the left. Almost all of these short IRTs come from right-right peck sequences. This topography tags them as functionally equivalent to pecks that terminate IRTs rather than pecks that initiate IRTs.

4. Mediating behavior in temporal control

Some accounts of behavior spaced in time have appealed to amount of responding as a mediator of temporal control (e.g., Laties et al., 1965). The organism is assumed to produce some chain of behavior during a long IRT that is strengthened by its relation to reinforcement at the end of the IRT; thus, long IRTs are created only indirectly, via differentiation of the length of this chain, which often consists of repetitious behavior. In this interpretation, the differentation of the temporal spacing of responses is a derivative of the differentiation of response number. If the differentiation of temporal spacing is called timing, then that of response number may be called counting, though it must be understood that both terms are metaphorical (cf. Davis and Pérusse, 1988).

One way to examine possible relations between timing and counting is to determine the functional properties of each within parallel procedures. An experimental example of the differential reinforcement of timing and counting in pigeons is provided here not only for its relevance to mediational accounts of timing but also as an illustration of molecular and molar analyses of behavior.

4.1. Differential reinforcement of timing and counting

A discrete-trial procedure was conducted in a two-key chamber comparable to that of Catania (1971). Each trial was initiated by lighting the left key amber. The first peck on this key lit the right key blue. Both keys stayed lit for the rest of the trial, and the trial ended with the first peck on the right key (Mechner, 1958; Mechner et al., 1963; cf. LeFever, 1973). A houselight, on throughout each session, was turned off during reinforcers (3-s access to food). Trials were separated by 20-s intertrial intervals, and sessions lasted 60 reinforcers.

In differential reinforcement of timing, the right peck was reinforced only if at least t s had elapsed since the first left peck, without reference to the number of subsequent left pecks. In differential reinforcement of counting, the right peck was reinforced only if it was preceded by at least n left pecks, without reference to the time elapsed since the first left peck. Both time and number of pecks from the first left peck to

14

the right peck were recorded in each trial of each procedure. Although left pecks after the first one had no consequences in timing, these pecks were likely candidates to enter into such a relation if timing were mediated by amount of behavior.

Conditions were arranged in the following order: timing with t values of 8, 4 and 2 s; counting with n values of 2, 4, 8 and 16, followed by attempts to shape perform-ance to higher values of n (one pigeon provided steady-state performance at 32 and another at 22); counting with n values of 16, 8 and 4 (one pigeon was dropped from the experiment because of illness after this sequence); and finally timing with t values of 2, 4 and 8 s. In all ascending sequences, several sessions were devoted to shaping of performance to the new criterion value before the start of steady-state conditions.

Mean data are based on the last 10 sessions of steady-state performance at each schedule value, where steady-state was determined by informal criteria based on visu-al inspection of the data. The minimum number of steady-state sessions for a condi-tion was 14 (counting procedure with n equal to 2); the range for the remaining condi-tions was 19 to 51, with higher parameter values typically requiring more sessions.

4.1.1. Molecular aspects of the data

A molecular analysis concentrates on the detailed properties of individual segments of behavior. In the present instance, such an analysis involves performances within individual trials as opposed to performances averaged over many trials or sessions.

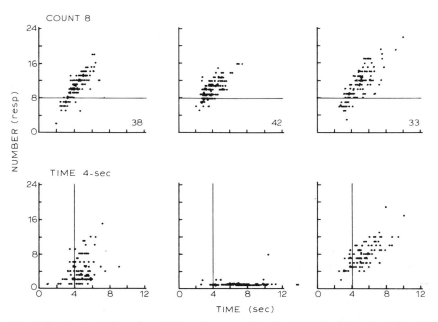

Fig. 6. Scatterplots of number of left pecks versus time from the first left peck to the right peck over single trials in COUNT 8 and TIME 4-s procedures for Pigeons 38, 42 and 33. These two parameter values were chosen for comparison because they produced similar time distributions.

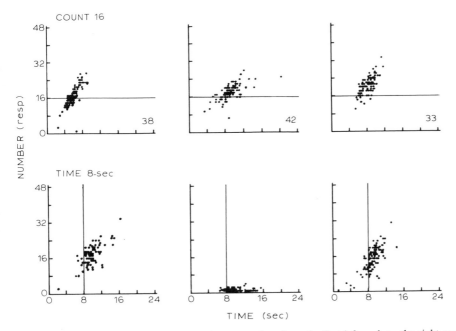

Fig. 7. Scatterplots of number of left pecks versus time from the first left peck to the right peck over single trials in COUNT 16 and TIME 8-s procedures for Pigeons 38, 42 and 33. These two parameter values were chosen for comparison because they produced similar time distributions.

Sample scatterplots of number versus time over single trials from late sessions of counting with n values of 8 and 16 and timing with t values of 4 and 8 s are shown for each pigeon in Figs. 6 and 7. The pairings were chosen on the basis of the similar ranges of the joint distributions. Number and time were highly correlated in both procedures (except in timing for Pigeon 42, who emitted only one or two left pecks on most timing trials); in other words, trials with more left-key pecks tended to be those with longer times to the first right-key peck. The magnitude of the correlations varied from pigeon to pigeon and from condition to condition, but for the present purposes the main point is that this relation was roughly the same in the counting procedure as in the timing procedure. There was no evidence that the dependency of time on number in the timing procedure was stronger than that of number on time in the counting procedure, as should be the case if timing were mediated in some way by number of responses.

4.1.2. Molar aspects of the data

The molar effects of the differential reinforcement of timing are shown in Fig. 8. The 3 birds have been assigned separate portions of the logarithmic X-axis to avoid overlap of their data at the 3 t values of 2, 4 and 8. Both time (T) and number (N) are plotted along a single logarithmic Y-axis. Arrows show ascending and descending

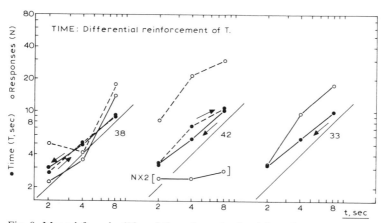

Fig. 8. Mean left pecks (N) and times from the first left peck to a right peck (T) as a function of t, the minimum value of T required by a schedule that differentially reinforced the time from the first left peck to the right peck. The data for Pigeons 38, 42 and 33, plotted in log-log coordinates, are displaced along the X-axis to avoid crowding. The diagonals show the function T = t.

series, and time and number data from corresponding conditions are indicated by common solid or dashed lines. For example, with a time value of 2 s in the ascending series for Pigeon 42 (dashed lines), the mean trial lasted slightly more than 3 s (filled circle at $t = 2$), and the mean pecks per trial was about 8 (unfilled circle at $t = 2$); for this pigeon only, the values of N in the descending series were multiplied by 2 before plotting to accommodate them on the graph (note the $N \times 2$ label; cf. the timing scatterplots for Pigeon 42 in Figs. 6 and 7).

In these log-log plots, obtained time was a roughly linear function of scheduled time for all 3 birds (filled circles) but obtained number was not (unfilled circles). A linear relation in log-log coordinates corresponds to a power function (the light diagonals show the function $T = t$, or a power function with an exponent of 1). These data are similar to those in other studies of temporal differentiation (e.g., Catania, 1970; Platt et al., 1973). Temporal dimensions of responding such as latency or IRT are related by a power function to the criterion for differentially reinforcing temporal properties of behavior:

$$T = ct^k$$

where T is obtained duration, t is the minimum duration eligible for reinforcement, and c and k are constants. The exponent k is typically about 0.9.

Effects of the differential reinforcement of counting are shown in Fig. 9. The format is similar to that in Fig. 8, except that the X-axis shows n (count) rather than t. Both time and number data are plotted along the single logarithmic Y-axis, with ascending and descending sequences indicated by arrows as in Fig. 9. The light diagonal lines show the function $N = n$.

The data for number in this figure are analogous to those for time in Fig. 8. In

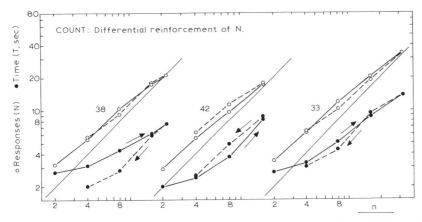

Fig. 9. Mean left pecks (N) and times from the first left peck to a right peck (T) as a function of n, the minimum value of N required by a schedule that differentially reinforced the number of left pecks that preceded the right peck. The data for Pigeons 38, 42 and 33, plotted in log-log coordinates, are displaced along the X-axis to avoid crowding. The diagonals show the function $N = n$.

the log-log plots for each bird, obtained number was a roughly linear function of scheduled number, but obtained time was not; the latter function paralleled number at higher values of n, but became concave upward at lower values. The similarity between timing and counting is that both functions are power functions with an exponent somewhat less than 1.0. But in both cases the dimension for which contingencies were arranged varied in a more orderly way than the other dimension (e.g., the unfilled circles for number and the filled circles for time for Pigeon 38 in Fig. 9). In agreement with the data at the molecular level, there is no more evidence that time depended on the number of responses emitted in the timing procedure than that number depended on time elapsed in the counting procedure. The property of responding that was differentially reinforced was the property that varied most consistently with the reinforcement criterion; the property not correlated with reinforcement was more variable. Given that neither set of data suggests that either measure of behavior depended upon the other, the two properties of behavior might best be considered independent of one another.

5. Conclusion: organisms as clocks or as counters

If the search for behavior mediating timing were successful, the outcome might be regarded as relevant to the organism's temporal receptor. But then it would be necessary to consider the nature of the receptors through which the organism discriminates properties of its own behavior. It is common for accounts of timing to speak of the organism as reading an internal clock, and a consequence of a successful search for behavioral mediators could be that the clock would come to be called a counter. It might then not be long before a search was mounted for still other behavior that could mediate the counting.

Meanwhile, although saying that the organism is reading its clock or resetting its counter sounds like talk about behavior, it might be difficult to identify responses distinguishable from the temporally distributed responses that characterize behavior under temporal control. If a rat presses a lever at a given moment, what sort of a response is its reading of its internal clock, and how could that response be studied independently of the rat's lever-pressing?

There is another alternative. It is inappropriate to leave the experimenter out of the story, and the relation between the organism and the experimenter is in some ways similar to that between a watch and someone who is interested in knowing the time. When an experimenter studies temporal discrimination or temporal differentiation in rat or pigeon, it may be best to speak not of the rat or pigeon reading its clock, but of the rat or pigeon as the clock that is read by the experimenter.

The experimenter may then be interested in what kind of a clock this organism is. Is it like a stopwatch? Can it be reset and, if so, what does it take to reset it? Is there a way to make the clock stop running temporarily? Will it pick up where it left off when it starts again? Is it limited to timing only one duration at a time? What sorts of alarms does it have, and how are they set or disabled? And so on. If it later turns out that behavior is involved in the way this clock works, it becomes appropriate also to ask what sort of a counter the organism is.

Some of the properties of clocks and counters have simple correspondences in the various temporal procedures outlined here. Others may suggest procedures that have not yet been adequately explored. It may therefore be useful, in considering the design of experiments on temporal discrimination or differentiation, to review these properties. Real as opposed to metaphorical clocks and counters are the tools used to arrange contingencies in experiments on temporal control. They should serve as reminders that the role of the environment in shaping temporally discriminated and differentiated behavior must not be ignored.

Acknowledgements

Crystal Archible, Edward Hamilton, Don S. Miller, and James Welsh contributed to the experiments illustrated by Figs. 3, 4 and 5. Kenneth Thurston and James Jans contributed to the research illustrated in Figs. 6 through 9, which was supported by NSF Grant BNS76-09723 to the University of Maryland Baltimore County.

References

Anger, D. (1956) The dependence of interresponse times upon the relative reinforcement of different interresponse times. J. Exp. Psychol. 52, 145–161.

Boren, J.J. (1961) Isolation of post-shock responding in a free operant avoidance procedure. Psychol. Rep. 9, 265–266.

Catania, A.C. (1970) Reinforcement schedules and psychophysical judgments: a study of some temporal properties of behavior. In: W.N. Schoenfeld (Ed.), The Theory of Reinforcement Schedules. Appleton-Century-Crofts, New York, pp. 1–42.

Catania, A.C. (1971) Reinforcement schedules: the role of responses preceding the one that produces the reinforcer. J. Exp. Anal. Behav. 15, 271–287.

Catania, A.C. (1973) The concept of the operant in the analysis of behavior. Behaviorism 1, 103–116.

Catania, A.C. and Reynolds, G.S. (1968) A quantitative analysis of the responding maintained by interval schedules of reinforcement. J. Exp. Anal. Behav. 11, 327–383.

Church, R.M. (1988) Theories of timing behavior. In: S.B. Klein and R.R. Mowrer (Eds.), Contemporary Learning Theory, Vol. 2. Erlbaum, Hillsdale, NJ, pp. 41–71.

Davis, H. and Pérusse, R. (1988) Numerical competence in animals: definitional issues, current evidence, and a new research agenda. Behav. Brain Sci. 11, 561–579.

Dews, P.B. (1970) The theory of fixed-interval responding. In: W.N. Schoenfeld (Ed.), The Theory of Reinforcement Schedules. Appleton-Century-Crofts, New York, pp. 43–61.

Eisler, H. (1984) Knowing before doing: discrimination by rats of a brief interruption of a tone. J. Exp. Anal. Behav. 41, 329–340.

Ferster, C.B. and Skinner, B.F. (1957) Schedules of Reinforcement. Appleton-Century-Crofts, New York.

Gibbon, J. and Allen, L. (Eds.) (1984) Timing and Time Perception. Ann. NY Acad. Sci. 423.

Hinson, J.M. and Higa, J.J. (1989) Discrete and continuous measures of dimensional stimulus control. J. Exp. Anal. Behav. 51, 199–214.

Jenkins, H.M. and Moore, B.R. (1973) The form of the auto-shaped response with food or water reinforcers. J. Exp. Anal. Behav. 20, 163–181.

Laties, V.G., Weiss, B., Clark, R.L. and Reynolds, M.D. (1965) Overt 'mediating' behavior during temporally spaced responding. J. Exp. Anal. Behav. 8, 107–116.

LeFever, F. (1973) Instrumental Response Chains and Timing Behavior. Unpublished doctoral dissertation, New York University, New York.

Mechner, F. (1958) Probability relations within response sequences under ratio reinforcement. J. Exp. Anal. Behav. 1, 109–221.

Mechner, F., Guevrekian, L. and Mechner, V. (1963) A fixed interval schedule in which the interval is initiated by a response. J. Exp. Anal. Behav. 6, 323–330.

Pavlov, I.P. (1927) Conditioned Reflexes (G.V. Anrep, Trans.). Oxford University Press, London.

Platt, J.R., Kuch, D.O. and Bitgood, S.C. (1973) Rats' lever-press duration as psychophysical judgments of time. J. Exp. Anal. Behav. 19, 239–250.

Reynolds, G.S. (1966) Discrimination and emission of temporal intervals by pigeons. J. Exp. Anal. Behav. 9, 65–68.

Reynolds, G.S. and Catania, A.C. (1962) Temporal discrimination in pigeons. Science 135, 314–315.

Richardson, W.K. and Clark, D.B. (1976) A comparison of the key-peck and treadle-press operants in the pigeon: differential-reinforcement-of-low-rate schedule of reinforcement. J. Exp. Anal. Behav. 26, 237–256.

Richelle, M. and Lejeune, H. (1980) Time in Animal Behaviour. Pergamon, Oxford, England.

Schoenfeld, W.N. (Ed.) (1970) The Theory of Reinforcement Schedules. Appleton-Century-Crofts, New York.

Shimp, C.P. (1983) The local organization of behavior: dissociations between a pigeon's behavior and self-reports of that behavior. J. Exp. Anal. Behav. 39, 61–68.

Shimp, C.P., Sabulsky, S.L. and Childers, L.J. (1989) Preference for starting and finishing behavior patterns. J. Exp. Anal. Behav. 52, 341–352.

Skinner, B.F. (1945) The operational analysis of psychological terms. Psychol. Rev. 42, 270–277.

Stubbs, D.A. (1968) The discrimination of stimulus duration by pigeons. J. Exp. Anal. Behav. 11, 223–238.

Experimental analysis of behavior, Part 2
Iversen and Lattal (eds.)
© *1991, Elsevier Science Publishers BV*

CHAPTER 2

Behavioral pharmacology

MARC N. BRANCH

Department of Psychology, University of Florida, Gainesville, FL 32611, U.S.A.

1. Introduction

Behavioral Pharmacology, as a discipline, is closely intertwined with the Experimental Analysis of Behavior, and, as a consequence, relies heavily on its methodology, theory and conceptual bases. In fact, it is possible to argue that were it not for the Experimental Analysis of Behavior there would be no research field known as Behavioral Pharmacology. This assertion is supported by several characteristics of research in Behavioral Pharmacology and also by an examination of the history of the field. As examples, consider the following distinguishing features of research in Behavioral Pharmacology. First, the discipline is concerned mainly with the *behavioral* actions of drugs, not their chemical or neurochemical effects. The development and analysis of techniques for understanding the behavior of individual subjects (Skinner, 1938; Ferster and Skinner, 1957; Sidman, 1960) serve as the research backbone of Behavioral Pharmacology. The concept of the operant (see Part 1, Ch. 3) in concert with other developments outlined in chapters in Part 1 have led to control of *reproducible* behavioral processes in individual subjects so that stable baselines may be established. As will be described more fully below, stable baselines are central in experimental pharmacology.

In addition to having provided the techniques most widely used, the Experimental Analysis of Behavior also has furnished many important concepts that enter into theoretical accounts in Behavioral Pharmacology. The goal of Behavioral Pharmacology is to identify *behavioral mechanisms* of drug action. Basic controlling relations like reinforcement, punishment and temporal control provide the theoretical grist for the behavioral pharmacologist's mill, just as heart rate, stroke volume and peripheral resistance serve the cardiovascular pharmacologist in understanding the mechanisms controlling blood pressure. That is, attempts are made to characterize a drug's effects on behavior in terms of how it interacts with or exemplifies basic behavioral processes.

Currently, much is left to be learned about behavioral mechanisms of action because the mechanisms themselves are in need of refinement and perhaps even discovery. All approaches to the study of behavior are comparatively young sciences, with basic laws and theories still to be developed. Because of this, it is important to note that the relationship between the Experimental Analysis of Behavior and Behavioral Pharmacology is not a 'one-way street'. Research on drug–behavior interactions not only makes use of the techniques and concepts of the Experimental Analysis of Behavior, it also provides information concerning the utility of those conceptualizations and in so doing contributes to their development and validation.

The relationship between Behavioral Pharmacology and the Experimental Analysis of Behavior also can be seen in the history of the two fields (see Pickens, 1977). Widespread use of drugs for behavioral (or 'psychological') purposes began in the 1950s with the advent of the drug chlorpromazine, a compound whose usefulness was discovered fortuitously in clinical practice. The success of chlorpromazine in alleviating some symptoms of psychosis provided the impetus for the identification and development of other drugs that might have behavioral uses. This in turn spurred interest in laboratory research on the behavioral effects of drugs. Peter B. Dews, a pharmacologist with interests in behavioral effects of drugs, was at Harvard University where B.F. Skinner and his colleagues were developing procedures that allowed one to maintain the same temporal organization of behavior in individual organisms over extended periods (cf. Ferster and Skinner, 1957). Specifically, by controlling the experimental environment in which the activity of interest was free to occur at any time, Skinner and his associates were able to bring a degree of precision to the control of behavior that had not been achieved using more traditional discrete-trial methods. Using these procedures, Dews began to conduct experiments that marked the beginning of Behavioral Pharmacology as an identifiable enterprise.

Major impetus for the field of Behavioral Pharmacology can be traced to Dews (1955). He studied effects of pentobarbital on key pecking of food-deprived pigeons. Some pigeons responded under a fixed-ratio (FR) 50 schedule food presentation and others responded under a fixed-interval (FI) 15-min schedule (see Part 1, Ch. 3). Once stable performance had developed, Dews tested a range of doses of pentobarbital by preceding some behavioral testing sessions with an injection of the drug into the pigeon's breast muscle. In this way he was able to assess the effects of a range of doses of pentobarbital. The results are summarized in Fig. 1. The drug effects, including their qualitative nature, depended on the dose administered. Under either schedule of reinforcement the drug acted either as a 'stimulant' or a 'depressant', depending on the dose. The more surprising finding, however, was the difference in drug effect for the two schedules at doses larger than 0.5 mg. At these doses, the drug acted so as to decrease key pecking under FI, but stimulated key pecking under FR at doses

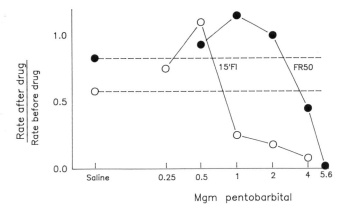

Fig. 1. Effects of pentobarbital on rate of key pecking of pigeons. Effects are expressed as a ratio of response rate under drug to response rate in the absence of drug (i.e., a value of 1.0 indicates no effect). Open circles show effects when pecking occurred under an FI 15-min schedule of food presentation, and closed circles show those obtained when pecking occurred under an FR 50 schedule. Also shown are effects of injecting the saline vehicle (symbols and dashed lines). (Reproduced from Dews, 1955, with permission of the publisher.)

of 1 or 2 mg. Note especially the divergence of effects at the doses of 1 and 2 mg. The qualitative nature of the drug's effect, i.e., whether it acted as a stimulant or a depressant, depended on the schedule of reinforcement rather than on the form of the behavior (key-pecking) or on the 'motivation' behind it (food deprivation). This was, and still is, a powerful demonstration of the importance of behavioral variables in determining drug effects. The results show that accurate prediction of the behavioral effects of drugs depends critically on the factors responsible for the occurrence of the behavior.

Following Dews' dramatic discovery, Behavioral Pharmacology emerged as a 'marriage' between pharmacology and the Experimental Analysis of Behavior. To describe the major strategies, tactics, and techniques of the discipline, therefore, it is necessary to be familiar with the principles of both pharmacology and the Experimental Analysis of Behavior. The chapters in Part 1 have provided the latter; the next section of this chapter is intended to help with the former.

2. General pharmacological principles

2.1. Drugs and receptors

Pharmacology is a somewhat unusual science because it is defined largely in terms of the independent variables, rather than the dependent variables, studied. The pharmacologist's major class of independent variables is drugs. Roughly defined, a drug is a nonnutritive (usually) chemical substance that affects living tissue. Behavioral pharmacologists study drugs that have or are suspected to have effects on behavior, and such drugs have several common general properties. For example, one characteristic of behaviorally active drugs is that large effects can be obtained from very small amounts. For example, the average body weight of an adult male human is about 150 lbs, which translates to a little over 68 000 g. A dose of diazepam (Valium) of 20 mg (i.e., 20 one-thousandth of a gram) given to a person this size will produce several hours of profound sedation. Even though drugs often can be characterized by the small amounts needed to produce significant effects, it is important to recognize that there is considerable variation both within and between drug classes in the amount needed to produce a particular effect. For example, an analgesic dose of oxycodone (Percodan[R]) for an adult human is 4.5 mg, whereas an equally effective dose of fentanyl (Innovar[R]) is 0.05 mg, i.e., nearly 100 times less fentanyl is needed.

A second, and more important, characteristic of behaviorally active drugs is that they generally affect nervous tissue, usually by combining with entities known as *receptors*. Receptors are localized structures with which drug molecules interact. These receptors are selective about the kinds of molecules with which they will interact. The interaction between a drug molecule and a receptor has been likened to that between a lock and key; the lock (receptor) can only be operated by a key (drug molecule) of the appropriate shape. The physiochemical characteristics of the drug molecule and the receptor site determine whether the 'fit' is appropriate. Although most behaviorally active drugs exert actions on receptors, there are some (e.g., alcohol) whose effects are characterized in terms of other types of interactions (e.g., alteration of cell membrane properties).

Receptor theory is the cornerstone of modern pharmacology (Goldstein et al., 1968; Cooper et al., 1982) by providing a description of factors that lead to specificity of drug action (as well as to the specificity of action within the nervous system). A particular drug produces a particular effect because it binds to (and thereby activates or inhibits) a specific type (or a few types) of receptor(s) but not with other types. Many types of receptors have been discovered (more than two dozen have been identified in the brain (Snyder, 1984)), and more are sure to be identified. Pharmacologists typically try to isolate systems that include only one or a limited number of receptor types so that drug–receptor interactions can be observed clearly. When drug effects on behavior are the topics of interest, however, the situation gets more complicated. A single behavioral process may involve many, if not all, of the known types of receptors (and probably some unknown ones). Even if a drug acts at only a single type of receptor site, activity at such sites modifies the functioning of neurons on which the receptors reside, and these neurons communicate via other receptor types with other neurons that exert their effects on still other neurons, and so on. Consequently, one must proceed with great caution when interpreting behavioral effects of drugs in terms of actions at specific receptors.

2.2. Procurement of drugs

One generally does not obtain drugs for research by going to a local pharmacist and having a prescription filled. Tablets, capsules and elixirs obtained at public pharmacies are special preparations that contain considerably more than just the drug itself. Compounds that control rate of release, stomach irritation, longevity of the preparation, and many other factors can be found in everyday pharmaceuticals. For research purposes, it is usually preferable to obtain samples of pure drug. Most drugs can be either purchased from general chemical supply companies or requested from drug manufacturers. Information on chemical properties and on how to store and prepare these drugs can be found in pharmacopoeias (e.g., *United States Pharmacopoeia and National Formulary* or *British Pharmacopoeia*) that can be found in most libraries that hold scientific books. Another useful source is the *Merck Index* which also provides chemical information. A good source for obtaining general information about the physiological actions and therapeutic uses of drugs is Gilman et al. (1985). Some highly restricted drugs (see below) are available in the United States only through the federal government via the National Institute on Drug Abuse (NIDA). In general, new experimental compounds must be obtained from the manufacturer; information regarding use and handling can be obtained from the supplier.

Behaviorally active drugs often are synthesized as salts. This feature of their composition makes it likely they will be soluble in water, a useful characteristic indeed. The active ingredient, however, is the base drug itself, not the drug in association with the molecule that makes it a salt, and sometimes it is important to characterize a drug's effects in terms of the amount of base administered. To achieve this, drugs may be synthesized in base form for administration, but this usually results in a water-insoluble chemical and therefore calls for special preparations for administration. More simply, the amount of base in a given mass of salt can be calculated on the basis of molecular weights. For example, cocaine usually comes as the hydrochloride salt. The molecular weight of cocaine is 303.4, and the molecular weight of cocaine hydrochloride is 339.8. Consequently, a given mass of cocaine hydrochloride is 89.3% cocaine base.

In order to monitor the sale and use of drugs more carefully, the Drug Enforcement Agency (DEA) of the United States Department of Justice has implemented a rating scale for drugs, and this agency is also in charge of licensing those who sell or dispense drugs in the US. To obtain drugs, one must either be licensed by the DEA (applications can be obtained by telephoning or writing to the nearest DEA office – they exist in all regions of the United States) or by working under the supervision of a licensed person. The scale places drugs into five 'schedules'. Drugs in Schedule I are those with no approved clinical use and that have high abuse potential (an example is LSD). Drugs in Schedule II are those that have high abuse potential but that also have approved clinical uses (an example is amphetamine). Drugs in the remaining three schedules, III–V, are ranked according to the risk associated with their use and are intended to include no drugs of abuse. To obtain drugs for research purposes, a licensed individual must submit to the agency or company from which the drug is to be obtained a specific order form published by DEA. Drugs in Schedule I are the most difficult to acquire, usually requiring not only the DEA order form but also a detailed research protocol. A useful outline of the responsibilities of a drug researcher can be obtained from Division 28 of the American Psychological Association.

2.3. The pharmacological preparation

General research strategies in Behavioral Pharmacology are those that have proven their worth in pharmacological research. The next section of this chapter therefore describes a standard pharmacological preparation. In parallel, a typical preparation in Behavioral Pharmacology will be described.

The essential components of a typical pharmacological preparation allow assessment of drug effects on an isolated strip of tissue (e.g., a piece of guinea pig ileum). The strip of muscle is removed from the guinea pig and suspended in a bath such that its contractions can be monitored continuously. Our comparison preparation from Behavioral Pharmacology will be the responding of a monkey under an FR 50 schedule of food presentation.

The two preparations have several characteristics in common. The environments in which the responses of the tissue strip and the responses of the monkeys are measured are highly controlled. The temperature and chemical composition of the bath in which the tissue resides are held constant in much the same way as the monkey's environment is controlled. The tissue is isolated in the sense that it is separated from its normal place in the body so that interactive influences are eliminated. Similarly, a part of the behavioral repertoire of the monkey is isolated for study. The piece of tissue is selected because it exemplifies certain functional properties (e.g., because it is a specific part of the digestive system, or because it is known to interact specifically with a certain class of drugs). Likewise, the monkey's performance is selected because of its functional properties or because of its known sensitivity to certain drug classes. In both cases direct and automatic recording of the dependent variable(s) minimizes the possible contribution of experimenter bias.

Once the preparation has been chosen and established, the next step is to establish a baseline, and it is here that a small but important difference between the two preparations is evident. With the isolated tissue strip, one simply waits for a kymograph record of contractions to 'settle down'. Once this happens, experimentation may begin. In the case of the monkey, by contrast, it is customary to establish a baseline of performance across several (sometimes many) test sessions. Performance must be relatively uniform within test sessions and also consistent from session to session.

Once a stable baseline has been established it is customary to test the effects of the drug *vehicle*, i.e., the solvent in which the drug is placed. Most drugs are provided in solid form and consequently must be dissolved or suspended in solution before being applied to the preparation. Usually, vehicles are chosen that do not exert any pharmacological action of their own. Sometimes, however, this is not possible because the drug of interest will dissolve only in active solvents. In either case, however, it is important to administer the vehicle by itself to determine its effects. In the case of an active vehicle, such a determination provides a reference value against which to compare the effects of the drug plus its vehicle. Also, such a determination allows assessment of the separate effects of the drug administration procedures. This is especially important in Behavioral Pharmacology because administration of the drug often requires unusual and repeated handling of the subject.

Following determination of vehicle effects and recovery of the baseline, experiments with the drug can begin. Both preparations allow for controlled application of precise amounts of drug. For the tissue preparation the drug is added to the bath, for the monkey it is added to the monkey (for details, see Section 2.7.1). At this point another difference arises. With the isolated tissue, the bath may be drained and refilled repeatedly so that the drug is 'washed' from the preparation. With the monkey, 'washing' is not possible. Instead normal metabolic processes clear the drug from the system. Consequently, with the tissue preparation, if the baseline is recovered following 'washing', additional drug or vehicle tests may proceed. With the monkey, the next drug or vehicle test awaits the time, once the drug has been cleared from the subject's system, when the session-to-session baseline has been recovered. For each preparation, each administration involves application of the same volume of fluid, be it vehicle or drug plus vehicle. In Behavioral Pharmacology the volume of fluid administered most often is held constant at 1.0 ml per kg of body weight.

Note that in both of the preceding cases, additional testing begins only if the previous baseline can be recovered. If baseline responding can be recovered following drug administration, the drug effects are said to be *reversible*. Reversibility is desirable because it allows complete determination of a drug's effects in a single preparation and thus avoids the complications that can arise from making comparisons across preparations (cf. Sidman, 1960; Johnston and Pennypacker, 1980). For the sake of simplicity, let us assume that in both our hypothetical preparations the effects are reversible.

Typically, the process of examining the effect of a certain amount (dose) of the drug and then recovering the baseline is carried out several times with a single preparation. This is done both to assess the reliability of the findings (i.e., do you get the same effect each time you test a particular dose?) and to allow determination of the effects of a range of doses. It is essential that effects of a range of doses be assessed. With an isolated-tissue preparation, effects of a range of doses can be examined in a single experimental session. With the monkey responding under the FR schedule, however, it can take much longer to obtain the same type of information. If, as described above, we must wait for the drug to clear from the monkey's system before we can test a new dose, then it may take weeks to obtain complete information. A technique exists, however, that can shorten the time needed to observe effects of several doses. The technique is called *cumulative dosing* and can be employed in either of the types of preparation we have been discussing. If a drug's effects last long enough then it is possible, after observing the effects of one amount, to add more drug to the preparation and thus effectively increase the active amount. For example, if with the isolated-tissue preparation we began by testing effects of Dose X and then, after observing its effects, added 2X more to the bath, then we would be observing the effects of a dose of 3X. Continued addition of other amounts would allow us to see effects of even larger doses. The same process can be used with the monkey preparation; within a single session, several doses could be examined.

Unambiguous interpretations of results obtained via cumulative dosing depend on there being no difference between data obtained this way and data obtained using the more standard technique. This is not always the case when behavioral preparations are used (Thompson et al., 1983). Consequently, when studying cumulative dosing with a particular drug in a given preparation one must determine if cumulative and intermittent dosing produce the same effect (cf. Sannerud and Young, 1986) before relying solely on cumulative dosing.

2.4. Dose–response functions

The foundation of pharmacology is the dose–response function. A dose–response (or dose–effect) curve is a graph in which the value of the dependent measure is plotted over dose (or amount) of drug. Fig. 2 exemplifies two of the types of curves commonly seen in pharmacology. The curve on the left is monotonic (i.e., it goes only in one direction) whereas the one on the right is bitonic.

By convention, the scale on the X-axis of a dose–response function is logarithmic (there are some exceptions, however), whereas Y-axes exhibit a wider range of scale types. There are a couple of reasons why this is so. One, in many pharmacological

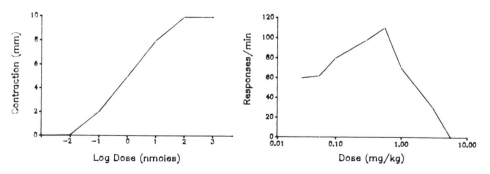

Fig. 2. Two hypothetical graded dose-response functions. The graph on the left shows mm of tissue contraction as a function of the logarithm of dose. The graph on the right shows response rate as a function of dose with a logarithmic X-axis.

preparations log dose–response curves are linear over a good portion of their range. This property makes curves easier to compare both statistically and visually. Two, use of a logarithmic scale allows a wide range of doses to be displayed on a single graph. Goldstein et al. (1968) discuss more fully justifications for the use of logarithmic scales.

Dose–effect curves are generally described as either graded or quantal. Graded functions are those in which the dependent variable is continuous. Both of the hypothetical preparations described above would yield a graded dose–response function, and the curves shown in Figs. 1 and 2 are graded dose–response functions. In Behavioral Pharmacology (and in pharmacology in general) either direct or relative measures of effect may be shown on the Y-axis of graphs of dose–effect functions. In Fig. 1, for example, drug effects are expressed as a proportion of the baseline, or nondrug, level. Because baseline values may differ among experimental subjects, it is common to see dose–effect functions expressed as a proportion of baseline level.

The quantal dose–effect curve results when an all-or-none dependent variable is employed. Two examples of an all-or-none response are death and loss of the righting reflex. (To test the righting reflex one places an animal on its back and determines whether it rights itself. Either it does or it does not, thus an all-or-none response is provided.) Quantal dose–effect curves provide information concerning individual differences among preparations. Fig. 3 illustrates two hypothetical quantal dose–response functions, one for the righting reflex and one for death. Plotted is the percent of subjects showing the effect at each dose. For example, at a dose of about 0.8 mg/kg 50% of the subjects tested have lost the righting reflex whereas only 1% of the subjects have died. Perpendicular lines to the X-axis from the point at which the dashed line from 50% on the Y-axis crosses each curve provide values for two commonly determined parameters: the ED_{50} and the LD_{50}. These two parameters (the Effective Dose producing a given effect in 50% of the subjects and the Lethal Dose killing 50% of the subjects) can be used to assess the safety margin of a drug as long

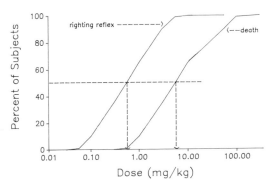

Fig. 3. Two hypothetical quantal dose-effect curves. The one on the left is for loss of righting reflex (see text) and the one on the right is for death. Descending vertical arrows that intersect the curves at the 50% point (dashed horizontal line) indicate the ED_{50} (effective dose) and LD_{50} (lethal dose).

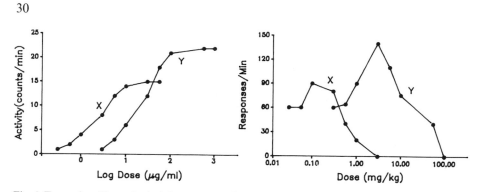

Fig. 4. Two pairs of hypothetical dose-response functions illustrating differences in potency and maximum effect. X and Y label curves for different drugs.

as the quantal dose–response functions are parallel (as they are in Fig. 3). The larger the ratio of LD_{50} to ED_{50}, the safer the drug. The size of this ratio, of course, depends on the effect chosen to determine the ED_{50}. For example, the safety margin for barbiturates is larger when the quantal response tested is sedation than when it is anesthesia.

Whether graded or quantal, dose–effect curves have four major characteristics: potency, slope, variability and maximum effect. These characteristics are illustrated in Fig. 4, which shows four curves, two monotonic dose–response functions and two bitonic functions. Potency refers to the absolute amount of drug needed to produce a given effect, and therefore refers, for a dose–effect function, to the placement of the curve along the X-axis. The smaller the amount needed to produce an effect the more potent is the drug. In Fig. 4, curves show that Drug X is more potent than Drug Y. From a therapeutic point of view, potency of a drug is one of its least important characteristics. As long as the amount of drug needed to produce a given effect is not so large as to prevent its administration, potency is of little concern.

The second and third characteristics of dose–effect functions, slope and variability, interact in important ways. Slope is related to the range of doses over which a drug goes from having no effect to having a maximum effect; the steeper the slope the narrower the range. Variability refers to the consistency of effects of a particular dose over repeated administrations. If the slope of the function is very steep and variability is large, then it is possible for the effects of a single dose to range from near minimum to near maximum. By contrast, if the slope is shallow, then variability becomes less important.

The fourth characteristic of a dose–response function is maximum effect, which refers to the largest value of the measured response that the drug can produce. In monotonic, increasing dose–response functions the magnitude of an effect often increases as dose increases until an effect is reached beyond which further increases in dose produce no additional effect. Maximum effect, of course, is a therapeutically important aspect of a dose–response curve. For example, increasing doses of aspirin and morphine both produce increased relief from pain; morphine, however, can produce a much greater effect. As a final important note concerning maximum effect, remember that with bitonic dose–effect curves (common in Behavioral Pharmacology) there are two maximum effects to consider: The maximum increasing effect and the maximum decreasing effect. In Fig. 3, the curves indicate that Drug X is more potent than Drug Y, but the maximum effect of Drug Y exceeds that of Drug X. For the bitonic curves, however, the description is more complicated. Although Drug Y produces a larger increasing maximum effect, the two drugs produce the same maximum decreasing effect.

2.5. Pharmacological factors that influence dose–effect relations

Many types of factors influence the characteristics of dose–response curves. One factor, environmental influence, is the major focus of Behavioral Pharmacology, and a good deal of the remainder of this chapter will deal with variables from this class. There are many other types of factors, however, of which any pharmacologist must be aware, and it is to these that we turn first. These factors can be divided into two categories, pharmacological and nonpharmacological.

2.5.1. Prior presence of same (or related) drug

If an experimental subject has been exposed previously to a drug, subsequently that drug may have different effects. In a simple case, consider administering a dose of the drug at time t_1 and then again at time t_2. If t_2 is close enough to t_1 so that some of the drug from the initial administration is still present, then the second administration of the drug may have an effect similar to that of a larger dose. The cumulative-dosing technique described earlier is based on this possibility.

Prior exposure to the same drug can also result in subsequent alterations of effects even though the drug from the initial administration(s) is no longer present. These effects occur most often when the drug has been presented continuously or repeatedly. Following a bout of repeated or continuous exposure to a drug, the dose–effect curve for that drug can be shifted either to the right (the drug is less potent) or to the left (the drug is more potent); the former result is called *tolerance* and the latter, *sensitization*. In cases where prior exposure to one drug results in a shift in the dose–response curve for a second drug the phenomena are called *cross-tolerance* or *cross-sensitization*, respectively. The demonstration of cross-tolerance or cross-sensitization is one method for identifying drugs that have similar actions.

2.5.2. Concurrent presence of other drugs

Another factor that can alter a dose–response function is the concurrent presence of another drug. The potency or the maximum effect of a drug can be altered if it is administered in combination with another drug. Two major categories of interaction can be observed. When a drug's potency or maximum effect is reduced when it is given with another drug, the interaction is called *antagonism*. Fig. 5 illustrates the

32

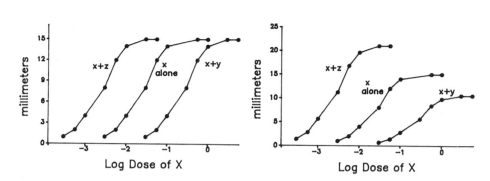

Fig. 5. Two sets of hypothetical dose-effects functions illustrating drug interactions. Each curve shows a function for a range of doses of Drug X. Curves labelled X+Z and X+Y show effects of a range of doses of X in combination with a fixed dose of either Drug Z or Drug Y.

two major kinds of antagonism. In the left panel three hypothetical dose–response curves are shown. Note that the curve for Drug X in the presence of a fixed dose of Drug Y is shifted to the right, indicating a loss of potency. A simple shift to the right in a dose–response function indicates a *surmountable*, or *competitive*, antagonism. That is, the effect of Drug X alone can be achieved by increasing the dose enough to overcome the antagonism.

The right panel of Fig. 5 illustrates another form of antagonism, an insurmountable, or noncompetitive, antagonism. Here, the dose–effect curve for Drug X in the presence of Drug Y reveals that certain magnitudes of effects that can be obtained by administering Drug X alone cannot be obtained when it is administered along with Drug Y.

The second major class of drug interactions falls under the heading, *synergism*. Synergism occurs when two drugs in combination produce a greater effect than either alone. Synergism can be observed simply as an increase in potency of a drug when it is given in combination with another drug (as depicted in the left panel of Fig. 5 for the curve labelled X+Z) or as a change in the maximum effect observable (as illustrated in the right panel of Fig. 5 for the curve labelled X+Z). More complex types of synergism are also possible in which both potency and maximum effect are changed. Sometimes a distinction is made between summation, wherein two drugs in combination produce an effect that is equal to the sum of their individual effects, and potentiation, wherein the two drugs produce an effect larger than the algebraic sum of their individual effects. It is important to realize that the curves in Fig. 5 do not characterize fully the nature of the interactions among Drugs X, Y and Z; a thorough description of the interaction would require that a 'family' of dose–response functions be determined. That is, the effects of X would need to be determined across a range of doses of Y and Z.

2.6. Nonpharmacological factors that influence dose–effect curves

Several nonpharmacological factors can influence dose–effect curves. One is the species of the subjects. For example, rats do not vomit, so if one wanted to study effects of drugs on emesis, rats would not be a good choice. Species differences can be more subtle, however. Consider an experiment by Byrd (1975) who studied effects of the analgesic drug morphine on the operant performance of baboons and chimpanzees. Even though comparable baseline behavior was established in the two species, drug effects were markedly different; baboons showed only decreases in performance whereas large increases were observed in chimps. Although this appears to be a species difference, it would be premature to conclude so. Even though reinforcement-schedule values and the measured rates of responding were the same in the two species, these equalities exist for the experimenter; they may not for the subjects. To demonstrate the species difference more conclusively both species must be studied under a range of schedule parameters, deprivation levels, response–effort requirements, stimulus conditions, reinforcer types, and other conditions. For example, the difference might disappear if the baboons were studied at a more extreme deprivation level. All this is to say that species comparisons are complex, and to appeal to a genetic basis for qualitative differences in drug effects is frequently premature if one has not conducted a thorough behavioral analysis.

Another factor that can influence a dose–effect curve is the size, or body weight, of a subject. A larger body frequently requires more drug to produce a given effect than does a smaller body, and this is especially true for drugs that have an affinity for body fat. Among members of a species, differences in body weight frequently are correlated with differences in body fat. Drug action depends critically on drug concentrations in the blood stream. Consequently, larger subjects with more fat may have more of the drug in fat, and less in blood, than do smaller subjects. To deal with this potential problem, drugs usually are given on a per-unit-body-weight basis. Most commonly, drugs are administered on a mg/kg basis. For drugs that do not have lipid affinity, adjusting for body weight is probably not crucial; most drugs of behavioral interest exert their actions on nervous tissue, and the amount of nervous tissue available is not highly correlated with total body weight (cf. MacPhail and Gollub, 1974).

A third factor influencing dose–response functions is sex of the subject. Many drugs produce effects on organs that are affected by and/or control the release of hormones, and because the hormonal systems are generally different for males and females of vertebrate species, drug effects can depend on the sex of the subject.

A fourth, and perhaps less obvious, determinant of dose–response functions is the time of day at which a drug is administered. Circadian rhythms can interact with many actions of drugs including behavioral effects. For example, Evans et al. (1973) studied the effects of several drugs on responding of rats maintained under a free-operant avoidance schedule (see Part 1, Ch. 5). A 12:12-h light-dark cycle was in effect, and avoidance performance was assessed both after 10 h in the dark and 10 h in the light. Scopolamine increased avoidance responding more during the light phase of each day than during the dark phase.

2.7. Time–response functions

In addition to dose–response functions, another important aspect of drug action is the time–response function. The effects of a particular drug dose change across time following its administration. Time–response functions have four major characteristics. The time from initial administration of the drug until the first measurable effect is called the *latency*; the time from initial administration to the beginning of the maximum effect usually is called *time to peak effect*; the time from the beginning to the end of the maximum effect is the *duration of peak effect*; and the time from the initial effect until no effect is seen is called the *duration of action* (cf. Levine, 1978).

Temporal characteristics of drug action are important in the design of experiments even when they are themselves not the direct focus of research. In Behavioral Pharmacology interest focuses most often on the action of a drug as it exerts its peak effect. Consequently, the drug is administered far enough in advance of exposure to the behavioral procedure so that measurements of the behavioral effects occur when the drug is exerting its maximum effect. Unless one is examining temporal aspects of drug effects, it is also important to arrange that the period of observation of drug effects does not extend beyond the end of the period of maximum effect. In many cases it is necessary to perform preliminary experiments on the temporal characteristics of a drug's effects to determine when to administer the drug and how long to monitor its effects.

Duration of drug action depends on factors that are involved in the absorption, distribution and elimination of the drug (cf. Levine, 1978). Most frequently, a behaviorally active drug is administered so that the blood supply distributes it to its site(s) of action; consequently, an important piece of information about a drug is its *half-life* in the blood stream. Half-life is the time it takes for the drug concentration in the blood to be reduced by 50%. In most cases this does not indicate one-half the duration of action because the amount of drug eliminated during any interval depends on the amount of drug present at the beginning of the period. Unfortunately, because values must be determined empirically, in many instances the half-life of a drug is not known.

Several classes of factors can influence the time-course of drug action. Processes responsible for absorption, distribution, and elimination all come into play. How long a drug's effects last depends largely on the processes involved in its elimination; metabolism and excretion are the main ways that drug action is ended. Many drugs undergo metabolism in the liver via enzymatic degradation.

Physical characteristics of a drug can determine its absorption and distribution. For example, some drugs (e.g., thiopental) have an affinity for fat. Once in the body, such drugs may be preferentially stored in fat, reducing the amount that initially gets to the site(s) of action, and then prolonging the total duration of action as the drug is slowly released from the fat. Another important phenomenon concerning drug distribution is the *blood-brain barrier*. The chemical constitution of some drugs (e.g. those with a charged nitrogen atom or very large molecules) is such that they do not readily enter the brain. The blood-brain barrier often provides a useful 'tool' to behavioral pharmacologists. For example, Vaillant (1964) compared the effects on food-reinforced pecking by pigeons of physostigmine (a drug that passes the blood-brain barrier) in combination with atropine (an antagonist of physostigmine that penetrates the blood-brain barrier) or methylatropine (an antagonist that does not readily cross the blood-brain barrier). In so doing he was able to isolate effects of physostigmine that were due to its actions in the brain.

2.7.1. Routes of administration

A major influence on the time course of drug action is the *route of administration*. The five most commonly used routes are listed in Table 1. The routes other than oral are called parenteral routes (i.e., they do not involve the alimentary tract), and all of the routes listed fall into the class of *systemic* routes of administration in that they

TABLE 1
Systemic routes of administration

Route (abbr.)	Description	Advantages	Disadvantages
Oral (p.o.)	By mouth	Some drugs cause tissue irritation if injected.	Uneven absorption due to variation in gut contents. Some drugs relatively ineffective by mouth
Subcutaneous (s.c.)	Inject just under skin	Even, relatively slow absorption	Cannot inject large volumes
Intramuscular (i.m.)	Inject into muscle mass (e.g., pigeon breast)	Rapid, even absorption	Some animals do not have enough muscle
Intravenous (i.v.)	Inject into vein	Very rapid absorption	Need to control rate of injection. Some animals may not have veins large enough
Intraperitoneal (i.p.)	Inject through abdominal wall into peritoneal space	Rapid absorption, simple technique	Inconsistent absorption due to injections into organs

are designed to get the drug into the circulatory system. Care must be taken when employing the i.m., s.c. or i.p. routes to make sure that the drug is not administered directly into the blood stream by accident. This usually can be prevented by 'aspirating' the syringe by drawing the plunger out a short distance to see whether any blood is drawn into the syringe after the needle has been inserted. The i.m. route is used most often with primates and pigeons, whereas the i.p. and s.c. routes are more common with rodents. Pigeons usually receive injections into the breast muscle, whereas primates usually are injected in the rump or leg. Subcutaneous injections to rodents usually are given by inserting the needle into pinched-up skin on the back of the animal's neck.

In some cases, instead of injecting a drug subcutaneously, either a pellet or an osmotic minipump can be implanted under the skin. Pellets are prepared so that the drug is released slowly across time to provide lengthy, continuous exposure to it. The minipumps, too, are constructed to result in slow, continuous release, and they have the advantage of producing a constant rate of release. The rate of release from an implanted pellet changes over time as the size of the pellet diminishes.

Less commonly used systemic routes of administration include inhalation and rectal administration. Current interest about the inhalation route centers on tobacco, marijuana and 'crack' cocaine smoking, and nasal insufflation of powdered cocaine.

In addition to systemic routes of administration, drugs sometimes are delivered directly to the brain either by placing them into brain loci or into cerebrospinal fluid. These routes circumvent the blood-brain barrier. Intracisternal (i.c.) and intracerebroventricular (i.c.v.t.) are two methods for placing a drug into the cerebrospinal fluid, the first by making an injection into the spinal fluid and the second by injecting into a brain ventricle. Another set of procedures involves stereotaxic placement of either cannulae or fine pipettes into specific brain locations.

Routes of administration can alter dose–response functions as well as time–response curves. Downs et al. (1980), for example, compared i.v., s.c., i.m. and oral routes of administration of several drugs. The parenteral routes resulted in roughly equivalent potency across routes for heroin, cocaine, d-amphetamine and phencyclidine (PCP), but heroin and PCP were 50 to 100 times less potent by the oral route. Cocaine was 16 times less potent orally, whereas d-amphetamine did not lose potency when administered p.o.

2.7.2. Behavioral factors

A final class of variables that can influence the time course of drug action is highly relevant to the present chapter; behavioral variables can modulate the temporal properties of drug effects. For example, Manning (1973) examined effects of orally administered tetrahydrocannabinol on performance of rhesus monkeys responding under a differential-reinforcement-of-low-rate (DRL) 60-s schedule of food presentation (cf. Part 1, Ch. 3). The drug occasionally was administered 3 h before daily 3-h sessions. Performance was disrupted more severely in the first half of the session than in the second half, seemingly illustrating the time course of drug action. When the drug was administered 4 h before a session, however, the pattern of drug effects across the session was identical to that observed when it was administered 3 h before. The temporal course of drug action across the session, therefore, depended on exposure to the behavioral procedure and was not simply a function of time since administration.

3. Behavioral pharmacology: principles and techniques

The report by Dews that was described earlier was followed by many experiments examining behavioral modification of drug effects. A particularly informative set of experiments was performed by Kelleher and Morse (1964). They trained squirrel monkeys to press a lever under a two-component multiple schedule of reinforcement (see Part 1, Ch. 3). One component was FR 30 and the other FI 10-min. For one group of subjects reinforcement was presentation of a food pellet; for the other group reinforcement was termination of a stimulus paired with intermittent electric shock presentation. (Specifically, after a given period of time, brief shocks were presented at short intervals. If the monkey satisfied the response requirement of the schedule, the prevailing stimuli and the shocks were terminated. This arrangement is called a stimulus–shock termination schedule.) Inspection of cumulative response records revealed that nearly identical performance patterns had been established in the two groups even though the motivation for performance was different. Kelleher and Morse examined effects of a range of doses of *d*-amphetamine, and the results are shown in Fig. 6. As the dose increased, performance under FI first increased and then

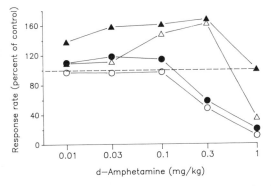

Fig. 6. Effects of amphetamine on rate of lever pressing by squirrel monkeys under a multiple FI 10-min FR 30 schedule. Effects are expressed as percentage of control rate of responding. Filled symbols are from a multiple schedule of food presentation; open symbols are from a multiple schedule of termination of a stimulus paired with electric shock delivery. Triangles show data from FI schedules; circles show those from FR schedules. The dashed horizontal line at 100% shows where points would fall if the drug produced no effect. (Adapted from Kelleher and Morse, 1964, with permission of the publisher.)

decreased, whereas performance under FR only decreased, and this happened regardless of the type of reinforcement. That is, the schedules of reinforcement were stronger determinants of the drug's effects than were the motivational operations. Again, then, we have a result that indicates that simplistic interpretations of drug effects are likely to be in error. Dews' results (Fig. 1) showed that behavioral effects of drugs cannot be predicted accurately from examining the form of the response. The findings of Kelleher and Morse add that simple predictions made on the basis of motivation (e.g., that different motivations will lead to different drug effects) also can be erroneous.

3.1. Rate-dependent drug effects

Results from experiments like those of Dews and of Kelleher and Morse led to substantial interest in characterizing drug effects on operant behavior. One approach was to focus on response rate under a schedule as a predictor of a drug's effects. For example, in Kelleher and Morse's study, response rates under the FR schedules were relatively high and those under the FI schedules lower. The drug, therefore, increased low rates but decreased high rates. For drugs usually categorized as stimulants, the generality of these *rate-dependent* effects is fairly substantial (cf. Dews and Wenger, 1977).

Under some conditions, the relation between response rate and drug effect is very orderly. For example, one method of generating a variety of response rates is to expose a subject to an FI schedule and collect response rates in equal-length segments of the interval. As an illustration, responses by a subject exposed to FI 10-min might be collected separately during each successive min of each interval so that an average rate for the 1st, 2nd and on up to the 10th min may be computed. This will yield 10 different average response rates ranging from very low rates (during early portions of the interval) to fairly high response rates (near the end of the interval). When a variety of response rates have been produced in an individual subject (e.g., by exposure to an FI schedule), data typically are presented as shown in Fig. 7. This is a 'rate-dependency' scatter plot showing proportional change in response rate following drug administration over control response rates. Each point shows the proportional change in average response rate following drug administration in a particular 10th of the fixed-interval over the average response rate during that 10th under non-drug conditions. The data shown are a typical result; low control rates are increased, whereas higher control rates are decreased.

Initially, rate-dependency seemed to serve as an organizing principle for a substantial variety of drug effects on schedule-controlled behavior, but its breadth of applicability has not proven so extensive. For example, the experiments of Kelleher and Morse described above are consistent with a rate-dependency account in that drug effects are predictable from baseline response rates (comparatively high rates under FR were decreased and comparatively low rates under FI were increased) rather than

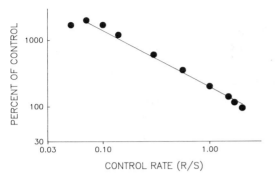

Fig. 7. A 'rate-dependency' scatter plot. For each value of control (i.e., baseline, or nondrug) rate the proportional change from baseline is plotted over it. The straight line was fit by the method of least-squares. (Adapted from McKearney and Barrett, 1978, with permission of the publisher.)

from motivational operations. Subsequent research, however, showed that even when equivalent rates and patterns of behavior were established using different motivational arrangements, drug effects depended on the motivational factors (e.g., McKearney, 1974; Barrett, 1976; Branch, 1979). For example, Fig. 8 shows data collected by McKearney (1974) from monkeys whose lever pressing was maintained under FI 5-min schedules of food presentation or electric-shock presentation (see Morse and Kelleher, 1977, for a discussion of how behavior can be maintained under schedules of intermittent, response-dependent electric shock presentation). Effects of morphine and chlorpromazine depended on the event scheduled as a consequence for lever pressing, with morphine producing increases only when responding was

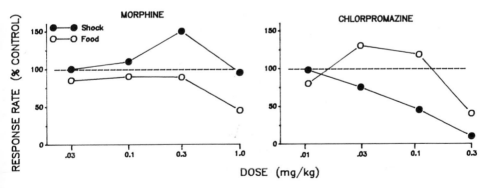

Fig. 8. Effects of morphine (left graph) or chlorpromazine (right graph) on lever pressing by squirrel monkeys maintained under a multiple FI 5-min (food presentation) FI 5-min (electric shock presentation) schedule. Effects are expressed as a percentage of control (i.e., nondrug) response rates. Note that morphine increased shock maintained performance while only decreasing food-reinforced responding, whereas chlorpromazine had an opposite pattern of effects. (Adapted from McKearney, 1974, with permission of the publisher.)

maintained by shock presentation and chlorpromazine producing increases only when lever pressing was maintained by food presentation.

In addition to data showing limits to the generality of the rate-dependency principle, the conceptual basis of the approach was challenged both with respect to the use of average rates within parts of an FI schedule as a method for examining rate dependency and with respect to characterizing the data. Branch and Gollub (1974) argued that the averages taken from segments of FI schedules frequently were not representative of interval-to-interval performance. Gonzalez and Byrd (1977) and Ksir (1981) suggested that an alternative view of rate-dependent effects is that different response rates become more similar as a result of drug administration (i.e., that stimulant drugs result in 'rate constancy' or 'rate convergence').

Nevertheless, that drug effects, especially those of drugs labeled stimulants, can be related to baseline rates is a well established fact (Kelleher and Morse, 1968; Sanger and Blackman, 1976; Dews and Wenger, 1977). Consequently, when interpreting drug effects it is important to take baseline performance into account. Experiments therefore should be designed so that differences in baseline performance are not confounded with other variables of interest. Otherwise, a confounded result is possible. For example, if one were interested in whether a drug differentially affected behavior under the stimulus control of auditory versus visual stimuli, it would be wise to ensure that baseline performances under the two types of stimuli were equivalent. If the baselines were not comparable, then a differential drug effect could be due either to the type of stimulus control or to the differences in baseline performance.

3.2. The importance of context

In addition to depending on baseline rate of responding, drug effects on schedule-controlled behavior have been shown to be influenced by other factors. One of these is the *context* in which schedule-controlled performance occurs. For example, McKearney and Barrett (1975) trained squirrel monkeys to press a lever under an FI 10-min schedule of food presentation. Then, every 30th response was followed by a brief electric shock. (Technically, this is a conjoint FI 10-min [food] FR 30 [shock] schedule; cf. Part 1, Ch. 3.) This suppressed performance (i.e., punishment occurred). This punished responding was studied under two different conditions. In one, each food presentation under the FI schedule was followed by a 10-min period in which a distinctive stimulus was present and responses were without programmed consequences (extinction). In the other, during the 10-min period following each reinforcement, a free-operant avoidance schedule was in effect; in the absence of lever pressing, brief electric shocks occurred every 5 s, whereas each lever press postponed shock for 25 s. Fig. 9 shows that the effects of *d*-amphetamine on FI performance were strongly influenced by the conditions in effect during the alternating 10-min periods, with response rates higher when the food-reinforced responding alternated with an avoidance schedule and lower when it alternated with extinction.

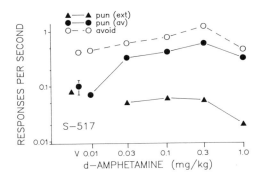

Fig. 9. Effects of *d*-amphetamine on lever pressing by a squirrel monkey that responded under a multiple schedule in which a component consisting of a conjoint FI 10-min (food presentation) FR 30 [electric shock presentation] (punishment) schedule alternated either with a 10-min period of extinction or a 10-min period of free-operant avoidance. Open circles: rate of lever pressing under the avoidance schedule. Filled circles: Rate of punished responding (i.e., during the FI) when it alternated with avoidance. Filled triangles: Rate of punished responding when it alternated with extinction. Note that the Y-axis is logarithmic. (Adapted from McKearney and Barrett, 1975, with permission of the publisher.)

These findings have important implications for experimental design. Frequently, procedures of the general type employed by McKearney and Barrett, i.e., those in which separate performances are controlled by different discriminative stimuli (multiple schedules), are used to study drug effects. To save time multiple schedules are often used to study the effect of a drug on more than one type of performance. When they are, however, drug effects in one component of the schedule may depend on what is going on in other components (cf. Part 1, Chs. 3 and 4).

3.3. Behavioral history

Behavioral history may influence how a drug affects schedule-controlled behavior. For example, Urbain et al. (1978) found that amphetamine increased response rates under an FI schedule in rats that had previously been exposed to DRL schedules but did not do so in subjects that had been exposed previously to FR schedules. The history of exposure to either DRL or FR schedules resulted in differences in baseline rates with FR-trained rats exhibiting higher rates than DRL-trained rats. So, explicit manipulation of behavioral history generated a result consistent with a rate-dependency analysis. Another striking illustration of the role of history was provided by Barrett (1977) who studied food-reinforced lever pressing of squirrel monkeys under an FI 5-min schedule of food presentation with the added contingency that each 50th response produced an electric shock (i.e., a conjoint FI 5-min [food] FR 50 [shock] schedule). The FR schedule of shock presentation punished behavior maintained by the FI schedule. Barrett determined the effects of amphetamine on this baseline performance both before and after intervening exposure to a free-operant shock-avoidance procedure. Before the experience with the avoidance schedule amphetamine decreased the rate of lever pressing under the FI schedule. After the exposure, however, despite no noticeable change in baseline performance, some doses of the drug produced large increases in response rate. That is, the qualitative nature of the drug's effect was changed by the intervening history of exposure to the avoidance contingencies.

Experience with a specific drug-behavior interaction can also modify a drug's later effects. For example, Glowa and Barrett (1983) studied the effects of pentobarbital on lever pressing of squirrel monkeys under an FI 5-min stimulus-shock termination schedule (cf. Kelleher and Morse, 1964). Each 30th response, however, produced a brief electric shock (i.e., the schedule was conjoint FI 5 min [stimulus-shock termination] FR 30 [shock]). The FR schedule of shock presentation punished responding maintained by the FI schedule of stimulus-shock termination. Initially, intermediate doses of pentobarbital increased response rate. Following determination of dose effects of morphine (which only decreased response rate), however, pentobarbital no longer increased response rates. Subsequent to exposure to a range of doses of amphetamine (a drug that increased response rates), rate increases followed administration of pentobarbital. Pentobarbital's effects, then, depended on the preceding drug–behavior interactions.

The examples just described illustrate the complexity of drug–behavior interactions. A thorough analysis of behavioral effects of a drug demands, first of all, systematic examination of a range of parameters of the behavioral procedure under scrutiny plus systematic manipulation of pharmacological variables (dose, route of administration etc.). In addition, consideration must be given to behavioral context, behavioral history and experience with particular drug–behavior interactions.

4. Interactions between drugs and behavioral processes

A major goal of Behavioral Pharmacology is to describe, characterize, and quantify how drugs modify or otherwise interact with fundamental behavioral processes. This section will illustrate how this has been attempted for several behavioral processes with a variety of drugs. Ideally, effects of a single drug across a range of behavioral processes should be described, but Behavioral Pharmacology is a young enough scientific field that such an analysis has not been completed for any single drug.

4.1. Drugs and stimulus control

The interaction of drugs with stimulus-control processes has been studied from several perspectives. Three issues of continuing interest have been: Degree of stimulus control as a determinant of a drug's effect, how internal (i.e., behavior-related) or external stimuli control behavior, and how temporal control of behavior is modified.

4.1.1. Degree of stimulus control

Two classes of techniques have been employed to examine the relations between degree of stimulus control and drug effects: (a) comparisons of performances that involve developing stimulus control versus completely established stimulus control and (b) comparisons of performances with different degrees of established stimulus control. An example of the former is Thompson's (1975, 1977) comparison of drug effects on performance under a repeated-acquisition procedure and on a similar task in which stimulus control was fully established. At the beginning of a trial three response keys were illuminated with one of four colors. A pigeon's peck on the appropriate key lit the keys by another of the four colors. A peck on either of the other two keys was counted as an 'error' and resulted in a short blackout followed by the keys being lit with the same color. When the second color was presented, another (usually) of the three keys was the 'correct' one. The sequence continued until each of the four colors had been presented and the 'correct' key pecked in its presence.

Reinforcement depended on accurate completion of this four-response chain of behavior. In a 'performance' condition, the sequence required for reinforcement was the same from session to session. In a 'learning' condition, the required sequence differed for each session. The performance condition, then, involved established stimulus control, whereas the learning condition involved developing stimulus control. Thompson (1977) examined the effects of cocaine on these two conditions and found that 'errors' were increased above baseline levels by lower doses under the learning condition than under the performance condition. These effects indicated that behavior in the process of coming under stimulus control was more sensitive to the drug's effects than was behavior under well-established stimulus control.

Different steady-state levels of stimulus control can also be established. For example, Katz (1982, 1983) trained pigeons under a conditional discrimination procedure in which reinforcement under an FI 5-min schedule could occur following pecks to either of two keys of either of two colors (red or amber). The color assigned to each of the two response keys alternated randomly after each peck, thus insuring that responding was controlled by key color and not location. The key color in the presence of which pecks could be reinforced depended on the level of illumination of the houselight. When it was on at full brightness pecks to one color could be reinforced, and when it was off pecks to the other color could be reinforced. Drug effects were observed under these conditions and also under conditions where the intensity of the houselight was reduced (from 22.4 ftL to 0.43 or 0.05 ftL), which diminished stimulus control by the key colors. Katz (1982, 1983) observed that promazine and pentobarbital decreased stimulus control by the low-intensity houselight but not by the high-intensity houselight. By contrast, amphetamine and cocaine did not disrupt stimulus control under either condition. These findings illustrate that effects of some drugs can depend on the degree of stimulus control exerted by external stimuli.

4.1.2. Internal and external stimulus control

Discriminative stimuli need not be exteroceptive, and the interaction of drugs and behavior under 'interoceptive' stimulus control also has been studied. One persistent question is whether drug effects on interoceptively or exteroceptively controlled behavior are the same. For example, Laties (1972) studied pigeons under a fixed-consecutive-number procedure (Mechner, 1958; see also Part 1, Ch. 3) under which 8 or more consecutive pecks on one response key followed by a peck on a second key was the sequence required for reinforcement. Two variations of the procedure were used. In one, the two response keys remained illuminated with the same color throughout; in the other, the eighth consecutive peck on the first key changed the color on the two keys. In the second case, therefore, the stimulus controlling pecking the second key was key color (an exteroceptive stimulus). In the former case, because key colors never changed, the stimulus controlling pecks on the second key was (were) that (those) arising from emitting the appropriate number of pecks on the first key. Effects of several drugs were examined under these two procedures. Amphetamine, scopolamine, chlorpromazine and promazine all led to considerable disruption of interoceptive stimulus control. Specifically, the number of times that the subjects pecked the second key after making fewer than 8 consecutive responses on the first key increased greatly following drug administration. Addition of the exteroceptive stimulus substantially attenuated the disruptive effects of amphetamine and scopolamine. Chlorpromazine and promazine continued to disrupt stimulus control, even for exteroceptive stimuli. Laties' results show that the source of stimulus control can determine drug effects. Drugs, therefore, may possibly be classified with respect to how they interact with interoceptive versus exteroceptive control. A caveat is in order, however; the two procedures used by Laties generated different degrees of stimulus control. As the results of the studies by Katz (described above) show, it is possible that this difference in degree of stimulus control contributed to the differences in drug effects. The development of procedures that produce comparable levels of control using exteroceptive or interoceptive stimuli will be necessary to sort out the relative contributions of the relevant variables.

4.1.3. Temporal control

Closely related to the study of effects of drugs on behavior controlled by interoceptive stimuli is the examination of drug effects on the temporal control of behavior. One important measurable aspect of a stimulus is its duration, which can control behavior via differential reinforcement (cf. Elsmore, 1971, 1972). Several procedures are available for the study of temporal control. These include the basic FI and DRL reinforcement schedules, the more recently developed 'peak procedure' (e.g., Roberts, 1981; Part 2, Ch. 1). For example, Meck and Church (1987) used the peak procedure to compare effects of physostigmine and neostigmine on temporal control (the comparison is of interest because the two drugs have similar actions outside the central nervous system, but only one, physostigmine, readily crosses the blood-brain barri-

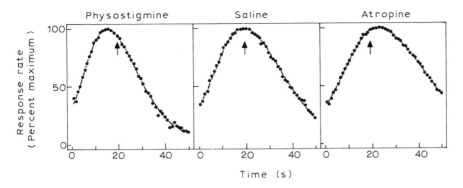

Fig. 10. Group-mean response rate during each second of 'peak' trials (see text), expressed as a percentage of the maximum average rate observed across all seconds, plotted over consecutive seconds. Each point is the average from ten subjects over the last 5 days of exposure to the experimental conditions. The left panel shows data from subjects exposed to physostigmine (0.03 mg/kg) before sessions; the center panel shows data from animals that received saline; the right panel shows data from subjects exposed to atropine (0.15 mg/kg). (Adapted from Meck and Church, 1987, with permission of the publisher.)

er). They trained rats to press a lever under a discrete-trial procedure in which two types of trials alternated randomly. One type was an FI 20-s schedule; white noise was presented and the 1st lever press after 20 s was reinforced. In the trial type, white noise was presented for 130 s, and lever pressing was not reinforced. After exposure to this procedure, behavior on trials without reinforcement developed characteristics indicative of temporal control; average response rates increased for about the first 20 s and then declined thereafter. The center panel of Fig. 10 illustrates the pattern averaged over 10 subjects. In subjects that were trained while exposed to pre-session administration of physostigmine, the pattern was altered; the peak of the distribution shifted left (see left panel of Fig. 10). Neostigmine produced effects that were indistinguishable from those observed when saline was administered. In other experiments, Meck and Church (1987) found that atropine (a drug that in many tissue systems has effects opposite those of physostigmine) shifted the peak to the right (see right panel of Fig. 10). Such findings help illustrate that drugs may differ in how they affect temporal control of behavior.

4.2. Drugs and punished behavior

Drug effects on punished behavior have been examined extensively (see Sepinwall and Cook, 1978, for a review). This line of investigation began with a now classic series of experiments by Geller and his colleagues (Geller and Seifter, 1960; Geller et al., 1962). Rats were first trained to respond under a variable-interval (VI) 2-min schedule of presentation of sweetened condensed milk. Next, when a clicker sounded, every lever press resulted in presentation of milk and also in the delivery of electric shock (0.6–0.75 mA) to the grid floor (i.e., a conjoint FR 1 [food] FR 1 [shock] sched-

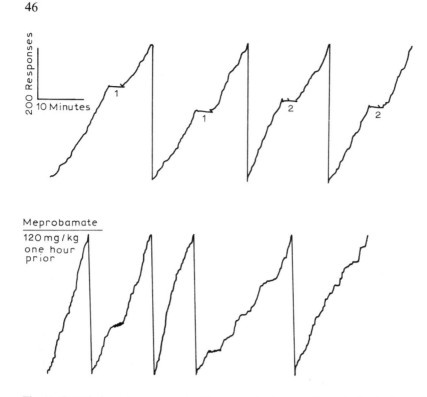

Fig. 11. Cumulative response records of lever pressing by rats. Pen up indicates that a VI 2-min schedule was in effect. Pen deflected indicates that each response resulted in both milk presentation and electric shock. Numerals under the periods with the pen deflected indicate the number of responses made during that period. The upper record is from a control session whereas the lower is from a session preceded by administration of 120 mg/kg of meprobamate. (Reproduced from Geller and Seifter, 1960, with permission of the publisher.)

ule). The top panel of Fig. 11 shows a cumulative record of typical performance under this procedure; responding was greatly suppressed during the periods with punishment. Several drugs, including amphetamine, chlordiazepoxide, meprobamate, pentobarbital and chlorpromazine, were administered to rats responding under this procedure. The lower panel of Fig. 11 shows effects produced by 120 mg/kg of meprobamate. Although this dose had relatively little effect on performance under the VI schedule alone, it substantially elevated responding during the clicker. This period is often called the 'conflict' period, and frequently procedures involving punishment of positively reinforced behavior are called 'conflict' procedures. Geller and his colleagues discovered that drugs that are used clinically as 'sedatives' or 'minor tranquilizers' (e.g., pentobarbital, chlordiazepoxide, meprobamate and phenobarbital) all attenuated the effects of punishment. By contrast, drugs from other classes did not.

Since the discoveries of Geller et al. research has characterized more accurately and completely how drugs interact with punished responding. For example, one possible confound in the studies by Geller et al. is that response rates were lower when punishment was present than when it was not. Therefore, the drug effects might have been due to these differences rather than specifically to the presence of punishment. Cook and Catania (1964) examined this possibility. They established responding by squirrel monkeys under concurrent schedules of food reinforcement (cf. Findley, 1958; Part 1, Ch. 6). Two VI schedules operated simultaneously, but reinforcement could be obtained from only one at a time via pressing one lever. Each schedule operated in the presence of a specific colored light, and the subject could alternate between schedules by pressing a second lever. One schedule was VI 6 min, and the other was conjoint VI 2 min [food] VI 2 min [shock]. Normally, higher response rates would prevail under the VI 2-min than under the VI 6-min schedule, but the superimposition of the schedule of shock presentation rendered the response rates under the two concurrent schedules roughly equal. That is, Cook and Catania, by adjusting shock intensity, successfully equated rates of punished and unpunished responding. They then examined effects of meprobamate. Fig. 12 shows that punished responding increased more than unpunished responding, suggesting a punishment-specific drug effect. Subsequent research with other 'sedatives' and other procedures has born out the original findings of Geller et al. (e.g., McMillan, 1973; Miczek and Lau, 1975; Branch et al., 1977; Dworkin et al., 1989) and has shown that these drugs do have effects that are specific to punishment (but see Wuttke and Kelleher, 1970).

An interesting limit to the generality of the effects of anxiolytic drugs on punished behavior was reported by McKearney (1976). Lever pressing of squirrel monkeys was maintained either by an FI 5-min schedule of food presentation or by an FI 5-min schedule of stimulus-shock termination (cf. Kelleher and Morse, 1964). Once relatively similar rates and temporal patterns of responding had been established, an additional punishment contingency was added whereby every 30th response was followed

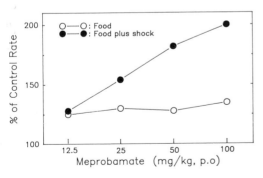

Fig. 12. Response rates, expressed as a percentage of control rate, as a function of dose of meprobamate. Filled circles show data from the concurrent schedule that included punishment, and open circles show data from unpunished responding. (Adapted from Cook and Catania, 1964, with permission of the publisher.)

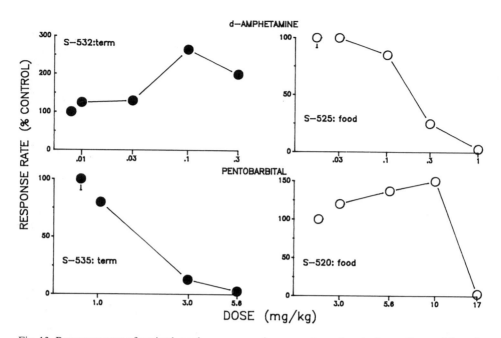

Fig. 13. Response rates of squirrel monkeys, expressed as percentage of control, over doses of *d*-amphetamine (upper graphs) or pentobarbital (lower graphs). Left panels show data for punished responding maintained by an FI schedule of termination of a stimulus correlated with shock, and right panels show data for punished responding maintained by food presentation. Bars on unconnected points show plus or minus one standard error for control sessions. Numbers preceded by S identify specific subjects. Note that the Y-axis scales differ among graphs. (Adapted from McKearney, 1976, with permission of the publisher.)

by a brief shock. Fig. 13 shows effects of selected doses of *d*-amphetamine, which usually suppresses punished responding, and pentobarbital, which usually increases the rate of punished behavior. The drug effects depended on the contingencies maintaining the punished performance. When responding was maintained by food presentation, the drugs had their 'typical' effects; pentobarbital increased and *d*-amphetamine decreased responding. When responding was maintained by termination of a stimulus-shock complex, however, the effects were reversed. These results illustrate an important fact; one must be careful not to oversimplify the description of a drug's effects on behavior. Before the advent of Behavioral Pharmacology, effects of drugs on 'behavior' were discussed, giving rise to terms like 'stimulant' and 'depressant'. Such terms, however, quickly became far too general. Subsequently, descriptions about drug effects on avoidance behavior, punished behavior, positively reinforced behavior, etc., gained popularity. Data such as those of McKearney, however, indicate that even these 'refinements' in descriptions of drug action may be incorrect. Behavioral Pharmacology has shown that drug effects depend critically on the specifics of the variables responsible for the behavior being examined. Seemingly minor characteristics of stimulus circumstances, scheduling of consequences, and other variables all can contribute to a drug's action on behavior. One of the major goals of Behavioral Pharmacology is to be able to offer meaningful, relatively general statements about drug–behavior interactions. These general statements, however, will have to be of a form that explains the complexity that already has been shown to exist.

Results such as those just described tell us something about behavior, too. In all the conditions he arranged, McKearney observed response suppression (i.e., what usually is called punishment). Yet, administration of drugs yielded effects that depended on the conditions of behavioral maintenance. This suggests that it may be an oversimplification to categorize simply as punishment all instances of response suppression via response-dependent presentation of stimuli. Punishment of postively reinforced behavior may be a different behavioral process than punishment of negatively reinforced behavior.

4.3. Drugs and conditional stimuli

Drugs may interact with stimuli that have developed the capacity, via the principles of respondent (also called Pavlovian or classical) conditioning, to elicit patterns of behavior. Such stimuli are called conditional stimuli (CSs), and the response patterns that are observed after CSs are called conditional responses. Interest in the interaction of drugs and CSs has focused largely on how drugs may alter the development of conditional responses. For example, Schindler et al. (1983) examined the interaction between morphine and the development of conditional responses. These investigators studied the nictitating membrane response of rabbits. A brief electric shock near the eye elicits movement of the membrane. In daily, 60-trial sessions brief shocks were preceded (by 800 ms) by either a tone or by a flickering light (30 trials of each

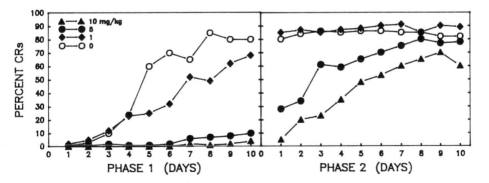

Fig. 14. Group-mean percentage of trials with a CR (nictitating membrane response by rabbits) over sessions during 10 sessions preceded by administration of morphine sulfate (left panel) and then over 10 subsequent sessions not preceded by drug administration (right panel). Open circles: No drug given in either phase. Diamonds: 1.0 mg/kg during Phase 1. Filled circles: 5 mg/kg during Phase 1. Triangles: 10 mg/kg during Phase 1. (Adapted from Schindler et al., 1983, with permission of the publisher.)

type); the 800-ms stimulus was thus the CS. Groups of subjects were exposed for 10 sessions (Phase 1) to these pairings under five different doses of morphine: 0, 0.2, 1, 5 or 10 mg/kg. Then, following a 5-day break, all subjects were exposed to another 10 sessions (Phase 2) of tone- or flickering light-shock pairings, but during this phase no subject received drugs. In this behavioral procedure, conditioning is indicated by nictitating membrane responses during the 800-ms CS prior to the shock. The results depicted in Fig. 14 show that mean levels of responding for the subjects that received 5 or 10 mg/kg of morphine remained low across the first 10 sessions, suggesting that the tone and flickering light had not become CSs.

Performance remained low after the 5-day break in these subjects, indicating that, indeed, morphine had retarded the development of conditional responses and had not simply blocked the performance of the conditional response. Subsequent experiments (e.g., Schindler et al., 1984) showed that morphine did not alter the effectiveness of electric shock as an elicitor of the nictitating response. This result further supports the view that morphine directly altered the formation of conditioned reflexes.

4.4. Drugs and conditioned reinforcement

The principles of respondent conditioning also are presumed to play a role in the development of conditioned reinforcers (Gollub, 1977), so examination of drug effects on behavior supported by conditioned reinforcement may be conceptualized partly as investigation of the interaction of drugs and established CSs. Following the pioneering work of Hill (1970), research on conditioned reinforcement and drugs has examined how drugs such as amphetamine, methylphenidate and pipradrol influence the effectiveness of conditioned reinforcers (e.g., Robbins, 1978; Beninger et al., 1981). For example, Files et al. (1989), using a within-subject design, trained pigeons to peck a response key during daily sessions made up of two parts. In the first part, which lasted for an unpredictable duration, pecks were reinforced according to a second-order schedule. Every 30 s, on the average, a peck could produce one of two consequences that lasted 3 s: either change of key color, houselight offset, tone presentation, and illumination of the feeder or all of the preceding plus elevation of the grain hopper. During the second part of each session, which lasted for 20 min, pecks no longer resulted in food presentation (i.e., extinction was in effect). Two types of extinction session could occur. In half of the sessions, simple extinction was in effect, i.e., pecks had no programmed consequences. During the remaining half of the sessions, pecks resulted in delivery, according to a random-interval 30-s schedule, of the stimulus complex correlated with food presentation. Because of its correlation with food, it was presumed that the stimulus complex would function as a conditioned reinforcer. Files et al. then examined the effects of methylphenidate on responding during extinction where responses either could or could not result in presentation of a conditioned reinforcer. Methylphenidate enhanced responding during extinction and did so to a greater degree when such responding occasionally resulted in conditioned reinforcement. These findings are consistent with those of others who have reported that methylphenidate enhances effects of conditioned reinforcers (e.g., Robbins, 1978).

4.5. Drugs and elicited behavior

When elicited behavior is studied in Behavioral Pharmacology, most frequently experimentation involves noxious stimuli such as heat or electric shock with an emphasis on how drugs interact with behavioral expressions of pain. Drugs with suspected analgesic activity routinely are administered to animals whose elicited reactions to noxious stimuli are then monitored. The two most commonly used procedures (with rodents) are the tail-flick test (D'Amour and Smith, 1941) and the hot-plate test (Woolfe and McDonald, 1944), although immersion of a rat's tail in either hot water (Janssen et al., 1963) or cold water (Pizziketti et al., 1985) is also sometimes used. In the tail-flick test a beam of light is focused on a small spot on the subject's tail and the latency either until the tail is 'flicked' to the side or until a preset maximum latency occurs (which prevents injury) is measured. In the hot-plate test, the subject is placed on a surface with a temperature (usually 55°C) that eventually will elicit paw withdrawal and paw licking. Latency to first paw lick is a common dependent variable. Drugs that are useful for alleviating pain (e.g., morphine) generally increase the latencies observed in the tail-flick or hot-plate tests. Such tests are limited because experiential variables can influence the results. For example, experience with the testing apparatus can influence latencies when drugs are given (e.g., Adams et al., 1969; Kayan et al., 1973; Bardo and Hughes, 1979). As a result, animals typically are tested only once in these procedures, so dose–response functions necessarily involve between-subject determinations. Because of this limitation, there has been interest in developing new procedures that do not limit the number of observations that can be made with a single subject. The next section details part of this endeavor.

4.6. Drugs and negative reinforcement

4.6.1. Escape responding
One possible reason that repeated exposure to hot-plate tests may change latencies irrespective of drug administration is that subjects develop an escape response. An escape response is one that terminates (or reduces the intensity of) an aversive stimulus (see Part 1, Ch. 5). Paw licking and jumping are such responses. Repeated exposure to a hot plate results in progressively shorter latencies to make the 'elicited' response. One approach to dealing with this 'problem' is to allow escape responding to occur in the design of the procedure. This approach is exemplified in 'shock titration' or 'fractional escape' procedures (Weiss and Laties, 1958, 1959, 1970).

An example of a comparison of two shock titration procedures is provided by Dykstra and McMillan (1977). In one procedure the intensity of continuous electric shock to a squirrel monkey's tail increased 0.25 mA every 2 s, but each press of a lever reduced the intensity by 0.25 mA. In the other procedure, shock intensity increased 0.25 mA every 7.5 s while each response reduced it by 0.25 mA. With both arrangements shock intensity increases as time passes while responses reduce shock intensity. The obtained level of shock, therefore, is controlled by the subject's behavior, and a given response rate can hold the average shock intensity at any of a range of levels, i.e., average shock intensity is not a direct function of response rate. Dykstra and McMillan (1977) found that although response rates were higher when shock intensity increased every 2 s, the shock intensity that the subject maintained was about the same under the two conditions. When morphine or methadone (both are drugs used to alleviate pain) was administered, shock intensity was maintained at higher levels than under nondrug conditions, with larger changes observed under the procedure in which intensity increased every 2 s.

4.6.2. Avoidance responding

As suggested in Part 1, Ch. 5, the study of negative reinforcement more frequently involves the use of avoidance procedures (i.e., the prevention or postponement of aversive stimulation) than the use of escape procedures like the shock-titration arrangement. Correspondingly, considerably more research in Behavioral Pharmacology has been conducted with avoidance than with escape procedures. Initial interest in the study of drugs and negative reinforcement involved procedures that included both avoidance and escape contingencies. For example, Cook and Weidley (1957) studied effects of several drugs using a pole-climb escape-avoidance procedure in which a warning stimulus was followed by electrification of a grid floor on which their subjects (rats) stood. A rat could avoid or escape from the shock by jumping onto a pole suspended from the ceiling. An interesting result was that chlorpromazine (a drug used in the treatment of psychoses) suppressed avoidance responding at doses that left escape responding intact. This result is in contrast to those of other types of drugs (e.g., barbiturates), which usually suppress both avoidance and escape responses at equivalent doses. A dissociation between effects on avoidance and escape responding continues to be evidence that a drug may be useful in the treatment of psychoses, although it is by no means a completely reliable 'screening test' for drugs that will be useful in this regard.

Although escape-avoidance procedures continue to be used in Behavioral Pharmacology, especially in efforts to 'screen' drugs, free-operant (Sidman) avoidance schedules (see Part 1, Ch. 5) play a prominent role in studying drug effects on behavior maintained by negative reinforcement. Despite, however, a great deal of research investigating effects of drugs on avoidance responding (cf. Seiden and Dykstra, 1977), there is still a great need for systematic behavioral analyses of the interplay between drugs and negatively reinforced behavior (cf. Galizio and Perone, 1987).

4.7. Behavioral factors in drug tolerance

Behavioral variables can influence not only effects of acutely administered drugs, but also may be critical in determining effects of repeated or chronic drug administration. An understanding of behavioral variables is important because repeated drug administration is very common therapeutically. As an example of how behavioral factors influence effects of repeated drug administration, consider the seminal experiments reported by Schuster et al. (1966). Three food-deprived rats were trained to press a lever under a multiple FI 30-s DRL 30-s schedule of food presentation. After determining acute effects of a range of doses of amphetamine, these investigators administered 1.0 mg/kg before each session for 30 consecutive days. Under acute conditions, the rats showed different effects under the 1.0 mg/kg dose. For two rats response rates under DRL and FI were increased; for the third rat rate under DRL was unchanged, but a substantial decrease was obtained under FI. Note that increases in response rate under DRL reduce reinforcement rate whereas increases in response rate under FI have little effect on reinforcement rate (see Part 1, Ch. 3). With chronic drug administration tolerance to amphetamine's effects was observed (i.e., the potency of the drug in inducing a behavioral change was reduced), but it was not uniformly obtained. Tolerance did not develop to the rate-increasing effects under FI, but did develop to the rate-increasing effects under DRL. Tolerance also was observed under FI in the rat whose performance was decreased following acute administration. Schuster et al. noted that tolerance occurred only under those schedules wherein the acute drug effect was to decrease reinforcement rate, and they suggested that this might be an important factor. This view has come to be known as the 'reinforcement loss hypothesis' or 'reinforcement density hypothesis' (for reviews see Corfield-Sumner and Stolerman, 1978, and Goudie and Demellweek, 1986). Stated simply, the notion is that if the acute effect of a particular dose of a drug is to reduce reinforcement rate, then tolerance is more likely to be observed, or will develop more rapidly, following repeated drug administration, than would be the case if the acute effect does not decrease reinforcement rate.

When tolerance to drug effects depends on behavioral factors, the tolerance is referred to as *behavioral tolerance* (cf. Dews, 1978) to distinguish it from pharmacological tolerance wherein tolerance develops simply as a result of repeated exposure to the drug. A common procedure to assess behavioral tolerance was first introduced by Chen (1968). An example is provided by Carlton and Wolgin (1971) who studied effects of amphetamine on milk drinking by rats. Three groups of food-deprived subjects were allowed to drink sweetened condensed milk for 30 min each day. Rats in Group A-S were given 3.0 mg/kg of *d*-amphetamine before each drinking session and were injected with isotonic saline after each session for 20 consecutive days. Subjects in Group S-A were injected with saline before sessions and amphetamine after sessions for 8 days and then they were exposed to the same regimen as that for Group A-S. Subjects in Group S-S (the control group) were given saline before and after

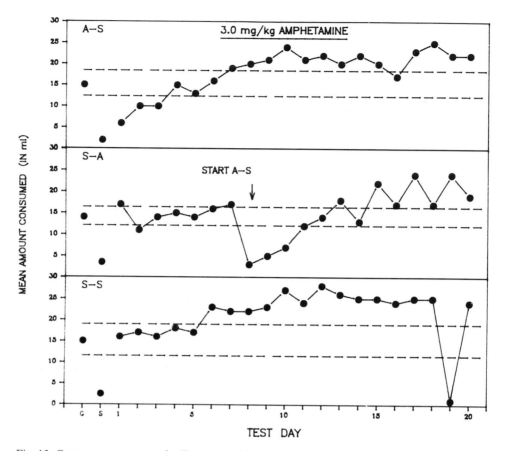

Fig. 15. Group-mean amount of milk consumed by rats across test days. Points above C show control levels and those above S the amount drunk after an initial test with 3.0 mg/kg of amphetamine. S-S indicates that subjects received injections of saline before and after test sessions except session 19, before which 3.0 mg/kg was administered. S-A indicates that subjects received saline before and amphetamine after each session. A-S indicates that subjects received amphetamine before and saline after test sessions. Dashed lines indicate the ranges of control values. (Adapted from Carlton and Wolgin, 1971, with permission of the publisher.)

sessions for 20 days except for the 19th day, on which they received amphetamine before the session rather than saline. Fig. 15 shows that subjects in Group A-S developed tolerance in 4 to 6 days to the suppressive effects of the drug. The most interesting findings concern Group S-A. Even though the subjects in this group received amphetamine with a frequency equal to that of Group A-S, they did not develop tolerance, as indicated by the data for the first day (Day 8) on which they received the drug before rather than after the session; tolerance, however, did develop once pre-session drug administration began. These findings indicate that in order for tolerance to develop, the subjects had to be exposed to the situation in which behavior was measured while under the influence of the drug. Simple drug exposure was not adequate. Carlton and Wolgin described the tolerance observed as 'contingent' tolerance. Such tolerance is also called 'learned tolerance' because the subject presumably 'learns' to respond more normally while in a drugged state as a result of being exposed to the contingencies of the behavioral test situation while under the influence of the drug. Comparison of pre-session versus post-session drug administration has been used to examine the possible contribution of behavioral factors to the development of tolerance to effects of several drugs (e.g., Campbell and Seiden, 1973; Branch, 1983; Branch and Sizemore, 1988).

The variables responsible for the development of 'contingent' tolerance presumably involve response-reinforcement contingencies. Tolerance to behavioral effects of drugs also has been discovered to depend in some cases on the operation of respondent (Pavlovian) conditioning processes. An early demonstration was provided by Siegel (1976) who studied effects of repeated morphine administration to rats. Two main groups were used; each received morphine (5 mg/kg, s.c.), but did so in distinctively different environments. Tests for tolerance to the analgesic effect of morphine revealed that tolerance was evident only if the animals were tested in the environment in which the drug had been administered repeatedly. When tested in the alternative environment, tolerance was not apparent. Seigel's interpretation of this finding was that the first environment came to function as a conditional stimulus (CS) because of the repeated pairing of that environment with morphine administration (the unconditional stimulus, or US). The CS is assumed to elicit a response *opposite* that of the US. That is, a *conditional compensatory response* is hypothesized to develop. Consequently, when the drug is given in the 'usual' environment, the conditional response (CR) opposes the drug effect and tolerance is observed. When the drug is administered in a new environment, no conditional response occurs and therefore tolerance is absent.

The view that tolerance can be mediated by conditional compensatory responses is still controversial (e.g., Baker and Tiffany, 1985), but the phenomenon of context-specific tolerance is well documented (Goudie and Demellweek, 1986) and occurs for many drugs. In addition, context-specific tolerance most surely depends on behavioral processes, whether they be those suggested by Seigel or others (e.g., habituation; cf. Baker and Tiffany, 1985).

Another way in which behavioral factors may play a role in the development of tolerance does not mesh easily with either the 'reinforcement loss' hypothesis or the phenomena associated with context-specific tolerance. For example, Hoffman et al. (1987) studied effects of repeated cocaine administration to pigeons trained to key peck under a multiple FR 5 FR 25 FR 125 schedule of food presentation. Following determination of the effects of a range of doses, a dose that reduced responding was administered before each daily session. After performance stabilized, sessions were preceded occasionally by administration of doses other than the usual daily dose so that a dose-response relationship could be determined. Tolerance developed under FR 5 and FR 25 but not under FR 125. This was especially evident at 10 mg/kg where performance under FR 5 and FR 25 recovered completely yet performance under FR 125 remained completely suppressed. That is, tolerance development depended on the FR parameter even though the drug initially produced reinforcement loss under all three ratios and even though the drug was always administered in the same context.

A related intriguing finding was reported by Genovese et al. (1988) who studied effects of repeated administration of physostigmine to groups of rats trained to press a lever under either an FR 10 or an FR 50 schedule of food presentation. Physostigmine (0.4 mg/kg, i.p.), when administered before daily sessions, initially suppressed responding under both schedules. When the drug was administered repeatedly before sessions, tolerance developed in the subjects responding under FR 10 but not in the subjects responding under FR 50. Interestingly, tolerance developed under FR 10, but not under FR 50, even in subjects that received the drug *after* each session. That is, the tolerance was dependent on the value of the FR schedule, but was not an instance of 'contingent' tolerance.

Tolerance to behavioral effects of drugs must be differentiated from the more general behavioral phenomenon of habituation (cf. Carlton, 1983). Habituation occurs when elicited responses diminish over repeated stimulus presentations. Correspondingly, tolerance is usually described as a diminished effect of a drug that is presented repeatedly. Because a drug may be thought of as a stimulus (see Section 5), it is possible that habituation could be involved in tolerance (cf. Baker and Tiffany, 1985). The key to discerning whether tolerance involves habituation is to examine dose-effect curves rather than simply to study the effect of a single dose. Dose-response curves are crucial in making the distinction because of the specificity of habituation; any change in the properties of a stimulus to which habituation has developed will result in at least a partial reinstatement of the habituated response. If tolerance and not habituation has developed, however, specific changes in the dose–effect function are expected. For example, suppose that Dose 1 produces a moderate increase in some measure of behavior, Dose 2 a decrease, and Dose 3 an even larger decrease. Next, repeated administration of Dose 2 attenuates its effect so that it no longer produces a decrease. Examining Doses 1 or 3 following repeated administration of Dose 2 might reveal that Dose 1 no longer produces an increase and that Dose 3 produces an increase. This is exactly what would be predicted if repeated administration of Dose 2 produced a surmountable tolerance (i.e., a simple shift to the right in the dose–effect curve), but would not be predicted by habituation. This again illustrates the importance of assessing the effects of a range of doses when determining effects of drugs.

With repeated drug administration, the most common technique for examining effects of a range of doses is what might be called a 'probe' procedure. An example is provided by Woolverton et al. (1978) who studied effects of repeated cocaine administration on milk drinking by rats. Some of the rats, after acute effects of a range of doses had been determined, received cocaine (16 mg/kg, i.p.) daily until performance became stable from session to session. Then, occasionally (i.e., not less than 4 days apart) other doses were substituted for the usual dose of 16.0 mg/kg. These 'probes' allowed the researchers to obtain dose–response functions during the period of repeated administration.

5. Stimulus functions of drugs

In addition to interacting with behavioral processes as described in the preceding section, drugs may participate in behavioral processes. That is, drugs may function as stimuli in much the same way as do lights, tones, and food presentation, and as such may serve eliciting, reinforcing, discriminative and other functions. We now turn to the study of drugs in this arena.

5.1. Drug administration as reinforcement

The study of drug administration as reinforcement was facilitated greatly by technical developments that allowed for intravenous drug injection to freely moving or relatively unrestricted animals. The techniques, developed by Weeks (1962), Thompson and Schuster (1964) and Yanagita et al. (1965), among others, involve the surgical implantation of chronic indwelling catheters, usually into the jugular vein, and the use of precision motorized syringe pumps. In general, reinforcement is most effective if consequences are immediate. Intravenous injection provides for a very short latency to onset of drug action and therefore is an ideal route of administration for studying drugs as reinforcers.

5.1.1. Identification of drug reinforcers
Research on response-contingent drug administration, or as it is more commonly called, drug self-administration, has been concerned with a number of issues, the first of which is the identification of drugs that can reinforce behavior. Two major types of techniques have been used to test drugs for effectiveness as reinforcers. The first is exemplified in work by Deneau et al. (1969) who first surgically prepared rhesus monkeys with indwelling venous catheters. The monkeys were studied in the two-lever apparatus illustrated in Fig. 16. They wore a harness connected to a mechanical arm that guided the tubing from the motorized syringe to the catheter and thereby prevented the monkey from damaging the catheter. Pressing one lever (A) resulted, according to an FR-1 schedule, in injection of drug; pressing the other lever (B) resulted in a sham operation of the injection machinery. Initially, saline was placed in the drug reservoir so that a baseline level of lever pressing could be assessed, and then subsequently, across sessions, drug solutions were placed in the reservoir. If drug administration is acting as reinforcement, and not simply increasing activity nonspecifically, then frequency of pressing lever A will increase relative to baseline

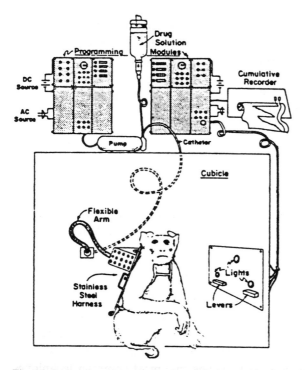

Fig. 16. System for automatic i.v. drug infusions in the rhesus monkey. The monkey is fitted with a steel harness connected to the wall of the cubicle by a metal coil. A catheter runs through the metal coil to an infusion pump. Drug delivery and monitoring of relevant responses are controlled by electronic circuitry. (Reproduced from Schuster and Johanson, 1974, with permission of the publisher.)

levels and relative to the rate of pressing lever B. Using this technique, Deneau et al. (1969) found doses of morphine, codeine, cocaine, amphetamine, pentobarbital, and alcohol that were effective as reinforcement. They did not discover any doses of chlorpromazine, mescaline, or caffeine that would maintain regular self-administration.

The second technique for assessing the reinforcing effectiveness of drug administration is illustrated in work by Hoffmeister and Goldberg (1973) who used a technique similar to that developed by Wilson et al. (1971) and Hoffmeister and Schlicting (1972), which is called a *cross-substitution* procedure. After preparing their rhesus monkeys with indwelling catheters, they initially trained the subjects to press a lever that resulted in the injection of 0.05 mg/kg of cocaine under an FR-10 schedule. This was accomplished by initially letting the animals administer 0.2 mg/kg under FR 1 and then gradually increasing the ratio while decreasing the amount of drug given per injection. Once performance was established under FR 10, testing of other drugs began. To observe the levels that a nonreinforcing substance would have, testing consisted of substituting saline for a few sessions, followed by sessions in which a drug other than cocaine was tested. Then responding was reestablished with cocaine injection as the consequence and the cycle repeated with other doses of the test drug or other test drugs. If a drug maintains performance at higher levels than saline administration it is identified as a reinforcer. Hoffmeister and Goldberg found several doses of morphine and amphetamine that acted as reinforcement. Imipramine, however, did not maintain performance at levels different than those seen with saline. Chlorpromazine led to performance at levels lower than those seen with saline, suggesting that its presentation as a consequence served as punishment.

The cross-substitution procedure has been adopted widely as a procedure for identifying reinforcing drugs. Once performance has been established with a highly effective reinforcer like cocaine, tests with other drugs can be made relatively quickly thus allowing for the prompt examination of a range of doses of several drugs. Because performance is established under intermittent reinforcement relatively large samples of operant behavior are produced, and one therefore can assess whether response-dependent drug administration results in the appropriate temporal pattern of performance.

5.1.2. Effectiveness of drug administration as reinforcement

Once drugs are identified as reinforcers a second question concerns their relative effectiveness in this regard. Drugs are compared with respect to their efficacy as reinforcers because those that are more effective as reinforcement seem to be more likely to be drugs of abuse (cf. Griffiths et al., 1979). The two most common techniques for comparing drugs or different doses of the same drug are discrete-trial choice procedures and progressive-ratio schedules.

An example of the progressive-ratio technique is provided by Griffiths et al. (1975) who studied i.v. drug self-administration in baboons. First, lever-pressing was established under an FR-160 schedule with 3 h intervening between drug administration and the next opportunity to respond. The 3-h timeout period allowed drug effects to dissipate so that direct facilitatory or suppressive effects of the drug on subsequent lever pressing could be avoided. Next, the ratio requirement was increased every 7 days (in the sequence 160, 320, 640, 1280, 4800) until the subject completed fewer than 3 ratios on each of 3 consecutive days. The value of the ratio at this juncture was defined as the 'breaking point', and the results with several doses of cocaine, methylphenidate, and secobarbital are shown in Fig. 17. Cocaine was a highly effective reinforcer at all the doses tested, whereas methylphenidate supported responding less well. Effects of secobarbital depended on dose, with the larger dose able to support more behavior.

In a series of experiments by Johanson and Schuster (1975) choice techniques were used to compare drugs as reinforcers. Their rhesus-monkey subjects were prepared with venous catheters and studied in a two-lever chamber. Red and green lights could be lit over either lever. After initial training to press the levers via reinforcement with cocaine, choice tests consisted of two 'sampling' periods followed by a choice phase. For example, in a test to compare cocaine with methylphenidate, the session began

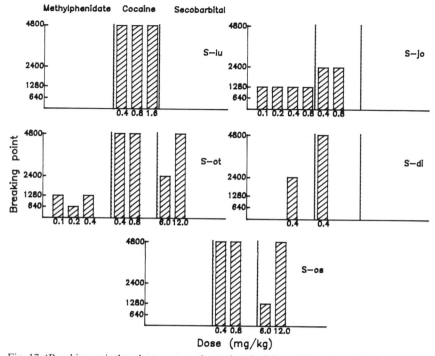

Fig. 17. 'Breaking point' under a progressive-ratio schedule as a function of dose for five baboons. Each set of coordinates is for a single subject. Within each graph the left set of bars show data obtained with methylphenidate, the center set, data obtained with cocaine, and the right set, data obtained with secobarbital. Only subject S-ot was tested with all three drugs. (Adapted from Griffiths et al., 1975, with permission of the publisher.)

with a red light lit over one of the levers. Completing an FR 5 resulted in an injection of cocaine followed by a 15-min timeout (determined from previous experimentation showing that an injection of cocaine or methylphenidate at the doses studied would not suppress responding for more than 15 min). Five such episodes, with the position of the red light, and therefore the active lever, alternating irregularly from injection to injection, constituted the first sampling period. The second sampling period had five illuminations of the green light over one or the other lever and injection of methylphenidate as a consequence for completing an FR 5 on the corresponding lever. Next, a 20-trial choice phase ensued in which, on each trial, one lever had the red light above it lit and the other had the green light over it lit. Position of red and green alternated irregularly across trials. Five lever presses under the red light resulted in injection of cocaine and 5 presses on the one under the green light resulted in injection of methylphenidate. As before, injections were followed by a 15-min timeout. Across blocks of sessions, 0.1 mg/kg injections of cocaine were compared with 0.075, 0.2 and 0.7 mg/kg injections of methylphenidate. The lowest dose of methylphenidate resulted in indifference (i.e., each choice phase resulted in about 10 selections of co-

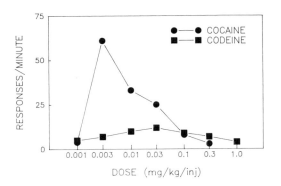

Fig. 18. Response rate by rhesus monkeys under an FR-30 schedule of injection of either cocaine (filled circles) or codeine (filled squares) as a function of dose per injection. (Adapted from Downs and Woods, 1974, with permission of the publisher.)

caine and 10 of methylphenidate), but the two higher doses resulted in eventual strong preference for methylphenidate, with the preference developing across fewer sessions for the highest dose. In addition illustrating a choice technique for comparing drugs as reinforcers, Johanson and Schuster's research again emphasizes the importance of examining a range of doses; methylphenidate and cocaine were about equally preferred for 0.075 mg/kg methylphenidate, but larger doses led to preference for methylphenidate. By and large, comparisons of different doses of the same drug in choice procedures have revealed consistent preference for larger doses.

In general, dose of a reinforcing drug determines patterns of drug self-administration, and the nature of the dose effect depends on the procedure used to examine reinforcing effectiveness. An example of how dose influences performance maintained by drug injection is provided in research by Downs and Woods (1974). Lever pressing by rhesus monkeys was maintained either by response-dependent injection (i.v.) of cocaine or codeine under an FR-30 schedule. Each injection lasted 14 s and was accompanied by a green stimulus light. Over blocks of sessions (at least 10 at each dose) a range of doses was tested. The results are displayed in Fig. 18, and the functions are typical for a wide variety of drugs in that as dose increases response rate first increases and then decreases (cf. Wilson et al., 1971; Hoffmeister and Schlicting, 1972; Goldberg, 1973).

Another determinant of i.v. drug self-administration is the rate of administration. Usually, the more rapidly a given dose is administered the more effective it is as reinforcement (Balster and Schuster, 1973). Pump limitations and the possibility of venous damage from pressure, however, limit the rate at which fluid can be injected. Usually, injection duration is about 5 to 10 s.

5.1.3. Separating a drug's reinforcing effects from its other effects
An important issue in studying drug self-administration is separating the reinforcing effect of the drug from its direct effects (either suppressive or facilitative) on the be-

havior that results in drug presentation. That is, after the drug has been self-administered once in a given session, subsequent performance may not only reflect the effectiveness of the drug as a consequence. It may also be affected by the drug more directly in much the same manner it might be if the performance were maintained by some other reinforcer (e.g., food). In some of the research described above, time-out periods followed drug administration to help overcome this possibility. Timeouts are an effective way to deal with the problem if they are long enough to exceed the drug's duration of action. Timeouts, therefore, are most useful if the drug has a relatively short duration of action. Another strategy is to limit the number of injections per session to one so that the only behavior measured is that which occurs before the drug is administered (cf. Kelleher, 1976). Sessions can be spaced so that even drugs with long durations of action can be tested. This strategy has the disadvantage of not providing a very large sample of behavior from each test session unless techniques are used that maintain a large sample by a single reinforcement. Procedures that generate a large sample of behavior with only a single consequence are second-order schedules.

A type of second-order schedule that maintains large samples of behavior is the FI (FR:S^P) schedule. That is, drug administration is correlated with a distinctive exteroceptive stimulus, S^P (e.g., a colored light). Each completion of the FR schedule results in brief presentation of S^P alone, and the completion of the first FR after the FI has elapsed results in drug injection. Arrangements such as this support much more behavior than a comparable FI schedule without the paired stimulus (e.g., Kelleher, 1976; Goldberg and Tang, 1977; Johanson, 1982). Goldberg and Tang (1977), for example, report the maintenance of average lever pressing rates in squirrel or rhesus monkeys of more than 60 resp/min even when drug administration occurred under a second-order FI 60-min (FR 30:S^P) schedule, i.e., when drug administrations occurred only at the end of a 60-min session. These high rates were maintained only when the S^P was presented at the end of each FR, indicating that this drug-correlated stimulus was important in the maintenance of performance. Interestingly, maintenance of performance with intramuscular injections (a route of administration that provides for a longer latency to drug action than i.v.) has been reported, using either morphine or cocaine injection as the scheduled consequence, under a second-order FI 60-min (FR 10:S^P) schedule (Goldberg et al., 1976). Drug-paired stimuli help to facilitate drug self-administration, and it is standard to have a distinctive stimulus paired with drug injection even when simple (rather than second-order) schedules are used.

Although much research on drug self-administration has involved i.v. administration, techniques also have been developed to induce oral (e.g., Meisch, 1977), intragastric (Woolverton and Schuster, 1983), and intracerebral (Goeders and Smith, 1987) administration. Little by way of comparing routes of administration, however, has yet been accomplished. Interestingly, one of the more widely used techniques for producing oral self-administration is to establish drug taking as schedule-induced, or adjunctive, behavior (cf. Falk, 1971). In these procedures, drinking of fluids can be generated by the proper temporal spacing of opportunities to eat. Such intermittent food presentation can generate oral intake of substances ranging from ethanol (e.g., Meisch and Henningfield, 1977) to cocaine (Tang and Falk, 1987).

Identification of factors that either enhance or diminish drug self-administration has been an evident research theme. As noted above, drug-paired stimuli seem to enhance performance maintained by drug injection, and rate of intermittent food presentation, via schedule-induction, also can modulate drug intake. Other factors also have important effects on the rate of behavior that results in drug administration. For example, food deprivation frequently enhances the effectiveness of a variety of drugs as reinforcers (cf. Carroll and Meisch, 1984), whereas concurrent access to some other reinforcer can decrease the amount of behavior allocated to obtaining a drug (e.g., Carroll, 1985; Samson and Grant, 1985). As one might expect, electric-shock punishment can be effective in suppressing drug-maintained performance (Grove and Schuster, 1974; Johanson, 1977), although this remains a much under-studied phenomenon.

5.2. Drugs as discriminative stimuli

Two general experimental approaches to studying drugs as discriminative stimuli have received much attention. These are called 'state-dependent learning' and 'drug-discrimination' procedures, respectively. Although research on state-dependent learning continues, far more effort has been directed towards establishing discriminative performances under the control of stimuli arising from drug administration, i.e., towards research on drug discrimination. (See Overton, 1984, for a discussion of the relative merits of state-dependent learning and drug-discrimination procedures.) An increase in research on drug discrimination is one of the most salient characteristics of Behavioral Pharmacology over the last two decades (cf. Stolerman and Shine, 1985). One reason for the preponderance of drug-discrimination over state-dependent learning studies is that with the former control of performance can be observed at doses considerably lower than those needed to produce state-dependent effects.

5.2.1. State-dependent learning

In state-dependent learning procedures (cf. Overton, 1964, 1968, 1971) a training phase is followed by a test phase, and comparisons usually are made between groups of subjects that differ with respect to conditions of training. For example, one group will be trained while under the influence of a drug whereas another group will not be drugged during training. Subsequently, subjects are re-exposed to the training situation. For half the subjects, this reexposure occurs under conditions where the drug is administered; for the other half the drug is not administered. Consequently, a minimum of four groups are needed to observe state-dependent learning. When performance is better when the testing condition is the same as the training condition (e.g., drug administered during training and during testing) than when it is not, then a state-dependent effect has been observed. That is, the drug can be considered a key part of the context (and therefore can be considered to be serving a discriminative function) in which the original training occurred, so that when it is absent there is a decrement in performance of the trained response.

5.2.2. Drug discrimination

The basic procedure for establishing a drug discrimination is conceptually simple; reinforce one type of activity following drug administration and reinforce some other activity following administration of either no drug or some other drug (or, in some cases, a different dose of the same drug). If differential performance is established (e.g., the subject makes Response A following drug administration and Response B following vehicle administration), then one may conclude that stimuli arising from the drug are acting in a discriminative fashion. This conceptual simplicity, however, overlooks complexities that are specific to using drugs as discriminative stimuli. For example, unlike more commonly used stimuli, the nature and timing of the onset and offset of stimuli arising from drug administration are difficult to control precisely. As a result, unlike conventional discrimination procedures in which each stimulus is presented within each test session, the different stimuli (usually the presence or absence of the drug) are presented across, rather than within sessions. For example, one technique is to precede the test session with injection of the drug or its vehicle on alternate days, with one set of contingencies in effect when the drug has been administered and another when it has not.

The conceptual simplicity of drug-discrimination procedures also belies the number of available procedures for studying it. Choices need to be made about the schedules of reinforcement in effect in each stimulus condition, the motivational operations, and the particular responses to be measured. Most commonly, food deprivation is the motivational operation, and the two schedules of reinforcement for the two responses are kept equal. For example, a common procedure is to reinforce responding on one lever according to a small FR schedule following drug administration and responding on the other lever according to an equal-valued FR schedule following vehicle administration (e.g., Colpaert and Janssen, 1982). When such a procedure is used, stimulus control usually is evaluated by examining data from before the first reinforcement of the session. This ensures that reinforcement itself does not serve a discriminative function. Because reinforcement is available for presses on only one of the two levers each session, reinforcer delivery for presses on a lever is perfectly correlated with the fact that only presses on that lever will be reinforced subsequently. Analysis of data from before the first reinforcement usually takes one of two forms; either the proportion of responses made to one of the options or the proportion of subjects that register a particular 'choice' is noted. (A 'choice' usually is defined as the option on which the response requirement is first completed.) In addition to FR schedules other variations in schedules, response and motivation are used, albeit relatively infrequently (Stolerman et al., 1989). Examples include aversively motivated (i.e., shock avoidance or escape) lever pressing (e.g., Shannon and Holtzman, 1976, 1979), arm choice in a T-maze (e.g., Overton, 1982), VI schedules (e.g., Kubena and Barry, 1969), FR schedules that reset if a response is made on the 'inappropriate' lever (e.g., Ator and Griffiths, 1986); and water reinforced performance (e.g., Overton and Hayes, 1984), among others. The importance, if any, of these differences in procedure has received little experimental attention (but see Overton, 1979; Overton and Hayes, 1984; Tomie et al., 1987). Much, then, is left to be discovered about procedural variables in the development and assessment of drug discrimination.

In contrast to the shortage of research on procedural determinants of performance under drug-discrimination tasks, a number of experiments have characterized the pharmacological implications of the nature of stimulus control by drugs. Two issues have dominated this research: (a) how training with one drug dose influences how other doses of the same drug control responding (i.e., stimulus generalization), and (b) whether training with one drug influences control exerted by other drugs (known as 'cross-generalization'). Frequently, both of these concerns are addressed in a single study. First, a discrimination is established using Drug A, and then, once asymptotic performance is established, other doses of A occasionally are substituted for the training dose of A. A typical result of such a procedure is shown in Fig. 19, which displays results from an experiment with rats by Kuhn et al. (1974) in which pressing one of two levers was reinforced (by presentation of water) following injection of 1.0 mg/kg *d*-amphetamine and pressing the other was reinforced following administra-

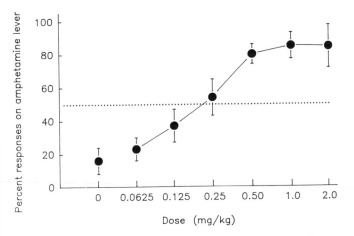

Fig. 19. Percentage of presses (i.e., [drug-lever responses]/[drug-lever responses + saline-lever responses] × 100) by rats during a 5-min test without reinforcement as a function of dose of *d*-amphetamine. Training was with 1.0 mg/kg *d*-amphetamine versus saline. The unconnected point above 0 shows the percentage of responses on this lever following administration of the vehicle. Vertical bars show plus or minus one standard error. (Adapted from Kuhn et al., 1974, with permission of the publisher.)

tion of saline before the session. After the establishment of a drug-saline discrimination, test sessions occasionally were conducted. These sessions lasted only 5 min and no reinforcement was forthcoming so that reinforcer delivery could not serve a discriminative function. Before each test session one of a range of doses was administered. Doses lower than 1.0 mg/kg resulted in relatively lower percentages of responding on the lever for which amphetamine served as the S^D. The dose larger than 1.0 mg/kg, however, tended to produce performance indistinguishable from that produced following administration of 1.0 mg/kg. That is, the generalization function was not symmetric about the training stimulus as is commonly seen using exteroceptive stimuli (e.g., Terrace, 1966; see Part 1, Ch. 7). This is the usual result when generalization tests are conducted following drug-discrimination training. Kuhn et al. (1974) also examined cross-generalization with a variety of drugs including LSD, mescaline, methamphetamine, and caffeine. In these tests, too, sessions lasted only 5 min and reinforcement was withheld. Only methamphetamine produced a dose–effect curve (generalization function) similar to that produced following administration of amphetamine; the other drugs resulted in performance similar to that seen with saline. This somewhat surprising outcome, i.e., that discriminable doses of drugs like LSD or mescaline result in responding similar to that following vehicle administration, is very common and quite useful. Following drug versus no-drug discrimination training only drugs that apparently share stimulus effects with the drug used for original training result in cross-generalization. This feature of the drug-discrimination procedure, which has been validated by studying drugs that are known to produce similar action at receptors, is useful in that it can help identify compounds that likely act at the same receptor. Consequently, drug-discrimination procedures have become a part of the arsenal for general pharmacology. Care must be taken, however, when using these procedures to answer pharmacological questions, especially those concerning drug–receptor interactions, for at least two reasons. First, it has been shown that the training dose of a drug is an important determinant of the outcome of cross-generalization tests (e.g., Shannon and Holtzman, 1979; Krimmer et al., 1984). Second, even when cross-generalization (i.e., Drug B produces effects of those like Drug A following discrimination training with A versus vehicle) is evident, one cannot conclude with certainty that the two drugs exert their primary action at the same site(s) in the nervous system. This is because of the possibility of 'downstream' effects. For example, Drug A could exert its primary action at Receptor X, the activation of which produces stimulation of Neuron Z. Neuron Z could, via a synapse involving Receptor W, activate Neuron Y, the stimulation of which provides the internal stimulus property responsible for the discrimination of Drug A. Now, if Drug B stimulates Receptor W, and therefore produces an effect similar to that of activation of Neuron Z, Drug B and Drug A will cross-generalize in a drug-discrimination paradigm despite not producing the same direct actions at the level of receptors. An additional complication arises in that a drug may have actions (either direct or indirect as just outlined) that involve several types of receptors, any of which, or some combi-

TABLE 2

Outcomes of cross-generalization tests following discrimination training with either pentobarbital or lora-zepam (+ indicates cross-generalization, − indicates no cross-generalization) (Reproduced from Ator and Griffiths, 1989, with permission of the publisher.)

Drug tested for generalization	Training drug	
	Lorazepam	Pentobarbital
Alprazolam	+	+
Chlordiazepoxide	+	+
Diazepam	+	+
Triazolam	+	+
Amobarbital	−	+
Pentobarbital	−	+
Phenobarbital	−	+
Secobarbital	−	+

nation of which, serves as the basis for discrimination. Evidence in support of such a view comes from Ator and Griffiths (1989) who used drug-discrimination techniques to examine drugs used for their sedative properties. Subjects were trained to discriminate either lorazepam or pentobarbital from saline in a drug-discrimination paradigm. Subsequently, several drugs were examined in cross-generalization tests. The results of these tests are summarized in Table 2. Even though training with either drug led to cross-generalization to drugs from the benzodiazepine class, only training with pentobarbital led to cross-generalization to drugs from the barbiturate class. These data indicate that the nature of stimulus control generated in drug-discrimination paradigms can be complex, indeed, and that a great deal of experimentation (often involving specific receptor-blocking agents) is needed before one can conclude with much certainty that a particular drug–receptor interaction serves as a foundation for discriminative control.

Although the focus of most research on drugs as discriminative stimuli has been directed at pharmacological questions, the procedures themselves also have been investigated. As noted earlier, Overton and his colleagues and Tomie and his have conducted research aimed at improving the speed with which experiments may be conducted. Research in this vein also includes that by Sannerud and Young (1987) who developed procedures for using cumulative dosing so that several drug doses may be used in a single generalization or cross-generalization test. In addition to these studies, other studies aim more directly at understanding the nature of stimulus control engendered under drug-discrimination procedures. For example, McMillan and Wenger (1984) used a signal-detection approach to examine the effectiveness of biasing operations in a drug-discrimination procedure. Their findings indicate that an attempt to isolate bias (i.e., control of choice responding that is not via the programmed discriminative stimuli) is viable. It remains to be seen if a behavioral model of two-response discrimination procedures (e.g., Davison and Tustin, 1978; McCarthy and Davison, 1982) will be useful in the analysis of drug discrimination.

5.3. Drugs as stimuli involved in Pavlovian processes

In addition to the Pavlovian-conditioning processes described earlier with relation to the establisment of tolerance, there is also evidence that drug administration can serve either as an unconditional stimulus (US) or as a conditional stimulus (CS) in establishing respondent conditioning. A striking example of the former is provided by Goldberg and Schuster (1967) who trained monkeys, which had been made physically dependent on morphine (by receiving injections of the drug every 6 h), to press a lever under an FR schedule of food presentation. During each daily session a 5-min tone was presented, initially followed immediately by an injection of saline. Subsequently, the tone was followed by an injection of nalorphine, a narcotic antagonist that precipitates an abstinence syndrome (i.e., 'withdrawal') in dependent subjects. After several experiences of the stimulus-nalorphine pairings, the subjects displayed abstinence signs (e.g., agitation, excessive salivation, emesis) during the stimulus that had been paired with nalorphine, indicating the formation of a dramatic conditioned response.

Attempts also have been made to establish drug administration as a CS in a Pavlovian conditioning paradigm. For example, Turner and Altshuler (1976) trained rats to press a lever under a VI 60-s schedule of food presentation. Then, off baseline, some subjects received injections of amphetamine or cocaine that were followed (15 min after injection) by exposure to a number of brief electric shocks, i.e., drug administration was paired with electric shocks. Other subjects were exposed to unpaired injections of either cocaine or amphetamine and electric shocks. Next, the drug was given prior to sessions in which the VI schedule operated. The drugs decreased responding in those subjects that had been exposed to drug-shock pairings but not in those that had received unpaired exposures.

The phenomenon of 'place learning' also can be conceptualized as involving respondent-conditioning processes. Place learning usually is studied in two interconnected compartments where each compartment is distinctive (e.g., Katz and Gormezano, 1979). Following assessment of pre-existing preference for one compartment or the other, animals are drugged and then confined to the less preferred compartment, after which preference is tested again. If the original preference is reversed the stimuli associated with the newly preferred compartment are assumed to be conditioned reinforcers because of the pairing with the drug. This technique is currently used as a rapid technique for assessing the reinforcing potential of drugs.

6. Drugs as tools for behavioral analysis

Although Behavioral Pharmacology usually is conceptualized as a discipline wherein techniques from the Experimental Analysis of Behavior are used to analyze drug effects, drug effects can aid in understanding behavioral processes. That is, there is a reciprocal relation between the Experimental Analysis of Behavior and Behavioral Pharmacology. The Experimental Analysis of Behavior is a young field and therefore can benefit from the behavioral implications of research in Behavioral Pharmacology.

Three strategies have been used in the understanding of behavioral processes via research on drugs. First, as noted in the preceding section, drugs can serve as reinforcers, or discriminative stimuli, or stimuli that enter into respondent-conditioning processes. Although not frequently recognized, when drugs serve any of these stimulus functions the generality of the behavioral concepts they exemplify is extended and the theoretical framework of the Experimental Analysis of Behavior is thereby strengthened. The concepts of reinforcement, discriminative stimulus, and conditional stimulus are validated by the fact that they can be used effectively to describe the behavioral effects of drugs. Research with drugs shows that these concepts can apply to stimuli other than the lights and tones generally used in laboratory research on behavior.

A second way in which drugs aid in the analysis of behavior is in their use as an added (usually disruptive) stimulus. The logic of this approach is illustrated in research by Branch et al. (1977) who studied effects of pentobarbital on punished responding by pigeons. A well-documented effect is that barbiturates increase responding that has been suppressed by electric-shock punishment. Branch et al. compared effects of pentobarbital on responding punished either by electric shock or by time out, and found that the drug increased only responding suppressed by electric-shock punishment; responding suppressed by timeout punishment was decreased further. In both cases punishment occurred in the absence of the drug, but the drug affected punished responding differently depending on the punishing stimulus. This indicates that the two conditions, although both meet the criteria for application of the term 'punishment', were not identical, i.e., the drug effect suggested that electric-shock punishment and timeout punishment may be slightly different behavioral processes. Perhaps positive punishment (response suppression via response-dependent presentation of a stimulus) and negative punishment (response suppression via response-dependent removal of a stimulus) need to be considered as separable behavioral processes.

The third approach to analyzing behavioral processes via drug action is to take advantage of drug-induced changes in performance. An example is provided in the work of Laties (1972) who studied behavior of pigeons under a fixed-consecutive-number (FCN) procedure (Mechner, 1958; see Section 4.1). For food presentation to occur a pigeon had to peck one key 8 or more consecutive times before pecking a second key. Pigeons perform quite accurately under such a procedure, with a preponderance of sequences on the first key being 8 pecks or longer. Not clear is what aspects of the situation are responsible for the accurate performance; is it the number of preceding pecks or is it the time taken to complete the requisite number of pecks (cf. Part 2, Ch. 1)? Haloperidol's effects bear on this issue. As the dose of haloperidol was increased, response rate on the first key was suppressed substantially, yet the proportion of sequences of consecutive pecks that was eight or longer was unchanged. That is, 'accuracy' was unaffected, even though time to complete each sequence was lengthened considerably. These data suggest that time to complete the 'run' was not crucial and thus support the view that something about the number of responses in each 'run' is the important factor.

7. Future directions

Much has been achieved in Behavioral Pharmacology considering its brief history. The importance of environmental and behavioral factors in the determination of drug effects is now widely appreciated. Procedures for predicting abuse liability are used routinely as are procedures for identifying drugs likely to be useful in the treatment of anxiety and other behavioral problems. Much is left to be accomplished, however. The theoretical framework established so far in behavior analysis has provided a useful starting point for Behavioral Pharmacology, but behavior theory is in need of refinement and elaboration. For example, most of the research in behavior analysis has been conducted by examining behavior in steady states, and there is no denying the importance to Behavioral Pharmacology of the ability to be able to generate steady-state performances that can be used as baselines. Nevertheless, much is left to be learned about the dynamics of behavior (i.e., about behavior in transition), and it is to this realm that the Experimental Analysis of Behavior could profitably look next. Approaches to the study of behavior in transition already show new promise. Especially useful in this regard are procedures that allow repeated observation of behavioral transitions in the same experimental subject. Such procedures permit determination of dose-effect functions in individual subjects (e.g., Thompson, 1977; Files et al., 1989; Watson and Blampied, 1989) and thus can be linked directly to the existing individual-subject data base already established as the foundation of the Experimental Analysis of Behavior.

Acknowledgement

Preparation of this chapter was supported by USPHS Grants DA-04074 and DA-04940.

References

Adams, W.J., Yeh, S.Y., Woods, L.A. and Mitchell, C.L. (1969) Drug–test interaction as a factor in the development of tolerance to the analgesic effect of morphine. J. Pharmacol. Exp. Ther. 168,251–257.

Ator, N.A. and Griffiths, R.R. (1986) Discriminative stimulus effects of atypical anxiolytics in baboons and rats. J. Pharmacol. Exp. Ther. 237,393–403.

Ator, N.A. and Griffiths, R.R. (1989) Asymmetrical cross-generalization in drug discrimination with lorazepam and pentobarbital training conditions. Drug Devel. Res. 16,355–364.

Baker, T.B. and Tiffany, S.T. (1985) Morphine tolerance as habituation. Psychol. Rev. 92,78–108.

Balster, R.L. and Schuster, C.R. (1973) Fixed-interval schedule of cocaine reinforcement: effect of dose and infusion duration. J. Exp. Anal. Behav. 20,119–129.

Bardo, M.T. and Hughes, R.A. (1979) Exposure to a nonfunctional hot plate as a factor in the assessment of morphine-induced analgesia and analgesic tolerance in rats. Pharmacol. Biochem. Behav. 10,481–485.

Barrett, J.E. (1976) Effects of alcohol, chlordiazepoxide, cocaine and pentobarbital on responding maintained under fixed–interval schedules of food or shock presentation. J. Pharmacol. Exp. Ther. 196,605–615.

Barrett, J.E. (1977) Behavioral history as a determinant of the effects of d-amphetamine on punished behavior. Science 198,67–69.

Beninger, R.J., Hanson, D.R. and Phillips, A.G. (1981) The acquisition of responding with conditioned reinforcement: effects of cocaine, (+)-amphetamine and pipradrol. Br. J. Pharmacol. 74,149–154.

Branch, M.N. (1979) Consequent events as determinants of drug effects on schedule-controlled behavior: modification of effects of cocaine and d-amphetamine following chronic amphetamine administration. J. Pharmacol. Exp. Ther. 210,354–360.

Branch, M.N. (1983) Behavioral tolerance to stimulating effects of pentobarbital: a within-subject determination. Pharmacol. Biochem. Behav. 18,25–30.

Branch, M.N. and Gollub, L.R. (1974) A detailed analysis of the effects of d-amphetamine on behavior under fixed-interval schedules. J. Exp. Anal. 21,519–539.

Branch, M.N., Nicholson, G. and Dworkin, S.I. (1977) Punishment-specific effects of pentobarbital: dependency on the type of punisher. J. Exp. Anal. Behav. 28,285–293.

Branch, M.N. and Sizemore, G.M. (1988) Behavioral tolerance to cocaine in squirrel monkeys: acute and chronic effects on complex operant behavior. Pharmacol. Biochem. Behav. 30,737–748.

Byrd, L.D. (1975) Contrasting effects of morphine on schedule-controlled behavior in the chimpanzee and baboon. J. Pharmacol. Exp. Ther. 193,861–869.

Campbell, J.C. and Seiden, L.S. (1973) Performance influence on the development of tolerance to amphetamine. Pharmacol. Biochem. Behav. 1,703–708.

Carlton, P.L. (1983) A Primer of Behavioral Pharmacology. Freeman, New York.

Carlton, P.L. and Wolgin, D.L. (1971) Contingent tolerance to the anorexigenic effects of amphetamine. Physiol. Behav. 7,221–223.

Carroll, M.E. (1985) Concurrent phencyclidine and saccharin access: presentation of an alternative reinforcer reduces drug intake. J. Exp. Anal. Behav. 43,131–144.

Carroll, M.E. and Meisch, R.A. (1984) Increased drug-reinforced behavior due to food deprivation. In: T. Thompson, P.B. Dews and J.E. Barrett (Eds.), Advances in Behavioral Pharmacology, Vol. 4. Academic Press, New York, pp. 47–88.

Chen, C. (1968) A study of the alcohol-tolerance effect and an introduction of a new behavioural technique. Psychopharmacologia 12,433–440.

Colpaert, F.C. and Janssen, P.A.J. (1982) Factors regulating drug cue sensitivity: limits of discriminability and the role of a progressively decreasing training dose in cocaine-saline discrimination. Neuropharmacology 21,1187–1194.

Cook, L. and Catania, A.C. (1964) Effects of drugs on avoidance and escape behavior. Fed. Proc. 23,818–835.

72

Cook, L. and Weidley, E. (1957) Behavioral effects of some psychopharmacological agents. Ann. NY Acad. Sci. 66,740–752.

Cooper, J.R., Bloom, F.E. and Roth, R.H. (1982) The Biochemical Basis of Neuropharmacology. Oxford, New York.

Corfield-Sumner, P.K. and Stolerman, I.P. (1978) Behavioral tolerance. In: D.E. Blackman and D.J. Sanger (Eds.), Contemporary Research in Behavioral Pharmacology. Plenum Press, New York, pp. 391–448.

D'Amour, F.E. and Smith, D.L. (1941) A method for determining loss of pain sensation. J. Pharmacol. Exp. Ther. 72,74–79.

Davison, M.C. and Tustin, R.D. (1978) The relation between the generalized matching law and signal-detection theory. J. Exp. Anal. Behav. 29,331–336.

Deneau, G., Yanagita, T. and Seevers, M.H. (1969) Self-administration of psychoactive substances by the monkey: a measure of psychological dependence. Psychopharmacologia 16,30–48.

Dews, P.B. (1955) Studies on behavior: I. Differential sensitivity to pentobarbital of pecking performance in pigeons depending on the schedule of reward. J. Pharmacol. Exp. Ther. 113,393–401.

Dews, P.B. (1978) Behavioral tolerance. In: N.A. Krasnegor (Ed.), Behavioral Tolerance: Research and Treatment Implications, NIDA Research Monograph 18, DHEW. U.S. Government Printing Office, Washington DC, pp. 18–26.

Dews, P.B. and Wenger, G.R. (1977) Rate dependency of the behavioral effects of amphetamine. In: T. Thompson and P.B. Dews (Eds.), Advances in Behavioral Pharmacology, Vol. 1. Academic Press, New York, pp. 167–227.

Downs, D.A., Miller, L.E., Wiley, J.N. and Johnston, D.E. (1980) Oral vs. parenteral drug effects on schedule-controlled behavior in rhesus monkeys. Life Sci. 26,1163–1168.

Downs, D.A. and Woods, J.H. (1974) Codeine- and cocaine-reinforced responding in rhesus monkeys: effects of dose on response rates under a fixed-ratio schedule. J. Pharmacol. Exp. Ther. 191,179–188.

Dworkin, S.I., Bimle, C. and Miyauchi, T. (1989) Differential effects of pentobarbital and cocaine on punished and nonpunished responding. J. Exp. Anal. Behav. 51,173–184.

Dykstra, L.A. and McMillan, D.E. (1977) Electric shock titration: effects of morphine, methadone, pentazocine, nalorphine, naloxone, diazepam and amphetamine. J. Pharmacol. Exp. Ther. 202,660–669.

Elsmore, T.F. (1971) Control of responding by stimulus duration. J. Exp. Anal. Behav. 16,81–87.

Elsmore, T.F. (1972) Effects of Δ-9-tetrahydrocannabinol on temporal and auditory discrimination performances of monkeys. Psychopharmacologia 26,62–72.

Evans, H.L., Ghiselli, W.B. and Patton, R.A. (1973) Diurnal rhythm in behavioral effects of methamphetamine, p-chloromethamphetamine and scopolamine. J. Pharmacol. Exp. Ther. 186,10–17.

Falk, J.L. (1971) The nature and determinants of adjunctive behavior. Physiol. Behav. 6,577–588.

Ferster, C.B. and Skinner, B.F. (1957) Schedules of Reinforcement. Appleton-Century-Crofts, New York.

Files, F.J., Branch, M.N. and Clody, D. (1989) Effects of methylphenidate on responding under extinction in the presence and absence of conditioned reinforcement. Behav. Pharmacol. 1, 113–121.

Findley, J.D. (1958) Preference and switching under concurrent scheduling. J. Exp. Anal. Behav. 1,123–144.

Galizio, M. and Perone, M. (1987) Variable-interval schedules of timeout from avoidance: effects of chlordiazepoxide, CGS 8216, morphine, and naltrexone. J. Exp. Anal. Behav. 47,115–126.

Geller, I., Kulak, J.T., Jr. and Seifter, J. (1962) The effects of chlordiazepoxide and chlorpromazine on a punishment discrimination. Psychopharmacologia 3,374–385.

Geller, I. and Seifter, J. (1960) The effects of meprobamate, barbiturates, d-amphetamine and promazine on experimentally induced conflict in the rat. Psychopharmacologia 1,482–492.

Genovese, R.F., Elsmore, T.F. and Witkin, J.M. (1988) Environmental influences on the development of tolerance to the effects of physostigmine on schedule-controlled behavior. Psychopharmacology 96,462–467.

Gilman, A.G., Goodman, L.S., Rall, T.W. and Murad, F. (1985) Goodman and Gilman's The Pharmacological Basis of Therapeutics, 7th Edn. Macmillan, New York.

Glowa, J.R. and Barrett, J.E. (1983) Drug history modifies the behavioral effects of pentobarbital. Science 220,333–335.

Goeders, N.E. and Smith, J.E. (1987) Intracranial self-administration methodologies. Neurosci. Biobehav. Rev. 11,319–329.

Goldberg, S.R. (1973) Comparable behavior maintained under fixed-ratio and second-order schedules of food presentation, cocaine injection or d-amphetamine injection in the squirrel monkey. J. Pharmacol. Exp. Ther. 186,18–30.

Goldberg, S.R., Morse, W.H. and Goldberg, D.M. (1976) Behavior maintained under a second-order schedule by intramuscular injection of morphine or cocaine in rhesus monkeys. J. Pharmacol. Exp. Ther. 199,278–286.

Goldberg, S.R. and Schuster, C.R. (1967) Conditioned suppression by a stimulus associated with nalorphine in morphine-dependent monkeys. J. Exp. Anal. Behav. 10,235–242.

Goldberg, S.R. and Tang, A.H. (1977) Behavior maintained under second-order schedules of intravenous morphine injection in squirrel and rhesus monkeys. Psychopharmacology 51,235–242.

Goldstein, A., Aronow, L. and Kalman, S.M. (1968) Principles of Drug Action: the Basis of Pharmacology. Harper & Row, New York.

Gollub, L.R. (1977) Conditioned reinforcement: schedule effects. In: W.K. Honig and J.E.R. Staddon (Eds.), Handbook of Operant Behavior. Prentice Hall, Englewood Cliffs, NJ, pp. 288–312.

Gonzales, F.A. and Byrd, L.D. (1977) Mathematics underlying the rate-dependency hypothesis. Science 195,546–550.

Goudie, A.J. and Demellweek, C. (1986) Conditioning factors in drug tolerance. In: S.R. Goldberg and I.P. Stolerman (Eds.), Behavioral Analysis of Drug Dependence. Academic Press, Orlando, FL, pp. 225–285.

Griffiths, R.R., Brady, J.V. and Bradford, L.D. (1979) Predicting the abuse liability of drugs with animal drug self-administration procedures: psychomotor stimulants and hallucinogens. In: T. Thompson and P.B. Dews (Eds.), Advances in Behavioral Pharmacology, Vol. 2. Academic Press, New York, pp. 163–208.

Griffiths, R.R., Findley, J.D., Brady, J.V., Dolan-Gutcher, K. and Robinson, W.W. (1975) Comparison of progressive-ratio performance maintained by cocaine, methylphenidate and secobarbital. Psychopharmacologia 43,81–83.

Grove, R.N. and Schuster, C.R. (1974) Suppression of cocaine self-administration by extinction and punishment. Pharmacol. Biochem. Behav. 2,199–208.

Hill, R.T. (1970) Facilition of conditioned reinforcement as a mechanism of psychomotor stimulation. In: E. Costa and S. Garattini (Eds.), Amphetamines and Related Compounds. Raven Press, New York, pp. 781–795.

Hoffman, S.H., Branch, M.N. and Sizemore, G.M. (1987) Cocaine tolerance: acute versus chronic effects as dependent upon fixed-ratio size. J. Exp. Anal. Behav. 47,363–376.

Hoffmeister, F. and Goldberg, S.R. (1973) A comparison of chlorpromazine, imipramine, morphine and D-amphetamine self administration in cocaine-dependent rhesus monkeys. J. Pharmacol. Exp. Ther. 187,8–14.

Hoffmeister, F. and Schlichting, U.U. (1972) Reinforcing properties of some opiates and opioids in rhesus monkeys with histories of cocaine and codeine self-administration. Psychopharmacologia 23,55–74.

Janssen, P.A.J., Niemegeers, C.J.E. and Dony, J.G.H. (1963) The inhibitory effect of fentanyl and other morphine-like analgesics on the warm water induced tail withdrawal reflex in rats. Arzneimittel Forsch. 13,502–507.

Johanson, C.E. (1977) The effects of electric shock on responding maintained by cocaine injections in a choice procedure in the rhesus monkey. Psychopharmacology 53,277–282.

Johanson, C.E. (1982) Behavior maintained under fixed-interval and second-order schedules of cocaine or pentobarbital in rhesus monkeys. J. Pharmacol. Exp. Ther. 221,384–393.

Johanson, C.E. and Schuster, C.R. (1975) A choice procedure for drug reinforcers: cocaine and methylphenidate in the rhesus monkey. J. Pharmacol. Exp. Ther. 193,676–688.

Johnston, J.M. and Pennypacker, H.S. (1980) Strategies and Tactics of Human Behavioral Research. Erlbaum, New York.

Katz, J.L. (1982) Effects of drugs on stimulus control of behavior. I. Independent assessment of effects on response rates and stimulus control. J. Pharmacol. Exp. Ther. 223,617–623.

Katz, J.L. (1983) Effects of drugs on stimulus control of behavior. II. Degree of stimulus control as a determinant of effect. J. Pharmacol. Exp. Ther. 226,756–763.

Katz, R.J. and Gormezano, G. (1979) A rapid and inexpensive technique for assessing the reinforcing effects of opiate drugs. Pharmacol. Biochem. Behav. 11,231–233.

Kayan, S., Ferguson, R.K. and Mitchell, C.L. (1973) An investigation of pharmacologic and behavioral tolerance to morphine in rats. J. Pharmacol. Exp. Ther. 185,300–306.

Kelleher, R.T. (1976) Characteristics of behavior controlled by scheduled injections of drugs. Pharmacol. Rev. 27,307–323.

Kelleher, R.T. and Morse, W.H. (1964) Escape behavior and punished behavior. Fed. Proc. 23,808–817.

Kelleher, R.T. and Morse, W.H. (1968) Determinants of the specificity of the behavioral effects of drugs. Ergeb. Physiol. Biol. Chem. Exp. Pharmakol. 60,1–56.

Krimmer, E.C., McGuire, M.S. and Barry, H. III. (1984) Effects of the training dose on generalization of morphine stimulus to clonidine. Pharmacol. Biochem. Behav. 20,669–673.

Ksir, C. (1981) Rate-convergent effects of drugs. In: T. Thompson, P.B. Dews and W.A. McKim (Eds.), Advances in Behavioral Pharmacology, Vol. 3. Academic Press, New York, pp. 39–59.

Kubena, R.K. and Barry, H. III. (1969) Two procedures for training differential responses in alcohol and nondrug conditions. J. Pharm. Sci. 58,99–101.

Kuhn, D.M., Appel, J.B. and Greenberg, I. (1974) An analysis of some discriminative properties of d-amphetamine. Psychopharmacologia 39,57–66.

Laties, V.G. (1972) The modification of drug effects on behavior by external discriminative stimuli. J. Pharmacol. Exp. Ther. 183,1–13.

Levine, R.R. (1978) Pharmacology: Drug Actions and Reactions, 2nd Edn. Little, Brown and Co., Boston.

MacPhail, R.C. and Gollub, L.R. (1974) Independence of the effects of d-amphetamine and food deprivation or body weight on the food consumption of rats. Psychopharmacologia 34,163–172.

Manning, F.J. (1973) Acute tolerance to the effects of Δ-9-tetrahydrocannabinol on spaced responding by monkeys. Pharmacol. Biochem. Behav. 1,665–671.

McCarthy, D. and Davidson, M. (1982) Independence of stimulus discriminability from absolute rate of reinforcement in a signal-detection procedure. J. Exp. Anal. Behav. 37,371–382.

McKearney, J.W. (1974) Effects of d-amphetamine, morphine and chlorpromazine on responding under fixed-interval schedules of food presentation or electric shock presentation. J. Pharmacol. Exp. Ther. 190,141–153.

McKearney, J.W. (1976) Punishment of responding under schedules of stimulus-shock termination: effects of d-amphetamine and pentobarbital. J. Exp. Anal. Behav. 26,281–287.

McKearney, J.W. and Barrett, J.E. (1975) Punished behavior: Increases in responding after d-amphetamine. Psychopharmacologia 41,23–26.

McKearney, J.W. and Barrett, J.E. (1978) Schedule-controlled behavior and the effects of drugs. In: D.E. Blackman and D.J. Sanger (Eds.), Contemporary Research in Behavioral Pharmacology. Plenum, New York, pp. 1–68.

McMillan, D.E. (1973) Drugs and punished responding: I. Rate-dependent effects under multiple schedules. J. Exp. Anal. Behav. 19,133–145.

McMillan, D.E. and Wenger, G.R. (1984) Bias of phencyclidine discrimination by the schedule of reinforcement. J. Exp. Anal. Behav. 42,51–66.

Mechner, F. (1958) Probability relations within response sequences under ratio reinforcement. J. Exp. Anal. Behav. 1,109–121.

Meck, W.H. and Church, R.M. (1987) Cholinergic modulation of the content of temporal memory. Behav. Neurosci. 101,457–464.

Meisch, R.A. (1977) Ethanol self-administration: infrahuman studies. In: T. Thompson and P.B. Dews (Eds.), Advances in Behavioral Pharmacology, Vol. 1, Academic Press, New York, pp. 36–84.

Meisch, R.A. and Henningfield, J.E. (1977) Drinking of ethanol by rhesus monkeys: experimental strategies for establishing ethanol as a reinforcer. In: M.H. Gross (Ed.), Alcohol Intoxication and Withdrawal, Vol. 3B. Plenum Press, New York, pp. 443–463.

Miczek, K.A. and Lau, P. (1975) Effects of scopolamine, physostigmine and chlordiazepoxide on punished and extinguished water consumption in rats. Psychopharmacologia 42,263–269.

Morse, W.H. and Kelleher, R.T. (1977) Determinants of reinforcement and punishment. In: W.K. Honig and J.E.R. Staddon (Eds.), Handbook of Operant Behavior. Prentice-Hall, Englewood Cliffs, NJ, pp. 174–200.

Overton, D.A. (1964) State-dependent or 'dissociated' learning produced with pentobarbital. J. Comp. Physiol. Psychol. 57,3–12.

Overton, D.A. (1968) Dissociated learning in drug states. In: D.H. Efron, J.O. Cole, J. Levine and R. Wittenborn (Eds.), Psychopharmacology: a Review of Progress, 1957–1967. U.S. Government Printing Office, Washington, DC, pp. 918–930.

Overton, D.A. (1971) Discriminative control of behavior by drug states. In: T. Thompson and R. Pickens (Eds.), Stimulus Properties of Drugs. Appleton-Century-Crofts, New York, pp. 87–110.

Overton, D.A. (1979) Influence of shaping procedures and schedules of reinforcement on performance in the two-bar drug discrimination task: a methodological report. Psychopharmacology 65,291–298.

Overton, D.A. (1982) Comparison of the degree of discriminability of various drugs using the T-maze drug discrimination paradigm. Psychopharmacology 76, 385–395.

Overton, D.A. (1984) State dependent learning and drug discriminations. In: L.L. Iversen, S.D. Iversen and S.H. Snyder (Eds.), Handbook of Psychopharmacology, Vol. 18. Plenum Press New York, pp. 59–127.

Overton, D.A. and Hayes, M.W. (1984) Optimal training parameters in the two-bar fixed-ratio drug discrimination task. Pharmacol. Biochem. Behav. 21,19–28.

Pickens, R. (1977) Behavioral pharmacology: a brief history. In: T. Thompson and P.B. Dews (Eds.), Advances in Behavioral Pharmacology, Vol. 1. Academic Press, New York, pp. 229–257.

Pizziketti, R.J., Pressman, N.S., Geller, E.B., Cowan, A. and Adler, M.W. (1985) Rat cold water tail-flick: a novel analgesic test that distinguishes opioid agonists from mixed agonist-antagonists. Eur. J. Pharmacol. 119,23–29.

Robbins, T.W. (1978) The acquisition of responding with conditioned reinforcement: effects of pipradrol, methylphenidate, d-amphetamine, and nomifensine. Psychopharmacology 58, 79–87.

Roberts, S. (1981) Isolation of an internal clock. J. Exp. Psychol.: Anim. Behav. Proc. 7,242–268.

Samson, H.H. and Grant, K.A. (1985) Chlordiazepoxide effects on ethanol self-administration: dependence on concurrent conditions. J. Exp. Anal. Behav. 43,353–364.

Sanger, D.J. and Blackman, D.E. (1976) Rate-dependent effects of drugs: a review of the literature. Pharmacol. Biochem. Behav. 4,73–83.

Sannerud, C.A. and Young, A.M. (1986) Modification of morphine tolerance by behavioral variables. J. Pharmacol. Exp. Ther., 237,75–81.

Sannerud, C.A. and Young, A.M. (1987) Environmental modification of tolerance to morphine discriminative stimulus properties in rats. Psychopharmacology 93,59–68.

Schindler, C.W., Gormezano, I. and Harvey, J.A. (1983) Effect of morphine on acquisition of the classically conditioned nictitating membrane response of the rabbit. J. Pharmacol. Exp. Ther. 227,639–643.

Schindler, C.W., Gormezano, I. and Harvey, J.A. (1984) Sensory and associative effects of morphine and naloxone in classical conditioning of the rabbit nictitating membrane response. Psychopharmacology 83,114–121.

Schuster, C.R., Dockens, W.S. and Woods, J.H. (1966) Behavioral variables affecting the development of amphetamine tolerance. Psychopharmacologia 9,170–182.

Schuster, C.R. and Johanson, C.E. (1974) The use of animal models for the study of drug abuse. In: R.J.

76

Gibbins, Y. Israel, H. Kalant, R.E. Popham, W. Schmidt and R.G. Smart (Eds.), Research Advances in Alcohol and Drug Problems, Vol. 1. John Wiley & Sons, New York, pp. 1–31.

Seiden, L.S. and Dykstra, L.A. (1977) Psychopharmacology: a Biochemical and Behavioral Approach. Van Nostrand Rheinhold, New York.

Shannon, H.E. and Holtzman, S.G. (1976) Evaluation of the discriminative effects of morphine in the rat. J. Pharmacol. Exp. Ther. 198,54–65.

Shannon, H.E. and Holtzman, S.G. (1979) Morphine training dose: a determinant of stimulus generalization to narcotic antagonists in the rat. Psychopharmacology 61,239–244.

Sepinwall, J. and Cook, L. (1978) Behavioral pharmacology of antianxiety drugs. In: L.L. Iversen, S.D. Iversen and S.H. Snyder (Eds.), Handbook of Psychopharmacology, Vol. 13. Plenum Press, New York, pp. 345–393.

Sidman, M. (1960) Tactics of Scientific Research. Basic Books, New York.

Siegel, S. (1976) Morphine analgesic tolerance: its situation specificity supports a Pavlovian conditioning model. Science 193,323–325.

Skinner, B.F. (1938) The Behavior of Organisms: an Experimental Analysis. Appleton-Century, New York.

Snyder, S.H. (1984) Drug and neurotransmitter receptors in the brain. Science 224,22–31.

Stolerman, I.P., Rasul, F. and Shine, P.J. (1989) Trends in drug discrimination research analysed with a cross-indexed bibliography, 1984–1987. Psychopharmacology 98,1–19.

Stolerman, I.P. and Shine, P.J. (1985) Trends in drug discrimination research analysed with a cross-indexed bibliography, 1982–1983. Psychopharmacology 86,1–11.

Tang, M. and Falk, J.L. (1987) Oral self administration of cocaine: chronic excessive intake by schedule induction. Pharmacol. Biochem. Behav. 28,517–519.

Terrace, H.S. (1966) Stimulus control. In: W.K. Honig (Ed.), Operant Behavior: Areas of Research and Application. Appleton-Century-Crofts, New York, pp. 271–344.

Thompson, D.M. (1975) Repeated acquisition of response sequences: stimulus control and drugs. J. Exp. Anal. Behav. 23,429–436.

Thompson, D.M. (1977) Development of tolerance to the disruptive effects of cocaine on repeated acquisition and performance of response sequences. J. Pharmacol. Exp. Ther. 203,294–302.

Thompson, D.M., Moerschbaecher, J.M. and Winsauer, P.J. (1983) Drug effects on repeated acquisition: comparison of cumulative and non-cumulative dosing. J. Exp. Anal. Behav., 39,175–184.

Thompson, T. and Schuster, C.R. (1964) Morphine self-administration, food-reinforced and avoidance behaviors in rhesus monkeys. Psychopharmacologia 5,87–94.

Tomie, A., Peoples, L. and Wagner, G.C. (1987) Effects of single or multiple choice trials per session on drug discrimination performance. Psychopharmacology 92,529–535.

Turner, E.G. and Altshuler, H.L. (1976) Conditioned suppression of an operant response using d-amphetamine as the conditioned stimulus. Psychopharmacology 50,139–143.

Urbain, C., Poling, A., Millam, J. and Thompson, T. (1978) d-Amphetamine and fixed-interval performance: effects of operant history. J. Exp. Anal. Behav. 29,385–392.

Vaillant, G. (1964) Antagonism between physostigmine and atropine on the behavior of the pigeon. Naunyn-Schmiedebergs Arch. exp. Path. u. Pharmak. 248,406–416.

Watson, J.E. and Blampied, N.M. (1989) Quantification of the effects of chlorpromazine on performance under delayed matching to sample in pigeons. J. Exp. Anal. Behav. 51,317–328.

Weeks, J.R. (1962) Experimental morphine addiction: method for automatic intravenous injections in unrestrained rats. Science 138,143–144.

Weiss, B. and Laties, V.G. (1958) Fractional escape and avoidance on a titration schedule. Science 128,1575–1576.

Weiss, B. and Laties, V.G. (1959) Titration behavior on various fractional escape programs. J. Exp. Anal. Behav. 2,227–248.

Weiss, B. and Laties, V.G. (1970) The psychophysics of pain and analgesia in animals. In: W.C. Stebbins

(Ed.), Animal Psychophysics: the Design and Conduct of Sensory Experiments. Appleton-Century-Crofts, New York, pp. 185–210.

Wilson, M.C., Hitomi, M. and Schuster, C.R. (1971) Psychomotor stimulant self-administration as a function of dosage per injection in the rhesus monkey. Psychopharmacologia 22,271–281.

Woolfe, G. and MacDonald, A.D. (1944) The evaluation of the analgesic action of pethidine hydrochloride (Demerol). J. Pharmacol. Exp. Ther. 80,300–307.

Woolverton, W.L., Kandel, D. and Schuster, C.R. (1978) Tolerance and cross-tolerance to cocaine and d-amphetamine. J. Pharmacol. Exp. Ther. 205,525–535.

Woolverton, W.L. and Schuster, C.R. (1983) Intragastric self-administration in rhesus monkeys under limited access conditions: methodological studies. J. Pharmacol. Methods, 10,93–106.

Wuttke, W. and Kelleher, R.T. (1970) Effects of some benzodiazepines on punished and unpunished behavior in the pigeon. J. Pharmacol. Exp. Ther. 172,397–405.

Yanagita, T., Deneau, G. and Seevers, M. (1965) Evaluation of pharmacological agents in the monkey by long-term intravenous self- or programmed-administration. Excerpta. Med. Int. Cong. Ser. 87,453–457.

Experimental analysis of behavior, Part 2
Iversen and Lattal (eds.)
© *1991, Elsevier Science Publishers BV*

CHAPTER 3

Behavioral neurochemistry: application of neurochemical and neuropharmacological techniques to the study of operant behavior

JAMES E. BARRETT

Department of Psychiatry, Uniformed Services University of the Health Sciences, 4301 Jones Bridge Road, Bethesda, MD 20814, U.S.A.

1. Introduction

The discovery and application of experimental techniques to study ongoing behavior has been one of the most significant contributions stemming from Skinner's pioneering work of over 50 years ago (Skinner, 1938). The intensive study of operant behavior that was initiated by Skinner's research and theory has permitted vivid resolution of behavior and identification of its controlling variables. Through the use of relatively straightforward techniques, complex dimensions of behavior and the multiple variables that control its occurrence and temporal distribution have become easily accessible. A number of fundamental principles of behavior have emerged that have widespread significance and application to fields well beyond those of the scientific study of behavior. At the time of his original work, Skinner (1938) noted that behavior might have certain 'neurological' correlates and, although clearly interested only in the scientific study of behavior, even suggested how a science that combined behavior and a 'physico-chemical' approach might best proceed:

> ... it may be assumed that a science of the nervous system will some day start from the direct observation of neural processes and frame its concepts and laws accordingly. It is with such a science that the neurological point of view must be concerned if it is to offer a convincing "explanation" of behavior. (p. 422)

At the time Skinner appeared most concerned with the fact that suitable techniques were not available for directly and reliably measuring changes in central nervous system (CNS) activity. This shortcoming, however, did not thwart attempts to provide accounts of behavior based on unmeasured neural processes. Although many individuals within the Experimental Analysis of Behavior have eschewed interest in domains other than behavior and its environment, this bias appears to stem, in part, from that time when CNS variables were not very accessible or objectively identifiable. Access to dynamic CNS functions that could provide the type of moment-to-moment simultaneous analyses of both behavioral and neurochemical effects of, for example, contingencies of reinforcement, has undoubtedly been extraordinarily difficult and frustrating. Even when techniques were developed that provided some access to CNS functions, these were often only static windows opened for a brief duration. As is well known, behavior unfolds over time and is a reflection of many variables both past and present. An appreciation and understanding of the reciprocal influences between behavior and neurochemistry must be able to capture what has to be an intriguingly dynamic interplay.

Many individuals recognized, however, that progress in the Experimental Analysis of Behavior did not have to await advances in other domains because principles formulated at the level of a behavior would remain coherent regardless of developments within other scientific fields. Over the past several years, a number of significant developments have occurred within related disciplines that have made the study of CNS correlates of behavior much more feasible for those so inclined. More recent techniques promise a view of behavioral and neurochemical interactions that approximates the type of resolution necessary and over a sufficient period of time to encourage advances in this field. Techniques are now available to measure directly and reliably neurochemical events and it is now possible to correlate those events with behavior. In some instances, neurochemical and neuropharmacological analyses are as quantifiable and objective as those used with behavior. They can be almost as instantaneous, thereby providing the experimenter with the type of reinforcement that derives from viewing changes in ongoing behavior that occur in response to manipulations of the environment. The purpose of studying such processes is not necessarily to 'explain' behavior as much as it is to determine the influence that behavior and behavioral variables have on neurochemistry and vice versa. The importance of variables controlling behavior is in no way diminished by such efforts. Techniques which yield a more detailed analysis of behavior by providing access to other variables can only extend and clarify basic behavioral processes.

Although behavioral neurochemistry is still in its infancy and without many empirical foundations, this area of research holds great promise. The purpose of this chapter is to provide information on some techniques that permit the simultaneous analysis of behavior and CNS functioning. Many of the initial steps in conducting this research, such as basic stereotaxic techniques, surgical preparation and anesthesia procedures, as well as intracerebral injections, have already been detailed clearly in previous publications and will be treated only briefly in this chapter. A list of available technical sources for these procedures and other relevant information is given in Section 11 of this chapter. The main focus will be on techniques that currently allow or promise the possibility of obtaining simultaneous measures of behavior and neurochemistry.

2. Fundamental procedures

Before pursuing any of the techniques reviewed in this chapter, extensive familiarity and skill with certain basic procedures routinely available in most physiological psychology laboratories is essential. Almost all of the methods and approaches described in this chapter necessitate the use of a stereotaxic instrument for precise location and placement of cannulae or probe devices used in the collection of fluid, the injection of a drug, or insertion of a recording electrode into specific brain regions. Most of the procedures reviewed in this chapter involve the collection of fluid from specific brain areas in awake, behaving animals and can be technically somewhat cumbersome. In addition to basic surgical skills, use of a stereotaxic instrument, administration and maintenance of anesthesia, animals must be monitored much more extensively than is typical or customary in most behavioral studies. This section reviews briefly some of these considerations.

2.1. Stereotaxic techniques

The use of stereotaxic instruments and stereotaxic atlases has been reviewed by Pellegrino and Cushman (1971). These authors also provide a list of additional references for stereotaxic atlases for use with several different species. Satisfactory histological methods for examining and locating the sites for cannula placement, extent of damage etc. also must be available once the particular study has been completed. These topics are treated in some detail in several specific texts in addition to the Pellegrino and Cushman article and should be consulted prior to embarking on studies of the nature described in this chapter (see also Bures et al., 1983; Joseph and Waddington, 1986).

2.2. Anesthesia

Fortunately, most regimens for the induction and maintenance of anesthesia have been worked out to provide sufficient depth to proceed safely, successfully and humanely. Waddington (1986) has provided a thorough description for inducing anesthesia in the rat and has also described in detail the basic procedure for conducting stereotaxic surgery with this species. Most studies with rats use barbiturate anesthesia (e.g., 50–60 mg/kg sodium pentobarbital administered intraperitoneally or i.p.), whereas in primates an inhalation anesthetic such as halothane (2% in oxygen) is used. Atropine sulfate (0.05 mg/kg, s.c.) is often given as a pre-anesthetic to rats to minimize bronchial and salivary secretions and prevent respiratory distress during surgery. With pigeons a mixture of 10 mg/kg pentobarbital sodium and 30–40 mg/kg ketamine HCl, both administered i.m., yields good levels of anesthesia that are safe; supplementary injections of 10 mg/kg ketamine will maintain these levels with no toxicity. Recovery from anesthesia should be reasonably slow and gradual to minimize trauma to the animal and to the devices that are implanted. Recovery from anesthesia should be permitted in a warm, clean area. Similarly, appropriate caging is essential to prevent the animal from damaging probes, cannulae or injury. This may involve housing the animals in cages without wire mesh or in larger cages that prevent the cannula or probes from being caught and pulled out.

2.3. Surgical preparation and procedure

Good surgical procedures that pay particular attention to the care of the animal prior to surgery, selection of appropriate surgical instruments, sterilization procedures, and preparation of the animal for surgery contribute substantially to the overall success of the study. It is essential to use sterile surgical techniques with non-human primates but, for most commonly used species such as the rat or pigeon, this is not necessary. However, as is obvious, the surgical instruments should be maintained in good condition and should be clean. A 'cold sterilization' method that appears to be particularly good is a combination of absolute alcohol (500 ml) and 19% zephiran (7 ml) both mixed with distilled water (500 ml). Instruments are allowed to soak for 30 min prior to surgery and then are rinsed in sterile distilled water immediately prior to use. A number of texts and articles are available on small-animal surgery that provide good overviews of the steps involved in these procedures (Meyer and Meyer, 1971; see also Section 11 under Stereotaxic and Surgical Procedures).

2.3.1. Preparation of the skull and insertion of the cannula

Once surgical anesthesia has been achieved and the skin area where the incision is to be made has been shaved or clipped and then scrubbed with betadine or a suitable alternative, the animal can be positioned in the stereotaxic instrument. The precise location of the incision depends on where the cannula or probe device is to be located but the incision must be large enough to permit sufficient reflection of the tissue to permit unencumbered access to the targeted site. Typically, the skin is held open with retractors. In most cases, 3 to 4 stainless steel screws will be inserted into the skull to anchor the cranioplastic cement that supports the cannula. Therefore, the periosteum must be scraped away and the surface of the skull that will be covered with the cement must be clean and dry at the time of preparation. Most screws for cement retention are self-tapping and can be inserted easily once the initial hole is made with a suitable size drill bit. The stainless steel screws should be threaded down far enough to provide a rigid anchor but should not compress the brain; additionally, the base of the screw head should not rest directly on the skull so that the cranioplastic cement can run underneath to ensure adequate support.

Once the retaining screws are inserted a hole can be made for the cannula to be lowered. These holes typically are opened with dental drills, proceeding carefully to avoid tissue damage. It usually is best to open an area large enough to visualize the surface of the brain, to expose and puncture the dura, and to ensure that the cannula is inserted without compression or deformation of the brain. Once the cannula is located at the proper depth, cranioplastic cement is applied to secure the cannula in place and protect it during subsequent experimentation. Initially, the cement should be mixed so that it flows easily around and under the mounting screws; subsequent applications can be more viscous and can be applied once each preceding application has dried. Cement that dries clear has several advantages over those that are opaque because it is easy to check for bleeding beneath the cement, and is easily removed, if necessary, without losing visualization of the skull or tissue below when drilling out the old cement. It is important to prevent direct contact of the cement with the skin drying because the hardening of the cement generates heat and can cause tissue damage and discomfort.

Most wounds are closed with autoclips applied carefully after application of topical antibiotic to the wound area. The wound should be cleaned daily with 3% hydrogen peroxide and the clips removed 7 to 10 days following surgery.

2.4. Monitoring behavior: technical considerations, anticipation and circumvention of problems

Many behavioral procedures that are used in behavioral neurochemistry are treated in other chapters in this volume. Many of the studies described briefly below require special modifications of the apparatus to minimize damage to the guide cannula, prevent damage to tubing connected to withdrawal pumps, etc. Most of these modifications are common-sense and do not require detailed elaboration. For example, pigeons with guide cannula cemented to the skull require a larger food aperture than is typically provided by most commercially manufactured grain magazines. The opening must be enlarged so that the height is minimally 9 cm so that when the pigeon inserts its head into this area, the cannula does not hit the top of the opening. In those instances where cerebrospinal fluid (CSF) or extracellular fluids are being withdrawn continuously throughout an experimental session, it is necessary to use a food cup mounted on the front panel of the chamber, just below the response keys. Pellets of pigeon checkers can be dispensed much the same way pellets are delivered for rats and monkeys (see Part 1, Ch. 1). We typically have used 97-mg pellets and have delivered 5 pellets per reinforcement.

One of the major problems confronting most attempts to collect fluid samples from behaving animals is that of keeping the tubing out of the way and inaccessible to the animal. Most investigators use a form of balance arm with an attached swivel that can be adjusted to move in response to the animal (see Fig. 1). Some compromises have to occur between maintaining the essential isolation of the experimental space and allowing the collection of the samples relatively quickly and without disturbing the animal. When performing microdialysis, push-pull perfusion and CSF withdrawal, many of the metabolites and neurotransmitters degrade rapidly when withdrawn from the brain and must be protected from degradation as quickly as pos-

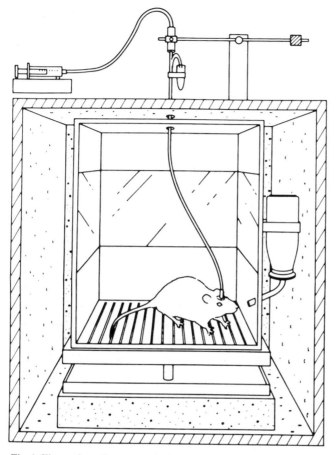

Fig. 1. Illustration of a rat attached to a balance arm and swivel for the unencumbered collection of dialysate from a microdialysis probe. Dialysis samples are collected outside the chamber in the microcentrifuge tube at the top. (Reproduced from Kuczenski and Segal, 1989, with permission of the publisher.)

sible. Therefore, it is important to minimize the length of tubing from which the samples are collected yet maintain the integrity of the experimental space so that behavior is not disturbed. This can be best accomplished by minimizing the distance between the top of the experimental chamber and the inside ceiling of the surrounding acoustical enclosure. In this manner the tubing can exit the experimental chamber and go only a short distance to the pump or collection device located directly on top of the acoustical chamber.

2.5. High-performance liquid chromatography with electrochemical detection

Most of the techniques described in this chapter for measuring neurochemical changes that correlate with behavior or drug administration require a means for detecting levels of neurotransmitters or their metabolites in CSF or in samples collected using other procedures such as microdialysis. The technique of high-performance liquid chromatography (HPLC), coupled with a method for electrochemical detection, provides a highly sensitive, rapid and selective means for determining picogram or smaller amounts of a wide variety of biologically and behaviorally active substances in fluid or tissue. Another distinct advantage is that analyses of several substances can be conducted simultaneously from a single sample thereby optimizing sample use and animal resources.

Although it had been known for some time that certain substances such as phenols and indoles were electrochemically active, it was not until the early 1970s that Adams and his colleagues recognized that the oxidation of tyrosine and tryptophan metabolites might permit the measurement of these substances in brain tissue (Adams and Marsden, 1982). As with all chromatographic techniques, HPLC separates various chemical species in a mixture; unlike other forms of chromatography (e.g., paper and gas), HPLC involves the use of a liquid mobile phase that is driven by a pump through a narrow analytical column that is tightly packed with small particles (see schematic in Fig. 2). The type and size of the packing material, together with the size of the column, as well as numerous other factors such as the specific composition of the mobile phase (pH, polarity etc.), are critical in determining the amount of time it takes biological substances contained in the mobile phase to pass through or elute from the column (retention time) and cross the electrochemical detector. The elec-

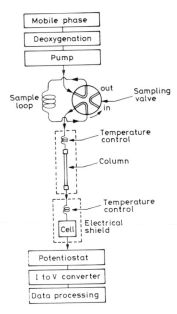

Fig. 2. Schematic illustration of the basic components of an HPLC system with electrochemical detection. (Reproduced from Kissinger, 1983, with permission of the publisher.)

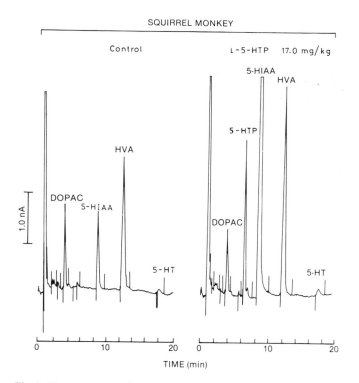

Fig. 3. Chromatogram of cerebrospinal fluid collected from a squirrel monkey under control (saline injection) conditions and after the administration of L-5-hydroxytryptophan (5-HTP). The graph shows the elution pattern of the metabolites.

trochemical cell is typically a thin-layer sandwich-type arrangement in which the volume at the detection area is very small, often less than 1 μl. It is at this point on the electrode surface that biologically electroactive compounds that have been inserted into the mobile phase are oxidized and the current produced at the working electrode surface amplified and converted into voltage which is then recorded on a strip chart or other type of recording or integrating device. An example of a chromatogram taken from an analysis of the CSF of a squirrel monkey after either saline or the administration of the serotonin precursor L-5-hydroxytryptophan (L-5-HTP) is shown in Fig. 3. The peaks show the order of elution of the metabolites of serotonin and dopamine clearly. Verification of the identification of these substances is determined by comparison of the elution times with known standards that also have been analyzed in the same system. The analysis of neurotransmitters and their metabolites by HPLC with electrochemical detection is a complicated and technical process that cannot adequately be treated in this chapter. Many of the principles involved are similar to those that will be covered later in this chapter when *in vivo* voltammetry is discussed. A list of excellent reviews and technical articles on HPLC techniques is provided in Section 11.

3. Push-pull perfusion and cerebrospinal fluid withdrawal

Push-pull perfusion techniques have been used extensively in physiology since their introduction in the late 1950s. Early experiments, reviewed by Myers and Knott (1986), consisted of a side-by-side configuration of tubing that was inserted into the forearm of a human subject to recover bradykinin. One piece of tubing introduced a perfusion medium (e.g., saline or Ringer's solution) into the area while, simultaneously, the other piece of tubing withdrew the perfusate which consisted of the perfusion solution and whatever physiological substances were available at the site being perfused (Fox and Hilton, 1958). Gaddum (1961) modified this technique to form a concentric cannula that could provide a more focused perfusion and performed the first observation of the release of acetylcholine from the caudate nucleus in brain (Gaddum, 1962). This procedure has been used extensively since its initial development (see Section 11).

An example of the usual concentric cannula arrangement is shown in Fig. 4. Typically, the outer guide tube is permanently implanted into the region of choice and kept closed with a 'dummy cannula' consisting of a stylet and a cap (Plastic Products Inc., Roanoke, VA 24022, supplies the cannula guide, cannula and caps and will custom make the assemblies). During experimentation, the longer assembly is inserted through the guide tube so that it extends beyond the tip of the guide. When the push-

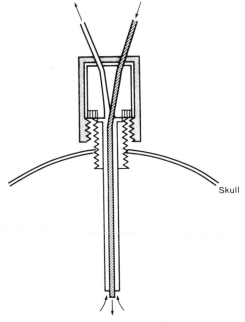

Push-Pull Perfusion Assembly

Fig. 4. Schematic of the push-pull cannula assembly.

pull perfusion begins, artificial CSF or an appropriate perfusion solution is infused through the push tubing where it exits and mixes with endogenous neuronal fluid and is retrieved by aspiration into the outer ('pull') tubing that leads to a collection device. Two pumps or syringe drivers are necessary and must be working reciprocally and be calibrated to infuse and withdraw at the same rate. Myers (1972, 1974, 1977) has written extensively on the methodology for conducting push-pull experiments and continues to provide innovative approaches with this technique. For example, a new 'micro push-pull' catheter system (Myers and Gurley-Orkin, 1985) has been described along with a recent double-lumen polyethylene cannula (Myers et al., 1985), each of which offer certain advantages to the more conventional push-pull system. At present, however, it appears that little additional work has been performed with these techniques, which may be due to the recent introduction of microdialysis procedures (described below). A number of factors are critical in determining the rate of recovery and extent of area perfused and extent of tissue damage. These have been evaluated systematically in model experiments and *in vivo* studies and include, most importantly, the rate at which the area is perfused and the length of the extension of the push tube beyond the outer pull tubing (Szerb, 1967; Yaksh and Yamamura, 1974).

3.1. Measurement of endogenous neurotransmitters and metabolites

One of the most frequent uses of the push-pull perfusion technique has been that of collecting neurotransmitters and their metabolites from ventricular space or from regional areas of the brain after systemic drug injections. Significantly, this procedure can be conducted in awake, freely-moving animals, thereby allowing a better assessment of neuronal activity within regionally specific areas of the brain than would be possible, for example, under anesthesia. Although this procedure permits repeated sampling from the same animal, it is restricted to only a limited number of times because of the formation of scar tissue, encapsulation of the cannula guide tip and cellular destruction. The push-pull perfusion approach became prominent when coupled with the powerful techniques of HPLC and electrochemical detection because analyses could be conducted using microliter amounts of perfusate (Nielsen and Moore, 1982). A number of experimenters have modified the push-pull technique to collect only CSF from ventricular space or cisterna magna, again concentrating on the use of repeated sampling techniques for long-term measures of neurochemical activity (e.g., Sarna et al., 1983; De La Riva and Yeo, 1985; Barrett and Nader, 1990). In these instances the guide cannula is implanted in or above the targeted site which is then punctured or tapped to collect CSF. Usually, CSF is withdrawn slowly by negative pressure and, in some cases, the system is open to air to minimize changes in ventricular pressure. This approach for monitoring neurochemical activity by measuring metabolites in CSF minimizes trauma to any specific brain area and can be maintained over much longer time periods.

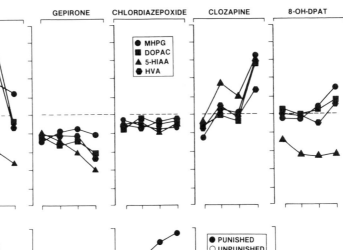
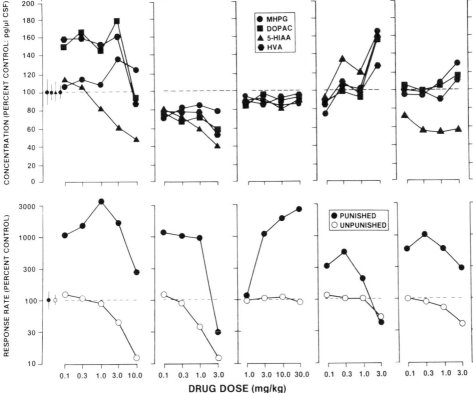

Fig. 5. Effects of various drugs on key pecking of pigeons under a multiple schedule of punished and un-punished responding (bottom) and changes in metabolite levels produced by those drugs (top). (Reproduced from Mansbach et al., 1988, with permission of the publisher.)

One technique that has been particularly successful for collecting CSF from pigeons over periods of up to 2 years has involved a slight modification of the system depicted in Fig. 4. Simply by changing the connections of the tubing, it is possible to collect CSF from the normal 'push' side of the cannula while leaving the 'pull' side open to air; gentle aspiration is by a Gilson Minipuls pump that withdraws CSF into silicone tubing at approximately 1 μl/min. The 10 to 20 μl sample is then immediately frozen on solid CO_2 until analysed by HPLC with electrochemical detection. Using this procedure, it was possible to examine a number of drugs that increase the punished behavior of pigeons and to correlate those neurochemical changes with behavioral effects under schedules of punishment (Mansbach et al., 1988; Barrett et al., 1989; Gleeson et al., 1989). One example of this approach is given in Fig. 5 where changes in the metabolites of norepinephrine (3-methoxy-4-hydroxyphenylethylene-glycol or MHPG), dopamine (homovanillic acid or HVA and dihydroxyphenylacetic

90

acid or DOPAC), and serotonin (5-hydroxyindoleacetic acid or 5-HIAA) are shown after different doses of various drugs; effects of those drugs on punished behavior are also provided in the lower portion of the figure. Different drugs produced different profiles of changes in metabolite levels despite their generally consistent rate-increasing effects on punished behavior. However, the different drugs operate through different neurotransmitter systems and such findings reveal the idiosyncratic neurochemical effects, despite a common behavioral outcome.

3.2. Simultaneous measurements of behavior

The application of push-pull perfusion techniques to study neurochemical changes correlated with ongoing behavior was pioneered by Sparber and his colleagues in the early 1970s (e.g., Tilson and Sparber, 1970; Sparber, 1975). At the time of this initial work, HPLC techniques for measuring neurotransmitter levels were not available and Sparber relied on measurements of radiolabelled norepinephrine by thin layer

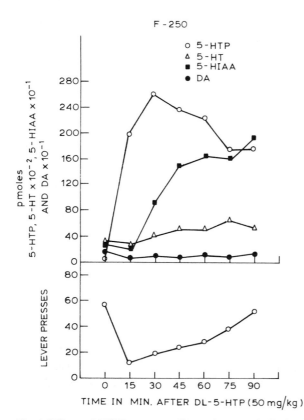

Fig. 6. Effects of 5-HTP on responding and on metabolite levels while a rat's responding was maintained under a variable-interval schedule; the animal was simultaneously perfused using a push-pull technique. (Adapted from Loullis et al., 1980, with permission of the publisher.)

chromatography in ventricular perfusate obtained while rats responded under fixed-ratio schedules of reinforcement; effects of extinction and exposure to electric shock also were studied. These were truly difficult experiments but provided the very first indication of the application and use of this technique to measure dynamic changes in neurochemistry that were correlated with behavioral processes. Few other experimenters, however, have attempted the combined analysis of neurochemistry and behavior controlled by schedules of reinforcement. In one study of this type, Loullis et al. (1980) measured behavioral and neurochemical effects of DL-5-hydroxytryptophan (5-HTP) in rats responding under a variable-interval 1-min schedule of food reinforcement. Perfusates were collected using a push-pull cannula inserted into the lateral hypothalamus while the animal responded under the schedule after injections of saline or 50 mg/kg of 5-HTP. This dose of 5-HTP produced large decreases in responding and also markedly increased levels of 5-HTP, 5-HIAA and 5-HT in the perfusate; levels of dopamine were unaffected as measured by HPLC with electrochemical detection (Fig. 6).

In experiments with pigeons, neurotransmitter metabolite measures in CSF have been obtained using the techniques described above after responding has been maintained under various schedules of reinforcement and punishment (Barrett and Hoffmann, 1991; Barrett et al., 1989). These studies demonstrate that behavioral contingencies can result in distinctive changes in neurochemistry and that such changes reflect the impact of environmental influences. Moreover, they provide encouragement for witnessing the dynamic interactions between behavior and neurochemistry of the type requested by Skinner over 50 years ago.

3.3. Advantages and disadvantages

Insertion of the cannula into specific brain regions has the advantage of regional and temporal specificity at the site of release, whereas collection of CSF represents a heterogeneous efflux of metabolites from both near and distant sites. Samples collected therefore may be both structurally and temporally remote from their actual release. Long-term neurochemical analyses of CNS activity are probably best accomplished by CSF collection rather that push-pull perfusion. Because the cannula is inserted into ventricular space, problems attendant with neuroglial occlusion, encapsulation by scar tissue and trauma stemming from repeated insertion of the assembly that occur with tissue perfusion are not encountered. However, even with a cannula implanted in the ventricle, the tip of the cannula can be occluded by the growth of choroid plexus. This can be prevented by inserting the cannula above the ventricle and puncturing the ventricle each time a sample is collected or, when actually implanted into the ventricle, by gently inserting a piece of wire to break through the occluded tip. As the field of neuroscience progresses, newer techniques such as microdialysis are likely to replace push-pull perfusion techniques because of the several advantages described below. However, techniques such as CSF collection, which permit neuro-

92

chemical analyses over long periods of time, should continue to provide useful information that is not possible even with microdialysis techniques. Furthermore, CSF analyses are used most frequently in clinical studies with humans, and similar studies with animals allow comparisons not otherwise possible with perfusions of specific brain regions. The decision as to which technique is most suitable actually depends on the objectives of the experiment (length of time analyses will be required, whether behavior will also be monitored etc.) and resources that may be available, with the recognition that it will be necessary to compromise and accept certain limitations or shortcomings regardless of the technique selected.

4. Microdialysis techniques

Although the push-pull cannula and its variations for sampling CSF have been useful techniques for investigating neurochemical processes, the development of the microdialysis device, which is actually a modification of the push-pull cannula, promises to be even more useful for obtaining information about brain chemistry. With microdialysis, the perfusion fluid is circulated within a semi-permeable membrane and never directly comes into contact with brain tissue. The membrane, located at the tip of the microdialysis probe, can be selected with a particular pore size or molecular weight cut-off that excludes certain compounds from entering the probe. This can prevent enzymatic degradation of the dialysate within the cannula and should permit

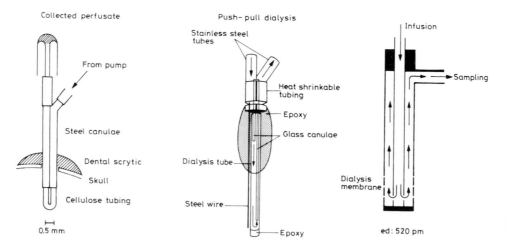

Fig. 7. Three types of probes used in brain microdialysis. The probe on the left is a loop-type probe, whereas the middle probe consists of a side-by-side arrangement of two tubes that are enclosed within a dialysis membrane. The steel wire is used to reinforce the probe (taken from Marsden, 1985). The probe on the right consists of a concentric arrangement of two tubes inserted into a dialysis membrane. (Reproduced from Benveniste, 1989, with permission of the publisher.)

a more accurate reflection of the actual neurochemical concentrations *in vivo*. Three types of microdialysis probes currently in use are shown in Fig. 7. One distinct advantage of these probes over the traditional push-pull perfusion cannula is that they minimize turbulence at the tip because they are self-contained systems and depend simply on the diffusion gradients across the membrane.

There are a number of factors that must be considered and evaluated when using microdialysis. Some of these have been explored in model experiments (Johnson and Justice, 1983) and factors affecting recovery both *in vitro* and *in vivo* have been treated in a recent review (Benveniste, 1989). Obvious factors that affect recovery involve the flow rate of the perfusion, concentration of the substances at the perfusion site, time since insertion of the probe (initial insertion of the probe releases numerous substances and equilibration at the site requires a period of at least 1 to 2 h), duration of time the site is being perfused, and the surface area of the membrane. Other factors such as the ionic composition of the perfusing solution also may be important (Moghaddam and Bunney, 1989). Individual probes should be calibrated before and after conducting microdialysis by evaluating recovery rates *in vitro* with solutions containing known concentrations of the substances of interest. Although a few investigators have repeatedly dialysed the same site in an individual animal, careful studies of recovery rates, tissue damage and drug effects on neurotransmitter release and repeated use of the same probe remain to be explored thoroughly. Such variables would be of critical concern to individuals interested in performing behavioral studies with animals where long-term behavioral and neurochemical measures are essential.

4.1. Measurement of neurotransmitter release

Dialysis in the awake, freely-moving animal is typically conducted by insertion of the microdialysis probe into a guide tube that has been previously implanted under anesthesia and targeted at the site of interest. The probe membrane can extend any distance beyond the tip of the guide cannula but the actual distance must depend on the size of the area that is being perfused. Dialysis studies have been conducted with a wide variety of drugs and have encompassed the analysis of a wide range of compounds such as catecholamines, amino acids and peptides (Ungerstedt and Hall-ström, 1987). Analyses of most of these substances have been with HPLC techniques with either electrochemical or fluorometric detection (Sharp et al., 1987). The recent introduction of microbore analytical columns has permitted the analysis of very small (1 μl) volumes collected within a short time period. Although still 'slow' in terms of ongoing behavioral and neurotransmitter release studies, the possibility of collecting samples within 1-min time periods is a significant development for studies in Behavioral Neurochemistry. In some cases the entire dialysis system, including the animal, has been connected directly to an HPLC system with 'on-line' analysis (Wages et al., 1986; Church and Justice, 1987).

Although microdialysis techniques have been available only for a relatively short period of time, the number of publications is extensive. A number of studies have examined release of dopamine (DA) and serotonin (5-HT) after the administration of drugs that have effects on these neurotransmitter systems. As an illustration of the technique and its potential application, two studies will be described that used microdialysis to examine neurochemical changes induced by drug administration. In one experiment (Sharp et al., 1986) the effects of the 5-HT releaser *p*-chloroamphetamine (PCA) were examined on extracellular levels of 5-HT and DA in the striatum and frontal cortex of anesthetized rats. Perfusates were collected every 20 min using loop-type dialysis probes with a flow rate of 2 μl/min. PCA produced an immediate release of 5-HT into both frontal cortex and striatum that declined over a 2-h period; increases in DA were also detected in the dialysate from striatum as well (Fig. 8). The time course of the effects of PCA on 5-HT parallel the behavioral effects of this drug in inducing the 5-HT behavioral syndrome, a constellation of behaviors that, in the rat, consists of reciprocal forepaw treading, lateral head weaving, hindlimb abduction, resting tremor, rigidity and Straub tail. Additionally, these results show that PCA, a drug with presumably selective effects on a single neurotransmitter also produces effects on other systems and suggest the need to consider DA in better evaluating PCA-induced changes in behavior.

Baseline levels of 5-HT in the dialysate are not always similar to those reported by Sharp et al. (1986). For example, Adell et al. (1989) found much lower levels of 5-HT in frontal cortex dialysates and comment that earlier studies collected samples within a few hours of inserting the probe, whereas in the Adell et al. study, samples were collected one day following probe insertion. This raises the possibility that 5-HT in certain experiments in which samples were collected less than several hours follow-

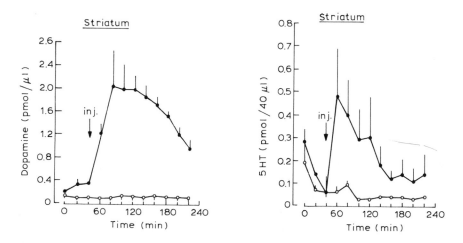

Fig. 8. Effects of *p*-chloroamphetamine on dopamine (left figure) and serotonin (right figure) release in striatum of rats collected using microdialysis procedures. (Reproduced from Sharp et al., 1984, with permission of the publisher.)

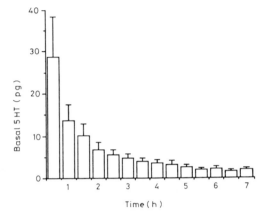

Fig. 9. Time-course of the release of serotonin collected in microdialysis perfusate (Reproduced from Auerbach et al., 1989, with permission of the publisher.)

ing insertion of the microdialysis probe may have come from platelets that accumulated around the probe or, as mentioned above, from terminals damaged by insertion of the probe (see Westerink et al., 1987).

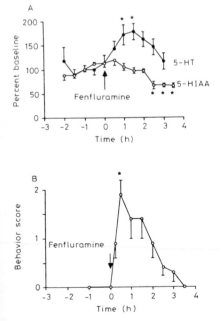

Fig. 10. Effects of fenfluramine on serotonin (5-HT) release and on the release of 5-hydroxyindoleacetic acid (5-HIAA), the 5-HT metabolite, as measured by microdialysis. The behavior score, shown in the lower portion of the figure, corresponds to the occurrence of the 5-HT syndrome. (Reproduced from Auerbach et al., 1989, with permission of the publisher.)

A second experiment examined synaptically released 5-HT in the hypothalamus of freely-moving rats after the administration of a number of drugs and after manipulation of concentrations of potassium or calcium in the dialysis solution (Auerbach et al., 1989). In this experiment, concentric microdialysis probes were inserted through implanted guide cannula and were perfused at a rate of 2 μl/min. Although for most experiments probes were inserted the evening before the experiment and the rats were perfused overnight, basal levels of 5-HT were examined from immediately after the probe was inserted and were determined for up to 8 h later. Fig. 9 shows that 5-HT levels were high immediately after insertion of the probe and declined to a steady level after approximately 5–6 h. These results suggest that at least 5 to 6 h should elapse before conducting analyses of 5-HT.

In other experiments Auerbach et al. (1989) showed release of 5-HT by fenfluramine, a known 5-HT releaser, with little or no effects on the 5-HT metabolite 5-HIAA (Fig. 10). It also was found in this study that increasing the concentration of potassium from 4 to 120 mM elevated 5-HT levels, whereas removal of calcium lowered levels of 5-HT in the perfusate. This study demonstrated that extracellular levels of 5-HT are sensitive to physiological and pharmacological manipulations.

4.2. Behavioral studies

As mentioned above, there are few studies at the present time that have measured neurotransmitter activity while making concomitant measurements of behavior. A recent experiment by Salamone et al. (1989), however, investigated the effects of lever pressing maintained by a continuous reinforcement schedule (CRF) of food presentation on neurochemical changes. In samples collected from the striatum of rats 60–120 min after the behavioral session, HVA levels were increased by 12–40% relative to baseline values. Experimentally naive control animals that were placed in the chamber but received neither food nor training to lever press did not show comparable effects. However, rats that received a food pellet every 30 s also showed elevated levels of striatal HVA, suggesting that this neurochemical change may be related to behavioral activation.

A recent study by Pettit and Justice (1989) used *in vivo* microdialysis to examine DA release in the nucleus accumbens during cocaine self-administration. In this experiment the extracellular concentration of DA in the nucleus accumbens increased and was maintained at high levels during the self-administration of cocaine. The possibility of examining neurochemical events correlated with drug self-administration as well as with the administration of other reinforcers is an exciting development for exploration of the possible neurobiological correlates of reinforcement.

The results of these and related experiments show a promising development towards a synthesis of behavioral studies and neurochemistry. As more individuals with behavioral training and orientation become familiar with these techniques and appreciate their ability to provide information about both behavior and neurochemistry, much more progress can be expected in both spheres of scientific endeavor.

5. *In vivo* voltammetry

The techniques described above provide neurochemical information over long periods of time with somewhat poor moment-to-moment resolution of neurochemical changes. Although it is possible to measure dialysate samples on a minute-to-minute basis, greater resolution and more instantaneous information about the relationships of neurochemistry and behavior are desirable. The technique of *in vivo* voltammetry allows this possibility. Voltammetric methods typically involve the miniaturization of the electrochemical techniques used with HPLC and electrochemical detection described above; i.e., the measurement of current flow at an electrode following the application of a potential. Unlike HPLC, however, there is no chromatographic separation of the compounds. Most studies using this technique use a three-electrode recording system with a high-quality current amplifier and increased shielding to minimize electrical interference. The 'working' electrodes are carbon (either paste, graphite-epoxy or fiber); an illustration of a carbon fiber electrode is shown in Fig. 11. The working electrode acts as an oxidizing agent so that when a suitable positive potential is applied, this causes *in situ* oxidation and electrons are transferred from the oxidizable compound to the electrode. The main factors that determine the ease at which a compound is oxidized are the presence of oxidizable groups such as OH or NH in the case of the indoleamines and the potential at which oxidation occurs. One of the major limitations of *in vivo* electrochemistry is that compounds with simi-

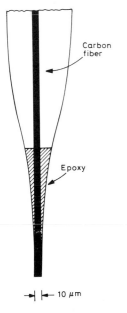

Fig. 11. Illustration of a carbon fiber electrode used in studies with *in vivo* voltammetry. (Reproduced from Cunningham and Justice, 1986, with permission of the publisher.)

lar chemical structures (e.g., DA and DOPAC or 5-HT and 5-HIAA) oxidize at similar potentials and there is a need for increased selectivity.

Measurement techniques are covered by Adams and Marsden (1982), Justice (1987) and Marsden et al. (1988). In brief, there are two main methods. In one, termed chronoamperometry, a square wave potential pulse is applied to the working electrode for a fixed time (e.g., +0.5 V for 1 s). The total current generated is measured during the last tenth of the time period; all compounds with oxidation potentials at or below the potential applied are oxidized, yielding a summed current response. In the second approach, a steadily increasing ramp potential with a pre-determined range is applied to the working electrode. The oxidation of a compound is recorded as a peak of current because, at its oxidation potential and above, all the compound at the electrode surface is oxidized. If there is a reasonable difference between the oxidation potentials of two compounds, they will produce separate oxidation peaks. Whereas the chronoamperometric procedure provides quantitative information, the ramp procedure and its variations (e.g., differential pulse voltammetry and normal pulse voltammetry) provide both quantitative and qualitative information.

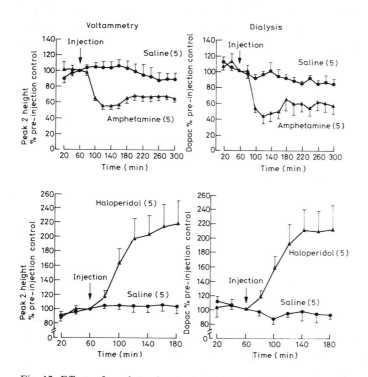

Fig. 12. Effects of amphetamine (top) and haloperidol (bottom) on release of the dopamine metabolite DOPAC as measured simultaneously from the striata of the same animal with dialysis and *in vivo* voltammetry. Note the correspondence between the two measures. (Adapted from Sharp et al., 1984, with permission of the publisher.)

5.1. Experimental studies

Sharp et al. (1984) compared voltammetry and microdialysis techniques by placing carbon fiber electrodes in one striatum and a dialysis loop in the contralateral striatum of anesthetized rats. Peak heights and extracellular levels of DOPAC and 5-HIAA were monitored after the administration of amphetamine or haloperidol. Fig. 12 shows that similar effects were obtained using the two different techniques. Compared to control injections of saline, both voltammetric and dialysis measures showed a marked drop in DOPAC levels after amphetamine that occurred at approximately the same time and persisted for over 4 h. Haloperidol also produced similar effects with both dialysis and voltammetry except that DOPAC levels were increased markedly following drug administration.

This study demonstrated that the two measures of neurochemical activity provide similar results when comparing changes in extracellular DOPAC in rat striatum. Although greater caution is required when evaluating oxidation peaks from voltammetry because many compounds oxidize at the same potential, combined studies of microdialysis and voltammetry verify that the voltammetric procedure is actually measuring a specific compound. Although a powerful technique, *in vivo* electrochemistry has certain limitations. At present, a limited number of neurotransmitter systems can be monitored and basal levels of release cannot be measured. Nevertheless, the rapid sensitivity of the system is a distinct advantage. When coupled with increasingly selective electrodes, this may provide the necessary means for monitoring rapid behavioral and neurochemical changes that, at the present time, are still elusive.

6. Neurochemical lesions

The possibility of localizing certain functions to discrete regions of the brain has long captured the attention of many scientists. Attempts to isolate the influence of any one structure or neurotransmitter system are particularly difficult because these structures and systems are under multiple interacting control and are reciprocally innervated in many cases. Physiological psychologists and neuroanatomists have developed a number of methods for examining the possible function of regional brain areas or certain neurotransmitter systems. These techniques range from ablation and electrolytic lesions, which remove or destroy certain regions, to chemical lesions which may destroy an anatomical structure or remove a chemical neurotransmitter (review and history by Breese, 1975; Schallert and Wilcox, 1985). Destruction of any one structure or system is not without influence on other structures and it may be difficult to localize effects because the consequences of removal or destruction of one area may be quite remote. Electrolytic or surgical lesions may have multiple other effects as well (Coyle, 1982).

Neurocytotoxins have many advantages over other techniques for examining the

CNS. The most important is that they are relatively selective and can induce neuronal degeneration with minimal effects on unrelated and proximal sites of neuronal activity. These compounds can be integrated with the specialized actions of cells and, through these actions, can alter any of a number of specialized processes such as synthesis, storage and uptake. Consequently, they can inactivate discrete neuronal processes. The use of chemical neurotoxins to aid in the study of behavioral processes such as reinforcement (reviewed below) illustrates the potential for these techniques in behavioral neuroscience.

Although a number of experimental studies were conducted with neurotoxins throughout the period of 1900 to 1960, the first transmitter specific neurotoxin, 6-hydroxydopamine (6-OHDA), was not introduced until 1967. This compound is accumulated by and subsequently destroys catecholaminergic neurons (Thoenen and Tranzer, 1968). Subsequently, compounds were discovered that also destroyed 5-HT containing terminals in the brain (Baumgarten et al., 1971), thereby allowing direct investigations of the effects of chemically removing the influence of these neurotransmitter systems on behavior. This section will review briefly the procedures for using 6-OHDA and the 5-HT neurotoxin, 5,7-dihydroxytryptamine (5,7-DHT), along with the possible use of kainic or ibotenic acid lesions and DSP-4 in behavioral studies.

Analyses of the results of any neurochemical lesion must involve a variety of behavioral and neurochemical assay procedures. In doing so, it should be remembered that the interpretation of lesion effects has several problems (Moore, 1978). Interpretations of the results shortly after the lesion may be complicated by residual anesthesia, trauma to the brain, and perturbance of normal CNS dynamics. Effects observed shortly after the lesion may be related more to these factors than the actual lesion. After lesioning a particular structure or neurotransmitter pathway a number of adaptive processes occur in the remaining presynaptic neurons as well as at postsynaptic sites. For example, presynaptically there may be increased activity of neurotransmitter synthesizing enzymes, increased basal levels of electrical activity, or decreases in the sensitivity of presynaptic inhibitory autoreceptors (Danysz et al., 1987). The result of all of these presynaptic processes results in an increase in neurotransmitter release from the remaining neurons. In response to the decreased stimulation resulting from the lesion, postsynaptic receptors may become more sensitive. This 'supersensitivity' may depend on the extent and severity of the lesion, the type of receptor, as well as the region in which the lesion is made. It is important to consider these different outcomes when evaluating the behavioral and pharmacological effects of the lesion.

Over a longer time period, several other processes may occur such as collateral sprouting and reinnervation in areas denervated by a distant lesion. These changes may account for some of the functional recovery that occurs over a relatively long period of time. Careful histological studies, together with correlational analyses of the functional changes in behavior and a careful evaluation of histological changes possibly brought about by behavior, make the need for a continuing reassessment of the lesion's effects an important consideration when conducting studies over a long-term period of time. As Moore (1978) has pointed out, the effects of the lesion are most likely modified not only by intrinsic events within the CNS but by the continuing interaction of the organism with its environment. Few studies have addressed this important issue about the reciprocal influences between behavior and lesion effects but it seems feasible that engaging in certain behavior that is related to or controlled by the lesioned system or site may facilitate recovery.

6.1. 6-Hydroxydopamine (6-OHDA)

As mentioned above, 6-OHDA can destroy dopaminergic and noradrenergic (NE) neurons. Because 6-OHDA does not readily cross the blood brain barrier, it must be administered directly into a brain site or into the cerebroventricular system. Studies summarized by Breese (1975) have demonstrated that following the administration of 6-OHDA there is a dose-dependent reduction of DA and NE, with the NE system being more sensitive to the effects than the DA system. To enhance specificity of the lesion, it has become common practice to administer uptake inhibitors before administration of 6-OHDA. Thus, for example, if interested in destroying DA neurons, administration of an NE uptake inhibitor such as desmethylimipramine (DMI) will limit the destruction of NE cells. Similarly, DA neurons can be protected by prior administration of a DA uptake inhibitor such as benztropine.

Detailed procedures for the administration of 6-OHDA, including presurgical treatment, doses, infusion procedures and evaluation of 6-OHDA neurotoxicity are provided by Schallert and Wilcox (1985); see also Section 11.

6.2. 5,7-Dihydroxytryptamine (5,7-DHT)

Relatively selective destruction of 5-HT neurons can be accomplished by administration of 5,7-DHT used, as mentioned above, in combination with DMI to prevent damage to NE neurons. Although other compounds are available for chemically inactivating the 5-HT system (e.g., p-chloroamphetamine), 5,7-DHT has become widely used because of its potency and selectivity for the 5-HT system. Many of the procedures for administration of 5,7-DHT are similar to those for 6-OHDA and are reviewed by Schallert and Wilcox (1985) and Breese (1975). As was the case with 6-OHDA, 5,7-DHT must be administered intraventricularly or directly into the brain region of interest such as the raphe nuclei.

6.3. DSP-4, AF64A, kainic acid and ibotenic acid lesions

DSP-4 and AF64A are two compounds based on aziridinium ions that are neurocytotoxic for NE and cholinergic neurons, respectively. Unlike the neurotoxins described above, DSP-4 can be administered peripherally, whereas AF64A requires central administration. Detailed procedures for the administration of AF64A are given by Schallert and Wilcox (1985), whereas Féty et al. (1986) described procedures for administering DSP-4.

Kainic and ibotenic acid are neuroexcitatory amino acids that are analogs of the neurotransmitter glutamic acid. These compounds selectively destroy neurons by means of their excitatory effects. Presumably, their administration results in a state of continuous depolarization and eventual depletion of cellular energy sources and death (Coyle, 1982). These compounds have been shown to destroy neuronal dendrites and perikarya (particularly those in the limbic system) but to spare axons of passage (Schwarcz et al., 1978; Coyle, 1982; Schallert and Wilcox, 1985). Kainic acid is not selective in all brain regions, may produce effects at distal sites, and has a high propensity for inducing seizures. Because the effects of ibotenic acid appear to be more direct, as well as localized, and because this substance has a lower likelihood for seizure activity, ibotenic acid offers several advantages and is replacing kainic acid as a neurotoxin. In view of the fact that excitatory neurotransmission plays an important role in the neurocytotoxic effects of ibotenic and kainic acid, the use of anesthetics which are also anticonvulsants (e.g., barbiturates) may attenuate the effects of the lesion. Prolonged anesthesia may antagonize the local neurotoxic effects and, although this may be overcome by higher doses of the neurotoxin, the substance may diffuse to other regions resulting in damage distant to the injection site as the anesthesia wears off (Coyle, 1985). Consequently, it may be best to use a brief inhalation anesthetic such as halothane so that the dose of the neurotoxin can be minimal and distant sites protected.

6.4. Effects on operant behavior

As would be expected, the amount of research using combined operant procedures and neurochemical toxins is related to the length of time these compounds have been available for use. A large number of studies have examined the effects of 6-OHDA and 5,7-DHT lesions on behavior maintained under a variety of schedules that have used various maintaining events (see reviews by Breese, 1975; Soubrie, 1986). Far fewer experiments have been conducted with the other neurotoxins reviewed in this chapter. Although a thorough review of these experiments is beyond the scope of this chapter, a few experiments will be described to show the potential application of these procedures to the study of operant behavior.

A number of studies that examined the effects of 6-OHDA lesions on behavior maintained by self-administration of cocaine and amphetamine are reviewed by Dworkin and Smith (1987, 1989). Dopaminergic lesions of the nucleus accumbens by administration of 6-OHDA, as well as kainic acid lesions in this area, decreased the intravenous self-administration of amphetamine and cocaine, whereas 5-HT lesions produced by 5,7-DHT did not affect this behavior. These studies would appear to suggest a critical role for DA and the nucleus accumbens in the maintenance of drug self-administration behavior. Several studies have evaluated the effects of 6-OHDA on behavior maintained under various schedules of reinforcement and typically have reported both transient and sustained increases in responding following the lesion. For example, Peterson and Sparber (1974) found that intracerebroventricular (i.c.v.) administration of 6-OHDA initially decreased response rates maintained under a fixed-ratio 30 schedule of food presentation but that rates gradually increased and remained elevated up to 156 days after the lesion. Similar effects occurred under interval-based schedules as well (Schoenfeld and Uretsky, 1972).

More recently, Morley et al. (1987a) have examined the effects of 6-OHDA lesions of the dorsal noradrenergic bundle on responding maintained under variable-interval schedules. This experiment focused on the quantitative analysis of operant performance and varied reinforcement rate from 8 to 350 per h to evaluate effects on parameters of Herrnstein's (1970) equation. Two parameters of that equation, R_{max}, which defines the theoretical maximum response rate, and K_H, which expresses the reinforcement frequency needed to maintain half the maximal response rate, were significantly higher in the lesioned animals, leading these authors to conclude that the 'value' of the reinforcer was reduced by the lesion without a corresponding impairment in the capacity to respond. This group has also examined the effects of DSP-4 on the behavioral changes induced by d-amphetamine under similar conditions (Morley et al., 1987b).

Several studies have examined the effects of i.c.v. administration of 5,7-DHT to rats trained under a punishment schedule and have found large increases in responding (review by Soubrie, 1986). Administration of 5,7-DHT into the ventral tegmentum produced a marked increase in punished responding and also impaired the initial acquisition of suppressed behavior under the punishment procedure (Tye et al., 1977). Based on these findings, together with several other reports linking the 5-HT system with the clinical effects of anxiolytic drugs, it has been suggested that 5-HT plays an important role in behavior suppressed under punishment procedures and in the clinical condition characterized as anxiety (Iversen, 1984; Barrett and Witkin, 1991).

7. Intracerebral injections

Under certain circumstances, it may be desirable to administer a drug directly to a particular site in the brain. This could occur, for example, under conditions where the drug of interest does not penetrate the blood-brain barrier or when one is interested in determining whether a specific region may be involved in a particular type of behavior. These techniques draw upon many of the procedures described in earlier portions of this chapter and involve stereotaxic surgery, implantation of a guide cannula, care and monitoring of the animal etc., and actually require little further elaboration here. The cannula systems are commercially available (e.g., Plastic Products) but can also be constructed from stainless steel tubing. Usually, guide cannulae are constructed from 22 or 26 gauge tubing with the internal or injector cannula constructed from 28 or 30 gauge tubing. In most cases the two cannulae are made so that when the injector is inserted through the guide tube it extends approximately 1 mm beyond the tip. This requires that the guide tube be stereotaxically implanted 1 mm above the targeted site. The system is closed by a 'dummy' cannula when no injections are occurring.

An important consideration in studies of this type is the volume injected into the brain. Clearly, the administration of a large volume of fluid into brain tissue can produce substantial mechanical displacement of tissue, and distortion, as well as potential tissue damage which could alter behavior. In addition to suitable control injections of artificial CSF or the injection vehicle, it is important to keep the injection volume as small and as slow as possible to minimize these effects as well as to prevent the diffusion of the drug away from the presumed site of action. The decision about volume depends to some extent on the size of the area being injected. When administering drugs into the ventricular system, it is possible to deliver larger volumes (up to 10 μl); however, when administering a drug into a specific region, the total volume is best kept between 0.5–1 μl delivered over a 1 min period.

Typically the injector is connected to a microliter syringe by flexible tubing and the injection performed either by hand, an automatic injector pump or by gravity, in which case the tubing is held at a certain height and the fluid allowed to flow into the region. The injector needle should remain in place for a 1–2-min period to allow the injection to diffuse. Otherwise the fluid may follow the withdrawal of the needle up the injection tract. Because only small volumes are administered, it is unnecessary to fill the syringe and tubing with the drug solution. Therefore, some recommend that a small bubble of air be inserted in the injection line between the drug solution and the remainder of the system which can be filled with distilled water or a more viscous substance such as oil. The bubble can serve as an index of infusion flow and may also act as a buffer to absorb some of the pressure changes associated with the injection (Greenshaw, 1985).

In addition to volume and rate of infusion, there are a number of other factors that should be considered when using intracerebral injections. Many of these are treated extensively in Myers (1974). As with other procedures involving the insertion of probes, cannula or other devices into the brain, it is essential to verify location and potential damage to the site and to adjacent areas. Additionally, some assessment of the extent of the diffusion of the injection should be made. This is accomplished by injecting methylene blue or a suitable dye prior to euthanising the animal. Although these experiments are difficult to conduct and require care, patience and detailed attention to many factors, they can be very informative in helping delineate the potential sites involved in certain behavioral processes.

8. Neurotransmitter turnover techniques and studies

The techniques that have been reviewed thus far in this chapter have involved methods for evaluating behavioral effects of neurochemical changes in awake, behaving animals. These techniques allow some interaction of behavioral contingencies with measurement of neurochemical activity over a period of time. A variety of other procedures are available that permit a detailed assessment of neurochemical changes induced by behavioral variables or drug administration but which involve *in vitro* analyses that require sacrificing the animal once exposed to the condition(s) of interest. There are a number of such techniques available. One is 2-deoxyglucose autoradiography (Porrino et al., 1984) which permits visualization of the loci of neuronal activity correlated with behavioral and pharmacological processes. More recently introduced molecular biological techniques can be used for studying gene expression (Gozes, 1988) and *in situ* hybridization (Uhl, 1988). Only two of these techniques, neurotransmitter turnover and receptor binding, will be discussed here because they have received the most recent attention from a combined approach to behavior and neurochemistry. Earlier experiments that examined neurotransmitter concentrations after various conditions, such as the initial experiments by Seiden and his colleagues have been summarized recently (Barrett and Nader, 1990). Studies of this type continue to be performed and provide useful behavioral and biochemical information when done using carefully established behavioral performances (Sakurai-Yamashita et al., 1989).

A number of different activities occur at the level of the neuron. These involve synthesis of the neurotransmitter, storage, release and reuptake mechanisms (Cooper et al., 1986). A number of studies have been conducted using neurotransmitter turnover measurements as indices of neurotransmitter activity and have correlated those effects with behavior (reviews by Dworkin and Smith, 1987, 1989). There are a number of approaches to the measurement of neurotransmitter turnover and the principles, as well as theory of turnover measures are complex (Pycock and Taberner, 1981). The method used by Smith, Dworkin and their colleagues has provided the most information on correlates of behavioral processes and will be used to illustrate this technique. Typically, animals are trained under a particular procedure for a number of sessions until responding has stabilized. Smith and Dworkin have used a number of procedures, including the Estes-Skinner procedure or conditioned emotional response, drug self-administration and punishment. Immediately prior to the final experimental sessions the animal, previously implanted with an intravenous catheter, is injected with a radioactive neurotransmitter precursor such as tyrosine for DA and NE or tryptophan for 5-HT, and then is sacrificed after the experimental session or at suitable times on the log-linear radioactive decay curve. Calculation of turnover rates, based on the product of the percentage of the total neurotransmitter synthesized per unit time and the neurotransmitter content in a brain region are calculated and compared across animals exposed to different experimental conditions.

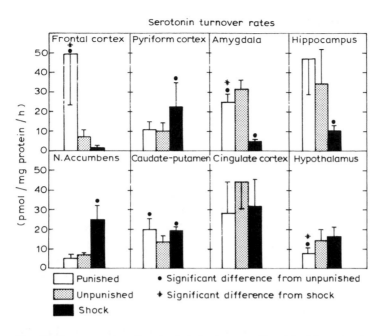

Fig. 13. Turnover rates of serotonin in brain areas of punished (open bars), unpunished (gray bars) and yoked-shock (filled bars) rats. An asterisk denotes a significant difference ($p < 0.05$) from the animals in the group that were not punished; a star denotes significant differences from the yoked-shock group. See text for details. (Adapted from Miyauchi et al., 1989, with permission of the publisher.)

One illustration of the use of this procedure was by Miyauchi et al. (1988) who examined neurochemical turnover correlates of punished behavior. In this experiment, triads of litter-mate rats were studied using yoked-control procedures. One rat was trained to respond under a random-ratio 100 schedule of food presentation (see Part 1, Ch. 3). A second subject received food under a variable-interval schedule with the reinforcement rate determined by the initial rat's behavior. Thus, when the rat responding under the random-ratio schedule received food, the next response by the second rat also produced food. The third rat received food independently of responding, whenever food was delivered to the first subject, thereby ensuring that the frequency of food presentation was identical for all three subjects. Subsequently, a random-ratio schedule of shock delivery was added to the random-ratio food-presentation schedule and was yoked to the rat receiving response-independent food. This procedure resulted in comparable low rates of punished (random-ratio schedule rat) and non-punished (variable-interval rat) responding and also allowed a control for the effects of food and shock independently of responding in the third rat.

After training under this procedure for a number of sessions, the animals were injected with radiolabelled precursors immediately before exposure to the session and then sacrificed 60–90 min later. Levels of the biogenic amines and amino acids (Miyauchi et al., 1989) in different brain regions were determined by HPLC with ei-

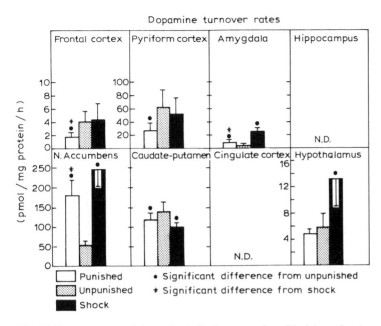

Fig. 14. Turnover rates of dopamine in brain areas of punished (open bars), unpunished (gray bars) and yoked-shock (filled bars) rats. An asterisk denotes significant difference ($p < 0.05$) from the group that was not punished; a star indicates a significant difference from the yoked-shock group. See text for details. (Adapted from Miyauchi et al., 1989, with permission of the publisher.)

ther electrochemical or fluorometric detection, respectively. Exposure to the punishment procedure increased 5-HT turnover in the frontal cortex and decreased it in the hypothalamus (Fig. 13), whereas DA turnover was decreased in the frontal cortex (Fig. 14). These effects did not occur in the animals that received response-independent shock, suggesting an effect specific to punishment.

These techniques can provide a wealth of information from a single animal with regard to regional differences in neurotransmitter turnover activity. When combined with the use of sophisticated and careful behavioral control procedures, such as those in the study described above, such techniques can yield useful significant information concerning the impact of behavioral processes on CNS activity.

9. Radioligand binding techniques and studies

Another approach to the study of neurochemical changes that might index behavioral processes involves the use of radioligand receptor binding techniques. Although these procedures are used extensively to identify and localize various receptor types in the CNS, at present, only a few studies have investigated the specific changes in parameters of receptor binding that may be produced by well-controlled behavioral procedures using schedules of reinforcement. In brief, these methods utilize radioactive ligands with high specific activity that are easily detectable, even in low concentrations, using suitable techniques. In a typical receptor-binding assay a radiolabelled ligand with high affinity for the receptor under study is incubated in a test tube with an amount of homogenized tissue. This mixture is washed and filtered leaving only ligand that is bound to the tissue. Because the ligand binds not only to its receptor (specific binding) but to other tissue as well (nonspecific binding), it is necessary to compare binding under conditions where access of the radioligand to specific receptor sites is blocked by the addition of a large amount of a nonradioactive competitor ligand that has a high affinity for the receptor. When this preparation is washed and filtered, there will be lower radioactive counts than in the first case because the radioactive ligand did not have access to the specific receptor sites that were blocked. This preparation, therefore, represents only nonspecific binding and the difference between the first preparation (total binding) and the second (nonspecific binding) represents binding to the specific receptor.

There are a number of additional considerations in receptor-binding studies (see Section 11) that warrant review but are beyond the scope afforded by this chapter. These techniques can provide information on the number of receptors in a particular tissue (so called B_{max}) as well as measures of the dissociation constant (K_d), which provides a measure of the affinity of a ligand for its receptor. The receptor-binding assay has been used to evaluate the mechanisms of action of a large number of behaviorally-active drugs and has been used as a preclinical screen for new drugs in drug development research. The proliferation of receptor or binding sites, with the identification of specific functional correlates of those sites, has been one of the most rapidly developing areas in the neurosciences.

Experiments conducted using operant procedures and receptor binding studies are few. Recently, however, Izenwasser et al. (1989) examined benzodiazepine receptor binding, as labelled by the benzodiazepine receptor antagonist [^{3}H]Ro 15-1788, in rats trained under the punishment and control procedures summarized above in which neurotransmitter turnover analyses were conducted. Benzodiazepine receptor binding (i.e., B_{max}) was significantly increased in the striatum of animals that received shocks, regardless of whether shock was response-produced (punishment) or response independent. Further, binding was higher in the striatum of animals that received response-independent shock compared to animals that received the same number of punishment shocks. Finally, increases in binding in the cerebellum occurred only in animals that received response-produced shock. Taken together, these results suggest that the specific contingencies of the punishment procedure can induce specific neurochemical changes in receptor activity. Binding was increased in certain regions of the brain depending on the manner in which the shocks occurred in relation to behavior. These studies represent the beginning phases of the type of research that will aid in an eventual clarification of the effects of behavioral variables on neurochemical processes.

10. Summary and conclusions

This chapter has reviewed some of the basic techniques used in the field of Behavioral Neurochemistry. Emphasis has been on techniques that have allowed the simultaneous measurement of operant behavior and neurochemistry. A central objective has been to provide an introduction and overview rather than an exhaustive description of the details involved in each procedure. Advances in behavior and neurochemistry over the past 25 years have been substantial. Techniques for the precise, systematic, and stable control of behavior have been developed that permit clear differentiation and analysis of behavioral processes involved in reinforcement and punishment. Similarly, progress in the fields of neurochemistry and neuroscience has also been substantial and rapid within the past few years. With the development of new techniques for monitoring neurochemical activity in parallel with ongoing behavior, it is now possible to begin a systematic analysis of the dynamic, reciprocal interrelations between behavior and neurochemistry. Neither behavior nor neurochemistry are static but the extent of their mutual influences are at present poorly understood. Many of the traditional barriers and theoretical objections raised from a behavioral viewpoint, focusing on the speculative nature of events within the CNS, are no longer valid. As demonstrated in this chapter, it is possible to measure neurochemical events directly and to do so almost immediately and with excellent temporal resolution.

Each of the techniques covered in this chapter has certain shortcomings or disadvantages. Nevertheless, the proper use of these techniques, in conjunction with the careful study of behavior promises to yield considerable information. As shown by the several experiments reviewed in this chapter, the sensitivity of neurochemical substrates to contingencies affecting behavior reaffirms the importance of studying and understanding behavior and its controlling variables. The interdisciplinary approach of behavioral neurochemistry should greatly enhance the scientific progress in both fields.

11. Technical sources

Stereotaxic and surgical procedures

Fox, F.G., Cohen, B.J. and Loew, F.M. (1984) Laboratory Animal Medicine. Academic Press, Orlando, FL.
Singh, D. and Avery, D.D. (1975) Physiological Techniques in Behavioral Research. Brooks Cole, Monterey, CA.

High-performance liquid chromatography

Adams, R.N. (1976) Probing the brain with electroanalytical techniques. Anal. Chem. 43,1128–1138.

Hashimoto, H. and Maruyama, Y. (1983) High-performance liquid chromatography with electrochemical detection. In: S. Parvez, T. Nagatsu, I. Nagatsu and H. Parvez (Eds.), Methods in Biogenic Amine Research. Elsevier, Amsterdam, pp. 35–74.

Kabra, P.M. and Marton, L.J. (Eds.) (1981) Liquid chromatography in clinical analysis. Humana, Clifton, NJ.

Kissinger, P.T. (1983) Determination of biogenic amines and their metabolites by liquid chromatography/electrochemistry. In: S. Parvez, T. Nagatsu, I. Nagatsu and H. Parvez (Eds.), Methods in Biogenic Amine Research. Elsevier, Amsterdam, pp. 75–99.

Lin, P.Y.T., Bulawa, M.C., Wong, P., Lin, L., Scott, J. and Blank, C.L. (1984) The determination of catecholamines, indoleamines, metabolites and related enzymatic activities using three micron liquid chromatography columns. J. Liquid Chromatogr. 7,509–538.

Mefford, I.N., Jurik, A., Noyce, N. and Barchas, J.D. (1983) Analysis of catecholamines, metabolites and sulfate conjugates in brain tissue and plasma by high-performance liquid chromatography with electrochemical detection. In: S. Parvez, T. Nagatsu, I. Nagatsu and H. Parvez (Eds.), Methods in Biogenic Amine Research. Elsevier, Amsterdam, pp. 101–112.

Push-pull perfusion and CSF withdrawal

Bayón, A. and Drucker-Colin, R. (1985) In Vivo Perfusion and Release of Neuroactive substances. Academic Press, New York.

Myers, R.D. and Knott, P.J. (1986) Neurochemical analysis of the conscious brain: voltammetry and push-pull perfusion. Ann. NY Acad. Sci. 473,1–560.

Philippu, A. (1984) Use of push-pull cannulae to determine the release of endogenous neurotransmitters in distinct brain areas of anaesthetized and freely moving animals. In: C.A. Marsden (Ed.), Measurement of Neurotransmitter Release In Vivo. John Wiley & Sons, London, pp. 3–37.

Pittman, Q.J., Disturnal, J., Riphagen, C., Veale, W.L. and Bauce, L. (1985) Perfusion techniques for neural tissue. In: A.A. Boulton and G.B. Baker (Eds.), Neuromethods: General Neurochemical Techniques, Vol. 1. Humana, Clifton, NJ, pp. 279–303.

Wightman, R.M., Plotsky, P.M., Strope, E., Delcore, R. Jr. and Adams, R.N. (1977) Liquid chromatographic monitoring of CSF metabolites. Brain Res. 131,345–349.

Microdialysis and voltammetry

Bauer, J.E., Kristensen, E.W., May, L.J., Wiedemann, D.J. and Wightman, R.M. (1988) Fast-scan voltammetry of biogenic amines. Anal. Chem. 60,1268–1272.

Gonon, F., Cespuglio, R., Buda, M. and Pujol, J.F. (1983) In vivo electrochemical detection of monoamine derivatives. In: S. Parvez, T. Nagatsu, I. Nagatsu and H.

Parvez (Eds.), Methods in Biogenic Research. Elsevier, Amsterdam, pp. 165–188.

Joseph, M.H., Fillenz, M., MacDonald, I.A. and Marsden, C.A. (1985) Monitoring Neurotransmitter Release During Behavior. Ellis Horwood, Chichester, U.K.

Marsden, C.A., Brazell, M.P. and Maidment, N.T. (1984) An introduction to in vivo electrochemistry. In: C.A. Marsden (Ed.), Measurement of Neurotransmitter Release. John Wiley & Sons, London, pp. 127–151.

Stamford, J.A. (1985) In vivo voltammetry: promise and perspective. Brain Res. Rev. 10,119–135.

Stamford, J.A. (1986) In vivo voltammetry: some methodological considerations. J. Neurosci. Methods 17,1–29.

Ungerstedt, U. (1984) Measurement of neurotransmitter release by intracranial dialysis. In: C.A. Marsden (Ed.), Measurement of Neurotransmitter Release in vivo. John Wiley & Sons, London, pp. 81–105.

Wightman, R.M., May, L.J. and Michael, A.C. (1988) Detection of dopamine dynamics in the brain. Anal. Chem. 60,769–779.

Wipf, D.O. and Wightman, R.M. (1988) Submicrosecond measurements with cyclic voltammetry. Anal. Chem. 60,2460–2464.

Neurochemical lesions

Björklund, A., Nobin, A. and Stenevi, U. (1973) The use of neurotoxic dihydroxytryptamines as tools for morphological studies and localized lesioning of central indolamine neurons. Z. Zellforsch. 145,479–501.

Jonsson, G. (1980) Chemical neurotoxins as denervation tools in neurobiology. Annu. Rev. Neurosci. 3,169–187.

Jonsson, G. (1981) Lesion methods in Neurobiology. In: C. Heym and W.-G. Forssman (Eds.), Techniques in Neuroanatomical Research. Springer-Verlag, New York, pp. 71–99.

Schallert, T. and Wilcox, R.E. (1985) Neurotransmitter selective brain lesions. In: A.A. Boulton and G.B. Baker (Eds.), Neuromethods: General Neurochemical Techniques, Vol. 1. Humana, Clifton, NJ, pp. 343–387.

Neurotransmitter turnover and radioligand binding

Pycock, C.J. and Taberner, P.V. (1981) Central Neurotransmitter Turnover. University Park Press, Baltimore MD.

Radioligand binding studies

Yamamura, H.I., Enna, S.J. and Kuhar, M.J. (Eds.) (1985) Neurotransmitter Receptor Binding, 2nd Edn. Raven Press, New York.

112

References

Adams, R.N. and Marsden, C.A. (1982) Electrochemical detection methods for monoamine measurements in vitro and in vivo. In: L.L. Iversen, S.D. Iversen and S.H. Snyder (Eds.), Handbook of Psychopharmacology, Vol. 15. Plenum Press, New York, pp. 1–74.

Adell, A., Sarna, G.S., Hutson, P.H. and Curzon, G. (1989) An in vivo dialysis and behavioural study of the release of 5-HT and p-chloroamphetamine in reserpine-treated rats. Br. J. Pharmacol. 97,206–212.

Auerbach, S.B., Minzenberg, M.J. and Wilkinson, L.O. (1989) Extracellular serotonin and 5-hydroxyindoleacetic acid in hypothalamus of the unanesthetized rat measured by in vivo dialysis coupled to high-performance liquid chromatography with electrochemical detection: dialysate serotonin reflects neuronal release. Brain Res. 499, 281–290.

Barrett, J.E. and Hoffmann, S.M. (1991) Neurochemical changes correlated with behavior maintained under fixed-interval and fixed-ratio schedules of reinforcement. J. Exp. Anal. Behav., in press.

Barrett, J.E., Hoffmann, S.M., Olmstead, S.N., Foust, M.J., Harrod, C. and Weissman, B.A. (1989) Behavioral and neurochemical effects of the serotonin (5-HT)$_{1A}$ receptor ligand spiroxatrine. Psychopharmacology 97, 319–325.

Barrett, J.E., Olmstead, S.N., Nader, M.A. and Gleeson, S. (1989) Neurochemical correlates of punishment. Society for Neuroscience Abstracts, Vol. 15, p. 557.

Barrett, J.E. and Nader, M.A. (1990) Neurochemical correlates of behavioral processes. Drug Dev. Res., 20, 313–335.

Barrett, J.E. and Witkin, J.M. (1991) Buspirone in animal models of anxiety. In: G. Tunnicliff, A. Eison and D. Taylor (Eds.), Buspirone: Mechanisms and Clinical Aspects. Academic Press, Orlando, FL, pp. 37–79.

Baumgarten, H.G., Björklund, A., Lachenmayer, L., Nobin, A. and Stenevi, U. (1971) Long-lasting selective depletion of brain serotonin by 5,6-dihydroxytryptamine. Acta. Physiol. Scand. (Suppl.) 373,1–15.

Benveniste, H. (1989) Brain microdialysis. J. Neurochem. 52,1667–1679.

Breese, G.R. (1975) Chemical and immunochemical lesions by specific neurotoxic substances and antisera. In: L.L. Iversen, S.D. Iversen and S.H. Snyder (Eds.), Handbook of Psychopharmacology, Vol. 1. Plenum Press, New York.

Bures, J., Buresová, O. and Huston, J. (1983) Techniques and Basic Experiments for the Study of Brain and Behavior, 2nd Edn. Elsevier, Amsterdam.

Church, W.H. and Justice, J.B., Jr. (1987) Rapid sampling and determination of extracellular dopamine in vivo. Anal. Chem. 59,712–716.

Cooper, J.R., Bloom, F.E. and Roth, R.H. (1986) The Biomedical basis of Neuropharmacology, 5th Edn. Oxford University Press, New York.

Coyle, J.T. (1982) Excitatory amino acid neurotoxins. In: L.L. Iversen, S.D. Iversen and S.H. Snyder (Eds.), Handbook of Psychopharmacology, Vol. 15. Plenum Press, New York, pp. 237–269.

Coyle, J.T. (1985) Neuron-specific cytotoxins. In: A. Lajtha (Ed.), Handbook of Neurochemistry, 2nd Edn., Vol. 9. Plenum Press, New York, pp. 299–329.

Cunningham, A.J. and Justice, J.B., Jr. (1986) Voltammetric and chromatographic monitoring of neurochemicals in vivo: progress and challenges. Am. Lab. 18,33–41.

Danysz, W., Fowler, C.J., Ahlenius, S. and Archer, T. (1987) 'Selective' lesions of brain neurotransmitters may be misleading. Trends Pharmacol. Sci. 8,45–46.

De La Riva, C.F. and Yeo, J.A.G. (1985) Repeated determination of cerebrospinal fluid amine metabolites by automated direct sampling from an implanted cannula in freely moving rats. J. Neurosci. Methods 14, 233–240.

Dworkin, S.I. and Smith, J.B. (1987) Neurobiological aspects of drug-seeking behavior. In: T. Thompson, P.B. Dews and J.E. Barrett, (Eds.), Neurobehavioral Pharmacology, Vol. 6. L. Erlbaum, Hillsdale, NJ, pp. 1–43.

Dworkin, S.I. and Smith, J.B. (1989) Assessment of neurochemical correlates of operant behavior. In:

A.A. Boulton, G.B. Baker and A.J. Greenshaw (Eds.), Neuromethods: Psychopharmacology, Vol. 13. Humana, Clifton, NJ, pp. 741–785.

Féty, R., Misère, V., Lambàs-Señas, L. and Renaud, B. (1986) Central and peripheral changes in catecholamine-synthesizing enzyme activities after systemic administration of the neurotoxin DSP-4. Eur. J. Pharmacol. 124,197–202.

Fox, R.H. and Hilton, S.M. (1958) Bradykinin formation in human skin as a factor in head vasodilatation. J. Physiol. 142,219–232.

Gaddum, J.H. (1961) Push pull cannulae. J. Physiol. 155,1–2P.

Gaddum, J.H. (1962) Substances released in nervous activity. In: W.D.M. Paton and P. Lindgren (Eds.), Pharmacological Analysis of Central Nervous Action. Pergamon Press, London, pp. 1–6.

Gleeson, S., Ahlers, S.T., Mansbach, R.S., Foust, J.M. and Barrett, J.E. (1989) Behavioral studies with anxiolytic drugs. VI. Effects on punished responding of drugs interacting with serotonin receptor subtypes. J. Pharmacol. Exp. Ther. 250,809–817.

Gozes, I. (1988) Gene expression, basic principles. In: F.W. Van Leeuwen, R.M. Buys, C.W. Pool and O. Pach (Eds.), Techniques in the Behavioral and Neural Sciences, Vol. 3, Molecular Neuroanatomy. Elsevier, New York, pp. 3–24.

Greenshaw, A.J. (1985) Electrical and chemical stimulation of brain tissue in vivo. In: A.A. Boulton and G.B. Baker (Eds.), Neuromethods: General Neurochemical Techniques, Vol. 1. Humana, Clifton, NJ, pp. 233–277.

Herrnstein, R.J. (1970) On the law of effect. J. Exp. Anal. Behav. 13,243–266.

Iversen, S.D. (1984) 5-HT and anxiety. Neuropharmacol. 23,1553–1560.

Izenwasser, S., Blake, M.J., Goeders, N.E. and Dworkin, S.I. (1989) Punishment modifies the effects of chlordiazepoxide and benzodiazepine receptors. Pharmacol. Biochem. Behav. 32,743–748.

Johnson, R.D. and Justice, J.B. (1983) Model studies for brain dialysis. Brain Res. Bull. 10,567–571.

Joseph, M.H. and Waddington, J.L. (1986) Working Methods in Neuropsychopharmacology. Manchester University Press, Manchester.

Justice, J.B., Jr. (1987) Voltammetry in the Neurosciences. Humana, Clifton, NJ.

Kissinger, P.T. (1983) Determination of biogenic amines and their metabolites by liquid chromatography/ electrochemistry. In: S. Parvez, T. Nagatsu, I. Nagatsu and H. Parvez (Eds.), Methods in Biogenic Amine Research. Elsevier, New York, pp. 75–99.

Kuczenski, R. and Segal, D. (1989) Concomitant characterization of behavioral and striatal neurotransmitter response to amphetamine using in vivo microdialysis. J. Neurosci. 9,2051–2065.

Loullis, C.C., Hingtgen, J.N., Shea, P.A. and Aprison, M.H. (1980) In vivo determination of endogenous biogenic amines in rat brain using HPLC and push-pull cannula. Pharmacol. Biochem. Behav. 12,959–963.

Mansbach, R.S., Harrod, C., Hoffmann, S.M., Nader, M.A., Lei, Z., Witkin, J.M. and Barrett, J.E. (1988) Behavioral studies with anxiolytic drugs. V. Behavioral and neurochemical analyses in pigeons of drugs that increase punished responding. J. Pharmacol. Exp. Ther. 246,114–120.

Marsden, C.A. (1985) In vivo monitoring of pharmacological and physiological changes in endogenous serotonin release and metabolism. In: A.R. Green (Ed.), Neuropharmacology of Serotonin. Oxford University Press, London, pp. 218–252.

Marsden, C.A., Joseph, M.H., Kruk, Z.L., Maidment, N.T., O'Neill, R.D., Schenk, J.O. and Stamford, J.A. (1988) In vivo voltammetry – present electrodes and methods. Neuroscience 25,389–400.

Meyer, P.M. and Meyer, D.R. (1971) Neurosurgical procedures with special reference to aspiration lesions. In: R.D. Myers (Ed.), Methods in Psychobiology, Vol. 1. Academic Press, New York, pp. 92–130.

Miyauchi, T., Dworkin, S.I., Co, C. and Smith, J.E. (1988) Specific effects of punishment on biogenic monoamine turnover in discrete rat brain regions. Brain Res. 454,40–50.

Miyauchi, T., Dworkin, S.I., Co, C. and Smith, J.E. (1989) Specific effects of punishment on amino acids turnover in discrete rat brain regions. Pharmacol. Biochem. Behav. 31,523–531.

Moghaddam, B. and Bunney, B.S. (1989) Ionic composition of microdialysis perfusing solution alters the

114

pharmacological responsiveness and basal outflow of striatal dopamine. J. Neurochem. 53,652–654.

Moore, R.Y. (1978) Surgical and chemical lesion techniques. In: L.L. Iversen, S.D. Iversen and S.H. Snyder (Eds.), Handbook of Psychopharmacology, Vol. 9. Plenum Press, New York, pp. 1–39.

Morley, M.J., Bradshaw, C.M. and Szabadi, E. (1987a) Effect of 6-hydroxydopamine-induced lesions of the dorsal noradrenergic bundle on steady-state operant behavior. Psychopharmacology 93,520–525.

Morley, M.J., Bradshaw, C.M. and Szabadi, E. (1987b) DSP alters the effect of d-amphetamine on variable-interval performance: analysis in terms of Herrnstein's equation. Psychopharmacology 92,247–253.

Myers, R.D. (1972) Methods for perfusing different structures of the brain. In: R.D. Myers (Ed.), Methods in Psychobiology, Vol. 2. Academic Press, New York, pp. 169–211.

Myers, R.D. (1974) Handbook of Drug and Chemical Stimulation of the Brain. Van Rostrand, Reinhold, NY.

Myers, R.D. (1977) Chronic Methods: intraventricular infusion, cerebrospinal fluid sampling, and push-pull perfusion. In: R.D. Myers (Ed.), Methods in Psychobiology, Vol. 3. Academic Press, New York, pp. 281–315.

Myers, R.D. and Gurley-Orkin, L. (1985) New 'micro push-pull' catheter system for localized perfusion of diminutive structures in brain. Brain Res. Bull. 14,1–7.

Myers, R.D. and Knott, P.J. (1986) Neurochemical analysis of the conscious brain: voltammetry and push-pull perfusion. Ann. NY Acad. Sci. 473,1–560.

Myers, R.D., Rezvani, A.H. and Gurley-Orkin, L.A. (1985) New double-lumen polyethylene cannula for push-pull perfusion of brain tissue in vivo. J. Neurosci. Methods. 12,205–218.

Nielsen, J.A. and Moore, K.E. (1982) Measurement of metabolites of dopamine and 5-hydroxytryptamine in cerebroventricular perfusates of unanesthetized, freely-moving rats: selective effects of drugs. Pharmacol. Biochem. Behav. 16,131–137.

Pellegrino, L.J. and Cushman, A.J. (1971) Use of the stereotaxic technique. In: R.D. Myers (Ed.), Methods in Psychobiology, Vol. 1. Academic Press, New York, pp. 67–90.

Peterson, D.W. and Sparber, S.B. (1974) Increased fixed-ratio performance and differential D- and L-amphetamine action following norepinephrine depletion by intraventricular 6-hydroxydopamine. J. Pharmacol. Exper. Ther. 191,349–357.

Pettit, H.O. and Justice, J.B., Jr. (1989) Dopamine in the nucleus accumbens during cocaine self-administration as studied by in vivo microdialysis. Pharmacol. Biochem. Behav. 34,899–904.

Porrino, L.J., Esposito, R.U., Seeger, T.F., Crane, A.M., Pert, A. and Sokoloff, L. (1984) Metabolic mapping of the brain during rewarding self-stimulation. Science 224,306–309.

Pycock, C.J. and Taberner, P.V. (1981) Central Neurotransmitter Turnover. University Park Press, Baltimore.

Sakurai-Yamashita, Y., Kataoka, Y., Yamashita, K., Miyazaki, A., Ushio, M., Mine, K., Niwa, M. and Ueki, S. (1989) Conflict behavior and dynamics of monoamines of various brain nuclei in rats. Neuropharmacology 28,1067–1073.

Salamone, J.D., Keller, R.W., Zigmond, M.J. and Stricker, E.M. (1989) Behavioral activation in rats increases striatal dopamine metabolism measured by dialysis perfusion. Brain Res. 487,215–224.

Sarna, G.S., Hutson, P.H., Tricklebank, M.D. and Curzon, G. (1983) Determination of brain 5-hydroxytryptamine turnover in freely moving rats using repeated sampling of cerebrospinal fluid. J. Neurochem. 40,383–388.

Schallert, T. and Wilcox, R.E. (1985) Neurotransmitter-selective brain lesions. In: A.A. Boulton and G.B. Baker (Eds.), Neuromethods: General Neurochemical Techniques, Vol. 1. Humana, Clifton, NJ, pp. 343–387.

Schoenfeld, R.I. and Uretsky, N.S. (1972) Operant behavior and catecholamine-containing neurons: prolonged increase in lever-pressing after 6-hydroxydopamine. Eur. J. Pharmacol. 20,357–362.

Schwarcz, R., Zaczek, R. and Coyle, J.T. (1978) Microinjection of kainic acid into the rat hippocampus. Eur. J. Pharmacol. 50,209–220.

Sharp, T., Maidment, N.T., Brazell, M.P., Zetterström, T., Ungerstedt, U., Bennett, G.W. and Marsden,

C.A. (1984) Changes in monoamine metabolites measured by simultaneous *in vivo* differential pulse voltammetry and intracerebral dialysis. Neuroscience 12,1213–1221.

Sharp, T., Zetterström, T., Christmanson, L. and Ungerstedt, U. (1986) *p*-Chloroamphetamine releases both serotonin and dopamine into rat grain dialysates in vivo. Neurosci. Lett. 72,320–324.

Sharp, T., Zetterström, T., Series, H.G., Carlsson, A., Grahame-Smith, D.G. and Ungerstedt, U. (1987) HPLC-EC analysis of catechols and indoles in rat brain dialysates. Life Sci. 41, 869–872.

Skinner, B.F. (1938) Behavior of Organisms. Appleton-Century-Crofts, New York.

Soubrie, P. (1986) Reconciling the role of central serotonin neurons in human and animal behavior. Behav. Brain Res. 9, 319–364.

Sparber, S. (1975) Neurochemical changes associated with schedule-controlled behavior. Fed. Proc. 34,1802–1812.

Szerb, J.E. (1967) Model experiments with Gaddum's push-pull cannulas. Can. J. Physiol. Pharmacol. 45,613–620.

Thoenen, H. and Tranzer, J.P. (1968) Chemical sympathectomy by selective destruction of adrenergic nerve endings with 6-hydroxydopamine. Nauyn-Schmiedeberg's Arch. Pharmakol. 261,271–288.

Tilson, H.A. and Sparber, S.B. (1970) On the use of the push-pull cannula as a means of measuring biochemical changes during ongoing behavior. Behav. Res. Methods Instr. 2,131–134.

Tye, N.C., Everitt, B.J. and Iversen, S.D. (1977) 5-Hydroxytryptamine and punishment. Nature 268,741–743.

Uhl, G.R. (1988) An approach to in situ hybridization using oligonucleotide cDNA probes. In: F.W. Van Leeuwen, R.M. Buÿs, C.W. Pool and O. Pach (Eds.), Techniques in the Behavioral and Neural Sciences, Vol. 3, Molecular Neuroanatomy. Elsevier, New York, pp. 25–41.

Ungerstedt, U. and Hallström, Å. (1987) In vivo microdialysis – a new approach to the analysis of neurotransmitters in the brain. Life Sci. 41,861–864.

Waddington, J.L. (1986) Psychopharmacological studies in rodents: stereotaxic intracerebral injections and behavioural assessment. In: M.H. Joseph and J.L. Waddington (Eds.), Working Methods in Neuropsychopharmacology. Manchester University Press, Manchester, pp. 1–40.

Wages, S.A., Church, W.H. and Justice, J.B., Jr. (1986) Sampling considerations for on-line microbore liquid chromatography of brain dialysate. Anal. Chem. 1649–1656.

Westerink, B.H.C., Damsma, G., Rollema, H., DeVries, J.B. and Horn, A.S. (1987) Scope and limitations of in vivo brain dialysis: a comparison of its application to various neurotransmitter systems. Life Sci. 41,1763–1776.

Yaksh, T.L. and Yamamura, H.I. (1974) Factors affecting performance of the push-pull cannula in brain. J. Appl. Physiol. 34,428–434.

Experimental analysis of behavior, Part 2
Iversen and Lattal (eds.)
© *1991, Elsevier Science Publishers BV*

CHAPTER 4

Behavioral ecology

E. FANTINO

Psychology Department C-009, University of California, San Diego, La Jolla, CA 92093-0109, U.S.A.

1. Introduction

Behavioral ecology is that division of biology that studies the organism's fitness as a function of the variables in its environment (ecological space). The area of Behavioral Ecology is characterized in part by a theoretical perspective that emphasizes 'inclusive fitness' as an organizing concept. Some of the areas addressed by behavioral ecologists include foraging (generally from the perspective of 'optimal foraging theory,' discussed in this chapter), territoriality, mate selection, kin recognition, weaning decisions, and thermoregulation. In this chapter we will emphasize the area that has received by far the most attention from researchers with a behavior-analytic background, namely foraging. This attention is quite predictable given traditional interest in behavior maintained by food and drink in behavior analysis and given that foraging theory emphasizes choice, a favorite topic of behavior analysis for three decades.

Behavioral ecologists have been attracted to behavior-analytic methodology because, after literally decades of refinement, this methodology promises to provide the ecologists with sharper tools to test more precisely their predictions, especially about decisions of foragers. Behavior analysts have been attracted to Behavioral Ecology in part as a way of applying principles that have evolved in the operant laboratory to a somewhat different range of phenomena and in part as a way of evaluating and perhaps adopting aspects of optimal foraging theory. The relation between behavior analysis and Behavioral Ecology has been discussed elsewhere (Fantino, 1985). For now it is sufficient to point out that this chapter will be a bit more theoretical than others in this volume. This stress stems from the theoretical emphasis that unifies Behavioral Ecology.

Although behavioral ecologists and behavior analysts have a range of interests, use somewhat different descriptive terms and have somewhat different methodological outlooks, there are many similarities between them including an emphasis on the environment, an emphasis on the whole organism, and a commitment to empirical test. Pulliam (1981), an ecologist, has argued for a theoretical correspondence between optimal foraging theory and reinforcement principles, and Fantino (1985) has suggested that both fields may profit from interdisciplinary work on common and complementary problems.

Behavioral ecologists have often emphasized research carried out in the organism's natural environment. To better test some of their theoretical predictions, however, they have increasingly conducted laboratory simulations of the natural environment. Behavior analysts also have moved in the direction of simulations in order to broaden the potential generality or external validity of their principles. External validity refers to the validity of generalizations made on the basis of internally valid conclusions to some other situation or population. Internal validity refers to the validity of conclusions drawn about changes in the behavior of the same sample of subjects on which the investigation was conducted. Both types of validity are central to the overall validity of any important conclusion. Thus, if alternative explanations of the behavior evident in the sample under study cannot be eliminated (low internal validity), generalization to other situations will be irrelevant. On the other hand, conclusions with high internal validity, that do not extend to the behavior of organisms beyond the immediate sample (low external validity), will not assist in understanding naturally occurring behavioral phenomena (for a fuller discussion of external versus internal validity see Fantino and Logan, 1979, pp. 478–479). Several experiments involving simulations of the natural environment will be discussed throughout this chapter. The value and appropriateness of simulations have been discussed by several behavior analysts. Here we review briefly some comments on this issue made by Baum (1983) and by Fantino and Abarca (1985).

Baum (1983) identified 'three artificialities' of the 'typical' experiment in behavior analysis. First, it takes place in a small box, rather than outdoors. Second, it takes up only a small portion of the organism's waking hours. Third, it provides food on a schedule that bears only slight resemblance to the manner in which food occurs in nature. At the same time, Baum points out similarities in the results from what has been done inside and outside the 'little box' and from what has been done with 1-h and 24-h sessions. He also cites his own study introducing locomotion in the chamber to better simulate 'travel' and to require the organism to hunt for its food even in the confines of the 'little box'. As Fantino and Abarca (1985) point out, Baum's locomotion procedure mitigates against another important shortcoming of typical operant analogues to foraging, namely the lack of spatial discreteness inherent in the typical operant situation. Olton et al. (1981), for example, have revealed a remarkable utilization of spatial memory in the rat. Although Baum (1982) found different choice relations as a function of different travel requirements, Dunn (1982) found relations analogous to those found by Baum although Dunn studied the same problem in the context of the 'little box' without locomotion. Dunn simulated travel by varying the number of responses required to switch from responding on one patch to responding on another.

Fantino and Abarca (1985) agreed with Baum (1983) that operant analogues to foraging contain potentially important artificialities and that more research is needed to explore the extent to which these artificialities affect the results obtained. They noted that their approach is to move slowly from the use of well-established procedures to the use of those better mimicking natural settings. In this way they hoped to increase the external validity of their results without breaking their moorings to the well studied operant choice procedures. They noted that only by altering their procedures gradually would they be in a position to assess which variables were responsible for any changing results.

Behavior analysts and behavioral ecologists have participated in many interdisciplinary efforts recently. Indeed the relation of behavior analysis to evolutionary phenomena has received considerable attention (e.g., Skinner, 1966, 1975, 1984; Fantino and Logan, 1979; Staddon, 1983; Fantino, 1985). The present chapter examines some of the ways behavior analysis has made contact with Behavioral Ecology. Generally, the methods are those of the operant laboratory applied to problems relevant to Behavioral Ecology. Often, however, the methodology is taken primarily from Behavioral Ecology and modified in ways of interest to behavior analysts. Many of these research efforts have been included in three volumes based on international and interdisciplinary conferences on foraging (Kamil and Sargent, 1981; Commons et al., 1987; Kamil et al., 1987). These conferences and other interdisciplinary activity and interest in foraging have exceeded what might have been anticipated a decade ago when, for example, Fantino and Logan (1979) ended their book with a call for more interdisciplinary research by ethologists, behavioral ecologists, and operant psychologists, noting that foraging was a natural area in which the theories and methodologies of these varied disciplines might complement one another successfully.

Many of the interactions between behavioral ecologists and behavior analysts have concerned the economic and temporal factors that influence foraging. Following a discussion of these, we shall present a brief review of work investigating the roles of memory, perception, and species differences in foraging. Finally, we will consider briefly areas of Behavioral Ecology other than foraging, for example, thermoregulation, circadian rhythms, territory defense and mate selection. This chapter reviews the methodologies in the subject area – behavioral ecology – that have been and are likely to be of interest and use to behavior analysts.

2. Foraging: methods for assessing economic and temporal variables

Much of Behavioral Ecology is concerned with problems of mate selection, territory defense, or foraging. Generally, choice is involved intimately with temporal and economic variables including molar variables, such as rate of reinforcement and long-term economic benefit, and molecular variables, such as delay of reinforcement and short-term economic gain. We begin with a review of economic considerations in foraging and the methods that have been developed for their assessment. This review is largely from the perspective of Collier (1987), who has pioneered many of the developments in this area.

2.1. Overview of economic methodology

Collier (1987) has noted in another volume of this series that experimental animals traditionally have been maintained in a 'welfare state' in which an experimenter provides the necessary resources. In the wild, however, the organism must find and acquire resources. Collier notes: "An efficient forager must make a number of economic (benefit/cost) decisions based on the structure of the environment before the resource is present. These decisions require knowledge of the benefit/cost structure of the habitat and the contingencies in the habitat. The consequences of foraging may be far removed from its initiation, and successful consequences may be infrequent" (1987, p. 55). Collier and his colleagues have identified several components of the chain of foraging behavior and have stressed the desirability, not of reproducing the natural environment but of mimicking central aspects of the environment's economic structure. Collier (1987) then reviews the procedures that have been developed to mimic that economic structure.

2.1.1. Search

The phase simulating an organism's search for its prey consists of: (1) search-initiating variables which may be simulated readily in the laboratory, for example, the light/dark cycle may be adjusted and monitored; (2) search strategies that maximize encounter rate; for example, the cost of search may be varied by varying search duration as in the studies reviewed below (Section 2.5); (3) search-terminating or 'giving-up' variables; for example, the benefits associated with staying or switching from a food patch, as in the studies reviewed below (Section 2.3). Search may be simulated in the laboratory by varying the requirement that a subject must satisfy to move a step closer to reinforcement. For example, a rat may be required to press a lever during a search phase. Completion of a specified number of lever presses changes the situation to one simulating prey handling.

2.1.2. Identification

Prey identification has been studied much less extensively than search within the operant framework. Below we discuss prey identification in terms of 'search images' and studies of crypticity using an operant paradigm (Section 4.1).

2.1.3. Procurement

The cost of obtaining or procuring a prey (once sought and identified) has been mim-

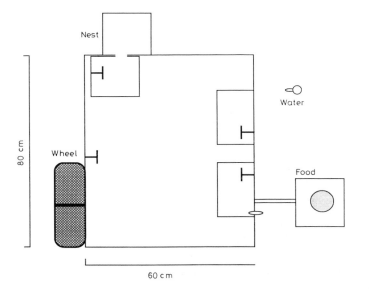

Fig. 1. An adaptation of Richter's multiple-activity cage developed by George Collier and his colleagues. Four activities – drinking, eating, nesting and wheel-running – are available. Access to each activity is controlled by lever-pressing (procurement cost). Entry into the wheel and nest is obtained by opening doors; access to water by advancing the cam-operated drinking tube; and access to food by turning on the pellet feeder. The cost of access to any of the four activities may be varied. This apparatus provides measures of the frequency of initiating bouts of behavior, the duration of these bouts, the amount of water or food consumed, the transitional probabilities between bouts, the transitional probabilities between episodes, and the distribution of bouts in time. (Reproduced from Collier, 1987, with permission of the publisher.)

icked extensively by Collier and his co-workers, for example, by varying the response effort, the kind of response, or the number of responses required to gain access to a meal. In a number of studies Collier's laboratory has shown that an increase in procurement cost results in the initiation of fewer meals but a compensatory increase in the size of these meals. In a typical experiment, completion of the procurement requirement allows the subject to receive unlimited access to the food (or other resources) until the subject itself abandons the resource (for example, a criterion might be 1 min without eating food). Fig. 1, from Collier (1987), shows the diagram of a large cage in which the cost of each of four activities may be manipulated by varying the number of bar presses the subject – in Collier's study rats – must emit in order to gain access to the activity. The large cage – described in detail in the figure caption – better simulates a natural environment than would a more restrictive rat cage. Fig. 2 shows the diagram of an apparatus used by Ackroff et al. (1986) to study diet selection. This apparatus permits the experimenter to address "the problem of the economics of abundance and availability. Some foods are rare and/or more costly. How does the animal solve this problem and over what time period? For example, does

122

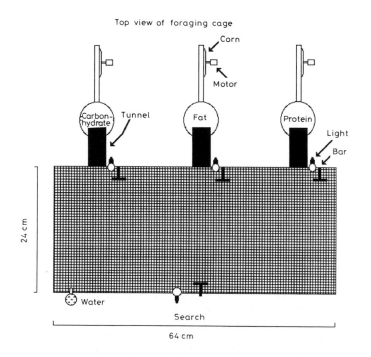

Fig. 2. An apparatus designed to study diet-selection in the foraging paradigm. Completing the requirement in the search bar (bottom) results in illumination of one of three procurement cue-lights, indicating
which macronutrient is available. The subject may accept the opportunity to respond on the bar near the
illuminated cue-lights; its response would then be reinforced by access to the macronutrient (top). Alternatively, the organism may reject the opportunity by making one bar press on the search bar or by waiting
30 s. In either case of rejection, the program returns to the search phase. The transitional probabilities
of acceptance of successively encountered nutrients as a function of the type and size of the preceding
meal may be studied with this apparatus. (Reproduced from Ackroff et al., 1986, with permission of the
publisher.)

he eat an expensive nutrient... less often but in larger meals?" (Collier, 1987, p. 63).
When the organism completes a lever-press requirement on the search bar at the bottom of Fig. 2 one of the three procurement cue-lights above one of three upper bars
indicates which macronutrient is now available. As in other studies with the succes-
sive-encounters procedure, the subject may accept or reject the proffered macronutrient. This apparatus and procedure may be used to vary search and procurement
costs. For example, the cost of a particular macronutrient may be varied selectively.
Ackroff et al. found that subjects will balance their diet over a time horizon of several
days (time horizons are discussed below, Section 2.8) and that protein was the least
'elastic' of the macronutrients in the sense that the size and frequency of protein
meals varied least with increasing costs.

2.1.4. Handling

Lea (1979), in developing his successive-encounter procedure, labeled the outcome phase 'handling', a convention that has been followed by most others using this procedure (see Section 2.5). Collier distinguishes between procurement and handling, and it is his procurement phase that corresponds most closely to the 'handling' encountered below (Fig. 3). For Collier 'handling' is a subsequent phase in which the prey, having been procured, must now be handled or 'prepared' for consumption (e.g. by shelling, killing, etc.). Although Collier notes that this process is difficult to simulate, he also notes that the effect of handling (preparation) cost may be mimicked by assessing choice between hulled and unhulled seeds.

2.1.5. Benefit

This variable may be manipulated by varying reinforcer magnitude (e.g., Ito and Fantino, 1986; see Section 2.9), that is, by varying access time to the reinforcer in the successive-choice procedure (Fig. 3) or, as Collier suggests, by varying the caloric density of the diet. For example, Johnson et al. (1986) found that rats regulated their calorie intake by eating meals of high-caloric-density foods less frequently.

2.1.6. Foraging versus consumption

Collier (1987) stresses the distinction between foraging and consumption, a distinction that has been overlooked often by others. He notes that many experimenters (including Krebs et al., 1978, see Section 2.4, and Ito and Fantino, 1986, see Section 2.5.) study consumption, which Collier characterizes as repeated "ingestion of small portions of food during a meal by experimenter-deprived animals" (Collier, 1987, p. 65) and treats consumption as if it were foraging. The constraints, however, are not on gaining access to a meal but are on meal ingestion. Foraging and consumption are described by different functions and have different sets of benefits and costs. Collier demonstrated the distinction between foraging and consumption by a simple experiment in which a procurement ratio must be completed to gain access to the food and a consumption ratio must then be completed for each pellet. He showed that the procurement ratio affected meal frequency and size but not within-meal rate of responding whereas the consumption ratio affected only within-meal rate of responding. Thus, Collier concludes that obtaining "access to resource (foraging) and using a resource (consumption) are independent processes which are affected by costs and benefits in different ways" (p. 68).

2.1.7. Simulation

Because lever pressing, and to a large extent, key pecking, does not resemble the natural elements comprising the foraging and consumption chain we have reviewed above, why use them in a simulation? In addition to the methodological convenience of simple repeatable responses that are measured easily, Collier notes that the lever press simulates the economic cost of predation and that the principles that have evolved from the study of operant responses such as bar presses parallel closely those that have been uncovered in field studies. Collier (1987) goes on to say:

> However, it is much easier to manipulate and quantify these relations in the laboratory because the bar-press units are equivalent. Is cost a common denominator of optimality decisions? One way to answer this question is to compare two means of varying cost, for example, bar-pressing and wheel-running. In Kanarek and Collier (1979), wheel-running was substituted for bar-pressing, that is, n turns of a running wheel were required to gain access to the feeder. The form of the functions relating cost (number of wheel turns) and meal frequency and size were exactly the same as those obtained with bar-pressing. Kacelnik et al. (1987) have shown that starlings bar-pressing for a 'load' in a field study performed as predicted by central place foraging theory (Orians and Pearson, 1979). (p. 69).

Economic considerations are helpful in providing a meaningful perspective with which to view foraging. Moreover, this perspective is consistent with recent trends in behavior analysis. For example, Hursh (1980), Rachlin et al. (1981) and others have emphasized the importance of economic variables for choice. This application to situations sharing important properties with the decision-making occurring in foraging follows readily from the more general principles of the effects of an economics-driven perspective of choice. We now turn to some of the variables implicated in simulations of foraging.

2.2. Methods for studying predation cost

A frequent 'cost' of foraging is the exposure of the forager to natural predation. Predators may adjust their own behavior to 'accommodate' their potential victim's foraging habits. Thus, Fantino and Logan (1979) have noted that reinforcers are sometimes arranged naturally on fixed-interval schedules, "for example, where prey or other food sources are prevalent only at certain times and places, such as water holes at dusk or flowers that secrete nectar at dawn. Under these circumstances the organism's investigation of these food locations may show a fixed-interval pattern quite comparable to that observed in the lab" (p. 495). Few studies in the behavior-analytic tradition, however, have simulated the effects of potential predators on foraging strategies. One exception is a series of studies by Fanselow and his associates. For example, Fanselow et al. (1988) simulated predation risk with the risk of infrequent electric shock and studied the effects of this risk on the meal patterns of rats. The rats could operate a response lever producing a food reinforcer, in a closed economy, according to chained fixed-ratio reinforcement schedules. This procedure allowed the rats to control the frequency and size of their meals. After acquiring responding on this chained schedule, shocks were delivered to the grid floor of the foraging compartment randomly in time and independently of the rat's behavior. Shocks could be avoided only if the animal remained in a nesting area at which foraging was not possible. Shock produced a reorganization of meal patterns: the rats ate larger, but less frequent meals. Fanselow et al. included an important control for the effects of shock that were spatially separate from the foraging context and that could not, therefore, reasonably be taken to simulate predation risk. That is, they assessed the effects of shocks outside the foraging situation on the rats' meal pattern. These spatially separate shocks did not modify the rats' meal patterns. Fanselow's technique is promising for simulating the effects of predation risk on foraging strategy.

Lima and Valone (1986), studying the effects of predation risk on diet selection, found that grey squirrels may prefer larger, but less energetically profitable items to smaller, but more energetically profitable ones, when the items may be carried to protective cover before consumption. This finding makes sense if one considers the implicit tradeoff between minimizing predation risk and maximizing foraging efficiency: if the squirrel is to minimize predation risk by finding cover before it eats, then carrying off larger items is more efficient. This tendency should be related directly to the distance covered, a prediction also supported by Lima and Valone's results.

Before continuing with an overview of methods for studying economic and temporal variables we will discuss and assess a widely influential principle in the Behavioral Ecology of foraging: Charnov's (1976) marginal-value theorem.

2.3 Assessing the marginal-value theorem

The marginal-valve theorem addresses the question of when foraging in a currently available depleting patch becomes less profitable than moving on to another patch. In simple terms, when the current rate of energy gain falls below the rate of energy gain in the environment as a whole, then the forager should move on to hopefully 'greener pastures'. Test of the theorem may depend on the time horizons over which the rates of energy gain should be assessed. If high future rates are not likely until the distant future, they will have less impact than more immediate energy gains, i.e., their effects will be 'discounted'. We will defer questions of the 'temporal horizons' over which foragers integrate rates of energy gain until Section 2.8. Nonetheless, in any situation involving discrete patches the forager may be giving up the chance for a fairly immediate food item (in the current patch) in exchange for a richer patch available only after a travel delay (e.g., Houston, 1987). Thus, one problem facing the forager is reminiscent of that facing subjects in standard operant self-control studies that pit immediately available small reinforcers against delayed larger reinforcers (e.g., Fantino 1966; Rachlin and Green, 1972). Subjects in these experiments generally are likely to choose the smaller more immediate reinforcer although they do appear sensitive to overall contingencies of reinforcement (see Section 2.6). Moreover, a number of species have been shown to perform in a manner at least roughly consistent with the marginal-value theorem (e.g., Stevens and Krebs, 1987).

What methods might be used in assessing whether a subject will leave one food source for a richer one even though it is giving up a more immediate reinforcer? An elegant demonstration is that of Wanchisen et al. (1988). They made use of a schedule of reinforcement that mimics a situation providing diminishing returns. Whereas a fixed-ratio schedule (FR) provides reinforcers for a fixed number of responses and resets at the same value following each reinforcer, a progressive-ratio (PR) schedule resets at a higher value following each reinforcer, thus corresponding to a source providing diminishing returns. In both conditions of Wanchisen et al., pigeons chose between such FR and PR schedules. At the outset the PR schedule provided reinforcers more often than the FR schedule (e.g., PR 1 versus FR 61). However, each time a reinforcer was obtained on the PR schedule its value increased by 20 responses (1, 21, 41, 61 etc.). The pigeon switched to the PR schedule approximately when the PR equalled the FR. In a subsequent condition, each completion of the FR reset the PR to its minimal value. In this condition, the pigeons chose the FR (thereby resetting the PR) well in advance of the equality point, i.e., they gave up responding on the PR even though the PR ratio was less than the FR. This result, consistent with an optimality analysis, will be discussed again later (Section 2.7).

Redhead and Tyler (1988) also used a progressive schedule to model food-patch depletion in a procedure in which responding on a second lever, unlike in the study of Wanchisen et al. only reset the schedule on the first and did not produce food. In addition, their subjects were rats, instead of pigeons, and their schedule was a progressive interval (PI) rather than a PR. In two conditions, the PI was always reset to its same initial value which could either be always rich ('stable good' condition) or always poor ('stable poor' condition). Both the stable good and the stable poor schedules arranged reinforcement on a progressive VI schedule in which the interval ranges increased with each successive interval, however, the interval lengths were shorter in the stable good schedule and increased at a slower rate. In a third condition, the environment was mixed, i.e., it contained both rich and poor PIs, and the patch type changed randomly each time a rat entered a patch. Their conditions permitted assessment of some predictions of the marginal-value theorem. Redhead and Tyler measured the time spent in a patch (residence time, i.e., the time from the first press on one lever to the next press on the other lever), the giving-up-time (i.e., the time from the earning of the last food pellet to the next press on the switching lever), and the interreinforcement interval before the subject switched out of a patch (i.e., the time between the last two pellets).

In one experiment, Redhead and Tyler found that rats spent more time in the rich patches than in the poor patches of the same variable environment. In addition, the rats spent more time in the patches of the poor stable environment than in the patches of the rich stable environment. Both of these results are consistent with the marginal-value theorem. The first result follows from the fact that more time will be spent in the better patch before it is depleted to the level of the 'environment' (the average of the rich and poor schedules). The second result follows from the fact that the poorer the environment, the longer it takes for a patch to be depleted to the level of the environment. The final interreinforcement interval data permitted confirmation of additional predictions of the theorem. For example, the rats left a patch in the rich stable condition at a shorter final interreinforcement interval than in the poor stable condition. In other words, the subjects left a patch in the richer environment at a higher rate of 'capture' (corresponding to a shorter interreinforcement interval) because the mean rate of capture in the richer environment was higher than in the poorer one.

The marginal-value theorem also implies that a forager will remain in a patch longer as travel requirement between the two patches increases. Thus, as the travel requirement increases, the size of the last interreinforcement interval should increase (correlated with a lower rate of 'capture'). Redhead and Tyler's second experiment assessed this prediction by increasing the time between pressing the switch lever and obtaining food by pressing the food lever. They studied two 'travel times', 5 and 25 s, and four groups of rats. The groups differed in terms of whether they were exposed to the stable rich or stable poor condition (as in their first experiment) and in the order in which they were exposed to short and long travel times (12 sessions for each travel time). Overall time in a patch increased sharply with increased travel time, as did the last interreinforcement interval duration before rats left the patch. These findings again confirmed the prediction of the marginal-value theorem. Other experiments reported in Redhead and Tyler (1988) support the marginal-value theorem and "demonstrate the value of modelling foraging strategies in operant apparatus ..." (p. 83).

2.4. Concurrent schedules and choice

Behavioral ecologists have utilized concurrent schedules to simulate aspects of naturally occurring foraging. For example, Krebs et al. (1978) used concurrent schedules to assess the patch-choice decisions of captured wild great tits (great tits, coal tits, marsh tits, and blue tits are all participants in the foraging literature; all belong to the same genus, parus, as the chickadees, which will be more familiar to North American readers). Nine great tits were trained to perform an operant response in an indoor aviary. Two identical feeding places, located at opposite ends of the aviary, each contained a disk enclosed in a shallow metal box. The disks each contained 72 holes; each hole housed a piece of mealworm. The bird had access to only one hole at a time through a small window at the top of the box. The bird had to hop on a perch next to the disk to obtain the next piece of food. The hops brought the next mealworm piece in line with the window on a variable-ratio (VR) schedule. After initial training, the birds were exposed to a series of treatments in which the VR schedule values were varied. Krebs et al. reported that the birds sampled both disks for an 'initial sampling period' after which they spent almost all of their time hopping on to the more profitable perch.

More recently, Houston (1986) analyzed field data assessing the time budgets and foraging effectiveness of pied wagtails. For these birds, choice data were described adequately by the generalized matching relation. In simple terms, this relation states that the proportion of responses to an alternative is equal to the proportion of reinforcers produced by responses on the two alternatives (Herrnstein 1961, 1970; Davison and McCarthy, 1988; Part 1, Ch. 6). Houston's data were collected at Port Meadow, Oxford, England, an area of open grassland two miles in length and half a mile wide. During the winter months, birds defend territories along the River Thames, which forms the western boundary. These birds may feed along the banks of the Thames, as the river washes food items (spiders and insects) onto its banks. The longer the time since a stretch of territory has been visited, the higher the feeding rate along that stretch. As Davies and Houston (1981) report, birds tend to walk around their territory in a regular circuit which, in principle, should lead to a fairly consistent degree of food availability. The results showed considerable deviation, however, probably because of intervening visits by intruders or because the defender chases an intruder leaving its place in the search circuit. There were also birds which fed in a flock on the meadow. Feeding rate in the flock was reasonably consistent on a given day and fairly resistant to depletion. Thus, the territory defenders sometimes left their territories when the feeding rate was low there, in order to feed with the flock. The flight to the flock required a travel time of about 30 s.

Watching individual birds for entire days permitted a determination of time allocated to foraging in the territory and in the flock and the numbers of comparable food items obtained (e.g. Davies and Houston, 1983). Houston (1986) found that wagtails match the time allocated to the obtained reinforcer allocations, but with a bias towards being in their territory. While consistent with the matching law the wagtail's time allocation pattern fails to maximize its overall rate of food intake. Houston argued that this failure of maximization makes good ecological sense as it may enhance the wagtails' chances of surviving the winter: "On some days the territories are the only possible feeding sites on the meadow. They are thus an important long-term asset for a wagtail, and the bias towards spending time on a territory may reflect this importance" (Houston, 1986, p. 18). In any event, Houston's analysis and the studies of Davies (1976) and Davies and Houston (1981) on which it builds, demonstrate the use of data collected in the field, rather than in the laboratory, for assessing principles for behavior analysis and behavioral ecology.

The concurrent-chain schedule is a type of concurrent schedule that has proven useful in operant analogs to foraging (see Fig. 3 in Part 1, Ch. 6 and that chapter for more detail on this procedure). For example, Fantino and Preston (1989) report an experiment in which the two outcome schedules (terminal links) were held constant at VI 20 s ('richer outcome') and VI 40 s ('poorer outcome') and in which the duration of the search schedule (initial link) leading to the poorer outcome was decreased from 60 s to zero (the duration of the search schedule leading to the richer outcome was always 60 s). Whereas most people's intuition as well as the theories of Killeen (1982) and Vaughan (1985) suggest that preference for the poorer outcome increases as it becomes more accessible, the delay-reduction hypothesis (Fantino, 1969) requires a decrease as the poorer outcome becomes sufficiently accessible. The results support delay-reduction. As search time to the poorer outcome becomes sufficiently short, preference for the richer outcome increases. This finding – that increased accessibility may lead to decreased acceptability – is discussed in more detail below.

2.5. Successive-encounter procedure

As Pulliam (1981) suggests, behavioral ecologists have not been successful in providing empirical support for many of their theoretical predictions. He notes that techniques developed in experimental laboratories may permit more powerful tests of these predictions. In fact, behavior analysts have modified some of their well-validated choice procedures and applied them to problems raised by behavioral ecologists. A particularly fruitful technique inspired by Collier and his associates (e.g., Collier, 1987) and further developed by Lea (1979) is the successive-encounter procedure, which mimics several aspects of the foraging situation. Lea's general procedure is shown in Fig. 3. A trial begins with a 'search state' in which a white keylight is present and responding at this key is reinforced on a fixed-interval (FI) X-s schedule with access to a choice phase. In the choice phase the white key light remains lit while a second key is now illumininated with red light (with a probability of p) or with green light (with a probability of $1-p$). In most studies, $p = 1-p = 0.5$, i.e., the red and green light are equiprobable and presented in a random order. In the choice phase, the subject can either peck the colored light once and commit to responding further in the presence of that light or it can peck the white light three times and return to the search state, i.e., the subject can either accept or reject the proffered outcome. In those rare cases where no response is made for 30 s the schedule also reverts to the search phase. When the outcome is accepted by pecking the colored light, the white light extinguishes and the key illuminated with colored light becomes the only one operative ('handling phase' in Fig. 3). Responses to the lit key in the handling phase produce food according to the associated schedule as shown in Fig. 3. Following food, the search state is reinstated. Using this procedure Lea mimicked variations in overall prey density by varying the FI value in the search state. The quality of the prey may be mimicked by varying the duration of the handling state, by varying the duration of food, or, optimally, by varying the type of food available. The reliability of a food source may be mimicked by providing food on only a percentage basis, i.e., a proportion of trials end with omission of food delivery. Of course, the appropriateness of these simulations, i.e., how well the simulation mimics the naturally-occurring variable, is always open to some question.

In his seminal study, Lea (1979) showed that pigeons' behavior became more selective as prey density varied from low to high values. In one set of conditions, Lea assessed preference for 5- versus 20-s handling durations (mimicked by FI 5-s and FI 20-s schedules, respectively) while varying the FI size in the search state across conditions. The optimal diet model (ODM) of optimal foraging theory requires that subjects always accept the more profitable outcome (FI 5 s) but that acceptance of the less profitable outcome depends on the search duration. The critical data are the pro-

130

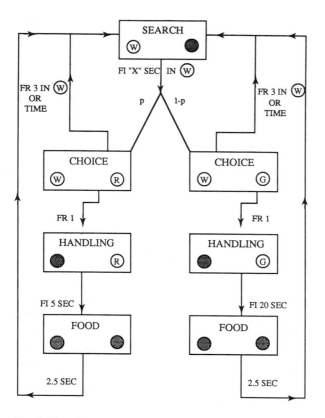

Fig. 3. Flowchart of the foraging schedule used by Lea (1979). The rectangles indicate the different states of the schedule; the state transition requirements are indicated next to the arrows. The circles indicate the keys and the letters the corresponding colors (R, red; G, green; W, white). The subject pecks a white key light in the search phase. These pecks are reinforced with an entry into the choice phase on a FI X schedule. With a probability of p, the choice phase consists of keys illuminated by white and red lights (left); with a probability of $1-p$ the choice is between keys illuminated by white and green lights (right). Generally, p equals 0.5. In the choice phase the organism may either accept the schedule of reinforcement associated with the colored key light by making a single response at that key or may reject that opportunity by waiting for a specified interval (which the subject rarely does) or by making three responses on the white key light. In the event of rejection the search phase is reinstated. If the organism accepts the schedule, it enters the handling phase in which a schedule of food reinforcement (providing 2.5 s of food) is available for responding at the only lit key. In the figure the schedule is FI 5 s in the presence of the red key light and FI 20 s in the presence of the green key light. Following food, the search phase is reinstated immediately. (Reproduced from Lea, 1979, with permission of the publisher.)

portions of acceptance of the two outcomes in the choice phase (the boxes marked 'choice' in Fig. 3). As required by the ODM, the more profitable outcome always was accepted (red always chosen in left choice box of Fig. 3).

Also, as required by the model, acceptance of the less profitable outcome (FI 20 s) increased as the FI duration in the search state increased (choice of green in right choice box of Fig. 3 is a positive function of 'X' in the search state). However, the pigeons showed a marked bias toward rejecting the less profitable outcome, that is, the less profitable outcome was rejected at FI values where the ODM appeared to require acceptance.

The discrepancy between theory and Lea's data may have a methodological source. In particular, based on operant research on choice Abarca and Fantino (1982) suggested that the use of VI instead of FI schedules in the handling states might produce data more compatible with the ODM. They repeated Lea's study with several variations, the most important of which were (1) the requirement for accepting or rejecting an outcome was made symmetrical, i.e., three responses in either case, and (2) VI schedules replaced FI schedules in the handling state. With those changes Abarca and Fantino showed that the mean data describing acceptance of the poorer outcome as a function of search duration crossed the $p = 0.50$ point at 7.5 s, or precisely the search time predicted by the ODM. To illustrate, at a search duration of 7.5 s the average overall duration to food from the onset of search equals 20 s (7.5 s of search plus (1/2) 20 s + (1/2) 5 s of handling), ignoring the 1–2 s to accept or reject the outcome. At this point the FI 20-s outcome constitutes neither an increase nor a decrease in mean delay to food. At search durations greater than 7.5 s the mean duration to food is greater than 20 s and the FI 20-s outcome represents a reduction in mean delay to food; therefore, it should be accepted. At search durations less than 7.5 s the mean duration to food is less than 20 s, the FI 20-s outcome represents an increase in mean delay to food, and should be rejected. The results support these predictions and, in so doing, both the ODM and the delay-reduction hypothesis (Fantino, 1969; see also Part 1, Ch. 6).

Lea's successive-choice procedure allows variations in several other variables central to foraging. Some of the variables assessed so far include providing food on a percentage basis and varying search and handling durations with unequal food durations (instead of unequal times to food as in the studies discussed above). These studies are reviewed later (Section 2.9). One aspect of the study with unequal food durations is more relevant here, however. Ito and Fantino (1986) varied the duration of the equal handling times while keeping search duration constant. Specifically they began with handling times arranged by equal VI 20-s schedules, shifted in the next condition to handling times arranged by equal VI 5-s schedules and finally returned to equal VI 20-s schedules in a third condition. According to both the ODM and the delay-reduction hypothesis, increasing a common handling time should have the opposite effect of increasing a common search time, that is, the longer the handling time the less acceptance of the poorer reinforcer (in this case the shorter duration reinforcer). This prediction, first derived by Fantino and Abarca (1985, p. 326), was confirmed as is shown in Fig. 4 because each of three pigeons was more likely to accept the shorter duration reinforcer (showing less selectivity) with the shorter handling time (note that for each subject percent acceptance is higher for VI 5-s handling schedules).

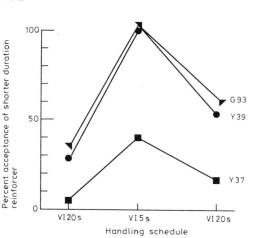

Fig. 4. Percent acceptance of the shorter-duration (3-s) reinforcer as a function of the values in the hand-ling state for each of the three pigeons. The experiment used the same basic procedure shown in Fig. 3 except that the requirement to accept or reject a schedule was symmetrical (FR 3 in each case), VI sched-ules were associated with the handling states, and the amount of the food reinforcer differed in the presence of the two key colors. The experimenters varied the duration of the equal VI schedules as indicated on the abcissa. Since the longer-duration reinforcer was always accepted (100% on ordinate) these data are not shown. As is typical in operant simulations of foraging the critical data are the percent acceptance of the less-preferred (here the shorter-duration) reinforcer. These data are shown on the ordinate and were obtained by dividing the number of acceptances by the total number of opportunities to accept the shorter-duration reinforcer, and then multiplying by 100 (to obtain percentages). For each pigeon data are the means of the percentages obtained in this manner over the last five sessions of each condition. (Re-produced from Ito and Fantino, 1986, with permission of the publisher.)

Finally, Fantino and Preston (1988a) used the successive-choice procedure to as-sess a counter-intuitive implication of the ODM and the delay-reduction hypothesis. As the less profitable outcome is encountered more frequently, i.e., as the search du-ration leading to it decreases, the predicted behavior eventually switches from that characteristic of a generalist feeder (accepting either outcome) to that typical of a specialist feeder (rejecting the less profitable, though increasingly accessible out-come). In other words, by manipulating search time to the less profitable outcome (while keeping search time to the more profitable outcome constant) one should find that increased accessibility should lead to decreased acceptability. This prediction, derived by Fantino and Preston (1988b), was confirmed and is shown in Fig. 5. Note that for each of four pigeons, the probability of accepting the poorer outcome (the VI 45-s schedule) was greater when the poorer outcome was least accessible (S_L, or search time leading to longer outcome, equalled 40s) than when the poorer outcome was most accessible (S_L equalled 10 s). The effects of accessibility on acceptability depend critically on methodological concerns. If accessibility is increased by increas-ing the probability of the less profitable outcome (decreasing p in Fig. 3) instead of increasing the encounter rate of the less profitable outcome, the opposite outcome

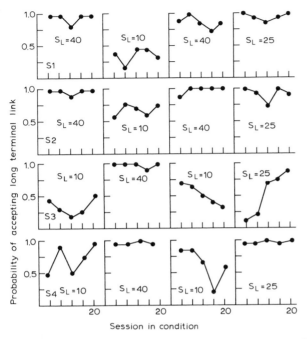

Fig. 5. These data were obtained in the same general manner as those described in Fig. 4, using the general procedure of Fig. 3. In this study, however, reinforcer amounts were equal and the VI schedules associated with the handling states were unequal. Unlike the earlier work, however, the search times leading to the two outcomes were unequal. While the search time leading to the short outcome was constant, that leading to the long (less-preferred) outcome was varied. The figure shows the probability of accepting the stimulus associated with the longer outcome (VI 45-s terminal-link) over the final five sessions in each of four conditions varying the search time leading to this longer outcome. (Reproduced from Fantino and Preston, 1988, with permission of the publisher.)

is both predicted and obtained. Specifically, in another phase of their study Fantino and Preston showed that increasing the probability of the less profitable outcome increases its acceptability.

2.6. Simultaneous-encounters procedure

Behavioral ecologists have developed simultaneous-encounters models of foraging that suggest how choices should be made between simultaneously-encountered, mutually-exclusive prey (Engen and Stenseth, 1984). They note that under certain circumstances the choice of an otherwise more profitable prey (i.e., one with a higher ratio of energy gain to handling time or E/h) should provide less overall benefit to the organism than another prey providing greater total energy gain divided by total time in the situation (i.e., a time frame longer than h). This distinction between an outcome that is more profitable on a short-term or molecular basis and one that is more profitable on a longer-term or molar basis parallels the much studied distinctions between impulsive and self-control selections and between molecular versus molar control of behavior. How may the simultaneous-encounters model be assessed empirically? Fantino and Preston (1989) reported a procedure they have used with both human and pigeon subjects. The procedure begins with a search phase during which X s elapse before the subject encounters a choice between responding on two side keys. The first response to either key commits the subject to that choice and darkens the other key. To ensure exposure to both outcomes, occasional forced-choice trials may be included. The model may be tested by arranging for two outcomes in which one has the longer-duration reinforcer but also the longer delay to reinforcer delivery. For example, in the pigeon case one outcome might be 10-s handling time leading to 4 s of food access (E_1/h_1 ratio $=0.4$) and the other 20-s handling time leading to 6-s food access (E_2/h_2 ratio $=0.3$). There is an 'indifference' search duration called S_I for which either outcome provides the same long-term payoff to the subject. For search durations less than S_I the subject should always choose the outcome with the higher profitability ratio, i.e. the larger of E_1/h_1 and E_2/h_2. For a search duration equal to S_I – the indifference point – either choice results in the same long-term payoff. For search durations greater than S_I, however, the subject should choose the outcome with the lower E/h ratio since it leads to greater long-term gains. For example in this case, when the search duration equals 10 s, both outcomes provide the same overall rate of food (1 s of food for every 5 s spent searching and handling). Thus, 10 s should be the indifference point. For search durations greater than 10 s the 6-s food access outcome should be preferred; for search duration less than 10 s the 4-s outcome should be preferred. Fantino and Preston (1989) report pilot data that support these predictions for both pigeons and humans. Experiments using this methodology not only should permit assessment of the simultaneous-encounters model but also should add to the growing literature assessing the relative behavioral control exerted by molar and molecular variables.

2.7. Progressive-ratio schedules

As noted in discussing the marginal-value theorem, PR schedules simulate increasing costs with increasing exposure to the situation. Although they did not relate their experiment to foraging, Hodos and Trumbule (1967) allowed chimpanzees to choose between FR and PR schedules. The larger the FR requirement, the greater the preference for the PR schedule. Indeed the chimps' choices approximated closely minimizing the cost of the reinforcer in terms of number of responses per reinforcer. Hineline and Sodetz (1987) reported similar results with monkeys. For purposes of indicating the actual techniques involved, the methods of two recent studies are described. First, Wanchisen et al. (1988) studied choice of FR versus PR schedules in pigeons under two conditions: 'No-Reset' and 'Reset,' discussed in Section 2.3. In their Reset procedure each completion of the FR reset the PR to its minimal value. If the pigeons waited until the PR value equalled the FR, their behavior would not be optimal. Subjects could minimize cost by switching to an FR 120 (and thereby resetting the PR to 1) when the PR value reached 60, rather then waiting until the equality point (120). In fact, the pigeons chose the FR well in advance of the equality point. These results not only support an optimality analysis but show that pigeons are sensitive to molar as well as molecular reinforcer rates in that the choice of the FR 120 when only 60 responses were required on the PR alternative involves minimizing future costs at the expense of immediate cost.

Bhatt and Wasserman (1987) trained pigeons on a PR schedule and on a multiple schedule (see Part 1, Ch. 3) that arranged for food at one of four constant rates. Following this training, the schedules were presented concurrently. The question was whether or not the pigeons would switch from selection of the PR schedule to an alternate fixed component of the multiple schedule in a way that maximized what Bhatt and Wasserman referred to as the benefit/cost ratio: time of access to food/ number pecks required to produce that access. The experimenters varied the benefit/ cost ratio in two ways: (1) varying the time of food access while holding the response requirement constant; (2) varying the response requirement while holding time of food access constant. Three conclusions were drawn that relate to an optimality analysis: (1) in both conditions, results were in qualitative agreement with an optimality analysis in that choice of the progressive schedule decreased as the benefit/cost ratio of the alternative fixed schedule increased: (2) subjects in the ratio group (response requirement varied) were more sensitive to changes in the benefit ratio than subjects in the time group (time of food access varied) a finding consistent with prior reports of greater sensitivity to delay than to amount of reinforcement (e.g., Fantino et al., 1972; Schneider, 1973); (3) subjects generally switched from the progressive to the fixed alternative sooner than was optimal, a finding somewhat at odds with those of Wanchisen et al. (1988) reported above, as they found that subjects tended to switch from the progressive schedule no earlier than at the equality point. Also, in a related series of studies by Lea (1976), pigeons switched at the point of equality, not the optimum point.

An important methodological point was stressed by Bhatt and Wasserman but is no less applicable to Wanchisen et al. (1988) and to most of the studies discussed in this chapter. They note that behavioral ecological theories of foraging – including Charnov's (1976) marginal-value theorem – assume that forager's decisions are based on extensive experience with the relevant situational variables, including prey value and patch characteristics. Bhatt and Wasserman explicity enhanced the likelihood that this complete knowledge was available to subjects by first training the subjects on the individual schedules that later were to comprise the choices. Thus the experimenter "guaranteed that the pigeons had learned the characteristics of the individual schedules before being confronted with the choice situation" (Bhatt and Wasserman, 1987, p. 41). Although most of the studies reviewed in this chapter did not go to such lengths to familiarize subjects with the contingencies prior to the choice phase, almost all of the studies exposed subjects extensively to the choices, thus ensuring at least a stable set of choice proportions by the time the critical choice data were collected.

2.8. Methods for assessing time horizons

Timberlake and his colleagues have called attention to the critical question of the time period ('time horizon') over which subjects integrate information in determining an optimal temporal distribution of foraging behavior (e.g., Timberlake et al., 1987, 1988). For example, consider a subject responding in an available food patch with the prospect of a much richer food patch becoming available in the future time. Obviously, if the richer patch is imminent, foraging on the currently available but poorer patch will be reduced. Timberlake's work sought to specify over what time period a richer future food patch would decrease current foraging. Timberlake et al. (1987), for example, varied the time to a patch providing food on a continuous basis (CRF) and observed the effects of this patch availability on the mean total number of food pellets consumed in a current PR patch. In this study the future patch was available 4, 8, 16, 32 or 64 min after the start of a session. The shorter the delay to the future richer patch, the fewer pellets were consumed in the PR patch. For the longer delays (32 and 64 min) there was no reduction in pellets consumed relative to a 'baseline' in which future food was delayed for 2 h. Thus, they placed the time horizon, under conditions of their study, at less than 32 min.

2.9. Other variables

Methods have been developed for the study of other variables affecting the economics of choice. In this section we consider briefly how three of these variables, reinforcer amount, probability of reinforcement, and deprivation have been assessed.

2.9.1. Reinforcer amount

Ito and Fantino (1986) used Lea's successive-choice procedure to investigate the effects of varying search and handling durations with unequal reinforcer amounts. They varied amount by the duration of time the food hopper was available to their pigeon subjects. The effect of varying search duration was the same when amounts differed as in earlier work (reviewed in Section 2.5) when delays to food differed. Fig. 6 shows that as the search duration increased, acceptance of the shorter duration reinforcer increased. Comparing the left and right panels of Fig. 6 shows that at each search duration acceptance of the shorter duration reinforcer was greater when it constituted 3-s access (left panel) than when it constituted 2-s access (right panel), where the longer-duration reinforcer was 6-s access in each case. Although Ito and Fantino varied access time to the reinforcer, one could instead vary reinforcer amount in terms of the number of food pellets or grain available, the intensity of the reinforcer (as in the sweetness of a sugar solution for a rat), or the number of presentations of the food hopper. In general, there is no reason to expect different results with these different methods of varying reinforcer magnitude, however without an empirical test one cannot be certain.

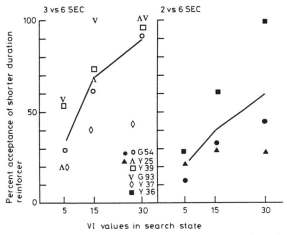

Fig. 6. These data, obtained in the same manner as those in Fig. 4, using the same general procedure as that described in Fig. 3, show percent acceptance of the shorter-duration (3-s or 2-s) reinforcer as a function of the duration of the search state. The left panel shows the results when reinforcer durations were 3-s and 6-s access to food, and the right panel shows the data when reinforcer durations were 2-s and 6-s access to food. The VI schedules associated with the handling states were equal. For each set of conditions, percent acceptance of the shorter-duration reinforcer increases as the equal search times increase. The longer-duration reinforcer (always 6 s) was always accepted; these data are not shown. The solid lines represent the means across pigeons. (Reproduced from Ito and Fantino, 1986, with permission of the publisher.)

2.9.2. Probability of reinforcement

Zeiler (1987) and Abarca et al. (1985) are among those who have assessed the effects of reinforcement probability in a foraging analog. In one condition of Zeiler's experiment, the alternative sources of food required equal numbers of responses, but the likelihood of obtaining food in each was varied. Specifically, the probability that successful completion of an FR requirement (FR 30 for two pigeons and FR 15 for a third) would result in food varied in increments of 0.1 from 0 to 1.0 on one of two keys. If this probability was p then the probability that the FR on the other key would result in food was $1-p$. On any given trial a given assignment remained in effect until the subject completed the FR on the appropriate key (correction procedure). In Zeiler's experiment, the pigeons departed from an optimality assumption of minimization of response output in two ways: (1) whereas optimal performance on the first choice of a trial was exclusive preference for the higher probability alternative (greater of p and $1-p$), the actual performance was more graded, resulting in a monotonic function of the likelihood of food delivery; (2) on subsequent choices of a trial subjects selected the same alternative repeatedly if it represented a higher probability of food even after an unsuccessful choice. Thus, subjects were not given to 'switch' after an unsuccessful ratio completion, a result somewhat unexpected in light of work with rats on the radial maze discussed below (where 'shifting' is commonplace, even after a successful trial). Abarca et al. (1985) used the successive-choice procedure and varied the percentage reinforcement for the less-delayed outcome (VI 5 s as opposed to VI 20 s which always resulted in food) between 10 and 100%. As usual with this procedure, the measures of choice were the mean probabilities of accepting the VI 5-s and the VI 20-s outcomes when each was available. No deviations from optimal performance were found with this procedure: the pigeon's responding was a function of variations in the percentage of reinforcement and the pigeon was always more likely to accept the outcome associated with the higher rate of reinforcement; when the percentage reinforcement for the VI 5 s was 25%, for example, both outcomes provided comparable reinforcer rates and both were accepted to a comparable degree.

2.9.3. Deprivation

The effects of both food and water deprivation on performance in a radial maze were examined by Dale and Roberts (1986). A diagram of this type of maze is presented in Fig. 7. Typically, food-deprived rats are released on the central platform and allowed access to the eight arms projecting out radially from the platform. The end of each arm generally contains a small piece of food. The rat can gather the eight pieces in any order. If performing with maximal efficiency this should take only eight choices. In fact, subjects typically learn to obtain all of the food in eight or nine choices. Dale and Roberts assessed response patterns as well as choice accuracy as a function of food and water deprivation. Rats deprived of either searched for the corresponding reward in the radial maze. Deprivation levels were 80 or 100% of pre-experimental free-feeding weights arrived at by restricting access to either food or water. Hence a 2×2 design was employed: 80% water deprivation; 100% water deprivation; 80% food deprivation; 100% food deprivation. Response patterns were assessed by computing the average angular distance between pairs of consecutively chosen arms, measured in 45° units (adjacent arms were 1 unit apart; opposite arms 4 units apart). Choice accuracy was assessed in two ways: (1) by the total number of errors (repeat visits to an arm) made before a subject attained a performance criterion of two consecutive trials with all eight arms chosen in the minimum eight choices; and (2) by the number of different arms chosen during a subject's first eight choices on each trial. Subjects were pretrained first on an open field, then on a straight runway before testing on the radial maze. On the radial maze subjects were given up to 15 min to enter all of the arms. The subjects' initial orientations were varied randomly over trials. For the first 10 days each subject received one trial. For the next 4 days subjects received three trials separated by 2-min stays in the home cage. A final methodological note concerns how choices were measured: Dale and Roberts recorded the sequence in which the arms were chosen manually, defining a choice as an entry by the subject to the point where the subject's entire body, up to the base of its tail, was inside the arm; the authors report that subjects rarely failed to continue to the end of the arm once they had entered it to this degree.

The water-deprived subjects learned the task more rapidly than the food-deprived

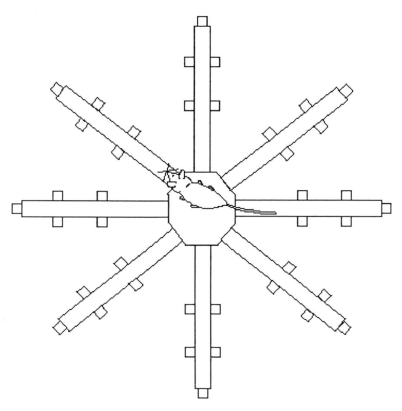

Fig. 7. A radial-arm maze. In the typical study, food-deprived rats are placed in the central platform and are allowed to choose freely among the eight arms. In the case where all eight arms contain food at their ends the optimal strategy involves choosing each arm once without repetition (since previously chosen arms no longer contain food). Deviations from optimality may be instructive. Although in most studies, including all discussed in the text, the food cups are at the end of the arms, one can also arrange for multiple food cups on each arm as shown. A recent study by Roberts and Ilersich (1989) used an arrangement of this type.

subjects and all four groups developed distinct response patterns. For example, water-deprived subjects generated lower mean angular distances between consecutively chosen arms. These results suggest that degree and type of deprivation may affect performance on the radial maze.

3. Methods for assessing memory

Foraging behavior involves more than choice, of course. Also intimately involved are remembering and discriminating. With respect to the former, behavioral ecologists and behavior analysts share a keen interest in how organisms remember location of food sources. In this section we consider two general types of procedures that have been utilized productively in the analysis of remembering. One involves the use of the radial maze in assessing spatial memory in central-place learners such as the rat. The second involves assessment of spatial memory in food-storing birds.

3.1. Spatial memory in the radial maze

The radial maze shown in Fig. 7 is a valuable apparatus in the study of spatial memory. Food-deprived rats typically are placed in the central platform and allowed to choose freely among the eight arms. Although the optimal strategy involves choosing each arm once without repetition (since previously chosen arms no longer contain food), deviations from optimality may be instructive. For example, Olton and Samuelson (1976) showed that rats reached asymptotic performance after 20 tests producing a near-optimal score of 7.9 different arms in their first 8 choices. To conclude that spatial memory is implicated, however, other more mundane alternatives must be ruled out. Olton et al. (1981) point out that the rat could achieve optimal performance in any of the following ways: (1) a response strategy involving always turning in a clockwise (or counter clockwise) manner after each return to the center platform, in this event the rat need remember only which arm it visited last; (2) intra-maze strategies based on cues from the food, such as odor or from the apparatus (subtle but distinct marks on the arms).

Olton and his colleagues eliminated the possible use of response strategies by taking the following precautions: (1) the rats were required to choose certain arms before allowing them free choice (this was accomplished by placing 'guillotine' doors at the entrance to each arm and by raising only one arm on 'forced-choice' trials); (2) All doors were closed for a period when the rat returned to the central platform, thus imposing a delay between the choice which would presumably disrupt any response patterns used to negotiate the eight arms efficiently. Despite these modifications rats continued to perform optimally (Olton et al., 1981).

Intramaze cues were eliminated by rotating the maze after the rat returned to the central platform. For some rats food was placed just beyond the end of each arm; when the maze was rotated the food retained its spatial location while the arm leading to that location changed. Nonetheless, rats continued to choose each spatial location just once, ruling out the importance of intramaze cues. Conversely, for other rats food was placed at the end of the arm, as usual, and optimal performance required choice of different arms, not different spatial locations. These rats performed at chance levels, indicating that intramaze cues were insufficient for task mastery (e.g., Olton and Collison, 1979).

It is not necessary to use food reward in the radial maze. Batson et al. (1986), for example, attached bottle caps to the ends of the maze arms which served as liquid containers for thirsty rats. Once the rat drank the 0.2 ml of water in a given cap, that cap remained empty for the duration of the rat's session on the maze (only one trial was conducted daily). Batson et al. studied the effects of altering the reward.

For example, in one experiment one maze location did not provide water (extinction) and the rats' preference for this arm declined. In a second experiment Batson et al. baited one arm with a preferred solution, sweet chocolate milk, and rats' preference for this arm was enhanced. Their most interesting manipulation occurred in their third experiment which involved taste-aversion learning. Batson et al. note that foraging animals occasionally encounter flavors that are toxic. Would rats learn to avoid not only consuming the toxic flavor but also learn to avoid the location that contains the aversive flavor consistently? Batson et al. utilized a conditioned taste aversion to a distinctive saccharin solution. In one study this aversive conditioning (saccharin-lithium pairings) was conducted in the maze. In a second study the aversive conditioning was conducted in the home cage and saccharin became one of the radial maze choices only afterwards. Rats in both studies learned to avoid the location containing the saccharin solution.

The radial maze also may be used to assess more fine-grained aspects of spatial memory. Specifically in an ingenious report Cook et al. (1985) investigated whether rats' excellent performance was due primarily to remembrance of choices past i.e., choices made in the arms preceding the present one (retrospective memory) or remembrance of choices to be made, i.e., choices in the arm forthcoming (prospective memory). If retrospective memory is critical, then the probability of an error should rise as a delay is inserted into later points in a twelve-arm radial maze (the later the delay the more difficult the rehearsal of the relatively large number of pre-delay choices made). On the other hand, if prospective memory is critical, then the probability of an error should decrease as the point of the interpolated delay is increased because there will be fewer post-delay choices to be remembered). Cook et al. found evidence for both processes: error rate increased as the point of interpolation increased over the early choices (supporting a retrospective view) but then decreased as the point of interpolation approached the end of the 12-choice sequence (supporting a prospective view). This type of methodology is likely to assist future assessments of memory.

3.2. Analyzing food storage

Food storage has been investigated extensively in studies of hoarding in rodents and food recovery in birds. We will consider the latter here. For issues and methods in rodent hoarding the reader may consult Phillips et al. (1989), Lea and Tarpy (1986), and Wong and Jones (1985). Some species of birds store food in various locations and then retrieve it as much as months later. In fact, as Shettleworth and Krebs (1986) have pointed out, birds such as marsh tits, Clark's nutcrackers, and black-capped chickadees appear to recall the locations of food items over longer temporal durations than either pigeons or rats retain spatial information in the laboratory. In their first experiment, Shettleworth and Krebs deprived marsh tits of food for 1-2 h and then exposed them to a test room which housed 98 storage sites (holes drilled in flat boards) and a bowl of hemp seeds. Each of the 98 holes was covered by an opaque flap. Prior to the start of each storage session a seed was hidden in about a quarter of the holes, chosen at random. Then the bird was permitted to store hemp seeds in the storage sites. During this process when the bird encountered seeds already in holes (experimenter-stored seeds), it would store its seed in a different site. After a bird had both encountered and stored about four seeds it was excluded from the test room for a 2-h food deprivation period. Following this period, the marsh tit was permitted to return to the room and search for seeds in the storage sites. The bowl of hemp seed was now absent and the only sources of seeds were those stored by the bird and those stored by the experimenter and previously encountered by the bird during storage. A central question: was remembering the location of stored seeds better than remembering the location of encountered seeds? The results of this experiment permitted an unambiguous answer of 'No.' Remembering was assessed by comparing the observed and expected number of seeds retrieved in the first 20 'holes'. For each of four marsh tits the observed number of seeds retrieved was significantly higher than the number expected if performance were random. However, encountered seeds were just as likely to be retrieved as stored seeds.

In their second experiment, Shettleworth and Krebs (1986) compared chickadees' retrieval of sunflower seeds, which had been stored or merely observed when the inaccessible seeds were behind plexiglas windows. In the test or recovery phase the experimenters added an important methodological control: only a random half of the observed or stored sites still contained seeds; the remaining half were now empty. If the chickadee was not retrieving on the basis of cues correlated with the presence of seeds then it should be just as likely to visit empty as full sites. Such a result would further implicate spatial remembering. To answer this question, recovery from stored and observed sites made empty during testing was compared to recovery from full sites. No significant differences were found between the proportions of full and empty sites visited during testing (among those sites that had previously contained seeds). Thus, the results support an interpretation in terms of spatial remembering of sites containing either stored or observed seeds.

Sherry et al. (1981) studied the role of remembering in stored food recovery with a different type of laboratory procedure. Marsh tits were admitted individually to an aviary containing three trays of moss, each divided into four sectors. In a 15-min baseline period the experimenters recorded how much time was spent in each sector of the moss when no food was available. This permitted assessment of baseline preferences and biases for particular sectors of the moss. In the next, storage, phase birds were given sunflower seeds and 15 min to store them in the moss. Following this storage phase the birds left the aviary. Twenty-four h later the test phase began: birds were given 15 min to search for stored seeds although no seeds were actually present (having been removed to eliminate sensory cues). If the birds' searching were random they would have been expected to allocate less than half of their time to sites where they had stored food. Instead about 90% of their time was spent searching in these sectors. Again spatial remembering, with accuracy up to at least 24 h after storage, is implicated. At the very least, studies such as those reviewed here demonstrate that birds have the capacity to use the spatial remembering cues inherent in food-storing situations. Moreover, the studies represent several ways to attack the role of spatial memory in foraging.

Sherry (1987) reviewed other techniques of studying foraging for stored food. In a field study, Cowie et al. (1981) labeled sunflower seeds radioactively and then tracked where marsh tits stored them. They then hid additional seeds either 10 cm away from the stored seed ('near control') or 100 cm away ('far control'). Marsh tits recovered the seeds they had cached much more quickly than either of the control seeds, suggesting that the stored food was not recovered randomly. Sherry (1987) also reviewed an intriguing B.A. thesis by Mott-Trille (1983), who investigated the birds' likelihood to store additional food as a function of the extent of random pilfering (by the experimenter). Indeed, the greater the degree of random pilfering (50% versus 25% versus 0%) the lower the number of seeds stored in a subsequent opportunity to store seeds freely. Finally, Sherry (1987) demonstrated that birds can apparently recall the type of food stored. When both sunflower and safflower seeds were offered *ad lib* to black-capped chickadees, the birds showed a strong (about 80%) preference to both eat and store sunflower seeds. Twenty-four h after storing equal numbers of both types of seeds the chickadees were given the opportunity to search for the stored seed (though in fact all seeds had been removed by the experimenter to control for actual detection of the seeds). Sunflower seeds were searched for at a level significantly above the control level but the less preferred safflower seeds were not.

4. Assessment of perception, species differences and areas other than foraging

Although scores of studies have used the technology of the operant laboratory to assess temporal, economic, and mnemonic variables in foraging, few have explored the wide range of additional areas of Behavioral Ecology. In this final section we mention some of the methods that have been used to address these other areas and point to a few potentially profitable research areas. Experimental psychologists have been much less active in simulating perceptual variables central to Behavioral Ecology than mnemonic variables; nonetheless, several important research areas have been the focus of interesting work in perception. After a consideration of this work we will address studies assessing species differences, thermoregulation, circadian rhythms, territory defense, and mate selection.

4.1. Perception

Tinbergen (1960) proposed that after a sufficient number of encounters with a cryptic prey type the predator forms a search image of that prey type. The predator is then more able to detect that prey type and therefore increase predation on that prey type. Pietrewicz and Kamil (1981) have studied the development of a search image, i.e., the change in ability to detect cryptic prey types, in an interesting simulation using behavior-analytic methodology.

Pietrewicz and Kamil used the concept-formation technology developed by Herrnstein and Loveland (1964) and by Herrnstein et al. (1976) to investigate how blue jays detect the cryptic Catocala moth. On each trial the experimenters projected a slide onto a large pecking key. Some slides included the Catocala moth, others included no moth. On trials including a moth, a peck at the slide produced a reinforcer (a meal worm for the food-deprived subject). On trials without a moth, the subject could peck a smaller key to advance to the next trial. If the subject made either a 'miss' (pecking the smaller key when a moth was projected) or a false alarm (pecking the larger key when no moth was projected), a long delay was inserted prior to the next trial. As Pietrewicz and Kamil (1981) noted: "This technique is particularly well suited to the study of prey detection. It allows exact control over the appearance of the prey and the order in which prey types occur and eliminates possible preferences for particular prey types on the basis of factors such as taste and capture or handling time" (p. 312).

Using this procedure the experimenters were able to demonstrate how naive and experienced predators detect cryptic prey. They also showed that repeated encounters with rare prey types increase their detectability. Pietrewicz and Kamil's work, thanks in part to its elegant methodology, sheds light on how predators deal with crypticity and how crypticity functions to reduce predation. It is possible that this methodology could also be extended to the study of kin recognition, at least to its visual components.

Other studies of the search image include those in which selection biases for an item by pigeons are affected by increased exposure to that item (Bond, 1983) and in which pre-exposure to an item causes chicks to eat that item at a faster rate (Dawkins, 1971). Gendron (1986) reported a study of search images in bobwhite quail involving an elegant procedure. The quail searched for cryptic prey in a large arena that was divided into quadrants, each of which had either zero or one prey item. Each quail searched the arena for a single prey type of a particular color for 9-12 trials. This procedure was repeated with six prey types that varied in degree of crypticity. Gendron found that the probability of detecting a prey item increased after several prey captures but decreased after 4–10 s elapsed without capturing any item. He suggested that the potency of a search image fluctuates with periodic reinforcement of search and decays between reinforced searches.

While the methods used in these studies of search image are elegant and promising, a recent critique by Guilford and Dawkins (1987) questions whether the results of these studies actually support the search-image hypothesis. They note that the results of these studies are equally consistent with a more parsimonious hypothesis, not involving search-image function. Their alternative search-rate hypothesis, based on one of Gendron and Staddon (1983), suggests that predators hunting for cryptic prey may simply reduce their search rate. By spending a longer time viewing each patch the predator is more likely to see cryptic prey. Guilford and Dawkins (1987) review the prior studies and suggest that they are inconclusive in deciding between the two hypotheses. They do suggest ways in which the hypotheses may be distinguished, however. For example, according to the search-image hypothesis learning to see one cryptic prey type may interfere with detecting other equally cryptic prey types; according to the search-rate hypothesis, however, detection of other cryptic prey types should also profit by the reduced search rate. Guilford and Dawkins' paper has promoted a lively controversy (see Guilford and Dawkins, 1989a,b; Hollis, 1989; Lawrence, 1989).

4.2. Species differences

Little attention has been paid by behavior analysts to comparative differences in feeding strategies. Zahorik and Houpt (1981) have assessed the ability of different species to acquire food aversions under what they regarded as optimal conditions. They deprived all subjects of their usual food for 16 h and then offered them a novel food. Following a 15-min trial with access to the novel food, half of the subjects received a swift-acting gastrointestinal poison and the other half received comparable quantities of saline. Two days later all subjects were redeprived of food and then offered a second novel food, again for 15 min. Subjects poisoned after eating the first novel food received saline after ingesting the second novel food, whereas subjects which received saline after ingesting the first novel food received poison after ingesting the second novel food. Zahorik and Houpt (1981) report studies of Jersey cows, sheep, goats, and ponies with this standard procedure. All four species of these large generalist herbivores developed food aversions to the novel food followed immediately by poison. While cross-species comparisons are difficult to make, their data are suggestive of comparable learning in the herbivores studied at least in the standard experiment used in this work.

Spetch and Edwards (1986) note that, unlike rats, pigeons do not display very accurate spatial memory when tested in the typical radial-arm apparatus without extended or special training (e.g., Roberts and Veldhuizen, 1985). But they reason that the choice of task may affect the degree of spatial memory displayed by members of a particular species. Spetch and Edwards found that they could demonstrate remembering within just a few trials by testing pigeons in either of two multiple-goal open-field test environments. In one environment, eight elevated food sites were located in an open room and the pigeon flew to (and ate from) the sites. In the second environment, an open room contained ground-feeding sites that the pigeons could walk to and eat from. Spetch and Edwards conclude that pigeons' display of accurate spatial memory may be facilitated by testing in environments resembling the natural feeding habitats of the species.

4.3. Thermoregulation

Recently attention has been directed to thermoregulation. Hypothermia is a means of conserving energy, including at times of deprivation. Rashotte and his colleagues have studied how subjects regulate their body temperature in response to environmental constraints (thermoregulation). Specifically, they have completed a series of elegant experiments assessing how pigeons cope with rising food costs in a closed economy. For example, Rashotte and Henderson (1988) assessed the time course of changes in feeding and body temperature to increased food cost. They raised food cost by increasing FR size from FR 6 to FR 1920 in a 24-h closed economy, i.e., one in which all of the subject's food is obtained by responding in the experimental chamber. They found that feeding was affected within the first day of exposure to the increased food cost: pigeons completed the larger FRs less frequently but ate more efficiently from the food hopper when it was produced (in terms of amount eaten per min of hopper time). Body temperature was affected later, declining to progressively lower resting levels during the dark phase of each 24-h period when the pigeon began to lose body weight (resulting from extended exposure to higher-cost food schedules). Presumably the reduced body temperature permits the pigeon to conserve energy in the face of declining resources. Rashotte's research on the energetic analysis of performance in the closed economy promises to be of continued interest to behavior analysts and behavioral ecologists.

4.4. Circadian rhythms

Research on circadian rhythms using behavior-analytic methods has assessed nonhuman behavior over extended time periods. As Terman (1983) has pointed out the reliable recurrence of a function over time – or rhythmicity – is a ubiquitous aspect of biological organization. He has noted that behavior displays daily rhythmicity as the likelihood of various operant behavior undergoes oscillations with 24-h periodicity. Terman also points out that, from another perspective, rhythmic control systems may influence the momentary likelihood of an operant response. Reviews of this area include those of Terman (1983) and Elsmore and Hursh (1982). In this brief section we examine the methods and results of one portion of a representative study by Boulos et al. (1980) on feeding schedules and the circadian organization of responding in Long-Evans rats. It should be cautioned, however, that many of the results obtained in studies of circadian organization in rats are not applicable to other species (see Boulos and Terman, 1980).

Boulos et al. (1980) noted that under a 24-h light-dark cycle with free access to food the temporal distribution of many of a subject's behavioral and physiological activities develop 24-h rhythms synchronized to the light-dark cycle. Such activities include drinking, body temperature, sleep, locomotive activity, and levels of hormones and of brain neurotransmitters. These rhythms may be modified by limiting food access to a few hours per day. Such feeding schedules may also modify the periodicity of various activities under constant lighting conditions. In this sense, daily feeding schedules share with light-dark cycles the ability to control daily biological rhythms. One such controlling relation studied by Boulos et al. (1980) is that between the feeding schedule and the rat's pattern of water intake. The experiments were conducted in continuous light with 11 rats, four of which had continuous access to electrical brain self-stimulation. The first condition was a baseline with continuous access to food and water. Food could be obtained by pressing a lever (each response produced food), water could be obtained merely by licking a spout (licks broke an infrared photobeam and were recorded). The second involved a 24-h feeding schedule in which food was available for lever-pressing only during an unsignalled 4-h period occurring at the same time each day. Following this experimental condition (which continued for 24-84 days) the subjects were returned to the baseline (free-feeding) condition. Fig. 8 shows the relative magnitude spectra of drinking for two rats (A and B) and the electrical brain self-stimulation spectra for a third rat (C) during the experimental (food-restricted, 24-h period) condition (food was available in hours 20 to 24). Note first that the peak for each rat is precisely at 24 h (24.00 ± 0.05 h) which contrasted with their peaks during the initial baseline condition (24.35-24.90 h for the eleven individual rats). Second, note that for B there is also a secondary peak at 24.60 h, suggesting the persistence of this rat's baseline rhythmicity. Third, note that the peaks below 24 h are exact harmonics of the one (for A and C) or two (for B) fundamentals. Upon returning to baseline, the 24-h periodicity disappeared gradually over 2-7 sessions and the baseline rhythmicity was reinstated for eight of the 11 subjects (for further details, see Boulos et al., 1980).

Not shown in the figure are the bouts of (ineffective) lever pressing on the food lever during the daily 20-h periods of food deprivation. All subjects showed accelerated lever pressing beginning 2-4 h prior to food availability. Commenting on these and related results Boulos and Terman (1980) suggest that a 'food-entrained mechanism' is responsible for the increases in lever pressing and locomotor activity prior to food delivery and may also be involved in similar increases in the activities of some intestinal enzymes and in body temperature. They surmise that a food-entrained mechanism may help the subject to better use the periodic recurrence of significant environmental events. The repetition of a reinforced behavioral pattern at the same time of day may prove advantageous to the organism (although in the case of predictable feeding habits by certain organisms, regularity may also prove advantageous to their predators, e.g., Fantino and Logan, 1979, p. 495).

In addition to the relation between feeding schedules and the circadian organization of responding, behavioral neurobiologists have demonstrated alternating dominance of cerebral hemispheric activity in humans and have shown that relative changes in electrocortical activity are correlated directly with changes in relative nostril dominance (the 'nasal cycle'). For example, right nostril dominance corresponds to enhanced verbal skills and left nostril dominance to enhanced spatial skills (e.g.,

148

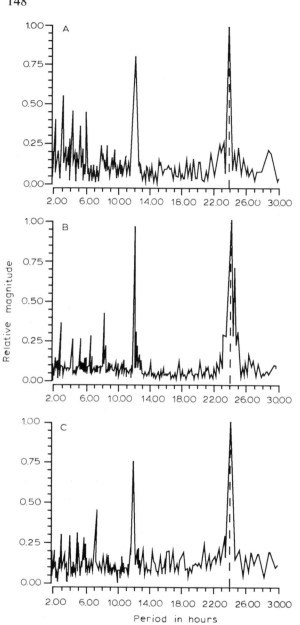

Fig. 8. Relative magnitude spectra of drinking (A and B) and electrical brain self-stimulation (C) of three rats all of which were deprived of food for 20 h, after which presses on a lever were reinforced with food (each response produced food) for a 4-h period. Water could be obtained at any time by licking a spout (licks broke a photobeam and were recorded). Rat C also had continuous access to electrical brain self-stimulation. The procedure was repeated continuously for 24–84 days (depending on the subject). Note that all three rats show a response peak at 24.00±0.05 h, that B also shows a peak at 24.6 h and that the peaks to the left of these are exact harmonics of these major peaks. Before and after this condition, subjects were exposed to baseline conditions in which food was unrestricted, as discussed in the text. (Reproduced from Boulos et al., 1980, with permission of the publisher.)

Werntz et al., 1983; Klein et al., 1986; for a review, see Shannahoff-Khalsa, in press). These relationships suggest fertile ground for research from a behavior-analytic perspective.

4.5. Territory defense and mate selection

Two crucial areas of Behavioral Ecology have received almost no attention from behavior analysts: territory defense and mate selection. Territory defense has important implications for foraging and also has direct implications for mate selection. The author does not know of any direct operant simulations of territory defense or mate selection. In principle, of course, relevant simulations could be constructed. It is not clear, however how to capture the meaningful aspects of mate selection in the laboratory. Certain choices and elicited responses could be studied. For example, subjects could respond in an operant chamber on schedules of reinforcement that permit access to a conspecific organism located in a large living chamber adjacent to the operant chamber. This conspecific could be an appropriate mate, in the study of mate selection, or an intruder, in the study of territory defense. Alternatively, operant responses could vary the distance of a potential mate or intruder observed through a window in the chamber (or on a video display). A procedure somewhat reminiscent of this has been used to study dominance by Temple and Foster (1988). In the area of mate selection, Domjan and his colleagues have analyzed what aspects of a female model produce sexual responses in male birds (e.g., Domjan et al., 1988). This work, of course, follows in the tradition of Tinbergen who used models to determine releasing stimuli for a variety of behaviors (e.g., Tinbergen, 1951) and is related to the larger topic of stimulus control (see Part 1, Ch. 7).

5. Conclusion

Once mating occurs, new organisms may be born, leading to a new set of 'foraging' decisions including a decision regarding the occurrence of weaning. Is this decision made by the nursing parent or by its offspring? While behavior analysts have thus far displayed little active interest in the topics covered in this final section, just a dozen years ago the very same might have been said about the temporal, economic, and mneumonic determinants of foraging. Research in these areas has suggested that the technology of the behavior analysis laboratory has important relevance for the study of foraging. More generally, as I noted elsewhere (Fantino, 1985), the increased interactions between behavior ecologists and behavior analysts have set the occasion for a synergistic advance in the Experimental Analysis of Behavior.

150

Acknowledgement

Preparation of this review was supported by NIMH Grant MH-20752 and NSF Grant BNS 83-02963 to the University of California at San Diego.

References

Abarca, N. and Fantino, E. (1982) Choice and foraging. J. Exp. Anal. Behav. 38, 117–123.

Abarca, N., Fantino, E. and Ito, M. (1985) Percentage reward in an operant analogue to foraging. Anim. Behav. 33, 1096–1101.

Ackroff, K., Schwartz, D. and Collier, G. (1986) Macronutrient selection by foraging rats. Physiol. Behav. 38, 71–80.

Batson, J.D., Best, M.R., Phillips, D.L., Patel, H. and Gilleland, K.R. (1986) Foraging on the radial arm maze: effects of altering the reward at a target location. Anim. Learn. Behav. 14, 241–248.

Baum, W.M. (1982) Choice, changeover, and travel. J. Exp. Anal. Behav. 38, 35–49.

Baum, W.M. (1983) Studying foraging in the psychological laboratory. In: R.L. Mellgren (Ed.), Animal Cognition and Behavior. North-Holland, Amsterdam, pp. 253–283.

Bhatt, R.S. and Wasserman, E.A. (1987) Choice behavior of pigeons on progressive and multiple schedules: a test of optimal foraging theory. J. Exp. Psychol.: Anim. Behav. Proc. 13, 40–51.

Bond, A.B. (1983) Visual search and selection of natural stimuli in the pigeon: the attention thresholds hypothesis. J. Exp. Psychol.: Anim. Behav. Proc. 9, 292–306.

Boulos, Z., Rosenwasser, A.M. and Terman, M. (1980) Feeding schedules and the circadian organization of behavior in the rat. Behav. Brain Res. 1, 39–65.

Boulos, Z. and Terman, M. (1980) Food availability and daily biological rhythms. Neurosci. Biobehav. Rev. 4, 119–131.

Charnov, E.L. (1976) Optimal foraging: the marginal value theorem. Theret. Pop. Biol. 9, 129–136.

Collier, G. (1987) Operant methodologies for studying feeding and drinking. In: F.M. Toates and N.E. Rowlands (Eds.), Feeding and Drinking. Elsevier, Amsterdam, pp 37–76.

Commons, M.L., Kacelnik, A. and Shettleworth, S.J. (1987) Quantitative Analyses of Behavior: Vol. 6, Foraging. Erlbaum, Hillsdale, New Jersey.

Cook, R.G., Brown, M.F. and Riley, D.A. (1985) Flexible memory processing by rats: use of prospective and retrospective information in the radial maze. J. Exp. Psychol.: Anim. Behav. Proc. 11, 453–469.

Cowie, R.J., Krebs, J.R. and Sherry, D.F. (1981) Food storing by marsh tits. Anim. Behav. 29, 1252–1259.

Dale, R.H.I. and Roberts, W.A. (1986) Variations in radial maze performance under different levels of food and water deprivation. Anim. Learn. Behav. 14, 60–64.

Davies, N.B. (1976) The feeding behaviour of some insectivorous birds. Unpublished doctoral dissertation, University of Oxford.

Davies, N.B. and Houston, A.I. (1981) Owners and satellites: the economics of territory defense in the pied wagtail, Motacilla alba. J. Anim. Eco. 50, 157–180.

Davies, N.B. and Houston, A.I. (1983) Time allocation between territories and flocks and owner-satellite conflict in foraging pied wagtails, Motacilla alba. J. Anim. Eco. 52, 621–634.

Davison, M. and McCarthy, D. (1988) The Matching Law: a Research Review. Erlbaum, Hillsdale, New Jersey.

Dawkins, M. (1971). Perceptual changes in chicks: another look at the 'search image' concept. Anim. Behav. 19, 566–574.

Domjan, M., O'Vary, D. and Greene, P. (1988) Conditioning of appetitive and consummatory sexual behavior in male Japanese quail. J. Exp. Anal. Behav. 50, 505–519.

Dunn, R.M. (1982) Choice, relative reinforcer duration and the changeover delay. J. Exp. Anal. Behav. 38, 313–319.

Elsmore, T.F. and Hursh, S.R. (1982) Circadian rhythms in operant behavior of animals under laboratory conditions. In: F.M. Brown and R.C. Braeler (Eds.), Rhythmic Aspects of Behavior. Erlbaum, Hillsdale, New Jersey, pp. 273–310.

Engen, S. and Stenseth, N.C. (1984) A general version of optimal foraging theory: the effect of simultaneous encounters. Theoret. Pop. Biol. 26, 192–204.

Fanselow, M.S., Lester, L.S. and Helmstetter, F.J. (1988) Changes in feeding and foraging patterns as an antipredator defensive strategy: a laboratory simulation using aversive stimulation in a closed economy. J. Exp. Anal. Behav. 50, 361–374.

Fantino, E. (1966) Immediate reward followed by extinction vs later reward without extinction. Psychon. Sci. 6, 233–234.

Fantino, E. (1969) Choice and rate of reinforcement. J. Exp. Anal. Behav. 12, 723–730.

Fantino, E. (1985) Behavior analysis and behavioral ecology: a synergistic coupling. Behav. Anal. 8, 151–157.

Fantino, E. and Abarca, N. (1985) Choice, optimal foraging, and the delay-reduction hypothesis. Behav. Brain Sci. 8, 315–362.

Fantino, E. and Logan, C.A. (1979) The Experimental Analysis of Behavior: a Biological Perspective. W.H. Freeman, San Francisco.

Fantino, E. and Preston, R.A. (1988a) The effects of accessibility on acceptability. J. Exp. Anal. Behav. 50, 395–403.

Fantino, E. and Preston, R.A. (1988b) Foraging for integration. Behav. Brain Sci. 11, 683–684.

Fantino, E. and Preston, R. (1989) The delay-reduction hypothesis: some new tests. In: N.W. Bond and D.A.T. Siddle (Eds.), Psychology: Issues and Applications. Elsevier, Amsterdam, pp. 457–467.

Fantino, E., Squires, N., Delbrück, N. and Peterson, C. (1972) Choice behavior and the accessibility of the reinforcer. J. Exp. Anal. Behav. 18, 35–53.

Gendron, R.P. (1986) Searching for cryptic prey: evidence for optimal search rates and the formation of search images in quail. Anim. Behav. 34, 898–912.

Gendron, R.P. and Staddon, J.E.R. (1983) Searching for cryptic prey: the effect of search rate. Am. Nat. 121, 172–186.

Guilford, T. and Dawkins, M.S. (1987) Search images not proven: a reappraisal of recent evidence. Anim. Behav. 35, 1838–1845.

Guilford, T. and Dawkins, M.S. (1989a) Search image versus search rate: a reply to Lawrence. Anim. Behav. 37, 160–162.

Guilford, T. and Dawkins, M.S. (1989b) Search image versus search rate: two different ways to enhance prey capture. Anim. Behav. 37, 163–165.

Herrnstein, R.J. (1961) Relative and absolute strength of response as a function of frequency of reinforcement. J. Exp. Anal. Behav. 4, 267–272.

Herrnstein, R.J. (1970) On the law of effect. J. Exp. Anal. Behav. 13, 243–266.

Herrnstein, R.J. and Loveland, D.H. (1964) Complex visual concept in the pigeon. Science 146, 549–551.

Herrnstein, R.J., Loveland, D.H. and Cable, C. (1976) Natural concepts in pigeons. J. Exp. Psychol: Anim. Behav. Proc. 2, 285–302.

Hineline, P.N. and Sodetz, F.J. (1987) Appetitive and aversive schedule preferences: schedule transitions as intervening events. In: M.L. Commons, J.E. Mazur, J.A. Nevin, and H. Rachlin (Eds.), Quantitative Analyses of Behavior, Vol. 5, The Effect of Delay and of Intervening Events on Reinforcement Value. Erlbaum, Hillsdale, New Jersey, pp. 141–157.

Hodos, W. and Trumbule, G.H. (1967) Strategies of schedule preference in chimpanzees. J. Exp. Anal. Behav. 10, 503–514.

Hollis, K.L. (1989). In search of a hypothetical construct: a reply to Guilford and Dawkins. Anim. Behav. 37, 162–163.

Houston, A. (1986) The matching law applies to wagtails' foraging in the wild. J. Exp. Anal. Behav. 45, 15–18.

152

Houston, A. (1987) The control of foraging decisions. In: M.L. Commons, A. Kacelnik and S.J. Shettleworth (Eds.), Quantitative Analyses of Behavior, Vol. 6, Foraging. Erlbaum, Hillsdale, New Jersey, pp. 41–61.

Hursh, S.R. (1980) Economic concepts for the analysis of behavior. J. Exp. Anal. Behav. 34, 219–238.

Ito, M. and Fantino, E. (1986) Choice, foraging, and reinforcer duration. J. Exp. Anal. Behav. 46, 93–103.

Johnson, D.F., Ackroff, K., Peters, J. and Collier, G. (1986) Changes in rat's meal patterns as a function of the caloric density of the diet. Physiol. Behav. 36, 929–936.

Kacelnik, A., Krebs, J.P. and Ens, B. (1987) Foraging in a changing environment: an experiment with starlings (*Sturnus vulgaris*). In: M.L. Commons, A. Kacelnik, and S.J. Shettleworth (Eds.), Quantitative Analyses of Behavior, Vol. 6, Foraging. Erlbaum, Hillsdale, New Jersey, pp. 63–87.

Kamil, A.C., Krebs, J.R. and Pulliam, H.R. (1987) Foraging Behavior. Plenum, New York.

Kamil, A.C. and Sargent, T.D. (1981) Foraging Behavior: Ecological, Ethological, and Psychological Approaches. Garland, New York.

Kanarek, R.B. and Collier, G. (1979) Patterns of eating as a function of the cost of a meal. Physiol. Behav. 23, 141–145.

Killeen, P.R. (1982) Incentive theory. II. Models for choice. J. Exp. Anal. Behav. 38, 217–232.

Klein, R., Pilon, D., Prosser, S. and Shannahoff-Khalsa, D. (1986) Nasal airflow asymmetries and human performance. Biol. Psychol. 23, 127–137.

Krebs, J.R., Kacelnik, A., and Taylor, P. (1978) Test of optimal sampling by foraging great tits. Nature 275, 27–31.

Lawrence, E.S. (1989) Why blackbirds overlook cryptic prey: search rate or search image? Anim. Behav. 37, 157–160.

Lea, S.E.G. (1976) Titration of schedule parameters by pigeons. J. Exp. Anal. Behav. 25, 43–54.

Lea, S.E.G. (1979) Foraging and reinforcement schedules in the pigeon: optimal and non-optimal aspects of choice. Anim. Behav. 27, 875–886.

Lea, S.E.G. and Tarpy, R.M. (1986) Hamsters' demand for food to eat and hoard as a function of deprivation and cost. Anim. Behav., 34, 1759–1768.

Lima, S.L. and Valone, T.J. (1986) Influence of predation risk on diet selection: a simple example in the grey squirrel. Anim. Behav. 34, 536–544.

Mott-Trille, R. (1983) Food storage: an inventory model. B.A. Thesis, University of Toronto, Canada.

Olton, D.S. and Collison, C. (1979) Intramaze cues and 'odor trails' fail to direct choice behavior on an elevated maze. Anim. Learn. Behav. 7, 221–223.

Olton, D.S., Handelmann, G.E. and Walker, J.A. (1981) Spatial memory and food searching strategies. In: A.C. Kamil and T.D. Sargent (Eds.), Foraging Behavior: Ecological, Ethological, and Psychological Approaches. Garland, New York, pp. 333–354.

Olton, D.S. and Samuelson, R.J. (1976) Remembrance of places passed: spatial memory in rats. J. Exp. Psychol.: Anim. Behav. Proc. 2, 97–116.

Orians, G.H., and Pearson, N.E. (1979) On the theory of central place foraging. In: D.J. Horn, G.R. Stairs and R.D. Mitchell (Eds.), Analysis of Ecological Systems. Ohio State University Press, Columbus, Ohio pp. 154–177.

Phillips, J.H., Robinson, A. and Davey, G.C.L. (1989) Food hoarding behaviour in the golden hamster (*Mesocricetus auratus*): effects of body weight loss and hoard-size discrimination. Q. J. Exp. Psychol. 41B, 33–47.

Pietrewicz, A.T. and Kamil, A.C. (1981) Search images and the detection of cryptic prey: an operant approach. In: A.C. Kamil and T.D. Sargent (Eds.), Foraging Behavior: Ecological, Ethological, and Psychological Approaches. Garland, New York, pp. 311–331.

Pulliam, H.R. (1981) Learning to forage optimally. In: A.C. Kamil and T.D. Sargent (Eds.), Foraging Behavior: Ecological, Ethological, and Psychological Approaches. Garland, New York, (pp. 379–388).

Rachlin, H., Battalio, R., Kagel, J. and Green, L. (1981) Maximization theory in behavioral psychology. Behav. Brain Sci. 4, 371–417.

Rachlin, H. and Green, L. (1972) Commitment, choice and self-control. J. Exp. Anal. Behav. 17, 15–22.

Rashotte, M.E. and Henderson, D. (1988) Coping with rising food costs in a closed economy: feeding behavior and nocturnal hypothermia in pigeons. J. Exp. Anal. Behav. 50: 441–456.

Redhead, E. and Tyler, P.A. (1988) An experimental analysis of optimal foraging behaviour in patchy environments. Q.J. Exp. Psychol. 40B, 83–102.

Roberts, W.A. and Ilersich, T.J. (1989). Foraging on the radial maze: the role of travel time, food accessibility, and the predictability of food location. J. Exp. Psychol.: Anim Behav. Proc., 15, 274–285.

Roberts, W.A. and Van Veldhuizen, N. (1985) Spatial memory in pigeons on the radial maze. J. Exp. Psychol.: Anim. Behav. Proc. 11, 241–260.

Schneider, J.W. (1973) Reinforcer effectiveness as a function of reinforcer rate and magnitude: a comparison of concurrent performances. J. Exp. Anal. Behav. 20, 461–471.

Shannahoff-Khalsa, D. (in press). Stress technology medicine: a new paradigm for stress and considerations for self-regulation. In: M. Brown, C. River and G. Koob (Eds.), Neurobiology and Neuroendocrinology of Stress. Marcel Dekker, New York.

Sherry, D.F. (1987) Foraging for stored food. In: M.L. Commons, A. Kacelnik and S.J. Shettleworth (Eds.), Quantitative Analyses of Behavior, Vol. 6, Foraging. Erlbaum, Hillsdale, New Jersey, pp. 209–227.

Sherry, D.F., Krebs, J.R. and Cowie, R.J. (1981) Memory for the location of stored food in marsh tits. Anim. Behav. 29, 1260–1266.

Shettleworth, S.J. and Krebs, J.R. (1986) Stored and encountered seeds: a comparison of two spatial memory tasks in marsh tits and chickadees. J. Exp. Psychol.: Anim. Behav. Proc. 12, 248–257.

Skinner, B.F. (1966) The phylogeny and ontogeny of behavior. Science 153, 1205–1213.

Skinner, B.F. (1975) The shaping of phylogenic behavior. J. Exp. Anal. Behav. 24, 117–120.

Skinner, B.F. (1984) The evolution of behavior. J. Exp. Anal. Behav. 41, 217–221.

Spetch, M.L. and Edwards, C.A. (1986) Spatial memory in pigeons (*Columbia livia*) in an open-field feeding environment. J. Comp. Psychol. 100, 266–278.

Staddon, J.E.R. (1983) Adaptive Behavior and Learning. Cambridge University Press, Cambridge, England.

Stevens, D.W. and Krebs, J.R. (1987) Foraging Theory. Princeton University Press, Princeton, N.J.

Temple, W. and Foster, M. (1988) Operant studies with farm animals. 24th International Congress of Psychology, Sydney, Austalia.

Terman, M. (1983) Behavioral analysis and circadian rhythms. In: M.D. Zeiler and P. Harzem (Eds.), Advances in Analysis of Behaviour, Vol. 3. Wiley, Chichester, England, pp. 103–141.

Timberlake, W., Gawley, D.J. and Lucas, G.A. (1987) Time horizons in rats foraging for food in temporally separated patches. J. Exp. Psychol: Anim. Behav. Proc. 13, 302–309.

Timberlake, W., Gawley, D.J. and Lucas, G.A. (1988) Time horizons in rats: the effect of operant control of access to future food. J. Exp. Anal. Behav. 50, 405–417.

Tinbergen, L. (1960) The natural control of insects in pinewoods. I. Factors influencing the intensity of predation by songbirds. Arch. Neerl. Zool. 13, 265–343.

Tinbergen, N. (1951) The Study of Instinct. Oxford University Press, New York.

Vaughan, W., Jr. (1985) Choice: a local analysis. J. Exp. Anal. Behav. 43, 383–405.

Wanchisen, B.A., Tatham, T.A. and Hineline, P.N. (1988) Pigeons' choices in situations of diminishing returns: fixed-versus progressive-ratio schedules. J. Exp. Anal. Behav., 50, 375–394.

Werntz, D.A., Bickford, R.G., Bloom, F.E. and Shannahoff-Khalsa, D.S. (1983) Alternating cerebral hemispheric activity and the lateralization of autonomic nervous function. Hum. Neurobiol. 2, 39–43.

Wong, R. and Jones, C.H. (1985) A comparative analysis of feeding and hoarding in hamsters and gerbils. Behav. Proc. 11, 301–308.

Zahorik, D.M. and Houpt, K.A. (1981) Species differences in feeding strategies, food hazards, and the ability to learn food aversions. In: A.C. Kamil and T.D. Sargent (Eds.), Foraging Behavior: Ecological, Ethological, and Psychological Approaches. Garland, New York, pp. 289–310.

Zeiler, M.D. (1987) On optimal choice strategies. J. Exp. Psychol.: Anim. Behav. Proc. 13, 31–39.

Experimental analysis of behavior, Part 2
Iversen and Lattal (eds.)
© *1991, Elsevier Science Publishers BV*

CHAPTER 5

The use of computers in the control and recording of behavior

LEWIS R. GOLLUB

Department of Psychology, University of Maryland at College Park, College Park, MD 20742, U.S.A.

1. Introduction

1.1. Impact of computers on operant research

Research requires control of the independent variables and accurate recording of the results. Computers permit experimenters to accomplish both goals more efficiently and economically than ever before. In recent years computers have become faster, easier to use, and capable of performing more tasks, while they have become cheaper and more reliable.

Computers also permit the researcher to conduct experiments that are simply not possible without them. They can create and present unlimited varieties of antecedent visual and auditory stimuli, arrange contingencies (relations between behavior and consequences), as well as define, record, and analyze behavior temporally, spatially, or in terms of other important dimensions such as force or location. Moreover, behavior can be studied at different levels of temporal integration, from millisecond by millisecond to aggregates over hours or weeks.

Computers also are useful in the undergraduate laboratory course covering Experimental Analysis of Behavior (Balsam et al., 1984; Vom Saal et al., 1984). Using computers in the teaching lab produces at least two additional benefits. First, it exposes students to contemporary research methods; second, it educates faculty about how to use computers in their own research. In addition, undergraduate and graduate students can use these computers for their own independent work.

In the area of Applied Behavioral Research, computers provide more reactive settings for human behavior. For example, changes in physiological parameters (biofeedback) can produce consequences according to flexible quantitative criteria as well as under the control of intermittent schedules of reinforcement (cf. Bermejo, 1988).

1.2. A brief overview of computers

Computers are devices that receive, manipulate, store, and report data. The data can be numeric, alphabetic, or graphic, although in the computer all data are in fact numeric. The unit of data is the bit (abbreviation of *bi*nary digi*t*) which takes the values 0 or 1. Thus, one bit can represent, as output, the on-or-off status of a stimulus, or, as input, whether or not a key is being pressed. Eight bits form a byte. One byte can represent the status of 8 responses or 8 stimuli, store one letter in a display of textual data, or be part of a graphic display. Two to 4 bytes can store numbers ranging in value up to 3.37×10^{38}.

Computer systems consist of two sets of resources: the *hardware*, or physical devices in which storage, computations, and control take place, and the *software*, or programs, which control what the hardware does. Fig. 1 shows the major components of typical microcomputer hardware. This chapter discusses the use of small computers ('personal computers' and some 'minicomputers') in behavioral research. This group of computers is defined by size (the computer occupying about 0.5 m³) and cost ($500–6000 for a reasonably complete system, exclusive of software). Distinctions among different classes of computers are constantly shifting, as advances in technology have made computers smaller and cheaper. Today's personal computers have the power and capabilities of 'main frame' computers of not many years ago! Of course, even the least expensive 'home computer' like the Commodore 64

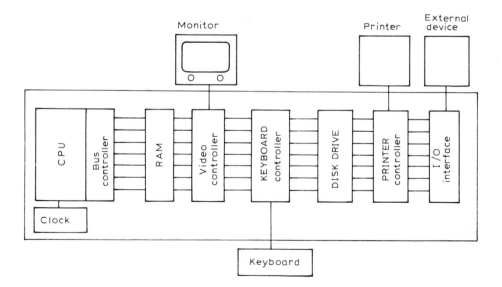

Fig. 1. Major parts of a microcomputer. Everything except the keyboard, monitor, and printer are usually contained in a single enclosure. The bus lines represent electrical connections among different components along which control and data signals are transmitted.

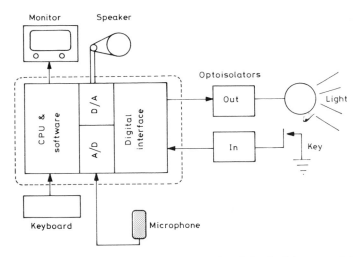

Fig. 2. Major components of computer use in a behavior laboratory. Interface is discussed in Section 2 of this chapter; software, in Section 5; stimuli (monitors and simple lights), in Section 3; and response input, in Section 4.

(Kallman, 1986) or Radio Shack Color Computer can be used in a behavioral laboratory (Reed, 1982; Crossman, 1984).

Fig. 2 illustrates the major parts of a computer system for a behavior laboratory, and the main topics of this chapter. The computer controls stimuli in the experimental chamber either by energizing lamps or feeders through an output interface and power isolators (opto-isolators or relays), or by creating and presenting complex visual or auditory stimuli. The organism's behavior operates either mechanical switches that are connected to an input interface through power isolators, or transducers of continuous variables like response force or vocalization, that are converted into appropriate numerical form by analog/digital converters.

1.3. Factors in the selection of a computer for laboratory use

Many different computers can be used for behavioral experiments. The primary criterion is whether a particular computer system will effectively conduct the experiments and collect the data. The computer system includes the computer, input and output interface, and software. Selection of a computer requires integrating all three elements.

Although it is theoretically true that most computers can accomplish the same tasks in the laboratory, there are considerable differences in the ease, cost, and speed with which a given computer system can carry out a specific goal. The relative importance of these factors will vary, of course, with individual circumstances. For example, research on a continuous variable like response force will emphasize the availability, cost, and quality of analog-to-digital (A/D) converters needed for that work.

TABLE 1

Major criteria for evaluating computer systems

Interfacing: ease of connecting the computer to experimental equipment to read inputs and control outputs (Sections 2, 3, 4).

Software for behavioral experiments: appropriateness and ease of use (Section 5).

Graphic (CRT) displays: special hardware, monitor, and software (Section 3).

Speed of operation, especially if more than one experiment is controlled by a computer.

Memory size.

Mass storage available (floppy disk and hard disk storage).

Cost of a computer system, calculated per experiment controlled, including all necessary hardware, interfacing, and software.

Availability of assistance for setting up hardware and software.

Graphic or sound generating capabilities, or availability of add-on components (Section 3).

Also, the circumstances under which an investigator conducts research will be important. For example, someone with little familiarity with computers and who needs to start behavioral experiments immediately might choose a 'turn-key' system (one that requires little more than plugging it in and turning it on). On the other hand, an experimenter with computer programming skills, with a program of research on the microanalysis of behavior and interactive reinforcement schedules, would value operating speed, available programming languages, and data storage capabilities.

Table 1 lists the main features of a laboratory computer system. These criteria are discussed briefly below, and in the other sections of the chapter, where indicated.

1.3.1. Interfacing

In virtually all laboratory experiments on operant behavior, the activity of the organism must be detected and recorded, and appropriate consequences (e.g., reinforcement) provided. How easily can external equipment be connected (interfaced) with the computer? Such connections are made with input-output (I/O) interface components. Interface hardware can either be integral to the computer, or an added component. If the latter, what components are available? Some computers have an 'open architecture' in that additional hardware components can easily be added just by plugging them into a socket that connects the component to the internal computer circuits (the bus). The Apple II was the first widely available computer with open architecture, followed by the IBM-PC and similar computers, colloquially called 'clones'. This label is inaccurate since they are not identical to the IBM computers.

The most important similarity was the use of the same microprocessor (Intel Corporation 8086, 8088, 80286 or 80386). The integral programs for basic computer operations, the BIOS and DOS or disk operating system (described below) were sometimes different from those of the IBM. In the remainder of this chapter, I will use the term PC to refer to the many similarly functioning computers related to the IBM-PC computer family. Although the letters PC abbreviate the term 'personal computer', and many personal computers are not related to the IBM-PC, this use of the term is almost universal.

1.3.2. Software availability

There are many considerations in selecting a programming language for behavioral experiments, including its ease of use, what it can do, and how it integrates with hardware. Software decisions are intimately related to hardware decisions. As discussed in Section 5, some computer software can be used only with specific computers. Programs written in general-purpose programming languages, like BASIC, Pascal, and C, are compatible with many different computers, so that such programs can be transported to a different computer with only minimal changes (usually in handling input and output). On the other hand, special experiment control languages, like SKED and Operant/PC, are tied to specific computers and specific hardware.

1.3.3. CRT display (monitor)

The monitor displays programs and data. Any sharp, bright, monochrome monitor is suitable for programming and data display. A monitor can also be used to present visual stimuli to the subject. In that case, additional criteria apply (see Section 4). With many computers, a second monitor with appropriate characteristics for stimulus presentation can be used with an additional graphic adapter card. The efficiency and memory capabilities of the graphic adapter to which the monitor is attached should be considered when making this selection. Characteristics of monitors used to display stimuli are discussed in Section 3.2.

1.3.4. Speed

The speed of operation of a computer, paced by an internal clock, determines how fast the microprocessor can perform arithmetic and logical operations, and how rapidly data can be stored or retrieved from memory. Speed can be important in experiments with graphic or auditory stimulus operations, or when a reinforcement contingency requires many calculations. In such experiments, a hardware math coprocessor chip can often improve speed dramatically. This chip performs many mathematical operations quite rapidly. Disk drives also affect overall operating speed when they store values representing complex stimuli. Hard disk drives transfer data faster than floppy drives and have a much greater storage capacity.

Timing of experimental events can be controlled by the computer's internal clock or by a plug-in timer or external clock. In my experience, a clock speed of 100/s is necessary with some animal species. Slower speeds can allow excessive time to pass between events, introducing a delay between a response and its consequence. (The topic has not been addressed empirically, but experimenters have observed differences in performance even with slow versus fast electromechanical equipment.) Investigators are cautioned to verify that a clock system is accurate.

PC computers operating under MS-DOS and PC-DOS present a particular problem. Although time values are displayed in units of 0.01 s, the actual unit of time keeping is 0.055 s (King, 1985). Using the internal timer to pace experiments would therefore introduce delays between response and consequence unless an alternative timing device is used. Two solutions exist for this problem. First, one can use a plug-in board with a faster clock; some I/O interface boards contain a clock. Second, the internal clock can be reprogrammed. Programs are available in C for 8088-based computers (Emerson, 1988b) and 80286-based (Emerson, 1988c; Granaas, 1989). See also Buhrer et al. (1987), Dlhopolsky (1988), and Graves and Bradley (1987), for other programs for PC computers, Flexser (1987) for the Tandy Color Computer, and Hormann and Allen (1987) for the Commodore 64/128.

1.3.5. Memory
The amount of available memory, measured in bytes, limits the size of experiment control programs, of stored stimuli, and, to some extent, the amount of data that can be collected. Although total memory size is usually not a concern, it can be crucial when the computer generates and displays visual or auditory stimuli, records and stores very large amounts of response information, or controls a number of independent experiments simultaneously. Memory can often be increased by adding memory chips or by a plug-in board.

1.3.6. Mass data storage
Large numbers of experimental programs and files of collected data soon become logistical problems. The main methods of storing data are on floppy disks and on hard disk. The latter can store the equivalent of 100 to 200 floppy disks. Even with a hard disk, data storage can still be a problem. If detailed performance records, for example of interresponse times, are collected every day from several subjects, the disk can fill up quickly. Plans should be made at the beginning for transferring data for permanent storage, and keeping duplicate records (back-ups) in case of accidental loss of the original data. As with paper records, the data format should facilitate later retrieval and analysis. Although many methods of storage can be used, a hard disk drive is a real advantage because of its large capacity and greater speed of operation.

1.3.7. Cost
Compare only the costs of total systems. System cost includes not only the computer hardware, peripheral devices, interface, and the software, but also the personnel costs to get the system functioning. Software costs vary greatly, from less than $100 for

some general purpose languages, to many times as much for special experiment control languages. Hardware costs should include an estimate of repair and upkeep along with original acquisition costs. There are many brands of computers, especially PCs, that differ in operational characteristics, keyboard and monitor, and compatibility with original IBM specifications. It is therefore advantageous to get expert advice, or consult reviews in computer magazines.

One important factor in cost is time-sharing: the ability of computer software to control several experiments simultaneously. The operation spreads the costs of the computer hardware across several experiments. The advantages of a time-sharing system are reduced costs per experiment and a centralized command station at one computer terminal. The disadvantages include reliance on a single computer which, when it fails, affects the entire experimental program.

Another cost factor is whether the computer can be used for other functions while experiments are under way. Some time-sharing systems permit data analysis and program preparation. The use of remote single-board computers (see below) also leaves the common computer free for other uses. Without this capability, additional computers may be needed for these necessary laboratory activities.

Three additional factors that may be difficult to quantify, but are often of great importance, also should be considered. (1) Advice and experience: many computer users have become expert working largely in isolation. This accomplishment usually entails a sizable expenditure of time and effort. Selecting hardware from a variety of manufacturers and writing, modifying, and verifying complex programs is time consuming. Further, most behavioral researchers do not have the professional skills to accomplish these tasks as rapidly or proficiently as trained computer scientists. Also, the immediate and concrete reinforcers of dealing with computers can maintain behavior incompatible with pursuing behavioral research. There are therefore advantages to acquiring hardware and software that have already been tested with the sort of research an investigator is planning. (2) Help: find an experienced user who is willing to help in the set-up stages of the program. (3) Determine the level and availability of support from the manufacturer. Is the software supplier available for telephone consultation in case of problems? Is there a support group or Special Interest Group (SIG) for the hardware or software? (I have benefitted immeasurably from SIGs on the Compuserve Information Service network dealing with the Tandy Color Computer, IBM Computers, Microsoft QuickBASIC and QuickC. There are also SIGs for many other brands of computers and general purpose software.)

One other hardware dimension should be mentioned: general-purpose computers versus dedicated single-board computers. The single-board computer is smaller and cheaper than a full-function computer. Because it is used as a peripheral processor, it may have limited (or no) displays, keyboard, or storage, with resultant cost savings. Solomon et al. (1983) discuss a group of single board computers (KIM, SYM-1, and AIM-65) that have been used in behavioral and physiological research. Typically several single board computers are connected to a single general-purpose computer which performs the functions of storing programs and data and displaying events. Walter and Palya (1984) introduced a single board computer with special interest for operant researchers. See Section 5.4. for further discussion.

2. Interfacing the computer to the experimental chamber

Most operant experiments involve studying the effects of contingencies between discrete behavioral events (a response occurs or doesn't) and discrete stimulus events (a stimulus is turned on or off). This section discusses the control of such discrete inputs and outputs; Sections 3 and 4 discuss control of more complex stimulus and response events, respectively.

2.1. Basic interfacing concepts

Interface equipment connects the computer and the experimental equipment. It performs two major functions: (1) matching the electrical and temporal characteristics of the computer to those of the external events, and (2) protecting the computer from electrical noise and destructive voltages. Interfacing is described from the viewpoint of the computer as output (O) or input (I). The output interface transfers signals from the computer out to external equipment, e.g. the lights, buzzers, and feeders, in an operant chamber. The input interface takes signals in to the computer from devices that measure behavior, e.g., switches connected to keys and levers.

A computer sends and receives data in parallel and serial formats. Parallel communication sends or receives all the bits of one byte simultaneously, on eight independent lines. Serial communication presents each bit in sequence, one at a time. Since input and output signals are logically parallel events, special circuits are required to transform signals between the computer and serial communications equipment (cf. Emerson, 1988d). Parallel communication typically is faster, and hardware costs are lower. Its main disadvantage is that the electrical characteristics of most parallel interface components limit their communication to relatively short distances (up to 10 m), unless some kind of amplification is provided, whereas typical serial communication equipment can be used over much longer distances.

The physical connection between computer and interface is made either through a built-in connector (jack) on the computer, or on a plug-in interface card. External jacks are usually found on less expensive computers, like the Commodore 64, where connections are made to a User Port (O'Dell and Jackson, 1986; see also Crossman, 1984). A user port is a socket or multi-terminal connection to the bus or input and ouput lines of the computer. External connections must be properly chosen so as not to interfere with the computer's operation. Buffering circuits with short connecting wires are required. In open-architecture computers, an I/O adapter board provides one level of buffering. The buffering is provided by a transistor or integrated circuit

TABLE 2
Converting a byte to its decimal equivalent

Binary number	1	0	1	0	0	1	0	1
Place	8	7	6	5	4	3	2	1
Decimal value ($2^{place-1}$)	128	64	32	16	8	4	2	1
Value	128		+32			+4		+1
Total	165							

component between the external signal lines and the computer's bus. PC computers define the input and output connections as 'ports': specific points of connection of the CPU to internal and external equipment. An external port is referenced by a port number that corresponds to switch settings on the I/O adapter card.

Outputs and inputs are typically handled in units of a byte. The value of a byte is determined in a similar way to that of the common decimal numbers, by place arithmetic, except that each digit represents increasing powers of 2 rather than of 10. For example, the binary number 10100101 has the (decimal) value 165, as shown in Table 2.

One byte can represent the status of 8 stimulus events, where each bit controls a specific output line. One value, e.g., 1, corresponds to a stimulus line on, and 0, to its being off. Thus, the byte 00000101 represents an output condition in which only stimuli numbered one and three are on. As the experiment progresses, the control program will change the value of different bits as the status of different devices is to be changed. Each change is brought about when the program transmits the output byte to the interface adapter card which controls the lights, feeders, recorders, and so on. Inputs are handled in a similar way, except that each bit represents the status of a response device, with value 1 when the bar is pressed, and 0 when it is not pressed.

2.2. Parallel interface devices

In order to illustrate the general principles of a parallel interface, this section will consider the most widely used hardware component in PC I/O boards. Many digital I/O interface adapters use the 8255 Peripheral Interface Adapter chip. The 8255 is a 40-pin semiconductor chip that contains a large-scale integrated circuit that can function in both input and output modes, controlling a total of 24 lines (represented by three 1-byte data registers). This chip, and interface boards that use it, permits 2 whole bytes (16 events) and the 2 halves (4 bits each) of the third byte to be separately designated for either input or output. Thus either 4, 8, 12, 16, 20 or 24 lines can be input or output. The specific input/output configuration is under program control. A 1-byte program register stores a value that determines the chip's operating mode. The control and data registers are accessed by signals sent to, or read from a specific port. For example, with the MetraByte PIO-12 interface card, one would first select a sequence of port addresses for the control and data registers by setting slide switches on the card. Then, before attempting input or output data transfers, the program would send a value to the port address of the control register, and clear (set to zero) all bits. For example, I have set the control switches selecting a base port address to 768. The control port is 3 greater than this base, or 771. To select 20 bytes for ouput and 4 bytes for input, the value 137 is output to the control port. The QuickBASIC instruction

OUT 771, 137

performs this operation, establishing that ports 768, 769 and half of 770 are outputs, and the other half of port 770 is input, and resets all ouputs to zero. Port addressing is needed in this application, and most compilers and interpreters include this operation. Functions like

OUT *outport*, *value*
and *value* = IN (*inport*)

where *outport* and *inport* are the port addresses of the designated connections, send and receive the output or input value, respectively.

The output registers of the 8255 hold the value of the last byte they receive (a process called 'latching'). The input byte reflects the momentary status of the input lines. The maximum output current of the 8255 chip is approximately 1.7 mA at 5 VDC, not enough to operate experimental equipment. The output must therefore be amplified. Relays, optoisolators, or semiconductor amplifiers provide the required power for external equipment and also electrical isolation. (See also Chute et al., 1987, and Genovese, 1988, for further discussion of these points.)

2.3. Digital inputs

In most behavioral experiments the organism operates a switch, such as a pigeon key, rat lever, and so on. This switch controls an electrical circuit that inputs a signal to the computer. Most experiments use the leading edge, or start, of the switch closure as the response. (Switches whose circuit is *opened* by a response, like Gerbrands pigeon keys, require a signal reversal when used in this sort of circuit. This reversal can either be in hardware, with a simple inverting transistor gate, or by a software step that inverts logically, e.g., by complementing the input value.) One variable in the experiment control program represents the status of the response lines, called an input buffer. Since this variable represents the *current* status of the input lines, the program must test for which inputs have turned on since the last examination of inputs. Table 3 shows subroutines written in C and QuickBASIC 4.5 that set the variable *respbuf* to the value of new responses.

Further discussion of the treatment of input signals is presented in Section 4.1.

TABLE 3
C and QuickBASIC functions for recording responses.

I. C function

```
setrespbuf()
{
static int oldbuf, newbuf;
  newbuf=inp (inputport); /* inp() reads a byte from
                              port inputport */
  respbuf=(oldbuf ∧ newbuf) & newbuf;
  oldbuf=newbuf;
}
```

```
II. QuickBASIC function
SUB setrespbuf
STATIC oldbuf AS INTEGER
 newbuf=INP (inputport)
 respbuf=(oldbuf XOR newbuf) AND newbuf
 oldbuf=newbuf
END SUB
```

2.4. Digital outputs

The most common method of output interfacing is to transmit a byte that represents the status of eight devices to a parallel I/O interface adapter controlling the eight devices. The output interface must provide a signal of sufficient electrical power and duration to operate equipment in the experimental chamber, and protect the computer from damaging external electrical inputs. Simple circuits that only amplify the 5 V signal from the computer bus or user port have been described (Blekkenhorst and Goldstein, 1983; Crossman, 1984). These circuits don't fully protect the computer from external voltages, since input and output share a common electrical connection. Methods of isolation are described below.

As previously noted, the 8255 chip used in most I/O adapters latches, or retains the status of, the most recent output byte sent by the program. For example, the QuickBASIC instruction to turn on channels 1 and 3 is OUT *portnumber*, 5, where 5 is the decimal value of the sum of bits 1 (value 1) and 3 (value 4), as shown in Table 2. Alternatively, some computers use 'memory-mapped I/O', in which certain locations in memory correspond to I/O buffers, and constantly reflect or determine the status of input and output conditions. The BASIC instruction POKE (address, value) performs the appropriate output function.

166

2.4.1. Electrical isolation of output devices

It is important to isolate the computer from external components. I recommend that all output devices be fully isolated. Two total isolation methods can be used: relays and optoisolators. I/O adapters that use the 8255 chip deliver only low current levels (1.7 mA) which can drive only solid state gates, or optoisolators that switch the experimental circuits. The low-power outputs can operate 5-VDC arc-suppressed Reed relays, and the relay's contacts switch the external power for the experimental equipment. Several companies (e.g., MetraByte and Alpha Products) provide modules using this design.

Optoisolators are encapsulated circuits in which a light-emitting diode (LED) controls a solid-state switch (e.g., O'Dell and Jackson, 1986). Optoisolators that drive DC or AC circuits are available in different power ratings. Since these modules have standard pin plugs, they are easily replaced if one malfunctions. OPTO-22 and other companies make widely available products. Fig. 3 shows a system used at the University of Maryland in which the optoisolators (E) are connected by a short cable to a parallel I/O card, a MetraByte PIO-12 (D), plugged into an expansion slot of a PC. The electrical outputs of the optoisolators can be carried long distances to the experimental chamber by standard wire cables (F).

One additional problem is electrical transients from AC motors or high current

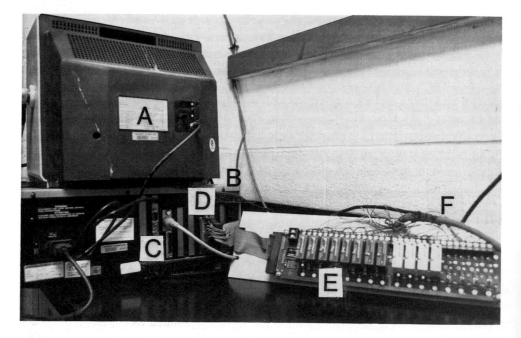

Fig. 3. Rear view of the computer connections in the author's laboratory. A: monitor (used for programming and data display). B: computer enclosure; C: monitor display adaptor card and jack; D: I/O interface adapter card and connector; E: optoisolation modules; F: cable going to experimental chamber.

DC solenoid operation. Transients can introduce spurious signals into the computer, changing data in memory or interfering with operation of the computer, or, at worst, damaging the computer. Total electrical isolation will reduce the effects of most transients, but may not eliminate all of them. Transients are transmitted through power lines and broadcast from motors. Transients are also more likely with relay than optoisolation circuits. Transient suppression at the source with diodes or transient suppression electronic components will usually prevent the problem. Since long lines can act like antennas and collect electrical noise, relay and optoisolation provide an important barrier between these spurious signals and the computer.

3. Controlling stimuli in behavioral experiments

Computers can control on/off stimulus sources like light bulbs and clickers, and also generate, store, manipulate, and present complex visual and auditory stimuli. Hardware and software exist for creating, arranging and modifying stimuli, and for manipulating numerous dimensions of the stimuli including orientation, color, masking, and movement (Proffitt and Kaiser, 1986).

Two main classes of stimulus production will be distinguished in this discussion: stimuli generated intact by external devices such as light bulbs, monochromators, fixed frequency generators, shock scramblers etc., and those generated by a computer, such as displays of textual material, graphic images, and auditory wave forms.

3.1. Digital stimulus control

On/off operation is obtained by a digital I/O interface controlling relays or optoisolators as described in Section 2.4. (Auditory stimuli should be turned on and off by an electronic switch rather than a relay controlling the output signal to avoid producing transient clicks.) The settings of some tone generators, amplifiers, and attenuators can be directly controlled by the output of the I/O controller (see, for example, Harrison, 1988). The experiment control program would output to the appropriate port the values corresponding to intensity, frequency etc. (The values depend on the coding scheme established by the manufacturer of the stimulus device.)

Slide projectors are convenient tools for presenting complex stimuli (Stoddard and Loftus, 1988). A sequence of pulses can move a tray of slides to a specific location. One characteristic of slide projectors should be considered however. Because the shutter in commercial slide projectors opens and closes gradually, an auxiliary high-speed shutter between the projector lens and the screen should be used in experiments where precise timing between stimulus onset and response is required (cf. Loftus et al., 1984, for a discussion of the relevant issues). Other stimuli and appropriate circuits include electric shock (Delay, 1985), and a microcontrolled stepping motor for manipulating physical objects (Finley, 1984).

3.2. *Computer generated stimuli*

A computer can be used to produce and present an infinite variety of visual and auditory stimuli. This use involves four basic steps: (1) generation of the stimulus in computer storable form, (2) storage and retrieval, (3) manipulation or alteration, and (4) creating a physical stimulus.

3.2.1. *Visual stimuli*

(1) *Generation*. Three basic methods exist for generating a visual stimulus: (i) an existing stimulus, e.g. a picture, can be transformed into digital form by a scanner, a video camera-like device that produces a digital representation of the scanned picture or text; (ii) complete graphic images are created by a graphic editing program, e.g., Microsoft Paint; and (iii) graphics instructions in general-purpose programming languages can produce a graphic display with functions that create lines, rectangles, and ellipses, and fill them with colors or patterns (as in vector graphics). For example, the following two instructions in QuickBASIC 4.5 create a circle at the center of the screen (the X and Y coordinates represented by the variables *xcenter* and *ycenter*) and fill it with a color represented by the variable *color*.

CIRCLE (*x*center, *y*center), radius, color
PAINT (*x*center, *y*center), color

The Amiga, Atari ST, and Macintosh computers have particularly effective graphics languages and special hardware components for producing and presenting visual and auditory stimuli that recommend them for experiments with these requirements (cf. Brooks, 1985; Anstis, 1986; Brooks and Bieber, 1988; Coney, 1989). In addition, the range and number of different colors that can be displayed vary greatly among computers, display drivers, and monitors.

(2) *Storage*. Graphic figures can be stored either in the form of the instructions that create them (called vector graphics) or as a bit-by-bit representation of the graphic display (a bit-mapped image). This bit-mapped storage contains a value for each point of the selected area within a rectangle that contains the selected section. For example, the colored disk created with the preceding instructions can be stored by the following instruction:

GET (*x*center – radius, *y*center – radius) –
        (*x*center + radius, *y*center + radius), disk

where the two parenthetical terms are the upper left and lower right corners of the rectangle, and *disk* is the name of a 2-dimensional array in which the values are stored.

Once a figure has been drawn and stored with a GET instruction, it can be displayed very rapidly any place on the screen with the PUT instruction, where *x* and *y* are the coordinates of the upper left corner of the figure:

PUT (x, y), disk

Bit image data are stored either in main computer memory or in memory on the monitor control card. With sufficient memory, multiple graphic images can be stored and rapidly alternated, to simulate motion.

The digital representations of graphic images created by different graphics languages and by scanners are usually incompatible. Additional programs may be needed to manipulate graphic data, or make data created by one language usable with another, e.g., to select a portion of an image, change its size, etc. Discussion of such graphics translators and editors is beyond the scope of this chapter.

(3) *Manipulation of the image.* A good graphics library is a valuable feature in a general-purpose programming language. A complex stimulus can be easily changed by changing a few variables in the program. In the preceding example, the screen location, size, and color of the disk are changed by assigning different values to the appropriate variables. The figure can be moved either by re-drawing it or, more rapidly, by the PUT function. In addition, variants of the stimulus, e.g., degraded stimuli that might be used in programmed instruction or of drug effects can be arranged by a bit-by-bit masking pattern (Brooks, 1987) or fragmenting the stimulus (Snodgrass et al., 1987).

(4) *Displaying the stimulus.* Graphic instructions require a certain amount of time to be executed. Drawing an image on a monitor while it is in view of the subject is not satisfactory because individual components, and slowly filling figures, will be presented, and time will pass from the beginning of a partial display until it is fully created on the monitor. Figures should be fully drawn prior to their display, and stored on disk or as data in the program. They can be presented rapidly in two ways. First, as previously described, with GET and PUT instructions that store the screen image in main RAM. Second, graphics adapter cards have independent storage memory and can often store two or more screen displays that can be presented rapidly. Portions of the display can be cleared by a PUT instruction of a rectangle of the background color.

Accurate timing of latencies can be affected by the way in which the monitor draws the display. Most monitors redraw their displays approximately 60 times/s. If a computer program creates a new display and begins timing a latency, the new display will start appearing on the monitor at a random place on the screen, and there will thus be an average delay of 8.33 ms until the full display appears. This value is about the size of variance with human reaction times. This problem can be eliminated by software routines that detect when a new display will be presented, and timing from that moment. Solutions are presented by Heathcote (1988) for the PC and by Wright (1986) for the Amiga 1000.

3.2.2. Graphics monitors

In most cases, visual stimuli will be presented on the screen of a monitor. Most monitors are like television sets, with a source of electrons guided to phosphors on the back side of the screen. Monochrome monitors that display only one color (white, green, and amber are common) have a single electron source, whereas color monitors create a range of colors by differentially energizing combinations of red, green, and blue phosphors. The important variables for monitors are the following.

The display is composed of an array of individual glowing phosphors called pixels (an abbreviation of *pic*ture *el*ements). The size of the pixel determines the 'grain' of the display. A large number of smaller pixels creates a less grainy, more realistic picture, easier to read text, and diagonal lines that appear continuous rather than step-like. (Tanner et al., 1989, present a software strategy that can reduce the staircase appearance of diagonal lines with analog monitor control.) For example, on the 13-inch monitor (measured diagonally), the display is 24 mm wide and 17 mm high. In PC systems, a medium resolution monitor using CGA standards has 320 vertical columns of dots × 200 lines. Textual stimuli (letters and numbers) are made up of 8 pixel × 8 pixel units. The EGA (Enhanced Graphics Adapter) standard provides a screen of 640 × 350 pixels with text characters of 8 × 14 pixels. VGA (Video Graphics Adapter) displays provide an even finer 640 × 480 pixel screen, or even more detailed, depending on the adapter card used. Monochrome monitors can achieve nearly the same resolution, 720 × 348 pixels, at considerably lower cost. Each step towards a less grainy color display entails a more expensive monitor and adapter, and a larger memory requirement for the storage of graphic data. If different colors are not needed, monochrome monitors create less grainy displays, and may be superior for figures and text at a lower cost than comparabale color monitors.

Several other problems of monitors should be considered.

(a) *Shape distortion.* Because the vertical and horizontal pixel separations are usually unequal, figures specified as circles and rectangles may not have the expected shape. Circles appear as ellipses, and squares, as rectangles. A simple solution is to draw a figure that is distorted in the opposite direction. Most CIRCLE functions have an aspect parameter that permits you to draw an ellipse that will be displayed as a circle. Similarly, squares can be drawn as rectangles, but displayed with sides of equal length.

(b) *Size.* Monitors occupy more than 30 × 30 × 30 cm and are nearly as large as a typical rat or pigeon chamber. When used with a small animal chamber, the placement of the monitor among the other components, e.g., the feeder and response keys, may be difficult. One solution may be to use a small television set that is driven from the RF output of many video display cards.

(c) *Relation of visual display and response.* The relation between the stimulus display and the response device is important (Cowey, 1968). The speed with which stimulus control develops to visual stimuli in pigeons is affected by whether or not the pigeon pecks on the discriminative stimuli (Sainsbury, 1971). With monitor displays, either the key can be next to the screen, invoking the problems noted above, or the pigeons can peck at the display itself (see Section 4.2 for methods of recording pecks on a large surface). If the monitor is mounted outside the chamber and the pigeon views it from afar, a problem of visual acuity can arise: the pigeon is relatively myopic for objects viewed down its beak (Hodos and Erichson, 1990) and since it pecks with beak raised (Hodos et al., 1976) a screen more than 25–33 cm away may be out of focus.

(d) *Screen distortion.* Characteristics of the display at different locations on the screen may vary. Because different locations are not equidistant from the electron source, intensity and color purity may vary from center to edge of the screen (cf. Smarte and Baron, 1988). In addition, screen surfaces vary from highly reflective to relatively matte. Finally, the characteristics of colors vary greatly among monitors. They are no worse than the ubiquitous 'Christmas tree bulb' or colored plastic pilot light lens, and can be calibrated.

3.3. Auditory stimuli

Auditory stimuli in experiments are presented by loudspeakers or headphones. The electrical energy that drives the speaker or headphone is typically produced by pure tone or noise generators or tape recordings. The computer greatly broadens the range and variety of auditory stimuli that can be studied, and can integrate stimulus production with other aspects of experimental control.

Three general methods for presenting auditory stimuli have been used. (1) The computer can control the output of external devices like tone generators or tape players through a digital I/O interface, as described in Section 2.4. (2) BASIC and other higher-level languages have a SOUND function that produces digital versions of pure tone stimuli. The BASIC function is

SOUND *frequency, duration*

where the two variables control the specific sound created. Ordinarily the sound is produced by the computer's internal speaker, but extension wires to the experimental chamber permit use of this method in experiments (I. Iversen, personal communication). (3) Noise and pure tones also can be produced by storing a numerical representation of the stimulus, which is decoded by a digital/analog convertor and amplified to drive loudspeakers. (See Wightman, 1978, for further details, as well as examples of FORTRAN computer code for representative stimuli.) This technique is the same as that used with bird song, described below.

Sound energy can be represented simply as the level of energy fluctuation over time. Repeated or organized sounds can, however, be analyzed and stored more effectively. For example, the Fourier transformation (Cooley and Tookey, 1965; Emerson, 1988a) can represent a continuous complex signal as a combination of harmonically related sinusoidal waves of differing intensities and relative phases. The numerical results of a Fourier transform are thus in an appropriate form for computer analysis, storage, manipulation and reproduction of the original or an altered sound. A sonographic transformation of bird song or human voice can be analyzed or altered, and then used to produce an auditory stimulus.

In a series of intriguing experiments, Dooling and his colleagues (e.g., Zoloth et al., 1980; Clark et al., 1983; Dooling et al., 1987), have investigated many parameters of song bird auditory discrimination and vocalization. A bird song is digitized by an A/D conversion and stored in numerical form. (See Section 4.3. for a discussion of analog/digital processing.) These values are then subjected to a discrete fast Fourier transform, which produces a compact numerical description of the sounds. When an auditory stimulus is required, the digital representation (or a modification thereof) is subjected to a reverse Fourier transform, and the resulting signal is converted to analog (D/A conversion). The resulting signal is amplified and fed to speakers in the chamber.

This method of presenting auditory stimuli has several advantages. First, the range of stimuli that can be presented is practically unlimited. Second, virtually any arbitrary change can be made to the stimulus–frequency shifts, duration changes, or combinations of different stimuli. Third, the order of presentation is completely arbitrary, compared to the serial order of stimuli on a tape recording. The preceding references provide information on both the apparatus and the computer programs used for this interesting work.

Analog to digital conversion consists essentially of measuring the amplitude of the input signal at a fixed rate, called the rate of digitization. In order to maintain a faithful representation of the input signal this rate must be sufficiently high. For bird song and speech, 20 kHz is considered adequate. Because of artifacts produced in the D/A conversion process, a low-pass filter, cutting off energy above 10 kHz, is used.

Speech sounds can also be presented and manipulated with a computer. Two different techniques are used. One is similar to the bird song procedures mentioned above. For example, Gibson (1987) described a system used with a Macintosh computer in which the digitized forms of speech stimuli were stored in separate data files for playback under program control. A second method utilizes special voice production hardware, such as specialized chips (Votrex, Federal Screw Works, Detroit) or boards. These chips require coded alphabetic input representing the phonemic values that the device can produce. Many parameters of speech sounds can be controlled, producing close approximations to natural speech.

4. Response measurement

This section is concerned with recording operant behavior with computers. Operant behavior is characterized by its relation to consequences (Part 1, Ch. 3). Most experiments rely on a functional definition of the operant class as whatever behavior operates the key (switch) and can control the consequence. Computers permit more precise measurement of the many parameters of behavior, e.g., temporal, spatial, and topographic. Contingencies can be placed on any of these variables, or they can be used as correlative measures, reflecting the effects of other manipulations.

Two types of response measurement will be discussed: (1) discrete responses, such as those producing switch closures, or categorized response location, and (2) continuous responses, such as location of the organism in space, and response force. (See also Part 2, Ch. 6).

4.1. Switch closures

Two special considerations arise in computer programs using switch closures to detect responses: (1) the correspondence between the actions of the experimental subject and the movements of the switch, and (2) artifacts due to mechanical oscillations of the switch (contact bounce). Genovese (1988) presents an excellent discussion of these problems.

Episodic responses, such as key pecks and lever presses, are defined by the apparatus rather than by a detailed topographic specification of behavior. Differences between what the organism does and what the apparatus records can be produced either by peculiarities of the response topography or of the recording switch. For example, a pigeon responding under ratio schedules of food reinforcement may make rapid multiple contacts of its beak with the key for each ballistic pecking movement towards the key (Jenkins and Moore, 1973; Hodos et al., 1976). These multiple contacts, some of which might have been too rapid to have been recorded with older electromechanical equipment, can be detected by computer equipment. The type of programming equipment used can thus change the definition of the response and the contingencies between behavior and consequences. Taking note of this relationship, Ferster and Skinner (1957) recommended that the pigeon key operate a sensitive, fast-acting relay that could follow rates of up to 15/s. Computer programs using polling rates of 100/s, or interrupt-driven systems, can respond to much higher rates that may represent different behavioral events or even artifactual sources. The experimenter needs to decide how to treat these rapid inputs. For example, one can simulate the standards of electromechanical equipment, limiting rapid responding either by software that ignores a response that follows too soon after another, or, by hardware, a one-shot multivibrator.

The second source of multiple switch outputs is more clearly artifactual. Mechanical switches, such as contact keys or snap-action switches attached to levers or pecking keys, predominate in operant laboratory equipment (see Part 1, Ch. 1). Because of the mechanical action of most switches, a single impulse applied to a key or lever initiates a period of oscillation because of the mechanical system of the lever and a return spring (or gravity). This oscillation, or contact bounce, produces multiple electrical signals (on-off cycles) for durations of 1–10 ms. Slower electromechanical equipment could not respond to these inputs. Transistorized programming circuits used a one-shot multivibrator, which produced a single timed output pulse for any duration of input pulse. Additional input pulses during an output, whether produced by bounce or behavior, had no effect.

The multivibrator solution can also be used with computers. An integrated circuit one-shot (type 74123) can be installed between the key and the I/O interface to provide a timed pulse of about 30 ms for each switch operation. Alternatively, the one-shot can be simulated in software by a timing loop that ignores additional inputs that occur within a given time since an earlier input.

Another hardware solution can be used with response switches that provide both on and off contacts, i.e., double-throw switches. A set-reset flip-flop can be controlled by the normally-open (NO) and normally-closed (NC) contacts of the switch, respectively. The '1' output of the flip-flop will be unaffected by bounce of either NO or NC contacts.

Some of these difficulties may be relieved by use of an electronic rather than a mechanical transducer of the pigeon's peck with a piezoelectric element. Complete directions for constructing such a key, which has the additional advantage of not requiring contact cleaning, is given by Stoddard (1987).

Physical connection to the computer is made either by having the switch drive a Reed relay that is connected to one line of an input port, or by an input optoisolator (see Section 2.4).

4.2. Recording response location

Recording the precise location of a response is useful not only for studying location as a dependent variable (e.g., Antonitis, 1951), but also for allowing a subject to respond directly to a stimulus on a computer monitor. Numerous experiments have made use of the recording of response location in a single continuous physical dimension. Multiple mechanical keys (Herrnstein, 1961; Cumming and Eckerman, 1965) and multiple response-interrupted visible light photocells (Gollub, 1966) have been used. Hori and Watanabe (1987) analyzed a TV camera output for fine-grained location of a pigeon's peck along a linear target (see Part 2, Ch. 6).

More recently, invisible light photocells have been used to detect peck location. Clauson et al. (1985) described a system in which the pigeon's beak interrupted infrared (IR) beams that were detected by photocells. Blough (1986) adapted this system (see below) to detect the horizontal location of a pigeon's peck with 12 pairs of IR emitter-photodetectors spaced (10.7–12) mm apart. In this application, adjacent pairs of outputs were treated as a single location, defining six regions. The output of each pair (at 5 VDC) can be connected directly to the input line of a parallel input adapter like the 8255 (see Section 2.3).

A similar technique is used to locate a response in two dimensions. Clauson et al. (1985) arranged horizontal and vertical arrays of four pairs of emitters and detectors in each dimension, so that 16 individual locations could be detected. Iversen and Mogensen (1988) described an apparatus for neurobehavioral studies in which a rat's nose pokes in 54 holes (a 9×6 array) are detected by photocell interruptions.

Commercial 'touch screens' are also available. Two technologies have been developed: (1) the screen surface uses conductive or capacitive sensing of the subject's beak, finger etc., and (2) closely spaced arrays of IR photocells. Elsmore et al. (1989) reported a system with a contact sensing screen for detecting contacts by nonhuman primates responding to graphic color stimuli on a monitor. There are a large variety of IR sensing devices, consisting of frames of IR emitters and detectors. These can be placed directly in front of a monitor screen which presents stimuli. The output of the array of IR detectors is connected to a serial port (RS-232 connection) of the computer. Software is provided to decode the signal into the horizontal and vertical locations of the contact. Because the stimulus display uses one monitor connection, provision must be made to connect a second monitor for use by the experimenter. Pisacreta and Rilling (1987) discuss the use of these devices in experiments with pigeons. Allan and Zeigler (1989) pointed out that adjusting the distance of an IR detector array from the monitor screen can increase its sensitivity for detecting pigeons' pecks.

4.3. Measurement of response force and extent

Measuring such continuous variables as force and duration of response makes good use of the fast operation and mass storage of modern computers. Fowler (1987) argued cogently for the valuable information that force measurement provides in studies of the behavioral effects of drugs. Although there are four different physical systems to measure response force, in most experiments a lever is connected to an isometric force transducer, such as a strain gage (see Fowler, 1987, for further discussion). A strain gage is a resistance network that changes value linearly with imposed force. A constant voltage input to the network produces an output voltage that varies linearly with force. This continuous signal is input to an analog/digital (A/D) converter, which produces a digital input proportional to the response force.

A/D converters can be purchased as plug-in boards for many different computers. (See Olivo, 1986, for a comprehensive discussion of A/D converters.) Game inputs on some computers (e.g., Radio Shack Color Computer, Apple II, or Atari ST) provide the same function (cf. Moss, 1984). Several parameters distinguish different A/D converters. (1) The sensitivity or fineness of measurement, determined by the size of the output data variable. An 8-bit converter produces 255 categories of force (2 to the 8th power minus 1), whereas a 12-bit converter produces 4095. (2) The sampling rate, i.e., the speed with which a signal is digitally coded. (3) The voltage ranges over which it operates. (4) Stability of the electronic components.

The control program will sample the output of the A/D converter, and read its value into a program variable. Fowler (1974, 1985, 1987) discussed several important programming considerations. For example, a threshold force is chosen, below which input changes are ignored. Some higher force level is designated as a minimal criterion response. By noting the number of time units that the response stays above threshold, a response duration can be defined. Titration schedules of force differentiation, with a somewhat different measurement system, have also been described by Elsner et al. (1988).

Other physical response systems can be studied in the same way. All that is needed is a transducer that produces (piezoelectric) or modulates (resistive or strain gage) a voltage that is turned into a numerical value by an A/D convertor. Techniques for studying the rabbit nictitating membrane response (NMR) have been developed by Gormezano and his associates (Gormezano and Gibbs, 1988), and for recording and analyzing it by computer (Scandrett and Gormezano, 1980; Marshall-Goodell et al., 1982). A system by which the rat startle response can be measured by connecting a suspended cage to a loudspeaker cone's magnet, was described by Silverman et al. (1988).

4.4. Recording the organism's spatial location

Pear and Eldridge (1984) described an ingenious system for detecting the location of a pigeon in 3 dimensions within an experimental chamber. The signals from two orthogonally oriented television cameras are processed by a special converter to produce digital information on the location of the pigeon's head. (The head and neck have been blackened so that they are readily detected against a white background.) The sampling rate used was 30/s. Location was used as an operant for which consequences were provided (Pear and Legris, 1987). This system was also used to provide information on correlative changes in location when key-pecking was reinforced under variable-interval schedules (Pear, 1985) or autoshaping procedures (Eldridge and Pear, 1987) (see Part 2, Ch. 6).

A similar procedure recorded social behavior, e.g., movement and interactions among two organisms, by marking each with a distinct color and using color tracking with the image from a color TV camera (Crawley et al., 1982). Strategies for designing optimal systems of recording from digitized video images were discussed quite comprehensively by Olivo and Thompson (1988) who also provide a list of equipment sources. Prepackaged commercial systems (camera, recorder, analyzer, and computer input generator) are available.

Events in an experimental space can be recorded on video tape for later analysis. Franks et al. (1989) describe equipment to control the recording. Later coding of events on the tape by an observer is discussed by Krauss et al. (1988).

4.5. Applied settings

The use of computers to aid the disabled is an important growing field. Just two applications will be mentioned here to indicate the range of behavioral studies that can be performed. The required movements to relieve prolonged skin pressure in the spinal cord injured can be monitored, and antecedent or consequent stimuli provided when pressure detectors in the seating pad are monitored by a small computer (Merbitz et al., 1985; Grip and Merbitz, 1986). Finally, a software system for biofeedback control under various schedules of reinforcement was described by Bermejo (1988).

5. Software for operant experiments

5.1. Introduction to computer software

Computer programs, or software, are used to control the functioning of the computer equipment, or hardware, for conducting experiments or analyzing data. In most computers, programs that control experiments or analyze data run in conjunction with an operating system. Operating systems, such as MS-DOS or PC-DOS, consist of a collection of programs and routines that control the execution of other programs, and the input and output of data with the keyboard, monitor, and external devices. Normally, operating system resources are 'transparent' to the user. For example, the BASIC program statement *WRITE* 'Hello.' displays *Hello.* on the terminal. But that simple instruction made use of various software resources.

Several 'layers' of programs, or program functions, are required. In PCs, for example, a Basic Input Output System (BIOS) provides elementary operating instructions for input and output connections of the computer CPU with the keyboard, memory, monitor controller, and external device controllers. Operating systems, such as MS-DOS, provide a collection of programs that facilitate the use of the computer's resources, e.g., to move or copy programs or data.

In addition, some experiment control languages, like SKED-11 and MED-PC, operate under a run-time system. This is a control program that has some of the features of an operating system, that permits the selection of new experimental programs, the starting and stopping of experiments, saving of data, while one or more experiments are being controlled.

Software development programs provide the tools to create the application programs that run the experiments. These may consist of either separate or integrated collections of three programs: (1) an editor to create the text or source version of the program, (2) a compiler that translates the source program into an object code version, similar to the machine code that directly governs hardware operations, and (3) a linker to create an executable version of the program that governs the computer. These may be separate programs or they may be built into an integrated development system for creating, editing, testing, and revising application programs. Examples include QuickC, QuickBASIC, and Turbo Pascal, and special-purpose programs like the SKED development system. The user program, operating either alone or in conjunction with an experiment run-time system program, also is responsible for recording the data of the experiment and storing or displaying them.

There are three general types of programming language for conducting behavioral experiments: (1) general purpose languages like BASIC, Pascal, and C, in which the built-in functions and features are used to control and record the real-time events of the experiment as well as manipulate graphic and numerical data; (2) special experiment control languages tailored to arranging experimental events and recording response, time, and event contingencies; and (3) a hybrid language with the syntax of a general purpose language while providing constructs to carry out experiments. The advantages and disadvantages of each type of language will be discussed below before a detailed consideration of the languages themselves.

Software is used also to analyze and summarize the results of an experiment. The data provided by the experiment control program will be input to an analysis program. Since the purpose of conducting an experiment is the analysis and interpretation of the results, it is essential that the control language permits the level of recording that is required for your experimental program. Some languages can create a complete record of all experimental events, while others can provide only summary records of the experimental session. It is also important that the data format is easily stored for later analysis. With perhaps several hours of experimentation in several concurrently running chambers, an immense quantity of data can accumulate in a relatively brief time. The effective analysis and archival storage of the data should be decided on early in the planning stages of the research, rather than when a crisis of insufficient resources, or missing information, arises. The experimenter can either write analysis programs in a general-purpose programming language, or use statistical packages or spreadsheet programs.

In selecting the type of experiment control language to use, the following points should be considered. General-purpose languages permit you to do everything that your computer is capable of, as long as you can program it. Many of the special-purpose languages allow you to schedule common behavioral procedures with less programming effort, but may make it difficult to use all of the computer's resources, e.g., for stimulus displays, computations, and so on. In other words, you may trade reduced flexibility (and probably increased expense) for programming time and effort. Examples of these different approaches will now be considered. For additional discussion see Balsam et al. (1985).

5.1.1. Critique of general-purpose programming languages (e.g., BASIC, C, Pascal)
Advantages. (1) Many programming languages are available as comprehensive development packages with an editor, compiler, and debugging facilities (e.g., Microsoft QuickBASIC, and Borland Turbo Pascal). Software development is therefore easier than using individual development tools. The simpler interpreted BASIC (e.g., GW-BASIC) has problems discussed below. (2) You can usually get help from local experienced programmers (e.g., computer science students). (3) These languages are flexible, and can control limitless applications. Experimental contingencies involving earlier performances (e.g., previous interresponse times) can be easily included (cf.

Kaplan, 1985b). (4) Portability to another type of computer is possible. For example, languages like C and Pascal are implemented on many different computers, and programs written within certain established guidelines (e.g., ANSI C) are adaptable to different compilers running on different computers. Only input and output functions may differ from one computer system to another. (5) Programming support from the software developer and from special interest groups (SIGs) on computer networks like Compuserve and USENET can help with hardware, software, and system problems (cf. Lehman, 1988).

Disadvantages. (1) A long start-up time may be required because many elementary programming requirements must be met before even simple experiments can be implemented (e.g., handling inputs and outputs, stepping recorders etc.). As Spencer and Emmett-Oglesby (1985, p. 295) said, "Behavioral scientists should not be forced to spend considerable amounts of time learning to program computers, regardless of how 'easy' the programming language is." Alternatively, the hybrid language EC-BASIC extends the standard BASIC language with experimental constructs like *turn-on* and *turnoff*. (2) Collegial support for behavioral applications may be limited if you choose a language that few other experimenters are using. (3) Complex or long programs may be difficult to trouble shoot, or may have hidden faults ('bugs') that arrange unplanned experimental events or faulty data recording. Of course similar problems can arise when using any programming language, but may be more likely with very flexible or unfamiliar languages.

5.1.2. Critique of special-purpose experiment control languages (e.g., MED-PC, SKED)

Advantages. (1) The programming constructs and language specifics are closely related to the vocabulary and control concepts of behavioral experiments. (2) Teaching the language to students may strengthen their understanding of experimental procedures. (3) Some languages permit the inclusion of sub-programs written in a general-purpose programming language. These sub-programs permit the use of resources not included in the original language design.

Disadvantages. (1) Each language is tied to a specific type of computer; therefore, there will be extra effort and cost if several different types of computer are used in or acquired for a laboratory. (2) The language usually requires specific proprietary interface hardware. (3) Some languages do not permit the inclusion of additional sub-programs, as described in (3) above. This may limit the behavioral contingencies that can be programmed, whether graphic or auditory stimulus devices can be controlled, and what data records can be made. (4) Since these languages are special-purpose, computer science consultants are probably not available. However, at least one user group for the state notation languages SKED and MED-PC has been formed (Announcement, 1988).

5.2. *Controlling experiments with a general-purpose programming language*

Although earlier behavioral programmers used machine code or assembly language (labelled 'low level' languages because they are close to the numeric code that the microprocessor itself uses), contemporary higher-level languages are easier to use and function nearly as well. High-level languages are characterized as "fairly close to natural languages like English" (Naiman, 1983). For example, the BASIC statement PRINT 'HELLO', which will print *HELLO* on the monitor screen, is easily understood without special training. The advantage of high-level languages (also including C, Pascal, FORTH, and PL/I) is that they are easier to learn and remember, and programs are easier to write, debug (locate and correct errors), and change than machine or assembly language. These advantages are obtained, however, at a cost. Programs written in higher-level languages are longer (in terms of storage on a disk) and may run more slowly than comparable programs written in assembly language. For most experimental applications, however, these differences are not great enough to be of concern.

There are four major higher-level languages used in behavioral experiments: BASIC, C, Pascal, and FORTH. Useful compilers or programming systems exist for all of these languages for most popular computer systems. Comparative evaluations are published in many magazines.

Choosing a computer language is like choosing an automobile. All will get you to your destination, but there will be differences in ease, elegance, and personal satisfaction. Therefore no completely objective evaluation of computer languages is possible. My own experience with each of these languages leads me to rank them as they are listed above.

BASIC was designed to be an immediately usable language, and most people find it easy to learn. Earlier versions of BASIC operated slowly because they ran with an interpreter. An interpreter translates BASIC statements to machine language on a line-by-line basis while the program is executing, and inherently runs more slowly and less efficiently than compiled BASIC. Interpreted BASIC also does not provide a full range of programming constructs. Missing were constructs for data storage, such as *records* for the logical combination of related data elements, and control operations like *SELECT CASE*, for directing program operation among a group of alternative possible paths, such as different schedule contingencies (cf. Kaplan, 1985a). Interpreted BASIC was built into computers in Read Only Memory, or ROM, or provided as GW-BASIC and BASICA with PC machines (cf. Deni, 1986). Recent versions of compiled BASIC, e.g., Microsoft's QuickBASIC 4.5 and Borland's Turbo BASIC, are fast, flexible and efficient. They provide integrated programming environments that combine the editing, compilation, and linking operations. The resulting executable program runs independently. These and other compilers give the programmer access to nearly all the low-level functions of the computer as do assembly language and C. The few missing concepts of one implementation (bit handling in

QuickBASIC) can be repaired either by a small assembly language function or by functions available from after-market suppliers, such as Pro-BASIC.

C is intermediate between assembly language and higher-level languages. C is more flexible than BASIC, but nonprofessional programmers find it somewhat more difficult to learn and use. It permits very low-level operations on bits and bytes and efficient use of memory, but has many of the features of higher-level languages including structured programming (described below), a wide array of logical, arithmetic, and character-manipulations, and various looping and testing constructs for program control. Anything can be done in C, and C programs generally execute as rapidly as those written in assembly language. As a passing note, I have written programs for many single and multiple key experiments in C and in QuickBASIC, as illustrated in Tables 3, 4 and 5.

Pascal has replaced BASIC (and BASIC's parent, FORTRAN) as the first language taught to computer science students. Like C, it emphasizes structured programming and also has a wide range of control structures for program flow. Pascal has been effectively used in scheduling operant experiments (Kaplan, 1985a; Schull and Kaminer, 1987).

FORTH is something entirely different. Originally developed in 1979 to control observatory telescopes by computers which at that time had limited and expensive memory, it is a marvel of compact and efficient coding. Many new users find it hard to learn, especially because some concepts, such as postfix or Polish notation, are the opposite of other computer languages. Nevertheless, it has its strong proponents (Orr, 1984; Svartdal, 1986; Watts, 1986).

The most important contemporary concept in computer programming is that of structured programming. Structured programming consists of a "a set of guidelines and techniques for writing programs as a nested set of single-entry, single-exit blocks of code, using a restricted number of constructs" (Yourdon and Constantine, 1979, p. 462). These blocks are re-usable sub-programs. For example, I have written functions in C, such as turnon (*x*) that turns on stimulus line *x* in addition to any other lines already on, and *setrespbuf* that determines what new responses have occurred since the last check (see Table 3). These functions are part of a library of functions that are used in every experiment control program. Program blocks not only save time and effort by being reusable, but also don't need to be debugged once they are properly tested.

5.3. The logic of experimental control

All but the simplest computer programs require planning. Creating the program from scratch at the keyboard is inefficient, and will probably result in a poor program. Since no general-purpose computer language contains the schedule notation terms of operant experiments (FI, FR, DRL etc.) it is important to have another notation system that helps the planning and coding of experiments. Snapper and his

182

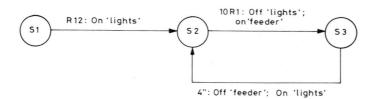

Fig. 4. State diagram for an FR 10 schedule. R12 is a response that starts the experiment; R1 is the organism's response; 'LIGHTS' and 'FEEDER' are symbolic names for specific output control lines connected to those components.

TABLE 4
SKED and QuickBASIC programs for an FR 10.

```
I.  FR 10 SKED Program
S.S.1,
S1,
 R12 : ON 'lights' → S2
S2,
 10 R1 : ON 'feeder';OFF'lights' →S2
S3,
 4" : ON 'lights';OFF 'feeder';Z1 →S1
S.S.2,
S1,
 'enough' Z1 →STOP


II. FR 10 QuickBASIC Program
lights = 1 : feeder = 2
OUT 768, lights 'turns on lights

DO ' Counts reinforcements
 count = 0
 DO ' Counts responses
  setrespbuf ' See Table 3
  IF respbuf AND responsel THEN
    count = count + 1
  END IF
 LOOP WHILE count < 10
 OUT 768, feeder
 starttime! = TIMER
 DO WHILE TIMER - starttime! < 4
 LOOP
 OUT 768, lights
 reinforcements = reinforcements + 1
LOOP WHILE reinforcements < enough
 OUT 768, 0 ' turns off everything
```

colleagues have adapted from engineering State Notation as "the language of process control" (cf. Snapper et al., 1970, 1982). This approach depicts an experimental procedure as a sequence of discrete states. In each state stimuli maintain a given status; rules (contingencies) specify the requirements for changing states. Fig. 4 shows a state diagram for a fixed-ratio (FR) schedule in which a given number of responses is required for reinforcer delivery. These diagrams are relatively easy to construct and to read, and guide the programmer very effectively into writing an experimental control program in both general-purpose and special purpose languages SKED and MED-PC discussed below (see also Part 1, Ch. 3).

The specific programming statements and the arrangement of statements obviously depend on the grammar of the programming language. Sample programs for the FR schedule shown in Fig. 4 are given in Table 4 in SKED and QuickBASIC.

Two types of program logic are used in programs controlling real-time processes like behavioral experiments: interrupt-driven and clock-polling. An interrupt process is initiated by a signal (e.g., a response or clock signal) that shifts control of the computer to a different part of the program; the interrupted operation restarts when the interrupt process is completed. Response to the interrupt signal is dealt with by a sub-program called an interrupt handler, which is very difficult for the nonprogrammer to write correctly. Clock polling is easier and quite reliable. In this logic the program continually checks for the passage of a short time period (a 'tick' of an electronic clock, usually every 10 ms, although 50 ms is sometimes used). At the tick, the status of response inputs is evaluated, e.g., by setting a response buffer variable to reflect the responses that have occurred, times are incremented, and then individual contingencies are evaluated.

The preceding program examples illustrate two things: (1) a BASIC program can be read fairly easily if meaningful names are used for functions and variables, and (2) a general-purpose higher-level language can entail considerable statement writing for even simple procedures. In addition, this method of programming does not permit multiple operations occurring simultaneously, as under concurrent contingencies. This feature is required also for controlling cumulative recorders fully. My solution to this problem is to program a series of independent contingencies, similar to the state sets described by Snapper et al. (1982). Table 5 illustrates this approach in QuickBASIC for a concurrent variable-interval variable-ratio (VI VR) schedule, which also shows control of the stepping motor of a cumulative recorder. Similar logic constructs can be used with C and Pascal programs.

5.4. Controlling experiments with special-purpose experiment control languages

For researchers whose main task is conducting experiments with specified contingencies between behavioral events and stimuli, a number of special-purpose computer languages are available. These languages have in common a grammar tied fairly closely to the flow of events in an experiment, either in terms of logical sequences,

TABLE 5
QuickBASIC program for concurrent VI 120– VR 50.

```
DO WHILE runstatus = ON
 IF tick THEN : ' tick function is TRUE every .01 s
 setrespbuf : 'See Table 2
   SELECT CASE state(1)
   CASE 1
    turnon (houselight AND keylight1)
    nextstate(1) = 2
   CASE 2
    IF reqt(1, VI, 120, 2) THEN
     turnoff (houselight AND keylight1)
     turnon (feeder)
     reinforcements = reinforcements + 1
     nextstate(1) = 3
    END IF
   CASE 3
    IF reqt(2, TIME, 4!, 0) THEN
     turnoff (feeder)
     turnon (houselight AND keylight1)
     nextstate(1) = 2
    END IF
 END SELECT

SELECT CASE state(2)
  CASE 1
   IF reqt(1, VR, 50!, 3) THEN
    turnoff (houselight AND keylight1)
    turnon (feeder)
    nextstate(2) = 2
   END IF
  CASE 2
   IF reqt(2, TIME, 4!, 0) THEN
    turnoff (feeder)
    turnon (houselight AND keylight1)
    reinforcements = reinforcements + 1
    nextstate(2) = 1
   END IF
 END SELECT

 SELECT CASE state(3)   'Stepper
   CASE 1
    IF resp(2) THEN
     turnon STEPPER
     nextstate(3) = 2
    END IF
   CASE 2
    IF reqt(1, TIME, .03, 0) THEN
     turnoff STEPPER
```

Continuation of TABLE 5
QuickBASIC program for concurrent VI 120–VR 50.

```
     nextstate(3) = 1
    END IF
  END SELECT
   IF reinforcement = maximumrfts THEN
    turnoff ALLLINES
    runstatus = STOPPED
   END IF
  END IF 'tick
LOOP
```

as in state notation, or in standard schedule notation. Table 6 summarizes the main features of these languages.

Judged from their operators manuals, all of these languages are appropriate for experiments on simple schedules. They are not, however, identical, since they are dependent on the use of specific computers. The several columns in Table 6 highlight some important differences. Several systems (Groups A and B) appear capable of arranging a wide variety of contingencies, whereas those in Group C are limited either

TABLE 6
Some features of special-purpose programming languages

Language	Computer System	Notation Language	Complimentary Language	Proprietary Hardware
A. Open systems: relatively unlimited contingencies				
SKED-11	PDP-11	SKED	Fortran-77	Yes
MED-PC	MS-DOS	Sked-like	Pascal	Yes
Conman	MS-DOS	Sked-like		No
Pastor	PDP-11	Pastor	Modula	No
B. Closed systems: limited contingencies or schedules				
OPN	MS-DOS			Yes
Operant/PC	MS-DOS			Yes/No
C. Semi-open systems: functions or Hardware Built around general purpose language				
FREDL	MS-DOS	Pascal		No
Apple-Psych	Apple II	Pascal		No
Lab-Forth	MS-DOS	Forth		No
Poeisis	MS-DOS	PL/I	PL/I	Yes
ECBASIC	Any	ECBASIC		Yes

to certain schedules, or to a maximum number of sequential components. In addition, some languages are integrated with general purpose computer languages, so that it is possible to incorporate either computational sections (e.g., to make the probability of reinforcing an interresponse time proportional to its frequency) or use the graphic functions of a computer.

Cost also needs to be considered. Most of the systems listed are proprietary, and are sold with specific licensing arrangements for use on either one computer or at one site. In addition, some systems are suitable for conducting several simultaneous experiments.

One system which is unique in this group is the ECBASIC system (specially modified BASIC) incorporated on the Walter-Palya interface board (Walter and Palya, 1984; Palya, 1988). This programming system is included as a ROM interpreter on a single-board computer with integral relay interface. Several relevant functions (e.g., TURNON, TURNOFF as well as functions for timing and counting events) were added to ECBASIC. The board also contains input and output buffering circuits (see Section 2). Control programs are written in ECBASIC using a text editor on any computer, and are then transmitted by a serial communication protocol (RS-232) to the individual control boards. The interface board can be located near the experimental chamber, thus simplifying wiring. Multiple boards can be controlled from any computer with serial communication capabilities. Signals to start the experiment can be issued either at the board or at the host computer. The boards can function in interpreted mode as stand-alone computers, or can be used solely as interfaces. Interpreted mode may run slowly for programs requiring large amounts of computation in the course of the experiment. The cost, however, may be less than that of the interfacing equipment needed for each station in a shared computer system. An ECBASIC system can be implemented with a minimal initial cost (cf. Pevey, 1988; Weisman and Palya, 1988). Circuits for the boards are in the public domain so that individual experimenters can construct their own, but soldering skills are necessary to produce reliable circuits.

5.5. Conclusions on software

The prospective user can compare systems in three ways: (1) examine a copy of the user's manual, which a manufacturer should be willing to lend you or sell at a nominal price. Is it clear? Does it appear to permit the experiments you will run? (2) Scan the Methods sections of journals publishing research similar to what you plan. Contact the authors. (3) Ask the manufacturer for a list of users; contact them. Once you adopt a programming language, you and your students or associates will probably continue using it for years. Your choice will also commit you to computers and hardware. No choice is perfect, and none is unusable. Pick those features that are most important to your present and foreseeable use of computers in research.

Many choices abound in the selection of graphics software and monitors. The experimenter can get useful comparative information from magazines such as BYTE and other publications oriented toward users of specific computers.

6. Conclusions and recommendations

Considering what computers can do in the operant laboratory, and how their cost compares to alternative methods of programming and recording behavioral data, it is clear why they are the method of choice. The selection of a computer system for an individual laboratory is not an easy decision. A number of factors enter into the choice. Because of the many relevant dimensions, there is no single recommendation for all users. It is hoped that this chapter will enable experimenters to review the possibilities and make profitable use of computers for a successful research program.

7. Sources for behavioral programming languages

SKED11. State Systems, Inc., P.O. Box 2215, Kalamazoo, MI 49003, U.S.A.

MED-PC. Med. Associates, Inc. Box 47, East Fairfield, VT 05448, U.S.A.

CONMAN. Spyder Systems, 4701 S. Rockport, Bloomington, IN 47401, U.S.A.

Pastor. J. Elsner, Institute of Toxicology, Swiss Federal Institute of Technology, Zürich, Switzerland.

OPN. M. W. Emmett-Oglesby, Department of Pharmacology, Texas College of Osteopathic Medicine, Fort Worth, TX 76107, U.S.A.

Operant/PC. Life Science Associates. One Fenimore Rd., Bayport, NY 11705, U.S.A.

FREDL. H.L. Kaplan, Addiction Research Foundation of Ontario, 33 Russell St., Toronto, Ontario, Canada M5S 2S1.

Apple-Psych. Suzanne Barnes, 1505 Northpark Blvd., F54, San Bernardino, CA 92407. U.S.A.

Lab-Forth. F. Svartdal, Institute of Social Science, University of Tromsö, Tromsö, Norway.

Poeisis. Poeisis Research, 4475 Yarmouth, Pensacola, FL 32514, U.S.A.

188

ECBASIC. W. Palya, Department of Psychology, Jacksonville State University, Jacksonville, AL 36265, U.S.A.

Acknowledgements

The author thanks Drs. R.J. Dooling, W. Hodos, and M. Penner for helpful information on stimulus control, and a Project FULCRUM grant from the University of Maryland Instructional Computing Programs for the computer equipment on which some of these behavioral control programs were developed.

References

Allan, R.W. and Zeigler, H.P. (1989) Measurement and control of pecking reponse location in the pigeon. Physiol. Behav. 45, 1215–1221.

Announcement. (1988) State-Table Users' Newsletter. J. Exp. Anal. Behav. 50, 504.

Anstis, S. (1986) Visual stimuli on the Commodore Amiga: a tutorial. Behav. Res. Methods Instr. Comput. 18, 535–541.

Antonitis, J.J. (1951) Response variability in the white rat during conditioning, extinction, and reconditioning. J. Exp. Psychol. 42, 273–281.

Balsam, P.D., Deich, J., O'Connor, K. and Scopatz, R. (1985) Microcomputers and conditioning research. Behav. Res. Methods Inst. Comput. 17, 537–545.

Balsam, P., Fifer, W., Sacks, S. and Silver, R. (1984) Microcomputers in psychology laboratory courses. Behav. Res. Methods Instr. Comput. 16, 150–152.

Bermejo, R. (1988) Biofeedback training program: multiple channels, displays, and schedules of reinforcement. Comput. Methods Programs Biomed. 27, 269–274.

Blekkenhorst, H. and Goldstein, S.R. (1983) A microcomputer interface to control reinforcement delivery. Behav. Res. Methods Instr. 15, 398.

Blough, D.S (1986) Odd-item search by pigeons: method, instrumentation, and uses. Behav. Res. Methods Instr. Comput. 18, 413–419.

Brooks, J.O., III (1985) Pictorial stimuli for the Apple Macintosh computer. Behav. Res. Methods Instr. Comput. 17, 409–410.

Brooks, J.O., III (1987) Enhancing and degrading visual stimuli. Behav. Res. Methods Instr. Comput. 19, 260–269.

Brooks, J.O., III and Bieber, L.L. (1988) Digitized nonobjects for use with the Apple Macintosh computer. Behav. Res. Methods Instr. Comput. 20, 433–434.

Buhrer, M., Sparrer, B. and Weitkunat, R. (1987) Interval timing routines for the IBM PC/XT/AT microcomputer family. Behav. Res. Methods Instr. Comput. 19, 327–334.

Chute, D.L., Gaeman, D. and Ziegler, T. (1987) MacLaboratory Controller: a switch and A/D interface between Apple's Macintosh and peripheral apparatus. Behav. Res. Methods Instr. Comput. 19, 205–209.

Clark, C., Dooling, R.J. and Bunnell, T. (1983) Analysis and synthesis of bird vocalizations: an FFT-based software system. Behav. Res. Methods Instr. 15, 251–253.

Clauson, H.D., Izatt, E.J. and Shimp, C.P. (1985) An infrared system for the detection of a pigeon's pecks at alphanumeric characters on a TV screen: the dependency of letter detection on the predictability of one letter by another. J. Exp. Anal. Behav. 43, 257–264.

Coney, J. (1989) An experimental control system for the Amiga microcomputer. Behav. Res. Methods Instr. Comput. 21, 391–393.

Cooley, J.W. and Tookey, J.A. (1965) An algorithm for the machine combination of complex Fourier series. Math. Comput. 19, 297–301.

Cowey, A. (1968) Discrimination. In: L. Weiscrantz (Ed.), Analysis of Behavioral Change. Harper & Row, New York, pp. 189–238.

Crawley, J.N., Szara, S., Pryor, G.T., Creveling, C.R. and Bernard, B.K. (1982) Development and evaluation of a computer-automated color TV tracking system for automatic recording of the social and exploratory behavior of small animals. J. Neurosci. Methods 5, 235–247.

Crossman, E.K. (1984) An inexpensive operant chamber interface for the VIC 20 microcomputer. Behav. Res. Methods Instr. Comput. 16, 338–340.

Cumming, W.W. and Eckerman, D.A. (1965) Stimulus control of a differentiated operant. Psychon. Sci. 3, 313–314.

Delay, E.R. (1985) A simple and inexpensive computer-compatible shock circuit Behav. Res. Methods Instr. Comput. 17, 114–115.

Deni, R. (1986) Programming Microcomputers for Psychology Experiments. Wadsworth, Belmont, CA.

Dlhopolsky, J.G. (1988) C language functions for millisecond timing on the IBM PC. Behav. Res. Methods Instr. Comput. 20, 560–565.

Dooling, R.J., Park, T.J., Brown, S.D., Okanoya, K. and Soli, S.D. (1987) Perceptual organization of acoustic stimuli by budgerigars (*Melopsittacus undulatus*): II. Vocal signals. J. Comp. Psychol. 101, 367–381.

Eldridge, G.D. and Pear, J.J. (1987) Topographical variations in behavior during autoshaping, automaintenance, and omission training. J. Exp. Anal. Behav. 47, 319–333.

Elsmore, T.F., Parkinson, J.K. and Mellgren, R.L. (1989) Video touch-screen stimulus-response surface for use with primates. Bull. Psychon. Soc. 27, 60–63.

Elsner, J., Fellman, C. and Zbinden, G. (1988) Response force titration for the assessment of the neuromuscular toxicity of 2,5-hexanedione in rats. Neurotox. Teratolog. 10, 3–13.

Emerson, P.L. (1988a) Compact C language Fourier analysis on small computers. Behav. Res. Methods Instr. Comput. 20, 423–426.

Emerson, P.L. (1988b) The best crude timer for MS-DOS implementations of C. Behav. Res. Methods Instr. Comput. 20, 583–584.

Emerson, P.L. (1988c) TIMEX: a simple IBM AT C language timer with extended resolution. Behav. Res. Methods Instr. Comput. 20, 566–572.

Emerson, P.L. (1988d) Using serial interfaces and the C language for real-time experiments. Behav. Res. Methods Instr. Comput. 20, 330–336.

Ferster C.B. and Skinner, B.F. (1957) Schedules of Reinforcement. Appleton- Century-Crofts, New York.

Finley, G.P. (1984) Microcontrolled stepping motors in behavior research: two application examples. Behav. Res. Methods Instr. Comput. 16, 288–293.

Flexser, A. J. (1987) Accurate display timing using an enhanced BASIC for the Tandy Color Computer. Behav. Res. Methods Instr. Comput. 19, 457–459.

Fowler, S.C. (1974) A minicomputer system for recording the dynamic properties of individual operant responses. Behav. Res. Methods Instr. 6, 288–292.

Fowler, S.C. (1985) Amplitude measures of operant response: implementation with Apple Pascal. Behav. Res. Methods Instr. Comput. 17, 301–306.

Fowler, S.C. (1987) Force and duration of operant response as dependent variables in behavioral pharmacology. In : T. Thompson, P.B. Dews and J.E. Barrett (Eds.), Advances in Behavioral Pharmacology, Vol 6, Neurobehavioral Pharmacology. Erlbaum, Hillside, NJ, pp. 83-127.

Franks, I.M., Nagelkerke, P. and Goodman, D. (1989) Computer controlled video: an inexpensive IBM based system. Comput. Educ. 13, 33–44.

Genovese, R.F. (1988) A strategy for microcomputer-controlled measurement of responses in the behavioral laboratory. Behav. Res. Methods Instr. Comput. 20, 1–5.

Gibson, J.M (1987) Using digitized auditory stimuli on the Macintosh computer. Behav. Res. Methods Instr. Comput. 19, 257–259.

Gollub, L.R. (1966) Stimulus generalization of response position in the rat. Psychon. Sci., 6, 433–434.

Gormezano, I. and Gibbs, C.M. (1988) Transduction of the rabbit's nictitating membrane response. Behav. Res. Methods Instr. Comput. 20, 18–21.

Granaas, M.M. (1989) TIMEX2: a modified C-language timer for PC AT class machines. Behav. Res. Methods Instr. Comput. 21, 619–622.

Graves, R. and Bradley, (1987) Millisecond interval timing and auditory reaction time programs for the IBM PC. Behav. Res. Methods Instr. Comput. 19, 30–35.

Grip, J.C. and Merbitz, C.T. (1986) Wheelchair-based mobile measurement of behavior for pressure sore prevention. Comput. Methods Programs Biomed. 22, 137–144.

Harrison, J.M. (1988) Control of responding by sounds of different quality: an evolutionary analysis. J. Exp. Anal. Behav. 50, 521–539.

Heathcote, A. (1988) Screen control and timing routines for the IBM microcomputer family using a high-level language.Behav. Res. Methods Instr. Comput. 20, 289–297.

Herrnstein, R.J. (1961) Stereotypy and intermittent reinforcement. Science 133, 2067–2069.

Hodos, W. and Erichson, J.T. (1990) Lower-field myopia in birds: an adaptation that keeps the ground in focus. Vision Res. 30, 653–657.

Hodos, W., Leibowitz, R.W. and Bonbright, J.C., Jr. (1976) Near-field visual acuity of pigeons: effects of head location and stimulus luminance. J. Exp. Anal. Behav. 25, 129–141.

Hori, K. and Watanabe, S. (1987) An application of the image processing system for detecting and controlling pigeon's peck location. Behav. Brain Res. 26, 75–78.

Hormann, C.A. and Allen, J.D. (1987) An accurate millisecond timer for the Commodore 64 or 128. Behav. Res. Methods Instr. Comput. 19, 36–41.

Iversen, I.H. and Mogensen, J. (1988) A multipurpose vertical holeboard with automated recording of spatial and temporal response patterns for rodents. J. Neurosci. Methods 25, 251–263.

Jenkins, H.M. and Moore, B.R. (1973) The form of the auto-shaped response with food or water reinforcers. J. Exp. Anal. Behav. 20, 163–181.

Kallman, H.J. (1986) A Commodore 64-based experimental psychology laboratory. Behav. Res. Methods Instr. Comput. 18, 222–227.

Kaplan, H.L. (1985a) Design decisions in a Pascal-based operant conditioning system. Behav. Res. Methods Instr. Comput. 17, 307–318.

Kaplan, H.L. (1985b) When do professional psychologists need professional programmers' tools? Behav. Res. Methods Instr. Comput. 17, 546–550.

King, R.A. (1985) The MS-DOS Handbook. Sybex, Berkeley, CA.

Krauss, R.M., Morrell-Samuels, P. and Hochberg, J. (1988) VIDEOLOGGER: a computerized multi-channel event recorder for analyzing videotapes. Behav. Res. Methods Instr. Comput. 20, 37–40.

Lehman, R.S. (1988) The languages we use. Behav. Res. Methods Instr. Comput. 20, 236–242.

Loftus, G.R., Gillispie, S., Tigre, R.A. and Nelson, W.W. (1984) An Apple II-based slide-projector laboratory. Behav. Res. Methods Instr. Comput. 16, 447–453.

Marshall-Goodell, B., Schreurs, B.G. and Gormezano, I. (1982) Ruler vs. Apple II/FIRST system analysis of analog signals in classical conditioning. Behav. Res. Methods Instr. 14, 519–525.

Merbitz, C.T., King, R.B. Bleiberg, J. and Grip, J.C. (1985) Wheelchair push-ups: measuring pressure relief frequency. Arch. Phys. Med. Rehab. 66, 433–438.

Moss, S.C. (1984) On-line Apple II for the recording and analysis of complex motor movements. Behav. Res. Methods Instr. Comput. 16, 19–24.

Naiman, A. (Ed.) (1983) Computer Dictionary for Beginners. Ballentine, New York.

O'Dell, J.W. and Jackson, D.E. (1986) The Commodore 64 and an interface system for controlling operant chambers. Behav. Res. Methods Instr. Comput. 18, 339–341.

Olivo, R.F. (1986) Selecting an analog-digital interface: a tutorial. Comput. Life Sci. Educ. 3, 83–93.

Olivo, R.F. and Thompson, M.C. (1988) Monitoring animals' movements using digitized video images. Behav. Res. Methods Instr. Comput. 20, 485–490.

Orr, J.L. (1984) Going FORTH in the laboratory. Behav. Res. Methods Instr. Comput. 16, 193–198.

Palya, W.L. (1988) An introduction to the Walter/Palya controller and ECBASIC. Behav. Res. Methods Instr. Comput. 20, 81–87.

Pear, J.J. (1985) Spatiotemporal patterns of behavior produced by variable-interval schedules of reinforcement. J. Exp. Anal. Behav. 44, 217–231.

Pear, J.J. and Eldridge, G.D. (1984) The operant-respondent distinction: future directions. J. Exp. Anal. Behav. 42, 453–467.

Pear, J.J. and Legris, J.A. (1987) Shaping by automated tracking of an arbitrary operant response. J. Exp. Anal. Behav. 47, 241–247.

Pevey, M.E. (1988) Using an IBM PC to network Walter/Palya experiment controllers. Behav. Res. Methods Instr. Comput. 20, 100–103.

Pisacreta, R. and Rilling, M. (1987) Infrared touch technology as a response detector in animal research. Behav. Res. Methods Instr. Comput. 19, 389–396.

Proffitt, D.R. and Kaiser, M.K. (1986) The use of computer graphics animation in motion perception research. Behav. Res. Methods Instr. Comput. 18, 487–492.

Reed, A.V. (1982) The Radio Shack Color Computer in the experimental Psychology laboratory. Behav. Res. Methods Instr. 14, 109–112.

Sainsbury, R.S. (1971) Effect of proximity of elements on the feature-positive effect. J. Exp. Anal. Behav. 16, 315–325.

Scandrett, J. and Gormezano, I. (1980) Microprocessor control and A/D data acquisition in classical conditioning. Behav. Res. Methods Instr. 12, 120–125.

Schull, J. and Kaminer, E.M. (1987) ESI: easy software interfacing tools for Turbo Pascal programming of digital input-output devices. Behav. Res. Methods Instr. Comput. 19, 199–204.

Silverman, R.W., Chang, A.S. and Russell, R.W. (1988) A microcomputer-controlled system for measuring reactivity in small animals. Behav. Res. Methods Instr. Comput. 20, 495–498.

Smarte, G. and Baron, N.M. (1988) Face to face. Byte 13(9), 243–252.

Snapper, A.G., Kadden, R.M. and Inglis, G.B. (1982) State notation of behavioral procedures. Behav. Res. Methods Instr. 14, 329–342.

Snapper, A.G., Knapp, J.Z. and Kushner, H.K. (1970) Mathematical description of schedules of reinforcement. In: W.N. Schoenfeld (Ed.), The Theory of Reinforcement Schedules. Appleton-Century-Crofts, New York, pp. 247–275.

Snodgrass, J.G., Smith, B., Feenen, K. and Corwin, J. (1987) Fragmenting pictures on the Apple Macintosh computer for experimental and clinical applications. Behav. Res. Methods Instr. Comput. 19, 270–274.

Solomon, P.R., Weisz, D.J., Clark, G.A., Hall, J. and Babcock, B.A. (1983) A microprocessor control system and solid state interface for controlling electrophysiological studies on conditioning. Behav. Res. Methods Instr., 15, 57–65.

Spencer, D.G., Jr. and Emmett-Oglesby, M.W. (1985) Parallel processing strategies in the application of microcomputers to the behavioral laboratory. Behav. Res. Methods Instr. Comput. 17, 294–300.

Stoddard, P.K. (1987) Inexpensive solid-state peck key for the operant conditioning of small birds. Behav. Res. Methods Instr. Comput. 19, 446–448.

Stoddard, P.K. and Loftus, G.R. (1988) An IBM XT-compatible, computer-based slide-projector laboratory. Behav. Res. Methods Instr. Comput. 20, 541–551.

Svartdal, F. (1986) LAB-FORTH software package. Behav. Res. Methods Instr. Comput. 18, 61–62.

Tanner, P.P., Jolicoeur, P., Cowan, W.B., Booth, K. and Fishman, F.D. (1989) Antialiasing: a technique for smoothing jagged lines on a computer graphics image–an implementation on the Amiga. Behav. Res. Methods Instr. Comput. 21, 59–66.

Vom Saal, W., Eckerman, D.A., Balsam, P. and McDaniel, C. (1984) Getting started with microcomputers in undergraduate education: hints and guidelines. Behav. Res. Methods Instr. Comput. 16, 144–146.

Walter, D.E. and Palya, W.L. (1984) An inexpensive experiment controller for stand-alone applications on distributed processing networks. Behav. Res. Methods Instr. Comput. 16, 125–134.

Watts, B.H. (1986) FORTH, a software solution to real-time computing problems. Behav. Res. Methods Instr. Comput. 18, 228–235.

Weisman, R. and Palya, W.L. (1988) Development and operating environments for a network of Walter/ Palya experiment controllers on the Macintosh computer. Behav. Res. Methods Instr. Comput. 20, 93–96.

Wightman, F.L. (1978) The minicomputer and research in hearing. In: M.S. Mayzner and T.R. Dolan (Eds.), Minicomputers in Sensory and Information-Processing Research. Erlbaum, Hillsdale, NJ, pp. 161–193.

Wright, R.D. (1986) Amiga 1000 hardware timing and reaction-time key interfacing. Behav. Res. Methods Instr. Comput. 18, 463–465.

Yourdon, E. and Constantine, L.L. (1979) Structured Design: Fundamentals of a Discipline of Computer Program and System Design, 2nd Edn. Prentice-Hall, Englewood Cliffs, N.J.

Zoloth, S., Dooling, R.J., Miller, R. and Peters, S. (1980) A minicomputer system for the synthesis of animal vocalizations. Z. Tierpsychol. 54, 151–162.

Experimental analysis of behavior, Part 2
Iversen and Lattal (eds.)
© *1991, Elsevier Science Publishers BV*

CHAPTER 6

Methods of analyzing behavior patterns

IVER H. IVERSEN

Department of Psychology, University of North Florida, Jacksonville, FL 32216, U.S.A.

1. Introduction

The scientific works of Pavlov, Thorndike, and Skinner have stood the test of time as important founding contributions to behavior analysis. These gentlemen are truly remarkable for their emphases on the scientific study of how the behavior of a single organism changes over time in an orderly way, depending upon experimental variables. Their data were reported as, for example, a single subject's drops of saliva plotted trial by trial (Pavlov, 1927), individual latencies of exit from a problem box (Thorndike, 1911), or cumulative presses on a lever plotted over a continuous time period (Skinner, 1938). These investigators rarely used average individual or group performance data and did not need to do statistical data evaluation because the obtained results were so striking to every observer. The inevitable, yet unexplained variability in behavior that occurred in their experiments, in spite of considerable regularity, only served as a source of inspiration for new experimentation to discover conditions that controlled the variability. This approach often is described as inductive because theoretical advances emerge from inspection of the data. The hypothetico-deductive approach, in contrast, focuses on formulating a theory or a hypothesis and in turn on designing experiments to generate data that will confirm or disconfirm the *a priori* expectation. The fit between theory and observation often is evaluated by means of statistical tests, and variability in data often is considered a nuisance rather than an inspiration.

Contemporary behavior analysis is a curious mixture of these approaches. The data handling methods developed by Pavlov, Thorndike, and Skinner, while certainly still practiced, often are combined with elements from the hypothetico-deductive method of averaging across subjects, conditions, or even groups of subjects. A description of contemporary methods of analyzing behavioral data will inevitably reflect this confluence of approaches. Many different trends characterize contemporary behavior analysis and some are even incompatible.

When data are averaged over N subjects to form a representative central tendency or mean, all N subjects are thereby treated as if they were equal in terms of the behavior they generate, when in fact they may be different. By averaging over the N subjects the variability among the subjects is ignored N times. In other words, a data analysis restricted to only the mean generates N degrees of ignorance. Once the behavior of individual subjects has been demonstrated to differ, subsequent aggregation of data across subjects reduces information and increases ignorance. Single-subject designs are used because data based on the individual subject are more accurate predictors of that individual's behavior than are data based on an average for a group of subjects. A similar logic pertains to the data from a single subject. One can provide a more accurate and useful prediction of what one subject will do at a given moment when data for that subject are analyzed in small time segments and conditional upon events within sessions than when data are based on an average for the whole session or from several sessions.

This chapter will present some examples of methods of analyzing patterns of behavior from the perspective of the inductive approach with an emphasis on the individual organism and close inspection of data. The chapter will cover some characteristic practices of data analysis that have been used extensively and some not-so-often used practices that take the investigator deep into the apparently chaotic infrastructure of behavior.

When analyzing behavioral data, an investigator can follow standard practices of data analyses or explore the data in novel, untried ways. The Experimental Analysis of Behavior is founded on the premise that behavior is orderly (Skinner, 1938). The goal for any investigator is to account for as much regularity in behavior as possible by pointing to critical environmental determinants of the behavior. Even when behavior appears irregular and chaotic one reasonably may presume that some uncontrolled determinants are responsible for the behavior patterns that one does see. The investigator's task then is to search for, rather than guess about, these determinants. In general, scientific discovery is said to stem from new accounts of previously disorderly data; a discovery can be made when such data are explained in terms of newly identified variables (Bernard, 1949; Sidman, 1960; Kuhn, 1970; Gleick, 1987). Indeed, new accounts of data may involve some form of reanalysis of well-known findings. Such new approaches may not necessarily be attractive at first because they can conflict with known and established ways of dealing with scientific information. Investigators who invest their efforts in examining systematic regularities in seemingly chaotic data therefore may face some hardship (Kuhn, 1970; Gleick, 1987).

A conflict of interest often faces the new investigator because the scientific community expects – and usually only accepts – reports of orderly data. Should time be spent on the disorderly data to possibly find some regularity that in turn may further a future understanding of the phenomenon at hand? Or should time be spent on producing reports that are acceptable immediately by conventional standards? Each new investigator faces this challenge (e.g., Bourdieu, 1975; Catania, 1981; Iversen, 1988).

Relevant sources on methods of collecting and analyzing data from the perspective of Experimental Analysis of Behavior are Baer and Parsonson (1981), Johnston and Pennypacker (1980), Parsonson and Baer (1978, 1986), and Sidman (1960). Several analysis methods for behavior patterns also have been developed by more ethologically oriented investigators (Sackett, 1978; Martin and Bateson, 1986; Suen and Ary, 1989). Martin and Bateson's short and easy introductory text is recommended for investigators new to the idea of analyzing behavior patterns. General sources on exploratory and graphical analyses of data are Cleveland (1985), Tufte (1983), Tukey (1977), and Wainer and Thissen (1981).

2. Local analysis of behavior

While overall response rate is reliable and useful as a measure of operant behavior, regularities in behavior do occur at more local levels. Local response rates refer to rate calculated over some time period shorter than the full session length. Several investigators have developed techniques to record and control local response rates directly. For fine-grained analyses of operant behavior, the time period studied can be as short as the time between two response instances. Indeed, in the words of Skinner (1938), "the main datum to be measured in the study of the dynamic laws of an operant is the length of time elapsing between a response and the response immediately preceding it or, in other words, the rate of responding" (p. 58).

2.1. Interresponse times (IRTs)

The time between two emissions of the same response often is called the interresponse time (IRT). Considerable research has been directed at determining the extent to which IRTs vary in an orderly manner and can be controlled by experimental manipulations (e.g., Anger, 1956; Blough, 1966; Morse, 1966; Shimp, 1969, 1979; Weiss, 1970; Silberberg et al., 1978; Platt, 1979; Gentry et al., 1983; Peele et al., 1984; Weiss et al., 1989). Based on the established sensitivity of IRT distributions to experimental manipulations, Platt (1979), Shimp (1979), and Weiss (1970) suggested that local changes in response rate are fundamental contributors to the overall response rate and therefore questioned the notion that overall response rate is the only way to deal with operant behavior.

2.1.1. Relative frequency, conditional probability and dwell time
To construct a frequency distribution of IRTs, one samples IRTs conditional upon their length. To determine the frequency of IRTs between say 1 and 2 s a count is

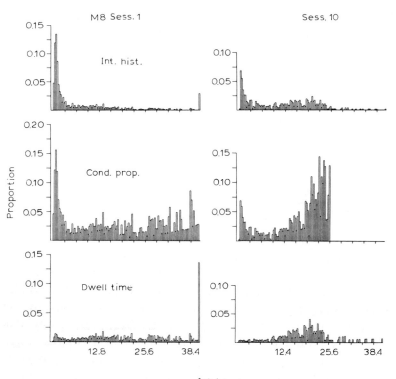

Irt (sec)

Fig. 1. Interresponse time (IRT) data from a monkey subject (M 8) responding under a DRL 20-s schedule of liquid (juice) reinforcement. IRTs were analyzed in 320 ms bins and are shown for Sessions 1 and 10. INT. HIST.: Interval histograms (relative frequency distributions) of IRTs. The number of IRTs in each class is divided by the total number of all IRTs. COND. PROB.: Conditional probabilities (interresponse times per opportunity, IRT/Op). The number of IRTs in a given class is divided by that number plus the number of all longer IRTs. DWELL TIME: Proportion of the session time spent by a given IRT. The number of IRTs in a given class multiplied by the class midpoint is expressed in proportion to the total session time. (Adapted from Weiss, 1970, with permission of the publisher.)

made each time an IRT within that range ends. This number is then divided by the total number of IRTs to yield the relative frequency of 1–2 s IRTs. IRTs are thus analyzed in classes of temporal intervals (e.g., 1–2 s, 2–3 s, 3–4 s etc.). The relative frequencies sum to 1.0. Relative frequency is a useful method of depicting IRT distributions because data from different phases of an experiment can be compared directly when the total number of IRTs changes across phases.

Fig. 1 shows three common types of IRT distributions. Data are from an experiment using monkey subjects pressing a lever under a differential-reinforcement-of-low-rate (DRL) 20-s schedule (Weiss, 1970); juice reinforcement was contingent on a pause between two consecutive lever presses of at least 20 s. Data in Fig. 1 are from Sessions 1 and 10 for one subject. The top interval histograms (INT. HIST.) show the proportion of IRTs in each interval, the relative frequency of IRTs. During Session 1, a peak is seen for very short IRTs. Summating the relative frequencies for the first 6 IRT classes (corresponding to IRTs shorter than about 2 s) yields a total relative frequency of approximately 0.5, indicating that half of all IRTs were shorter than 2 s. The last column of IRTs is a sort of 'wastebasket' that represents all excessively long IRTs, in this case IRTs longer than 41 s. By Session 10, a second peak occurs around the 20-s value and the relative frequency of short IRTs has decreased considerably, although there is still a peak at short IRTs (the total relative frequency of IRTs shorter than 2 s is now about 0.2). Notice that the excessively long IRTs have disappeared by Session 10.

Anger (1956) introduced another analysis of IRTs. He calculated the probability of terminating an IRT conditional upon the number of opportunities to terminate that IRT. This probability is called interresponse times per opportunity (IRTs/Op); see also Part 2, Chs. 1 and 7. When the probability of terminating an IRT is independent of the length of the IRT, the IRTs/Op is constant for all lengths of IRTs; deviations from a constant IRTs/Op therefore indicate differential control by time since the last response. The IRTs/Op is now more commonly called conditional probability and is calculated by dividing the number of IRTs terminating in a class by the number of IRTs in that class plus the number of all longer IRTs. Commonly, this measure is not reported when the denominator is less than some small number (e.g., 20). The middle graphs in Fig. 1 present conditional probabilities (COND. PROB.) calculated from the data in the interval histogram. For Session 1, the early peak is evident in the conditional probability plot. By Session 10, the conditional probability distribution peaks at around 20 s; given that about 20 s have passed since IRT onset, the probability of terminating an IRT increases considerably compared with the probability of terminating the IRT earlier, say after 10 s. The formation of the second peak in the conditional probability distribution usually is interpreted as an instance of temporal control by the DRL schedule. The bimodality of the IRT distribution is more evident in the conditional probability plot than in the interval histogram. Conditional probability calculations can be used, therefore, to analyze trends in the data that may be less apparent with relative frequency plots. (Notice that no data are given for IRTs longer than 25.6 s for Session 10 because fewer than 20 IRTs occurred in these classes.)

The lower graph presents the proportion of the total session time spent by a given IRT (DWELL TIME). The dwell time for a given IRT bin is a weighted IRT distribution calculated by multiplying the number of IRTs in a bin by the midpoint of the bin width (e.g., for the 4–5 s bin, the number of IRTs in that bin is multiplied by 4.5 s) and dividing by the total time allocated to all IRTs (see also Shimp, 1967). For Session 1, the proportion of the total session time occupied by the longest IRTs was thus about 0.14. The initial peak in the interval histogram is difficult to detect in the dwell-time analysis because those IRTs are so short. Even though half of all IRTs were less than about 2 s, their added duration is very short compared with the added duration of the fewer but substantially longer IRTs. Dwell time by Session 10 revealed a clear unimodal distribution with a peak around the DRL value of 20 s. Based on these findings, Weiss (1970) argued that in this experiment, dwell time was perhaps the most revealing index of temporal control of IRTs by the DRL schedule.

2.1.2. An example of microanalysis: fixed-interval responding

Distributions of IRTs customarily are summarized by the mean, median, or mode IRT. Sometimes, however, this practice may do injustice to the information regarding IRT control that can be available in the original distributions. Visual presentation of IRT distributions improves the analysis of behavior patterns by communicating considerably more information so that other investigators can confirm trends in the data that are not revealed by the summarizing statistics. Indeed, unheeded trends in the data may be discovered by other investigators. Fig. 2 presents a microanalysis of performance of one pigeon's key pecking maintained under a fixed-interval (FI) 5-min schedule (Gentry et al., 1983); the first response to occur after 5 min was reinforced. IRTs were analyzed in 100-ms bins and are plotted by ordinal position for the first 320 responses in the 5-min interval. Responses were grouped in fours to increase the sample size of IRTs. The height of each group's peak is the relative frequency of that IRT for that ordinal-response position. Gentry et al. (1983, p. 332) described their figure as follows:

> Several features of FI responding are revealed in this figure. First, there is a ridge of very short IRTs whose relative frequency changes little through the interval. Second, as responding proceeds, moderate IRTs rise in frequency. Third, there is a rapid drop in the relative frequency of very long IRTs as responding proceeds. One striking aspect of this figure is the lack of obvious acceleration that would be indicated by a mound of IRTs moving toward the shorter values. Instead, as the relative frequency of long IRTs decreases, the relative frequency of the shorter IRT modes increases. Plots based upon time from the beginning of the interval show similar relations.

This analysis illustrates how different interpretations of FI performance can be separated through microanalysis. When a cumulative record shows a progressively increased local response rate (a scallop), the customary interpretation is that the local response rate is positively accelerated through the interreinforcement interval (i.e., IRTs should decrease progressively through the interval). Data from a microanalysis would have appeared rather differently had this been correct; one would have expected a gradual progression of IRTs from long to short as a wave of peaks moving from the lower left corner to the upper right corner in Fig. 2. Instead, the microanalysis reveals a progressive change in types of IRTs. Long IRTs (5 s or longer) decrease in frequency quickly as a function of ordinal position and the frequency of IRTs slightly less than 1 s increases slowly; ultra-short IRTs (200–300 ms) occur at the same frequency at all ordinal response positions. In other words, the FI scallop results from a gradual shortening of pauses (long IRTs) that separate bursts of responding at a fixed local rate (clusters of short IRTs).

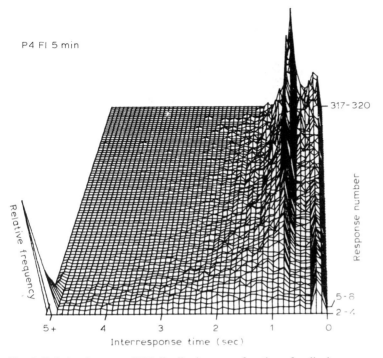

P4 FI 5 min

Relative frequency

Response number

317-320

5-8

2-4

5+   4   3   2   1   0

Interresponse time (sec)

Fig. 2. Relative frequency IRT distributions as a function of ordinal response position. Data are from one pigeon (Bird P4) responding under a FI 5-min schedule of food reinforcement. Responses are grouped by 4 to increase sample size; the first IRT after reinforcement is excluded, so the first group, 2–4, represents 3 IRTs only. The relative frequency in the last bin (5 + s) was decreased by one half to maintain perspective of the figure. The data represent responding for each FI period of 21 sessions (420 periods in all). (Adapted from Gentry et al., 1983, with permission of the publisher.)

2.1.3. The IRT as a unit of behavior

The IRT is not constant, but instead changes from moment to moment. A fundamental question is how this variation is controlled by the prevailing schedule of reinforcement. When specific IRTs are selected for reinforcement, the IRT distribution changes (e.g., Anger, 1956; Shimp, 1969). The susceptibility of IRTs to reinforcement argues in favor of considering the IRT as a dynamic property of behavior. The IRT therefore can be a functional unit of analysis but it is hardly an invariant or structural unit (e.g., Shimp, 1979; Zeiler, 1986; Arbuckle and Lattal, 1988). The importance of reinforcement of IRTs in interpretations of how schedules of reinforcement control behavior has been emphasized since Skinner (1938) and was the basis for studying several types of schedules in Ferster and Skinner (1957); see also Part 1, Ch. 3.

The issue of how reinforcement of IRTs determines overall response rate is illustrated by an example (Peele et al., 1984). Response rate is considerably higher under a variable-ratio (VR) schedule than under a variable-interval (VI) schedule with comparable overall reinforcement rates. Under VR, the distribution of reinforced IRTs peaks at very short IRTs with few long IRTs ever being reinforced. Under VI, on the other hand, reinforcement of longer IRTs is common. First, Peele et al. confirmed this difference in an experiment using pigeons as subjects. Next, the reinforcement of IRTs was manipulated so that under VI only short IRTs could be reinforced thereby making the VI similar to the VR in terms of distribution of reinforced IRTs. The overall response rate under VI changed and became similar to that under VR. Peele et al. then reversed the manipulation and made the distribution of reinforced IRTs under VR similar to that seen under regular VI. The overall response rate again changed so that the VR and VI performance became similar. Peele et al. concluded that IRT reinforcement accounts for the higher overall response rate under VR schedules than under VI schedules.

IRTs also have been subjected to sequential analyses to determine the extent to which the length of an IRT depends upon the length of the preceding IRT (e.g., Blough, 1963; Shull, 1971; Shimp, 1973; Real, 1983; Weiss et al., 1989). The analysis can be extended further to involve the time between two different responses such as the pecks on two keys; Silberberg et al. (1978), for example, studied sequences of left and right key pecks in pigeons under different arrangements of concurrent reinforcement schedules.

3. Levels of analysis

Levels of analysis refer to how much data are averaged for a conceptual unit. Considerable diversity exists in the literature regarding what should be proper conceptual units of analysis. Response rate has served well, and important functional relations have been determined at the level of responding averaged over hours or days. Conceptual analyses at levels that encompass even more data have gained ground. For example, the mean rate of responding over the last 5 sessions of each of 10 different experimental conditions may be plotted against the values of the manipulated variable. Next, the slope of the function relating the 10 mean response rates to the 10 values of the experimental variable is calculated, and this single number now represents a higher-order conceptual unit of analysis. Theoretical advances often are stated in terms of such molar analyses of the data. Several examples of this approach are described in Part 1, Ch. 6 and Part 2, Ch. 7.

The molar analysis typically is contrasted with what is called a molecular analysis. While neither type of analysis has ever been well defined, molar usually refers to aggregation of data over relatively long time periods (e.g., whole-session data) whereas molecular refers to collection of data over shorter time periods (e.g., within-session data); time periods are most often left unspecified in theoretical discussions. Another difference is the method of treating variability in data. When a molar analysis sums data over several sessions, within-session variability will cancel or neutralize when averaged. On the other hand, a molecular analysis may focus on this variable data and try to determine functional relations in moment-to-moment patterns of behavior by sampling behavior across time segments with similar antecedent conditions. The molar and molecular methods of analysis engender different types of results and focus on different types of controlling variables. Functional relations established with either method of analysis should be considered valid within the domain of the analysis method used but may not be valid within the domain of different analysis methods. That is, a principle established at the molar level may not hold at the molecular level, and vice versa.

Debates over levels of analysis are not unique to operant conditioning. Gleick (1987) discussed the notion of self similarity, which refers to the generality of a scientific principle regardless of level of analysis, or scale. If a principle, true at one scale, also is true at other scales, then the principle is self similar. When the same functional relation holds at the next level of magnification, the function is general. But when each change in scale brings about a new phenomenon, the choice of scale is of course crucial. How one's choice of scale or level of analysis influences the conclusion one draws from data will be illustrated with two empirical examples from the literature on stimulus generalization and concurrent reinforcement schedules.

3.1. Overall versus local generalization gradients

Generalization gradients obtained in stimulus control research often are assumed to be direct measures of sensory capabilities. The relevant issue is whether the shape of a gradient is the same for different scales of analysis or methods of data sampling. Gray (1976) asked the basic question of self similarity in an assessment of stimulus control along a dimension of wavelength in pigeons (see Part 1, Ch. 7 for methods of stimulus generalization). Pecking a key with a 570-nm visual stimulus was reinforced with grain on a DRL 8-s schedule. The stimulus was presented in 45-s trials with 3-s intertrial intervals (dark key). To determine the degree of stimulus generalization to other wavelengths after this single-stimulus training, 12 test stimuli were presented, one at a time, in 45-s trials; during these trials pecking the key was not reinforced. The wavelength of the test stimuli ranged from 560 to 582 nm in 2-nm steps (including the 570 nm stimulus). To maintain responding over several sessions, additional trials with the original training stimulus (570 nm) were interspersed with the test stimuli and pecking was reinforced on the DRL 8-s schedule during these trials. Gray first provided an overall analysis of the data. The mean number of responses emitted to each of the 12 test stimuli was calculated over the last 18 sessions of testing. The top data in Fig. 3 present the obtained gradients showing percent of total responses at each stimulus value for 5 birds. These data suggest that stimulus control (peaked gradients) was obtained for two birds only (Birds 4 and 5). The remaining 3 birds responded to the test stimuli in practically the same way as they did to the training stimulus and thus showed little evidence of stimulus control (i.e., their gradients were almost flat).

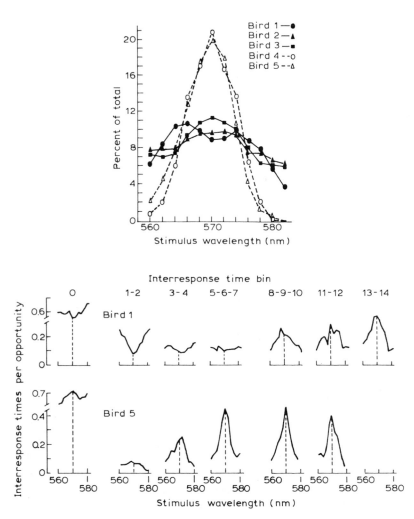

Fig. 3. Generalization gradients to visual stimuli after single-stimulus (570 nm) training on a DRL 8-s schedule of food reinforcement. *Top*: Percent of total responses to each of 12 stimuli during extinction for each of 5 pigeons. Data are based on 18 days of steady-state generalization with reinforced trials at the training stimulus (570 nm) interspersed with the test stimuli. *Bottom*: Generalization gradients calculated for interresponse times per opportunity for different lengths of interresponse times. Bin 0 corresponds to 0–1 s IRTs, Bin 1 to 1–2 s IRTs, etc. Data are presented for Birds 1 and 5. (Adapted from Gray, 1976, with permission of the publisher.)

To search for other evidence of stimulus control, Gray analyzed the data at a smaller scale to see if responding in different classes of IRTs might be controlled differently by the wavelength stimuli. The IRTs were classified into 16, 1-s bins (labelled 0–15). Next, for each bin Gray calculated the IRTs/Op (i.e., the number of IRTs in each bin was divided by the number of IRTs in that bin plus the number of IRTs in all longer bins; see Section 2.1.1). The results of this analysis of stimulus control conditional upon IRT bin are presented for Birds 1 and 5 in the lower part of Fig. 3. IRTs/Op are presented for each wavelength and for groups of IRT bins. The shape of the gradients evidently depends upon which IRT bin you look at. For the shortest IRTs of 0–1 s (Bin 0), the gradient is virtually flat for each bird. The next class, 1–2 s IRTs, produced an inverted (V-shaped) gradient for Bird 1 and a flat gradient for Bird 5. For classes of longer IRTs, the gradients progressed from flat to steep with a peak at the training stimulus.

The results of this more detailed analysis reveal that the conclusion one draws about stimulus control depends upon how one looks at the data. For Bird 1, in particular, an analysis based on all responses shows no stimulus control (top graph in Fig. 3). In contrast, an analysis that divides this class of 'all responses' into subclasses based on IRT length shows that the wavelength did indeed control responding. Peaked gradients were obtained for IRTs close to or longer than the reinforced IRT (8 s). But flat or inverted gradients were obtained for very short IRTs. Gray (1976) suggested that "rate of response is not an appropriate measure of stimulus control in the DRL situation [because] averaging responses regardless of IRT length obscures evidence of stimulus control" (p. 206). In Gray's experiment, wavelength did not control overall response rate but instead controlled the distribution of IRTs. Different scales of measurement thus generated different conclusions about the controlling variables of the response.

More generally, one cannot necessarily assume that all responses or all IRTs are controlled in the same manner by the manipulated stimuli during stimulus generalization. Therefore, flat or intermediate slopes of gradients do not, by nature, reflect absence of control. Instead, they may reflect the investigator's averaging of several rather different response categories. For further illustrations of this issue see Blough (1965), Gray (1976), Ray (1967), Ray and Sidman (1970), Stoddard and Sidman (1971), and for a literature review see Bickel and Etzel (1985).

3.2. Overall versus local relative response rate

Relative response rate has become a common way of presenting data from experiments involving two operanda, as in concurrent reinforcement schedules (e.g., Part 1, Ch. 6). For example, two VI schedules can be arranged simultaneously, one on each operandum. The relative rate between the two responses on the two separate operanda is determined by dividing the number of responses to one key by the total responses to both keys. Usually, only the relative rate for one response is presented. If all responses occur to Key 1 then the relative rate to that key is 1.0. When no responses occur to Key 1 (but some, at least one, occur to Key 2) then the relative rate to Key 1 is 0.0. The relative rate is 0.5 if equal numbers of responses occur to each key. With concurrent schedules, relative response and reinforcement rates customarily are sampled over the whole session and then averaged for the last several sessions of each experimental condition. An often reported finding is that the overall relative response rate matches the relative reinforcement rate (e.g., Herrnstein 1961, 1970). This means, that if, for example, 75% of the reinforcers are presented for responding on Key 1, then one can predict that 75% of the responses are emitted to Key 1. Herrnstein's Matching Law has been influential in the area of operant conditioning and has generated a considerable amount of theoretical and empirical work on choice (see Part 1, Ch. 6 and Part 2, Ch.7).

An important question regarding generality is whether the principle of matching is self similar. In other words, does the relative response rate stay the same for time periods shorter than the full session length? To answer this question, some investigators have analyzed relative response rates at scales smaller than the whole session. The importance of levels of analysis for the generality of the matching principle has been debated often (e.g., Herrnstein and Vaughan, 1980; Real, 1983). One critique of analyzing relative response rates only at the level of the whole session is that the matching of overall relative response and reinforcement rates may in fact result from averaging over many choices, no one of which obeys the matching principle (Shimp, 1969). A striking example of this problem was provided by Silberberg and Fantino (1970). Pigeons' pecking on two keys was maintained by food on concurrent VI VI schedules with a changeover delay (COD). The COD is a short time period after a changeover from one key to the other during which a reinforcer cannot be delivered; the COD usually is programmed to prevent rapid alternation between the keys (see Part 1, Ch. 6). Generally, pigeons peck the key faster during the COD than after the COD (Catania, 1966). Silberberg and Fantino asked the basic question of self similarity: Do these different local relative rates of pecking during and after the COD each match the overall relative reinforcement rates as does the overall relative re-

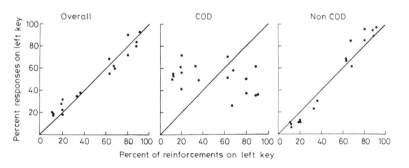

Fig. 4. Relative response rate on the left key under a two-key concurrent VI VI schedule of food reinforcement as a function of relative reinforcement rate. *Left*: Overall relative response rate. *Middle*: Relative response rate during the changeover delay (COD) only. *Right*: Relative response rate during non-COD periods only. Each point represents the performance of a single pigeon averaged over the last 5 sessions of a single procedure (6 pigeons each had 3 procedures). The overall relative reinforcement rates were varied across 3 experimental conditions and the COD was fixed for each pigeon but varied among the 6 pigeons from 0.88 s to 3.5 s. (Adapted from Silberberg and Fantino, 1970, with permission of the publisher.)

sponse rate? To answer this question, Silberberg and Fantino sampled key pecks conditional upon whether they occurred during a COD or after a COD. Thus, three types of relative response rate were calculated: Relative rate for the whole session, relative rate during COD periods only, and relative rate during non-COD periods. The 3 diagrams in Fig. 4 relate each of these relative response rates to the overall reinforcement rate (expressed as percent of reinforcements on the left key). The relative reinforcement rate was manipulated across several values in different conditions of the experiment.

Considering all responses in the session, regardless of whether they occurred during COD or non-COD periods, relative response rate matched relative reinforcement rate, as the left-hand diagram indicates. However, when relative rate during COD only was plotted against overall relative reinforcement rate (middle diagram), the relative response rate was unaffected by the reinforcement rate. For the non-COD periods, the relative rate did increase with the relative reinforcement rate, but also deviated systematically from strict matching, as the right-hand diagram reveals. In fact, for most points, more non-COD responses occurred on the key providing more reinforcement than would be expected by strict matching. So, this data analysis indicates that the manipulated reinforcement rate had different effects upon COD and non-COD responses. Silberberg and Fantino concluded that matching occurred on a gross level although it did not occur for either COD or non-COD responses. Overall matching occurred when COD and non-COD responses were added together. Silberberg and Fantino discussed the possibility that overall matching is an artifact of averaging responses that have different relations to the experimental variables. Apparently, a key peck occurring during a COD is different from a key peck occurring after the COD.

Although overall relative response rates change in an orderly manner as a function of several variables, local relative response rates also may change in an orderly way rather than remain constant or vary haphazardly. Different scales of analysis may provide different information regarding choice behavior. As progress generally proceeds from little to more information, a broader understanding of concurrent performances may be obtained as investigators more routinely include within-session response changes for analysis and control. For related analyses of momentary response changes in concurrent schedules see Henton and Iversen, (1978), Hinson and Staddon (1983), Real and Dreyfus (1985), Shimp (1979), and Silberberg et al. (1978).

3.3. Theoretical levels of analysis

Levels of data analysis can have profound implications for how one formulates a general statement, let alone a theory, about behavior. Consider two Responses A and B that can occur in the same 1-hour time segment. If Response A occurs at a rate of 30 resp/min and Response B at 60 resp/min, one could use this data as support for an argument, based on a molar analysis, that Response B has a higher 'value' than Response A. The explanatory concept of value is meant to be static. A procedure that increases the value of Response B should increase the rate of Response B and perhaps decrease the rate of Response A. If the data-sampling strategy is changed so that the responses are instead sampled and analyzed in very short time segments, say 1-min periods, Response A may dominate in some intervals even though Response B has a higher overall rate. The static notion of value pertains only to the overall measure of behavior and is not meant to wax and wane from one moment to the next. Therefore, value does not explain why Response A occurs more often than does Response B during some intervals. To explain the local variation in responses one needs to find a determinant that changes at that level. Such a determinant may differ conceptually and dimensionally from the overall explanatory variable of value. Different levels of data analysis thus may engender very different levels of explanation too.

The issue of levels of analysis is embedded in practically all conditioning techniques. As an example consider the following experiment (Iversen, 1981). Rats' lever pressing was first reinforced on a VI schedule. Next, the procedure was changed to that of signalled delay of reinforcement so that a 2-s signal preceded each reinforcer delivery. When a reinforcer was set up by the VI schedule, the next lever press turned on the signal and the reinforcer was delivered 2 s later. The signal was a light located directly above the lever. The typical result of adding a signalled delay to reinforcement is a reduction in overall response rate. One level of explanation would suggest that the delay procedure reduced 'response strength', hence the lowered response rate. In a search for an explanation at another level, the rats were observed directly. The new behavior of orienting toward the signal source had been generated by the change to signalled reinforcement. This behavior occurred not only during the signals but also frequently in the absence of the signal and thereby interrupted lever pressing substantially. The reduction in response rate generated by the signalled delay procedure could thus be explained rather differently by invoking the actual response of observing the signal source. This experiment illustrates the conflict between different levels of analysis. Using strength, one attempts to explain behavior at a level where behavior does not occur. Strength is not on par with responding versus not responding at a given moment. By referring to the generation of an observing response, on the other hand, one invokes an explanation that is on par with the response to be explained. The observing response occurs in a dimension that is the same as that of lever pressing, and the presence versus absence of observing can be identified at any point in time.

Skinner (1950) addressed the conceptual implications of different levels of behavior analysis:

A third type of learning theory is illustrated by terms like preferring, choosing, discriminating, and matching. An effort may be made to define these solely in terms of behavior, but in traditional practice they refer to processes in another dimensional system. A response to one of two available stimuli may be called choice, but it is commoner to say that it is the result of choice, meaning by the latter a theoretical pre-behavioral activity. The higher mental processes are the best examples of theories of this sort; neurological parallels have not been well worked out. The appeal to theory is encouraged by the fact that choosing (like discriminating, matching, and so on) is not a particular piece of behavior. It is not a response or an act with specified topography. The term characterizes a larger segment of behavior in relation to other variables or events (p. 210).

4. Partitioning behavior

A difficult issue in behavior analysis is selection of the proper unit of a response (e.g., Thompson and Zeiler, 1986). Pragmatic considerations have allowed behavior to be divided into brief instances (e.g., key pecks and lever presses) as easy 'on-off' units, which are convenient to measure and count. However, Skinner (1953) warned that the ultimate continuous nature of behavior must not be forgotten. Some techniques that examine continuity of behavior are outlined below.

4.1. Descriptive and functional operant

A given response instance is measured in terms of some of its physical properties, and reinforcer delivery is contingent upon certain criteria within these properties. Catania (1973) noted that some confusion can stem from a failure to recognize that responses may change in properties other than those upon which the reinforcer depends. Catania suggested a distinction between the descriptive and the functional operant. The descriptive operant refers to the defined, measurable physical properties of the response class for which consequences are arranged. A simple example for pigeons is the class defined as responses that activate the switch attached to the key. Pecks can differ in location, force, duration etc., but as long as they activate the switch they belong to the descriptive class. The functional class, on the other hand, is the class of responses generated by the consequences arranged for responses in the first class. Pecks that start to occur at a force too weak to activate the key, at too short a duration, or at places other than on the key etc., are members of the functional class in addition to the pecks that activate the key. The usual measures of key pecking or lever pressing do not always do justice to the many dimensions of responding that may be affected by a contingency between only one response dimension and reinforcement.

4.2. Off key pecking

When a pigeon's peck on a key is reinforced with food, the pigeon will not only peck the key frequently but also peck surrounding areas, next to the key. This off key pecking can be so prevalent in some procedures that the paint or finish of the surrounding wall wears off from thousands of off key pecks. Because only pecks on the key

Fig. 5. Carbon-paper recording of pigeons' off key pecking under a negative automaintenance procedure. Both keys were lit green for 8 s; food reinforcement occurred at the end of trials unless either key was pecked. Data are shown for 2 pigeons (Birds 687 and 696) and are based on one 50-trial session. (Adapted from Barrera, 1974, with permission of the publisher.)

produce the reinforcer (the descriptive operant), off key pecking is a type of behavior that is generated indirectly through the direct reinforcement of pecking the key. Pecking the key and off key pecking together constitute the functional operant because both are generated by the peck-reinforcer contingency. Observing such behavior is a simple matter, but measuring and analyzing it is a challenge. Bachrach (1966) placed layers of paper and carbon paper around the key; off key pecks thereby left marks on the paper corresponding to their location. Fig. 5 illustrates carbon-paper scatter records of the spatial pattern of off key pecking for 2 of 8 pigeons from an experiment with food-omission contingencies (Barrera, 1974). After varying intertrial intervals 2 keys were lit green for 8 s, and if no peak occurred to either key, food presentation followed offset of the light; however, if a peck occurred to either key while green, food presentation was omitted and the lights turned off. Gradually, after an initial high rate of pecking one or both of the green keys, pecking ceased and the reinforcement rate increased. All pigeons persisted, however, in off key pecking on the wall around one or both of the keys. These visual displays vividly relate the extent of this aberrant behavior, which normally is ignored because it is not recorded. Without these data, the conclusion is that peck-contingent food omission suppresses pecking; with these data, however, the conclusion is that pecking is not suppressed but instead redirected. The carbon-paper method also can be used to measure the location of pecking on the key (Skinner, 1965; Jenkins and Sainsbury, 1970). With a different procedure, using key-peck contingent shock presentation, which generally suppresses food-reinforced key pecking in pigeons, Dunham et al. (1969) similarly observed off key pecking and arranged for this pecking to be recorded automatically by a sensing plate surrounding the key. With this method the frequency, but not the spatial location, was the measured property of off key pecking.

4.3. Spatial response location

The notion of the functional operant as somehow encompassing more than the descriptive operant raises some fundamental questions about operant behavior. How much wider is the functional class than the descriptive class? Or, more concretely, how far away from a key will a pigeon peck when only pecks to the key are reinforced? Is the boundary between what is explicitly reinforced and what is observed fixed for a given response? Or does the boundary vary with the experimental conditions? Is the variability in responding within the functional operant determined in some way or simply irrelevant noise that can be disregarded? These questions have been asked routinely in behavior analysis and have led to development of techniques for the control and analysis of moment-to-moment behavior changes. Some of these techniques are categorized below with respect to the number of response dimensions involved.

4.3.1. Response location in one dimension

Measuring the spatial location of a response has been accomplished using a variety of devices (e.g., Antonitis, 1951; Herrick, 1964; Eckerman and Lanson, 1969). For a high resolution of peck location, Hori and Watanabe (1987) used a 22×2 cm horizontal key. The exact location of a peck on this key was measured via a TV camera located above the box. Each detected key peck stored a digitized image of the peck's location in a microcomputer with a processing time of only 40 ms. Interestingly, this system's accuracy in detecting peck location was checked visually by using the carbon-paper method mentioned above. The relative frequency distributions of peck location along the key are presented for two experimental conditions for one pigeon in Fig. 6. Using a discrete-trial procedure, the houselight turned on and a single key peck within a 1-cm target area was reinforced with food; pecks outside this target turned off the houselight and initiated a timeout period. First, when the target area

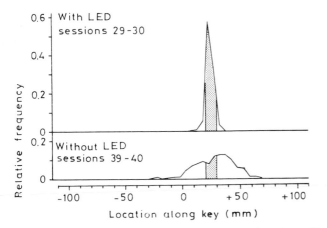

Fig. 6. Relative frequency distributions of peck location along a 22×2 cm horizontal key for one pigeon. Trials were indicated by the houselight; pecking the target area (shaded) was reinforced with food. With LED, the target area was lit; without LED, the target area was not lit. Location 0 indicates the center of the key. The resolution of peck detection allowed for 5-mm class intervals. (Adapted from Hori and Watanabe, 1987, with permission of the publisher.)

was lit during trials (LED), the location distribution was narrow with the majority of the pecks occurring within the target area (on 80–90% of the trials). Next, without the target lit during trials, pecking occurred over a much wider area with only 28–32% of the pecks within the target. The presence versus absence of the target light thus affected the frequency of pecking outside the target area. The variation in peck location was symmetrical around the target area in all conditions. These data illustrate the difference between the descriptive and functional operant. The distribution of responses in the class of the functional operant conforms closely to the boundary set for the descriptive operant (shaded area) when the target was lit. But without the target lit, the distribution of the functional operant is considerably wider than that of the descriptive operant. The width of the functional operant thus is dependent upon exact procedural details and not a characteristic of the subject or the response.

4.3.2. Response location in two dimensions

Allan and Zeigler (1989) compared two automated methods of sampling response location in two dimensions around a target area. With one method, an array of infrared light emitters and detectors is arranged to form a matrix of horizontal and vertical beams, as shown at A in Fig. 7. This matrix is placed in front of a response surface, pecks on which are recorded with microswitches (B in Fig. 7). With the second method, a Mylar touch panel is positioned on the surface of a computer monitor (C in Fig. 7), which is accessible through a response window. With both arrangements, a 2.54 cm circular white stimulus is rear projected onto the response surface. In a test of the detection systems, one pigeon was exposed to a discrete-trial fixed-ratio (FR) 10 schedule of food presentation. While the stimulus was projected on the response surface during trials, reinforcement was contingent on 10 pecks but independent of peck location. Peck location was monitored continuously. The infrared device was used first for 30 sessions and then the Mylar touch device was used for 10 sessions. The location data are presented in 3-dimensional frequency distributions in Fig. 8 for the two detection devices for one pigeon. The lower diagram shows the relative position of the stimulus. For each plot the height of a spike shows the frequency of pecks at that location. For the Mylar device (A) there are more but shorter spikes than for the infrared device (B) because of the higher resolution for the Mylar device. For both devices, the majority of the pecks are distributed around the upper left border of the target. The percent of pecks falling within the stimulus was 33.6 for the Mylar device and 38.0 for the infrared device. In a final condition using the infrared device, peaks were only reinforced for locations within the stimulus; the percent of pecks falling within the stimulus then increased to 61.0 (data are not shown) indicating that the contours of the two-dimensional response map were sensitive to differential reinforcement of peck location. Related automated analyses of spatial response location in two dimensions have been implemented in a wide range of experimental situations for rats, pigeons, and monkeys (e.g., Blough, 1977; Clauson et al., 1985; Scott and Platt, 1985; Iversen and Mogensen, 1988; Rumbaugh et al., 1989).

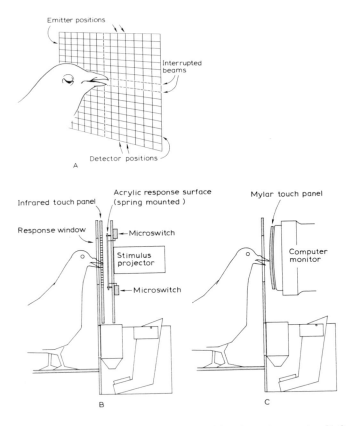

Fig. 7. (A) Schematic view of a pigeon pecking through a matrix of infrared beams. Infrared emitters are positioned on the top and on the left side of the matrix with corresponding detectors positioned opposite the emitters. Dashed lines represent interrupted infrared beams. The emitters and detectors are spaced every 0.588 cm. With the beaks open, adjacent beams may be broken simultaneously and a peck is recorded as a point midway between the two adjacent beams. This feature increases the effective resolution of the device to 0.279 cm. (B) Schematic view of the infrared touch location system, indicating positions of the front panel with a 10 × 12 cm response window, the infrared touch panel, the spring-loaded acrylic response surface with 2 of the microswitches, and the stimulus projector. (C) Schematic view of the Mylar touch device. The touch panel is attached to the computer monitor. The surface of the device is covered with an additional thin sheet of Mylar to protect it from damage caused by repeated beak contacts. (Adapted from Allan and Zeigler, 1989, with permission of the publisher.)

4.3.3. Response location in three dimensions

Tracking a given response automatically in space is a difficult task. By using visual observational technique alone one can obtain a great deal of information about a subject's behavior. But continuously tracking the spatial coordinates of a response in quantitative terms has to be performed automatically to be accurate and reliable. Pear and his associates (Pear and Eldridge, 1984; Pear, 1985; Eldridge and Pear, 1987; Pear and Legris, 1987) have designed a computer-controlled system that con-

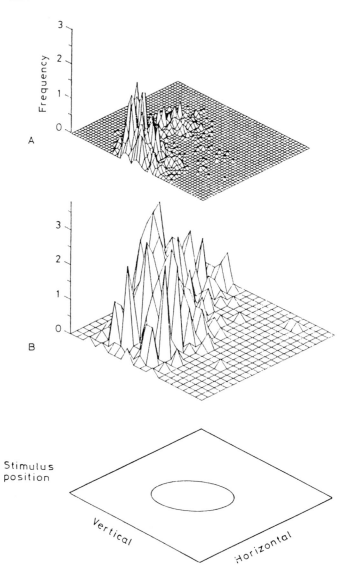

Fig. 8. Response location data for the last 5 sessions of each condition. (A) Mylar detection device. (B) Infrared device. Differences between the grid representations of the two devices reflect the higher resolution of the Mylar screen. Because the pigeon's responses tended to be confined to a small area of the grid, the data represent only a subset of the total number of locations accessible through the response windows. (Reproduced from Allan and Zeigler, 1989, with permission of the publisher.)

tinuously tracks the head of a pigeon. Two TV cameras, perpendicular to two adjacent transparent walls of the chamber, are connected to video-analyzing equipment. The white pigeon's head is painted black and, because the rest of the chamber is white as well, the black spot detected by the TV cameras is the pigeon's head. The design

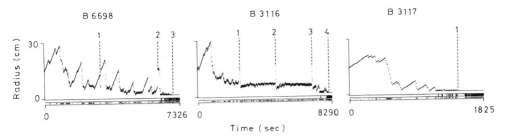

Fig. 9. Data showing automated shaping of a pigeon's behavior of placing the head inside an invisible 3-cm sphere of fixed location. Data are the radius of the shaping sphere, which contracted or expanded depending upon the distance between the pigeon's head and the target sphere. Each data point represents an average of 3 1/30 s periods. All shaping sessions and one additional session are shown for 3 birds (session number is indicated in numerals, 1–4). Vertical marks in the top band below each graph indicate target responses (head in the target sphere). Marks in the bottom band indicate reinforcements. Notice that the time scales are different for the 3 pigeons. (Reproduced from Pear and Legris, 1987, with permission of the publisher.)

was used to track head movement in various behavioral procedures such as shaping, VI schedules, extinction, multiple schedules, and autoshaping.

In one experiment on automated shaping (Pear and Legris, 1987), an arbitrary, fixed, 3-cm diameter spherical region was the invisible target location for the pigeon's head. To shape the target response (placing the head inside the sphere), a shaping sphere, concentric with the target sphere, was programmed to expand or contract depending on the pigeon's behavior. When the pigeon's head contacted the shaping sphere, a reinforcer was presented and the radius of the sphere contracted by 1 cm; for every 10 s without a contact with the shaping sphere, the radius was expanded by 0.25 cm. Fig. 9 presents automated shaping of placing the head within the invisible target sphere, which occurred within 1 to 4 sessions for 3 pigeons. Data show moment-to-moment changes in the radius of the shaping sphere. The radius increases when the pigeon's head is far from the target and decreases when the pigeon's head makes contact with the shaping sphere. This method combined video recording with precise specification of an effective shaping parameter to control moment-to-moment changes in behavior during shaping.

Digitized videodisplays will no doubt be used more often as computer analysis of the images will become easier with advances in technology. Spruijt and Gispen (1983) described a method for automated monitoring of rat behavior. Every 4th s a digitized picture of a rat's behavior was stored as a screen image in the computer's graphic memory. Based on the parameters on the videodisplay, the software detected human-defined behavior categories such as grooming, sitting, sleeping and rearing.

A similar technique was developed by Kernan et al. (1980) whereby 40 separate behavior acts in monkeys were automatically monitored and analyzed. Three video cameras, one from each of two sides and one from the top, simultaneously sent images to video discriminators, which in turn converted and sent the signals to a com-

214

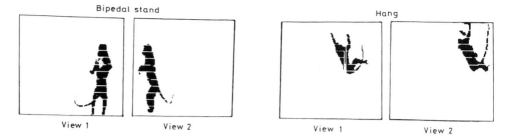

Fig. 10. Examples of digitized images of behavioral acts in a monkey as seen from two video cameras. Bipedal stand and hang were behavioral acts identified automatically via the computerized pattern recognition system. (Adapted from Kernan et al., 1980, with permission of the publisher.)

puter. The automated pattern recognition method is complex and will not be described here. Fig. 10 presents examples of the digitized videoimages from the two side cameras of specific behaviors that could be detected automatically. Kernan et al.'s system classified the 40 behavior acts with a reliability comparable to that of trained human observers. With a more recent development for rat behavior (Kernan et al., 1987; Kernan et al., 1989), the automated pattern recognition system can sample behavior at a rate of one frame per second. Apparently, these techniques have not been used for operant conditioning research but are obvious candidates for future developments of research on, for example, shaping and response differentiation.

4.3.4. Multi-dimensional response classes

A conditioned response does not occur in only a single location. Variability in response location seems inevitable and has been considered important enough to warrant advances in automated techniques that quantify this aspect of behavior in great detail. For example, a response-reinforcer contingency generates more than the response topography necessary for reinforcer delivery. A given response is rarely repeated with the exact same force, duration and location. Yet, the typical key peck or lever press is treated as if the same response is repeated over and over as when we speak of rate of responding. The apparent inconsistency here stems from the fact that the repeated responses have several elements in common such as striking a key, yet differ in some other properties such as location or duration. The response class is defined by some of the common elements, usually consequences such as activating a certain detection device. Studying only one kind of element of the response may lead to conclusions that do not pertain to other elements. The variability in response location portrayed above provides visual aids to an understanding of the difference between descriptive and functional operants (cf. Section 4.1). Consider the data in Fig. 6 from Hori and Watanabe's (1987) experiment. The peck-food contingency generated pecks not only within but also outside the target area. These pecks were never reinforced, yet persisted. The class of functional operants thus encompasses not only pecks to the target area but also pecks outside. In addition, other elements of pecking, such as duration or force, may be functionally related to the peck-food contingency and would similarly be part of the functional operant. Thus, the operant response has many dimensions only few of which are studied customarily. The technology seems to be available for mapping of response classes and a conceptual step forward from the operant as being a one-dimensional response class to the operant as a set of response classes or a multi-dimensional response class.

4.4. Methods of analyzing response differentiation

Even though responses in one class are defined as having one characteristic in common, usually a consequence, they do differ in other respects. For example, if all pecks to a key activate the microswitch and are reinforced, then they have that property in common, but pecks could still be unevenly distributed on the key's surface so that 10% occurred to the lower half and the rest to the upper half of the key. If one arranged the contingency of reinforcement so that pecks would be reinforced only when they occurred to the lower half of the key, the pigeon would shift the distribution of pecks to that part of the key. This differentiation of peck location within the class of key pecking is an essential feature of operant conditioning. Several studies are available on differentiation of response rate, duration of response episodes, inter-response times, response location, and even beak separation in pigeons. Two studies are described in detail below. The first is a classic analysis of large-scale differentiation of spatial response location. The second is a novel analysis of small-scale differentiation of beak separation.

4.4.1. Differentiation of response location
Using pigeons as subjects, Eckerman et al. (1980) arranged 20, 1.2-cm wide keys horizontally on one wall of a chamber with a feeder opening beneath. Pecks were recorded separately for each key. In all conditions, pecks were reinforced only if they occurred to either of two adjacent target keys; all keys were illuminated evenly. The location of the target keys was changed systematically across sessions. First, the target was the two rightmost keys. Then the target location was displaced in steps of 1, 2, 3 or 6 keys per step. For example, with 3 keys per step, the target would move over 3 keys between sessions starting at the rightmost position. From session to session, the target location continued to step toward the left until the leftmost pair of keys became the target. Then the target would step back toward the right. The procedure of displacing the target from one outer position to the other (e.g., from right to left) is called one sweep.

Some of the complex data generated by this procedure are presented in Fig. 11. Data are from one pigeon at step size 3. Absolute frequency distributions of peck location are presented for each step from the first sweep at step size 3. For each step, the distribution for pecks emitted prior to the 25th reinforcer (initial performance) is shown as a frequency polygon without Xs, and the distribution of pecks during

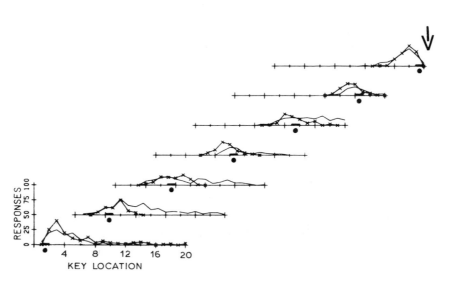

Fig. 11. Frequency of pecks at each of 20 locations on a strip of keys. The target location (2 adjacent keys) moved along the strip in steps of 3 keys between sessions. The target locations are indicated by a dot under the abscissa. Data are shown for the first sweep. The distribution of pecks emitted prior to the 25th reinforcer at a location (initial performance) is shown as a frequency polygon without Xs; the distribution during the last 25 reinforcers (final performance) is shown as a frequency polygon with Xs. Data are from one pigeon (Bird 433). (Adapted from Eckerman et al., 1980, with permission of the publisher.)

the last 25 reinforcers (final performance) is shown as a frequency polygon with Xs. Each target location is indicated by a dot under the abscissa. Because each target covers two adjacent keys, the frequency of pecks to these two keys always totals 25 for each distribution.

Starting at the beginning of the sweep (arrow in Fig. 11), the initial and final distributions overlap because the pigeon has had extensive prior training pecking this target location. In the next session the target is moved 3 keys to the left. The initial distribution shows a peck at the previous target location from the session before but also pecks at keys to the left of this location. This variability in peck location generated by non reinforcement of pecks to the prior target allows some pecks to be reinforced at the new target location. The final distribution of pecks at the new target location is shifted to the left compared with the initial distribution. In general, a similar process takes place each session; the initial distribution peaks around the prior target location, and the final distribution peaks around the current target location. Across sessions, the two distributions thus move along the key-location dimension in accord with the movement of the target location.

An important precursor for successful differentiation of response location is some degree of variability in location, seen as the relative width of the initial distribution at each step. If this distribution is not wide enough to cover the new target location, then pecks will extinguish, and the distribution will not shift. Eckerman et al. found that the widths of both initial and final distributions increased with step size. Degree of variability around a prior target therefore is not a fixed property of behavior but can be determined explicitly by experimental arrangements.

The data-presentation technique developed by Eckerman et al. (1980) is an excellent example of an effective analysis of an enormous amount of data representing variable behavior under several experimental conditions. Average peck location would have been a poor representative of the obtained performances. Once the basic procedure is understood, Fig. 11 effectively communicates how the shifting criterion for one component of the response class (peck location) changed the frequency distribution of that component. For related work see Galbicka and Platt (1989).

4.4.2. *Differentiation of beak separation in pigeons*

An important question regarding generality of response differentiation would be to determine whether scale of analysis matters. The spatial domain of peck location can be considered wide because the whole body has to move. A much narrower scale would be differentiation of individual response components. A given response instance can be considered an assembly of discrete components rather than a unitary response. For example, the pigeon's key peck may be analyzed into locomotion, head transport, and beak separation. These components are mediated by different effector systems and therefore might be dissociated experimentally. To determine if response differentiation holds at this much smaller scale of analysis, so that one component may be conditioned to change while the others remain the same, Deich et al. (1988) measured beak separation and key contact (pecking) separately. Beak separation is anatomically different from key contact because beak separation is not mechanically constrained by key contact (i.e., the key can be contacted with open or closed beak). Fig. 12A depicts Deich et al.'s technique. A Hall-effect device, which outputs a voltage corresponding to the strength of an applied magnetic field, was fixed on the upper beak and a small magnet under the lower beak. After pretraining with intermittent reinforcement of key pecking, baseline values of beak separation were determined during discrete-trial continuous reinforcement. A trial began when a key was lit red. The first peck to the red key was reinforced with food and turned the light off. After 2 s a new trial began, etc. Next, larger or smaller interbeak distances were differentially conditioned. For larger distances (up), the criterion for reinforcement was that the associated interbeak distance should be in the 80th percentile of the distribution of distances for the preceding session. Conversely, differential reinforcement of smaller distances (down) required that distances were in the 20th percentile of the distribution for the preceding session. Fig. 12B presents relative frequency distributions (percentages) of interbeak distance (gape) during initial baseline and for the final session

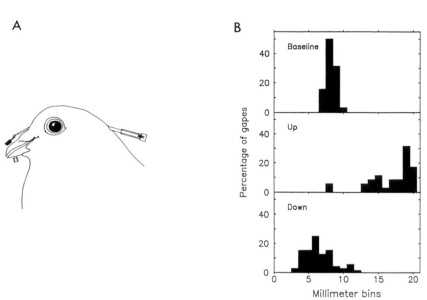

Fig. 12. (A) Diagram of the Hall-effect assembly of a samarium-cobolt magnet on the lower beak and a Hall-effect IC on the upper beak. The electrode assembly exiting the scalp was connected to a swivel linking the Hall-effect device on the pigeon to the monitoring equipment while leaving the pigeon free to move. (B) Relative frequency distributions of interbeak distances (gapes) during baseline, differentiation of larger distances (Up), and differentiation of smaller distances (Down). Data are shown for one pigeon (Bird 85-01). (Adapted from Deich et al., 1988, with permission of the publisher.)

of each response differentiation condition for one bird. Relative to baseline, differential reinforcement of beak separation produced clear shifts in the frequency distributions with enlargement of beak separation when the criterion went up and lessening of beak separation when the criterion went down. The frequency distributions for up and down were practically non overlapping. In addition, each differential reinforcement procedure induced interbeak distances that were absent during baseline. Almost all beak separations were larger under upward conditioning than under baseline, and more than 50% of the beak separations were smaller under downward conditioning than under baseline. Note that this induction of new interbeak distances is not necessary to produce reinforcement. Hence, once again, new response instances were generated outside of the criterion required for reinforcement (i.e., the functional operant is a wider class than the descriptive operant, Section 4.1).

The data demonstrate that even a subtle, small scale, motor movement, such as beak separation, can be brought under operant control by contingencies of reinforcement. This successful bidirectional differentiation (both up and down) of beak separation in the pigeon confirms that response differentiation as a process is general across different levels of analysis. An interesting parallel can be drawn between this differentiation of small-scale motor movement in pigeons and the differential conditioning of infinitesimal thumb contractions in humans (Hefferline and Keenan, 1963).

Entirely new combinations of response topographies, never seen before in a subject's response repertoire, can be generated through the systematic application of response differentiation techniques. Response differentiation is one of the most powerful methods Experimental Analysis of Behavior has to offer for it allows the experimenter to change the form of existing behavior (see Part 1, Ch. 2). The dynamic properties of operant behavior are probably defined and also restricted by the processes of response differentiation. Galbicka (1988), in a review of response differentiation, similarly argued that "response differentiation is an integral part of all operant conditioning. Response differentiation is operant conditioning, and vice versa" (p. 343).

5. Multi-behavioral analyses

The data analysis methods engendered by results from experiments where the topography of only one response is recorded can become quite complex, as indicated above. But when two or more responses are recorded, the analysis often is seen as formidable. As with one-response analyses, the data can be analyzed at many levels. One can record the total frequencies of several responses and convert them to proportions. On the other hand, one can analyze how the responses relate to each other, how a change in one response at one moment affects the remaining responses in the next moment. An emphasis upon the patterning and sequences of several behaviors requires detailed data analyses that are demanding and time consuming. Yet, such analyses can reveal data indicating that patterns and sequences among multiple recorded behaviors are orderly and controllable rather than random or haphazard.

Some of the earliest systematic multi-behavioral approaches were those of Wendt (1936) and Zener (1937) who interpreted inhibition of conditioned reflexes as competition among different behaviors. More recently, the sequential structure and conditional organization of measured responses in the domain of Pavlovian conditioning have been documented by several investigators (e.g., Ray and Brown, 1975; Henton and Iversen, 1978; Henton, 1981a, 1981b; Holland, 1988). Within the area of operant conditioning, the multi-behavioral approaches have dealt primarily with sequential structures among two operants (e.g., Silberberg et al., 1978), temporal control of schedule-induced behaviors (e.g., Staddon and Simmelhag, 1971; Staddon, 1977; Roper, 1978), competition among behaviors (e.g., Dunham, 1971, 1972; Henton and Iversen, 1978), behavior-field analyses of extinction (Wong, 1977; Osborne and Black, 1978), and mediational properties of collateral behavior during spaced responding (e.g., Laties et al., 1965; McIntire et al., 1983).

5.1. Observing and recording multiple behaviors

Multi-behavioral analyses are complicated by the fact that behaviors of differing to-pographies are recorded simultaneously. A wide range of approaches has been tried and new technological developments allow for continuous improvements. Delprato (1986), Henton and Iversen (1978), Lyon (1982), Ray and Delprato (1989), and Thompson and Lubinski (1986) have reviewed and discussed different multi-behavioral analyses.

5.1.1. Visual observation

The simplest approach is to observe the subject during an experimental session. Most sound-attenuating chambers have a peephole through which one can see the subject. A further step is to add a television camera so that behavior can be monitored at distance or videotaped. The playback of a video can be synchronized with a clock so that response episodes can be timed in duration and with respect to scheduled events (e.g., Epstein, 1985). In an experiment where autogrooming in vervet monkeys was reinforced with food, Iversen et al. (1984) transcribed behavior from a videotape. Scratching was reinforced with food on a VR-5 schedule with the stipulation that the same form of scratching could not be reinforced on two successive occasions; this was done to generate variability in form of scratching. Reinforcers were delivered by an experimenter while the subject was monitored during the session. After sessions, the videotape was replayed several times until 3 observers agreed upon the transcript; as part of the analysis the tape was replayed in slow motion as well. Fig. 13 presents a transcript of the first part of one session and identifies the body location scratched and the hand or foot used for scratching. Each symbol identifies one bout. Filled and unfilled circles refer to scratching with the right and left hand, and filled

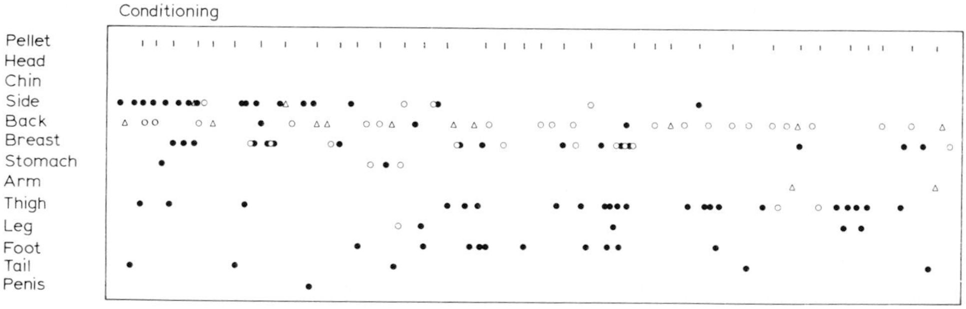

Fig. 13. Behavioral record showing individual bouts of scratching for one monkey during a session of conditioning of scratching on a VR 5 schedule with the stipulation that the same scratching form could not be reinforced successively. Scratching form is shown with respect to location on the body. Symbols indicate the hand or foot involved in the scratching burst. Filled circles: right hand; unfilled circles: left hand. Filled triangles: right foot; unfilled triangles: left foot. Marks in the upper row indicate pellet deliveries. (Adapted from Iversen et al., 1984, with permission of the publisher.)

and unfilled triangles refer to scratching with the right and left foot. The first symbol thus represents scratching the side with the right hand. Pellet deliveries are indicated by marks in the upper row. The frequency and variety of scratching can be read directly from the graph. Considering each combination of area scratched and hand or foot used in scratching as a separate form, 18 different forms occurred. This method of recording and collecting behavioral data should be useful in situations where topographical variability is at issue. In our experiment, we could not predict which new form of scratching would be induced by the contingencies because the objective was to vary the form of scratching. Yet, any form the subject emitted could be retrieved from the videotape, given a name, and counted.

5.1.2. Transfer of observational information to quantitative data

Several experimenters have combined observational technique with automated recording. The observed behaviors are recorded indirectly. One method is to press an electric switch each time a given response occurs. The switch closure can be used as a direct input to electronic equipment. Thus, the duration and frequency of bouts of a given behavior can be recorded and compared with other behaviors that are recorded automatically. Consider an experiment designed to provide an exhaustive record of the amount of time a rat spends exploring, grooming, and standing in addition to the amount of time spent lever pressing, contacting a food cup, and licking a water spout. The latter 3 responses can be recorded automatically. The first 3 can be determined by visual observation. One switch is activated each time and for as long as exploration occurs, a second switch when grooming occurs, and a third switch when standing occurs. These responses must be defined so that the criteria for recording are the same from session to session. When more than two switches are used, however, some measurement errors invariably occor. Because the objective is to provide a complete account of the observed responses, the observer cannot look away from the subject. As a consequence, the observer may on occasion press the wrong switch. Therefore, a system must be used so that manual recording can proceed without looking at the switches. The use of a modified joystick has been a successful method for the author. The stick can move in 4 directions. Four switches inside the joystick correspond to the 4 positions of the stick. Movement of the stick in one direction activates one switch only. Each direction of the stick is associated with a separate response to be recorded and looking at the joystick while recording therefore is unnecessary. The differential feedback from the movement of the stick in space has proven sufficient to prevent errors in recording that can occur when several switches are arranged in a line.

5.2. Automated recording

Several techniques are available to record responses other than the prototypical lever press or key peck. The most common techniques involving touch detectors and photocells to record water drinking and hoppertending are described in Part 1, Ch. 1 and Part 2, Ch. 5. Less commonly used methods are described here.

Experimental chambers with several compartments date back to the multiple activity cage for rats designed by Richter (1927). With modern designs, switches in the floor detect which compartment the rat visits at a given time (e.g., McIntire et al., 1983). The type of activity specific for the compartment, such as licking or running in a wheel, can be recorded as well. Floorboards that monitor pigeons' positions through switches beneath the floor also have been used (Killeen, 1975; Matthews and Lerer, 1987). Similar arrangements can monitor spatial location of mice (Henton and Spohn, 1980). In a black box with fluorescent houselight, 9 photocells in the ceiling were calibrated so that the reflection of the white mouse in a specified area activated the photocell above. The subject's position could be analyzed on a moment-to-moment basis using this procedure (Henton 1981a, b).

A subject's proximity or orientation to a feature in the environment such as a stimulus source, a food cup, or a lever can also be recorded with several types of photocell devices or with proximity detectors. Typically such arrangements are custom made (e.g., Zucker, 1969).

A unique method of recording several responses incorporates the movements of the subject directly. Henton (in Henton and Iversen, 1978) fixed a directional light emitter to the midline of the skull of rats. Photocells were placed at various critical locations within the chamber such as near the food cup and near the source of a discriminative stimulus. In addition, photocells were placed beneath the transparent floor to record downward orientation of the head. Because of the singular source of light (on top of the rat's head) the activation of a given photocell corresponded to the rat's activity at a given moment. Blough (1977) reported a similar approach using pigeons. A photocell was mounted on the bird's head, and light sources at different places within the environment emitted different flicker rates of infrared light. When a pigeon oriented in the direction of a particular source, the photocell on the pigeon's head generated a particular flicker rate, and the direction of observation could be recorded. These innovative techniques can be arranged to record a variety of behaviors, all automatically.

The possible simultaneous use of the various methods of automated recording mentioned above combined with the newer approaches of computer analysis of digitized videoimages (e.g., Kernan et al., 1980; Spruijt and Gispen, 1983; Pear and Legris, 1987; Kernan et al., 1989) may allow for detailed, accurate, and completely automated monitoring of subject behavior during experimental sessions. With the recent advances of computers, sophisticated analyses of the complex data generated from such procedures may soon become familiar research tools.

5.3. The event recorder

On-line displays of multiple behaviors during sessions can be provided through the use of multi-channel event recorders. The event recorder advances the recording paper at a constant speed, and several recording pens can displace either briefly or continuously depending upon the input. The event recorder can simultaneously record different responses and their relation to one another and to experimental variables. The sequences and patterns of the recorded responses are apparent immediately on event records for the trained observer. Event records therefore are as useful as cumulative records (Part 1, Chs. 1 and 3) for monitoring progress during sessions and for data analysis and display.

Considerable information about how two or more responses are interrelated can be revealed on event records. Fig. 14 presents an event record showing 2 responses of one pigeon. Pecking the left of two keys was reinforced on a VI 120-s schedule with a limited hold of 3.6 s, and a signalled VI 120-s operated on the key to the right. Observing responses toward the right key were recorded with a photocell under the key; a single houselight was positioned so that movements of the head toward the right key would occlude the photocell. In addition to the event records, Fig. 14 presents the IRT distribution of pecks on the left VI key. The event record shows that VI-key pecking (Trace A) occurred in clusters of several pecks interrupted by longer IRTs. These long IRTs usually occurred when the bird oriented toward the other key, as indicated on Trace B. The signalled VI schedule on the right key thus influenced the pattern of pecking the left VI key by controlling orienting toward the right key

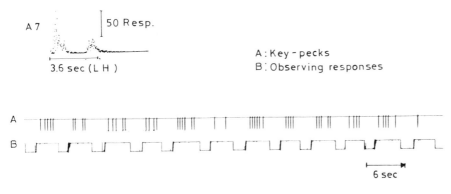

Fig. 14. Event record showing pecks on one key maintained by food under a VI 120-s schedule with a limited hold (LH) of 3.6 s. With a LH, the reinforcer set up on the VI schedule is available only for the time specified by the LH; if no response occurs during the LH, the VI timer advances to the next interval and the reinforcer set up is cancelled. A signalled VI 120-s schedule operated on a second key. Each time the signalled VI schedule set up a reinforcer the second key was lit white and a peck was reinforced; this results in pecking only during the signal. No signals happened to occur during the 80-s event-recorder segment shown here; hence, signals and pecks on the second key are not shown. Observing toward the second key was recorded by a photocell placed under that key. When the pigeon's head extended toward the second key the photocell was occluded from the single source of houselight. (A) Pecks on the left key with VI and LH. (B) Occlusion of the photocell under the right key with signalled VI. A frequency distribution of IRTs in pecking the VI key is presented above the event record. IRT width is indicated with respect to the LH. Data are from one pigeon (Bird A 7). (Data are from an unpublished experiment by Iversen.)

224

in the absence of the signal. The limited-hold contingency on the VI schedule also affected the pattern of responding. Episodes of observing rarely were longer than the 3.6-s limited hold. In turn, the long IRTs associated with observing the right key were just under 3.6 s, as indicated by the second peak of the IRT distribution. The event record illustrates the vivid interplay between the two topographically dissimilar responses.

Event records also can demonstrate how experimental events control several responses on a moment-to-moment basis. Interactions between lever pressing reinforced with food on an FR 60 schedule and water drinking in rats are shown in Fig. 15. With free access to a water tube, licking typically will occur during the pause after FR reinforcement. The experimental question was whether a dislocation of licking from the postreinforcement period into the run period of the FR schedule might produce a simultaneous dislocation of the pause in FR responding (Henton and Iversen, 1978). A retractable drinking tube was placed near the lever so that licking and lever pressing could occur simultaneously. Access to licking was manipulated by inserting

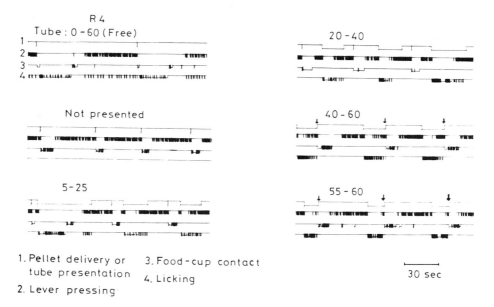

1. Pellet delivery or   3. Food-cup contact
   tube presentation   4. Licking
2. Lever pressing

30 sec

Fig. 15. Sample event records showing the effect of dislocating collateral licking to within the run period of lever pressing under an FR 60 schedule of food reinforcement. Numbers refer to ordinal location of access to a retractable drinking tube. The procedural conditions each lasted several sessions and were: Free access to the tube (0–60), no access, tube only accessible from the 5th to the 25th lever press (5–25), from 20 to 40, from 40–60, and from 55–60. A brief deflection of Pen 1 indicates pellet delivery; an extended deflection indicates tube position (except for free access). When tube retraction and pellet delivery coincide (i.e., at the 40–60 and 55–60 tube positions), pellet delivery is indicated by an arrow. Pen 2 shows lever presses, Pen 3 food-cup contact, and Pen 4 licking the tube. All behaviors were recorded automatically. Data are from one subject (Rat R 4). (Adapted from Henton and Iversen, 1978, with permission of the publisher.)

the tube at different positions within the FR schedule, as indicated in Fig. 15. With free access, licking occurred in an extended burst after pellet delivery with a considerable pause in lever pressing. With the tube not presented licking was absent, of course, and the FR pause was relatively short. With the tube available at a position within the FR run (e.g., from the 5th to the 25th lever press) the lick burst moved. This dislocation of the lick burst entirely changed the typical 'break and run' pattern of FR responding. The pause after reinforcement contracted, and a new pause appeared at the position of the lick burst. Such response interactions can be verified directly, 'on the spot', on the event records as they occur, without any other type of data analysis. Evidently, the hallmark of FR performance, the break and run pattern, may be modified instantly by altering the pattern of a single collateral response.

To illustrate the rich information segments of event records can provide, a few additional features of the response–interaction data in Fig. 15 are highlighted. First, the lick burst and the associated pause in lever pressing are decreasing functions of the ordinal position of the lick burst within the FR schedule. Second, with free tube access licking occurred in two patterns, an extended burst after the pellet and brief bursts during the period of high lever pressing rate. Third, with the tube not presented, the bout of food-cup contact that followed pellet delivery expanded compared with free tube access, indicating some interaction between licking and food-cup contact as well. Fourth, with the 5–25 tube position, the postreinforcement pause was shorter than when the tube was not presented, indicating that tube presentation also may strengthen lever pressing. This latter finding points to the dual role of licking; lever pressing is suppressed during periods where licking occurs but can be facilitated during periods leading up to water access.

5.3.1. Measuring from event records

Event records not only provide visual impressions of the patterns of responding, they also allow detailed measures of the temporal and sequential organization of the various responses recorded. Thus, event records provide information that can be sampled depending upon theoretical perspective. One can measure the length of individual bouts of responding by placing a ruler along the record and convert the distance to time. Time between bouts can be measured similarly.

Direct measurement on event records may appear time consuming and unnecessary especially with the advent of computers. To measure behavior in detail using a computer, however, the investigator needs to know in advance what the computer should search for. Initial careful inspection and measurement of multi-behavioral organization from event records can save considerable amounts of time otherwise spent programming. More important, event records may reveal patterns and trends that otherwise might go unrecognized. In a short period of time one can get an impression of the behavioral organization from simple measurements on the event record. The following example from an experiment I conducted illustrates this issue.

Lever pressing in rats was reinforced with food according to a VI 60-s schedule.

The objective of the experiment was to determine time allocation to collateral responses, which are not-explicitly reinforced responses. Lever pressing, proximity to the lever (i.e., being within a distance of 1 mm), contact with the food cup, and running in an activity wheel were recorded automatically by switches, drinkometers, and proximity detectors. Exploration, standing on hind legs, and face and body grooming were recorded by observational technique using the joystick method described above. While observing the subjects I noted that whenever a rat began body grooming, the bout would last several seconds, and the associated IRT in lever pressing therefore would be relatively long. This observation suggested that individual IRTs might be predicted based upon which collateral response occurs at IRT onset, i.e., right after a lever press. To verify this possibility, I measured each individual IRT on the event record and determined for the IRT which collateral response occurred within 0.5 s after the lever press. Thus, IRTs were sampled conditional upon which collateral response occurred at IRT onset. If the rat remained near the lever, the ensuing IRT was noted on one sheet for lever proximity. If the rat began running in the wheel within 0.5 s after a lever press, the IRT was noted on a separate sheet for wheel running, and so on for all 7 collateral responses. After collecting data for about 50 IRTs, the pattern in the data was clear. Short IRTs occurred when the rat remained near the lever, intermediate IRTs occurred when the rat changed over to sniffing the food cup or to running in the wheel, and long IRTs occurred when the rat began body grooming. This meant that IRT length was conditional upon the type of collateral response that occurred at IRT onset. Put simply, I could predict roughly the length of a given single IRT based upon what else the rat did right after having pressed the lever. Of course, all IRTs were measured eventually from the event records and for several rats (see Henton and Iversen, 1978). Yet, the initial impression of differential prediction of individual IRTs from measuring just a handful of IRTs for one rat was sufficient to motivate a substantial analysis of all IRTs. Frankly, without the success of this impetuous analysis, I would not have undertaken the very time consuming complete analysis.

5.3.2. Future of event records

As for cumulative records, event records are not presented for scientific communication as much now as they used to be. This is unfortunate because behaviors other than the single operant come to life on event records. A pause in operant responding is not a dead space implying lack of behavior. For example, through inspection of event records of properly recorded multiple behaviors, the action of an 'inhibitory' stimulus may be understood as changes in concurrent behavior rather than in terms of inhibitory processes inferred from changes in only one response. With experience, the viewer of event records can determine quickly how several responses are interrelated by glancing at the record. In fact, after years of working with event records one can almost see the subject responding in much the same way as musicians after years of working with musical notation report almost hearing the music when glancing at a score.

Event records force the viewer to examine the behavioral data in real time. One can find patterns and sequences that are not expected, and one can measure directly from event records how experimental events affect the behavioral composition. The lawfulness that may exist in behavior from one moment to the next can be determined and verified solely by inspection of event records. As with cumulative records, event records have a direct authority because they are in fact made by the experimental subject and therefore minimize questions regarding objectivity in data collection and presentation. Perhaps the most important aspect of event records is that when they are used as a vehicle for data presentation, other investigators can inspect the data directly and come up with interpretations on their own. Event records thus serve an archival purpose and may be used to answer unexpected questions.

5.4. How to analyze multi-behavioral data

Given the complexity of multi-behavioral data, general strategies of analysis will not be presented here. Instead, selected examples will illustrate some attempts at studying interactions and sequences among different responses.

5.4.1. Response interactions

When several responses are recorded simultaneously a common way to present the data is to calculate the time allocated to each response. Access to one response can be manipulated and the changes in time allocated to the remaining responses can be determined (e.g., Dunham 1972; Dunham and Grantmyre, 1982; Lyons and Cheney, 1984).

Changes in time allocation can be assessed at several levels of analysis from overall session allocation to allocation in particular time zones within sessions. With FI schedules, for example, time allocation to different responses can be shown as a function of time within the interval. Fig. 16A shows data for one rat from an experiment by Roper (1978) where lever pressing was reinforced with food on an FI 60-s schedule. Roper recorded eating, drinking, general activity, wheel running, grooming, visits to the food tray, and lever contact. Data are shown for each recorded response and are presented as frequency of occurrence. Availability and time within the interreinforcement interval determined where the different responses occurred. With free access to both drinking and running, drinking followed eating and was replaced gradually with wheel running. With free access to drinking only, drinking expanded and general activity peaked earlier in the interreinforcement interval; grooming partly replaced wheel running. Toward the end of the FI period, lever pressing increased in frequency along with visits to the food tray while running, grooming, and general activity decreased in frequency.

A time zone also can be defined with respect to ongoing behavior. Thus, time allocation to one response can be analyzed in relation to pauses in a second response.

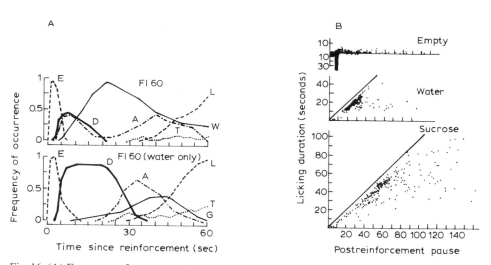

Fig. 16. (A) Frequency of occurrence of each activity as a function of time since food reinforcement delivered contingent on lever pressing on an FI 60-s schedule. E = eat; D = drink; A = general activity; W = in running wheel; T = visit food tray; L = contact lever. Activities in which frequency of occurrence failed to exceed 0.05 have been omitted. Data are from one subject (Rat 4). (Adapted from Roper, 1978, with permission of the publisher.) (B) Scatter plots of licking duration and individual postreinforcement pauses in lever pressing maintained under an FR 60 schedule of food presentation. A water bottle connected to a spout near the lever contained water, was empty, or contained a 2.5% sucrose solution in different phases of the experiment. With an empty bottle the frequency distribution of pauses without licking is shown as an inverted histogram (i.e., the descending Y-axis shows frequency of pauses without licking). Data are the last 200 pauses for each condition and are shown for one subject (Rat R1). (Adapted from Iversen, 1976, with permission of the publisher.)

Fig. 16B presents the results of such an analysis. Under an FR schedule of food reinforcement for lever pressing in rats, access to water was manipulated so that the bottle was either empty, contained water, or a mild sucrose solution. The time allocated to individual bouts of licking was analyzed during all time zones defined as the postreinforcement pauses in lever pressing (i.e., time from pellet delivery to initiation of lever pressing). Each dot in Fig. 16B thus shows an individual pause and the associated duration of licking. Data are presented for one rat for the last 200 pauses of each conditon (Iversen, 1976). With the bottle empty, licking did not occur in most pauses; the downwards-pointing Y-axis shows a frequency distribution of pauses without licking. With water in the bottle, licking occurred in practically all pauses and pause length correlated with lick duration except for some very long pauses. With sucrose in the water, lick length increased considerably and the postreinforcement pauses expanded correspondingly. These methods of data analysis are useful in assessing moment-to-moment interactions among different responses.

5.4.2. Response sequences

Response sequences have been analyzed in many different procedures. An impressive

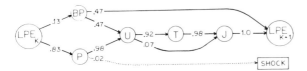

Fig. 17. Conditional probabilities of different activities during lever press avoidance (response-shock inter-val = 15 s, shock-shock interval = 5 s). LPE = lever pressing; BP = back paw lever holding; P = prone posi-tion; U = upward movement; T = turning; J = jumping. Low-probability behaviors have been omitted for clarity, so the sum of the probabilities at each fork may sum to less than 1.0. Data are shown for one subject (Rat 47). (Adapted from Hann and Roberts, 1984, with permission of the publisher.)

early work analyzed sequences of lever pressing and approach to the food tray in rats responding on a continuous reinforcement schedule (Frick and Miller, 1951). Using automated recording of each response, clear patterns of sequential dependen-cies emerged in the data. Frick and Miller stated that "taking sequential dependen-cies into account materially decreased uncertainty regarding the individual animal's behavior" (p. 24). Sequential analyses reveal some degree of pattern or order in the recorded behavior that enables predictions of behavior that surpass those based on response rate alone. A more recent example will illustrate a typical multi-behavioral analysis method. Hann and Roberts (1984) studied lever press shock avoidance in rats (see Part 1, Ch. 5). Rats were videotaped and tapes were analyzed by different observers. Fig. 17 shows the sequential pattern of responses between consecutive lever presses for one rat. The calculation of transition probabilities is basically sim-ple. If 100 lever presses occur and 40 are followed by jumping and 60 by turning, then the transition probabilities from lever pressing to these two responses would be 0.4 and 0.6, respectively. The rat chosen for display was avoiding well with a lever pressing rate of 10.3 resp/min and a shock rate of 0.21 shocks/min. The most typical sequence between successive lever presses was prone position/upward movement/turning/jumping (P-U-T-J). Even though prone position was most likely to be fol-lowed by upward movement (0.98), prone position was nonetheless the only response that reliably preceded shock. This observation questions the notion that lever press-ing occurs because it is the only response not followed by shock. In fact, prone posi-tion was the response most likely to follow a lever press. Different compositions were obtained for the remaining 5 rats, but all rats developed reliable sequences rather than random patterns. Hann and Roberts suggested that avoidance responding should be viewed within a context of sequences of activities or response chains. Anal-yses of response chains may be critical for an understanding of why some rats are poor at avoidance tasks. In addition, how drugs and toxins affect avoidance behavior may be elucidated further through response-chain analyses.

5.4.3. Assessing generality of response patterns
Using observational technique and measuring response patterns from event records

230

pose a particular challenge regarding observer bias. However, when particular response patterns established through observation and hand measurement can be replicated later by other investigators using automated recording and analysis, then these response patterns become general findings. Consequently, the issue of observer bias becomes of minimal importance when findings can be replicated either by other observers or by automated recording.

The experiment related above (Section 5.3.1) regarding prediction of individual IRTs based on observational technique in fact was replicated by another investigator using completely automated recording of all responses and computerized data analysis (Henton, 1985). Rats' lever pressing was maintained by food under a VI 50-s schedule. Wheel running, water drinking, and food-cup contact were measured automatically. Separate distributions of IRTs were recorded for IRTs initiated by a changeover to each of these collateral responses. Fig. 18 gives the distributions of all IRTs regardless of collateral response (top row) and the distributions of IRTs conditional on which collateral response occurred after a lever press. Consider first lever press IRTs initiated by wheel running (second row). These IRT distributions differ from the distribution based on all IRTs. When wheel running occurred, IRTs were generally in the last bin of longer than 10 s. A changeover to drinking similarly en-

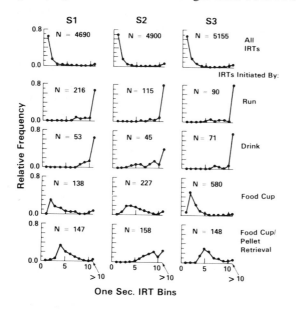

Fig. 18. Distributions of interresponse times (IRTs) in lever pressing maintained under a VI 50-s schedule of food reinforcement. Top row shows distributions of all IRTs. Rows 2–5 show distributions of IRTs initiated by a changeover to wheel running, drinking, food-cup response in the absence of pellet delivery, and food-cup response after pellet delivery. For all distributions, relative frequency is the number of IRTs in each 1-s bin divided by the total IRTs in all bins (N). IRTs at 10 s or greater are combined in the final bin of each distribution. Data are from each of 3 rats. (Reproduced from Henton, 1985, with permission of the publisher.)

gendered a distribution that peaked at the longest IRTs. For IRTs initiated by food cup activity not associated with pellet retrieval, IRT distributions peaked at relatively short IRTS. Last, IRTs initiated by food-cup activity at pellet retrieval peaked at intermediate IRTs.

5.4.4. Levels of analysis in multi-behavioral data

The final example of data analysis indicates that degree of prediction in behavior analysis may improve instead of getting worse as investigative efforts are expanded into moment-to-moment analyses of response sequences.

In an experiment with rats pressing a lever for food pellets under a VI 60-s schedule, I recorded exploration, standing, wheel running, face grooming, body grooming, food cup contact, and lever contact (Iversen, 1986). Table 1 presents overall sequential dependencies among these responses. (Lever pressing was immersed in lever contact and is not identified separately in the Table). The transitions from all episodes of each response were calculated. Rows show transition probabilities from one response ($N-1$) to each of the other responses (N). Because the behavioral record was exhaustive, a transition from one response to itself was not defined (hence the diagonal blanks). Columns show conditional probabilities of a changeover to one response (N) for each of the immediately preceding responses ($N-1$).

The first row shows that explore was followed more often by lever activity ($p=0.5$) than by any other activity. Run, on the other hand, was followed by lever activity almost exclusively ($p=0.95$), as indicated in the third row. The conditional probabili-

TABLE 1

Sequential dependencies between recorded responses in conditioning for Rat 4

$N-1$		Explore	Stand	Run	Face groom	Body groom	Lever activity	Food-cup activity
Explore	(198)		0.30	0.17	0.02	0.00	0.50	0.01
Stand	(36)	0.11		0.17	0.03	0.00	0.61	0.08
Run	(109)	0.01	0.00		0.00	0.00	0.95	0.04
Face groom	(4)	0.00	0.00	0.00		0.00	1.00	0.00
Body groom	(0)	–	–	–	–		–	–
Lever act.	(272)	0.60	0.00	0.09	0.00	0.00		0.31
Food cup act.	(94)	0.28	0.00	0.24	0.00	0.00	0.48	

Note. $N-1$ stands for preceding response, N stands for following response. Probabilities were calculated from the data from the last session. The frequencies of each response are given in the second column. Dashes indicate nonoccurrence of a response, and zero probabilities indicate absence of a transition to a response. The behavioral record was exhaustive, therefore a transition from one response to itself was not defined (hence the diagonal blanks). (Reproduced from Iversen, 1986, with permission of the publisher.)

232

ties in columns reveal, for example, that explore was most likely to follow lever activity ($p=0.60$) and least likely to follow run ($p=0.01$). The most clearcut finding is, of course, that the rat is not as likely to engage in one response as it is to engage in another. The responses therefore are not homogeneously distributed in time.

The sequential analysis can be carried further. The transitions in Table 1 represent averages based on all episodes of the same topography. Thus, when calculating the transition probability from explore to run all episodes of exploration are considered. After having observed the subjects and studied the event records one can often make predictions that are more accurate than these overall transition probabilities. In a search for such moment-to-moment regularities in behavior sequences, transition probabilities were calculated conditional upon their position within a sequence of behaviors. Wheel running occurred often and the sequential transitions were calculated from one run bout to the next. Thus, the responses from one run bout to the next might be run, lever, explore, stand, lever, and then run. The results of this analysis

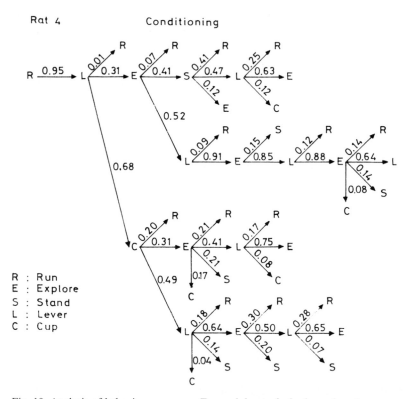

Fig. 19. Analysis of behavior sequences. For each bout of wheel running, the sequence of behaviors was calculated up to the next bout of running. Transition probabilities are relative frequencies. For frequencies of 5 or less, relative frequencies were not calculated. Therefore, not all transitions shown here end in running. Data are from one subject (Rat 4) and are from one session of lever pressing maintained by food on a VI 60-s schedule. (Reproduced from Iversen, 1986, with permission of the publisher.)

of behavior sequences are presented in Fig. 19. Data are from the same rat and session that provided the data in Table 1. The most notable finding is that a given transition is not equally probable. Consider the transition from lever to run (L-R). As the position of this transition progresses in the interrun interval, the L-R probability increases. In the top branch, the L-R probability increases from $p = 0.01$ to 0.25, in the 2nd branch the probability increases from $p = 0.09$ to 0.12, and in the 4th branch from $p = 0.18$ to 0.28. The L-E transition probability also increased within the interrun sequence. On the other hand, some transition probabilities decreased. The lever-cup (L-C) transition decreased from $p = 0.68$ to $p = 0.12$ in the 1st branch, from $p = 0.68$ to $p = 0.08$ from the 1st to the 3rd branch, and from $p = 0.68$ to $p = 0.04$ from the 1st to the 4th branch. Some transitions (L-S and E-R) showed no systematic trends.

As noted in Section 3, different levels of analysis may generate different conclusions about the data. The sequential analysis in terms of subunits in Fig. 19 showed that transition probabilities are positionally dependent. The probability of changing from Response A to Response B is not always the same; the transition depends upon the sequential position of Response A. This type of analysis is only a beginning, however. The duration of individual bouts could be analyzed as well. Transition probabilities would, with further analysis, become much more certain. The accuracy in prediction improved when the data were analyzed for interrun sequences compared with the overall sequences. For example, the overall lever-cup transition of 0.31 in Table 1 did not accurately describe the different lever-cup transitions of 0.68, 0.12 and 0.04 in different branches of the interrun sequence in Fig. 19.

Sequential analysis of multi-behavioral data is not particularly common. However, the attempts that have been made have generated data revealing that neglecting the sequential composition may lead to erroneous conclusions about how experimental events affect behavior. Perhaps the most important finding is that predictions about which behavior will occur at a given moment are more accurate when based on a detailed moment-to-moment sequential analysis than when based upon an analysis that disregards the momentary controlling events. For related literature see Dunham and Grantmyre (1982), Henton (1981a, b), Innis et al. (1983), McIntire et al. (1983), Ray and Delprato (1989) and Spruijt and Gispen (1984).

6. Conclusion

The empirical examples provided above indicate that advances in data analysis progress through steps of less and less aggregation combined with identification of new controlling variables at each step. For example, stimulus generalization gradients may differ depending on how session data are segmented (Section 3.1). Similarly, IRT distributions may differ when IRTs are sampled conditional upon the moment-to-moment occurrence of collateral behavior (Section 5.4.3). Even though successive emissions of the same response can be of the same topography they may nonetheless differ in terms of their relation to controlling variables. Pecks on a key in one time zone are 'tagged' by the contingency of reinforcement operating during that zone, and pecks in a second time zone are tagged differently if the conditions of reinforcement differ in that time zone. The different local rates of pecking during COD and non-COD periods provide one case in point (Section 3.2). When one encounters unexplained variability in behavior between conditions presumed to be equal, the behavior could possibly be tagged differently by unknown variables. Progress from variability to explanation then consists of the identification of the conditions (the tags) that are responsible for the variation one sees in the data. Once such conditions are identified, for example by conditional data analysis, a next step is to conduct an experimental analysis where the conditions that before were considered equal are now dissociated experimentally. When the different conditions reliably produce different data, a functional relation has been obtained (Sidman, 1960).

Advances in scientific discovery can take place through less and less aggregation along both independent and dependent variables. Reduced aggregation along the dependent variable corresponds to improved sampling conditions (e.g., increased sensitivity of recording spatial response location). Reduced aggregation along the independent variable, on the other hand, corresponds to refinement in experimental control (e.g., differential reinforcement of small-scale motor behavior). Scientific progress is associated with reduced aggregation along both variables. However, aggregation done after progress is made may have some unfortunate consequences. For example, a well established finding is that overall response rate maintained under a VI schedule of reinforcement is a function of rate of reinforcement provided by the VI schedule. This means that behavior differs under different experimental conditions. Once this function is obtained, progress would be reversed if one were to consider the different reinforcement rates the same by representing them by one value, the overall average reinforcement rate. In a crude analogy, a composer of a piece of music would be more than insulted if someone were to represent the piece by playing it as one, average note. Investigators who have labored to obtain a functional relation, showing how the response rate of a subject depends upon an identified and manipulated experimental variable, similarly are sensitive to aggregation along 'their' independent variable because this is tantamount to neglecting the experimental control, sought so hard. Even though aggregation along the independent variable is not a method of analysis, it is nonetheless a recognized tactic in the sociology of science (e.g, Kuhn, 1970; Gleick, 1987), as when one group of investigators neglects the functional relations obtained by another group of investigators working on the same problems.

Conflicting approaches in data treatment prevail within science of behavior, and a common consensus is lacking as to what is the right or wrong method of analysis. Contemporary approaches range from the study of behavior in great detail to aggregation of as much data as possible. Szechtman et al. (1988), for example, argued that "in order to provide meaningful correlations between brain mechanisms and behavior, the analysis of behavior will require as much sophistication and attention to detail as does the analysis of the brain" (p. 172). On the other hand, Baum (1989) proposed that "with maturity, a science of behavior should be able to make quantitative predictions. Since quantitative predictions are only possible with molar laws, behavioral analysis can progress toward this goal only by looking beyond momentary events to molar variables and molar relations." (p. 176). The contrast between these views may be rooted in differences in underlying philosophy regarding what constitutes an explanation of behavior. Nonetheless, the difference between these views is considerable and might conceivably be a source of hardship for new investigators who favor one view but happen to be exposed to the social contingencies of the opposing view.

When different levels of data analysis force different conclusions about how behavior is controlled, a natural question is where to set the boundary between determinism and noise. Maybe tradition has dictated that an analysis stops when data become chaotic and unpredictable. Some new developments within contemporary science recognize that seemingly chaotic events can stem from deterministic sources; even popular books have been written on the subject (e.g., Eigen and Winkler, 1981; Prigogine and Stengers, 1984; Gleick, 1987). For example, mathematical description is not necessarily restricted to molar data analyses only. In a review of some new methods, Steen (1988) thus wrote that "mathematical science has become the science of patterns, with theory built on relations among patterns and on applications derived from the fit between pattern and observation" (p. 611). Similarly, Jurs (1986) described how pattern recognition methods can be used to find functional relations in complex data and even to build quantitative models (e.g., in chemistry). Also, Bradshaw et al. (1983) provided a provocative computerized simulation of scientific discovery that generates quantitative relations solely by means of data-driven induction in advance of theory formulation. Additional examples of quantitative pattern analyses of moment-to-moment events within other areas of the neurosciences are provided in Tam et al. (1988) and Montgomery (1989).

Which level of analysis to select is a difficult problem. Response rate calculated over a whole session has been the prevaling analysis method for decades. IRTs also can be units of analysis, showing functional relations with experimental variables. Concurrent response events within IRTs can serve as units as well, as when collateral response topography can be used to predict IRT length. Even a part of a response can be a unit, as when interbeak distance was differentially reinforced. Each of these units of analysis is valid because replicable functional relations can be established within the domain of the analytic unit. Given the wide range of successful application of conditioning techniques involving units both large and small, units of analysis could profitably be considered as functional and not structural. Baer (1982) discussed whether behavior has a necessary structure, that is, should units of analysis be fixed or can they vary? Baer (1986) suggested that the proper unit is whatever emerges

236

when a contingency is applied. Units of analysis can therefore themselves be considered as scientific findings rather than based on *a priori* assumptions regarding behavior structure. As behavior recording and control techniques become more refined, behavior units and scales of analysis may become smaller, and possibly new functional relations may be obtained. A functional relation established at one level of analysis may therefore not be the final answer because explanations of behavior in terms of other functional relations established at subunits of analysis may be discovered later.

References

Allan, R.W. and Zeigler, H.P. (1989) Measurement and control of pecking response location in the pigeon. Physiol. Behav. 45, 1215–1221.

Anger, D. (1956) The dependence of interresponse times upon the relative reinforcement of different interresponse times. J. Exp. Psychol. 52, 145–161.

Antonitis, J.J. (1951) Response variability in the white rat during conditioning, extinction, and reconditioning. J. Exp. Psychol. 42, 273–281.

Arbuckle, J.L. and Lattal, K.A. (1988) Changes in functional response units with briefly delayed reinforcement. J. Exp. Anal. Behav. 49, 249–263.

Bachrach, A.J. (1966) A simple method of obtaining a scatter distribution of offkey pigeon pecking. J. Exp. Anal. Behav. 9, 152.

Baer, D.M. (1982) The imposition of structure on behavior and the demolition of behavioral structures. In: D.J. Bernstein (Ed.), Nebraska Symposium on Motivation: Response Structure and Organization. University of Nebraska Press, Lincoln, pp. 217–254.

Baer, D.M. (1986) In application, frequency is not the only estimate of the probability of behavior units. In: T. Thompson and M.D. Zeiler (Eds.), Analysis and Integration of Behavioral Units. Erlbaum, Hillsdale, NJ, pp. 117–136.

Baer, D.M. and Parsonson, B.S. (1981) Applied changes from steady state: still a problem in the visual analysis of data. In: C.M. Bradshaw, E. Szabadi and C.F. Lowe (Eds.), Quantification of Steady-State Operant Behaviour. Elsevier, Amsterdam, pp. 273–285.

Barrera, F.J. (1974) Centrifugal selection of signal-directed pecking. J. Exp. Anal. Behav. 22, 341–355.

Baum, W.M. (1989) Quantitative prediction and molar description of the environment. Behav. Anal. 12, 167–176.

Bernard, C. (1949) An Introduction to the Study of Experimental Medicine. (H.C. Greene, Trans.). H. Schuman, New York.

Bickel, W.K. and Etzel, B.C. (1985) The quantal nature of controlling stimulus-response relations as measured in tests of stimulus generalization. J. Exp. Anal. Behav. 44, 245–270.

Blough, D.S. (1963) Interresponse time as a function of continuous variables: a new method and some data. J. Exp. Anal. Behav. 6, 237–246.

Blough, D.S. (1965) Definition and measurement in generalization research. In: D.I. Mostofsky (Ed.), Stimulus Generalization. Stanford University Press, Stanford, CA, pp. 30–37.

Blough, D.S. (1966) The reinforcement of least-frequent interresponse times. J. Exp. Anal. Behav. 9, 581–591.

Blough, D.S. (1977) Visual search by pigeons: hunt and peck method. Science 196, 1013–1014.

Bourdieu, P. (1975) The specificity of the scientific field and the social conditions of the progress of reason. Sociol. Sci. Inform. 14 (6), 19–47.

Bradshaw, G.F., Langley, P.W. and Simon, H.A. (1983) Studying scientific discovery by computer simulation. Science 222, 971–975.

Catania, A.C. (1966) Concurrent operants. In: W.K. Honig (Ed.), Operant Behavior: Areas of Research and Application. Appleton-Century-Crofts, New York, pp. 213–270.

Catania, A.C. (1973) The concept of the operant in the analysis of behavior. Behaviorism 1, 103–116.

Catania, A.C. (1981) Discussion: the flight from experimental analysis. In: C.M. Bradshaw, E., Scabadi and C.F. Lowe, (Eds.), Quantification of Steady-State Operant Behaviour. Elsevier, Amsterdam, pp. 49–64.

Clauson, H.D., Izatt, E.J. and Shimp, C.P. (1985) An infrared system for the detection of a pigeon's pecks at alphanumeric characters on a TV screen: the dependency of letter detection on the predictability of one letter by another. J. Exp. Anal. Behav. 43, 257–264.

Cleveland, W.S. (1985) The Elements of Graphing Data. Wadsworth, Monterey, CA.

Deich, J.D., Allan, R.W. and Zeigler, H.P. (1988) Conjunctive differentiation of gape during food-reinforced keypecking in the pigeon. Anim. Learn. Behav. 16, 268–276.

Delprato, D.J. (1986) Response patterns. In: H.W. Reese and L.J. Parrott (Eds.), Behavior Science: Philosophical, Methodological and Empirical Advances. Erlbaum, Hillsdale, NJ, pp. 61–113.

Dunham, P.J. (1971) Punishment: method and theory. Psychol. Rev. 78, 58–70.

Dunham, P.J. (1972) Some effects of punishment upon unpunished responding. J. Exp. Anal. Behav. 17, 443–450.

Dunham, P.J. and Grantmyre, J. (1982) Changes in a multiple response repertoire during response contingent punishment and response restriction: sequential relationships. J. Exp. Anal. Behav. 37, 123–133.

Dunham, P.J., Mariner, A. and Adams, H. (1969) Enhancement of off-key pecking by on-key punishment. J. Exp. Anal. Behav. 12, 789–797.

Eckerman, D.A., Hienz, R.D., Stern, S. and Kowlowitz, V. (1980) Shaping the location of a pigeon's peck: effect of rate and size of shaping steps. J. Exp. Anal. Behav. 33, 299–310.

Eckerman, D.A. and Lanson, R.N. (1969) Variability of response location for pigeons responding under continuous reinforcement, intermittent reinforcement, and extinction. J. Exp. Anal. Behav. 12, 73–80.

Eigen, M. and Winkler, R. (1981) Laws of the Game: How the Principles of Nature Govern Chance. Harper & Row, New York.

Eldridge, G.D. and Pear, J.J. (1987) Topographical variations in behavior during autoshaping, automaintenance, and omission training. J. Exp. Anal. Behav. 47, 319–333.

Epstein, R. (1985) The spontaneous interconnection of three repertoires. Psychol. Rec. 35, 131–141.

Ferster, C.B. and Skinner, B.F. (1957) Schedules of Reinforcement. Appleton-Century-Crofts, New York.

Frick, F.C. and Miller, G.A. (1951) A statistical description of operant conditioning. Am. J. Psychol. 64, 20–36.

Galbicka, G. (1988) Differentiating The Behavior of Organisms. J. Exp. Anal. Behav. 50, 343–354.

Galbicka, G. and Platt, J.R. (1989) Response-reinforcer contingency and spatially defined operants: testing an invariance property of phi. J. Exp. Anal. Behav. 51, 145–162.

Gentry, G.D., Weiss, B. and Laties, V.G. (1983) The microanalysis of fixed-interval responding. J. Exp. Anal. Behav. 39, 327–343.

Gleick, J. (1987) Chaos: Making a New Science. Penguin Books, New York.

Gray, V.A. (1976) Stimulus control of differential-reinforcement-of-low-rate responding. J. Exp. Anal. Behav. 25, 199–207.

Hann, D.M. and Roberts, A.E. (1984) Free operant avoidance behavior in hooded rats: IRTs and response chains. Anim. Learn. Behav. 12, 175–183.

Hefferline, R.F. and Keenan, B. (1963) Amplitude-induction gradient of a small-scale (covert) operant. J. Exp. Anal. Behav. 6, 307–315.

Henton, W.W. (1981a) Concurrent classical conditioning. Psychol. Rec. 31, 395–411.

Henton, W.W. (1981b) Kupalov conditioning: molecular control of response sequences. Psychol. Rec. 31, 489–509.

Henton, W.W. (1985) Interresponse times and the molecular control of behavior: IRTs conditional upon changeovers to alternate behaviors. Psychol. Rec. 35, 549–557.

Henton, W.W. and Iversen, I.H. (1978) Classical Conditioning and Operant Conditioning: a Response Pattern Analysis. Springer Verlag, New York.

Henton, W.W. and Spohn, W.D. (1980) Classical conditioning with compound unconditioned stimuli. Psychol. Rec. 30, 47–60.

Herrick, R.M. (1964) The successive differentiation of a lever displacement response. J. Exp. Anal. Behav. 7, 211–215.

Herrnstein, R.J. (1961) Relative and absolute strength of a response as a function of frequency of reinforcement. J. Exp. Anal. Behav. 4, 267–272.

Herrnstein, R.J. (1970) On the law of effect. J. Exp. Anal. Behav. 13, 243–266.

Herrnstein, R.J. and Vaughan, W. (1980) Melioration and behavioral allocation. In: J.E.R. Staddon (Ed.), Limits to Action: the Allocation of Individual Behavior. Academic Press, New York, pp. 143–176.

Hinson, J.M. and Staddon, J.E.R. (1983) Matching, maximizing, and hill-climbing. J. Exp. Anal. Behav. 40, 321–331.

Holland, P.C. (1988) Excitation and inhibition in unblocking. J. Exp. Psychol.: Anim. Behav. Proc. 14, 261–279.

Hori, K. and Watanabe, S. (1987) An application of the image processing system for detecting and controlling pigeon's peck location. Behav. Brain Res. 26, 75–78.

Innis, N.K., Simmelhag-Grant, V.L. and Staddon, J.E.R. (1983) Behavior induced by periodic food delivery: the effects of interfood interval. J. Exp. Anal. Behav. 39, 309–322.

Iversen, I.H. (1976) Interactions between reinforced responses and collateral responses. Psychol. Rec. 36, 399–413.

Iversen, I.H. (1981) Response interactions with signaled delay of reinforcement. Behav. Anal. Lett. 1, 3–9.

Iversen, I.H. (1986) Time allocation, sequential, and kinematic analyses of behaviors controlled by an aperiodic reinforcement schedule. Psychol. Rec. 36, 239–255.

Iversen, I.H. (1988) Tactics of graphic design: a review of Tufte's The Visual Display of Quantitative Information. J. Exp. Anal. Behav. 49, 171–189.

Iversen, I.H. and Mogensen, J. (1988) A multipurpose vertical holeboard with automated recording of spatial and temporal visit patterns for rodents. J. Neurosci. Methods 25, 251–263.

Iversen, I.H., Ragnarsdottir, G.A. and Randrup, K. (1984) Operant conditioning of autogrooming in vervet monkeys (Cercopithecus aethiops). J. Exp. Anal. Behav. 42, 171–189.

Jenkins, H.M. and Sainsbury, R.S. (1970) Discrimination learning with the distinctive feature on positive or negative trials. In: D.I. Mostofsky (Ed.), Attention: Contemporary Theory and Analysis. Appleton-Century-Crofts, New York, pp. 239–273.

Johnston, J.M. and Pennypacker, H.S. (1980) Strategies and Tactics of Human Behavioral Research. Erlbaum, New York.

Jurs, P.C. (1986) Pattern recognition used to investigate multivariate data in analytical chemistry. Science 232, 1219–1224.

Kernan, W.J., Higby, W.J., Hopper, D.L., Cunningham, W. and Lloyd, W.E. (1980) Pattern recognition of behavioral events in the nonhuman primate. Behav. Res. Methods Instrument. 12, 524–534.

Kernan, W.J., Mullenix, P.J. and Hopper, D.L. (1987) Pattern recognition of rat behavior. Pharm. Biochem. Behav. 27, 559–564.

Kernan, W.J., Mullenix, P.J. and Hopper, D.L. (1989) Time structure analysis of behavioral acts using a computer pattern recognition system. Pharm. Biochem. Behav. 34, 863–869.

Killeen, P.R. (1975) On the temporal control of behavior. Psychol. Rev. 82, 89–115.

Kuhn, T.S. (1970) The Structure of Scientific Revolutions, 2nd Edn. University of Chicago Press, Chicago.

Laties, V.G., Weiss, B., Clark, R.L. and Reynolds, M.D. (1965) Overt 'mediating' behavior during temporally spaced responding. J. Exp. Anal. Behav. 8, 107–116.

Lyon, D.O. (1982) Concurrent behavior: are the interpretations mutually exclusive. Behav. Anal. 5, 175–187.

Lyons, C.A. and Cheney, C.D. (1984) Time allocation in a multiresponse environment: effects of restricting response classes. J. Exp. Anal. Behav. 41, 279–289.

Martin, P. and Bateson, P. (1986) Measuring Behaviour: an Introductory Guide. Cambridge University Press, Cambridge.

Matthews, T.J. and Lerer, B.E. (1987) Behavior patterns in pigeons during autoshaping with an incremental conditioned stimulus. Anim. Learn. Behav. 15, 69–75.

McIntire, K., Lundervold, D., Calmes, H., Jones, C. and Allard, S. (1983) Temporal control in a complex environment: an analysis of schedule-related behavior. J. Exp. Anal. Behav. 39, 465–478.

Montgomery, E.B. (1989) A new method for relating behavior to neuronal activity in performing monkeys. J. Neurosci. Methods 28, 197–204.

Morse, W.H. (1966) Intermittent reinforcement. In: W.K. Honig (Ed.), Operant Behavior: Areas of Research and Application. Appleton-Century-Crofts, New York, pp. 52–108.

Osborne, B. and Black, A.H. (1978) A detailed analysis of behavior during the transition from acquisition to extinction in rats with fornix lesions. Behav. Biol. 23, 271–290.

Parsonson, B.S. and Baer, D.M. (1978) The analysis and presentation of graphic data. In: T.R. Kratochwill (Ed.), Single-Subject Research: Strategies for Evaluating Change. Academic Press, New York, pp. 101–165.

Parsonson, B.S. and Baer, D.M. (1986) The graphic analysis of data. In: A. Poling and R.W. Fuqua (Eds.), Research Methods in Applied Behavior Analysis. Plenum Press, New York, pp. 157–186.

Pavlov, I.P. (1927) Conditioned Reflexes (G.V. Anrep, Trans.). Oxford University Press, London.

Pear, J.J. (1985) Spatiotemporal patterns of behavior produced by variable-interval schedules of reinforcement. J. Exp. Anal. Behav. 44, 217–231.

Pear, J.J. and Eldridge, G.D. (1984) The operant-respondent distinction: future directions. J. Exp. Anal. Behav. 42, 453–467.

Pear, J.J. and Legris, J.A. (1987) Shaping by automated tracking of an arbitrary operant response. J. Exp. Anal. Behav. 47, 241–247.

Peele, D.B., Casey, J. and Silberberg, A. (1984) Primacy of interresponse-time reinforcement in accounting for rate differences under variable-ratio and variable-interval schedules. J. Exp. Psychol.: Anim. Behav. Proc. 10, 149–167.

Platt, J.R. (1979) Interresponse-time shaping by variable-interval-like interresponse-time reinforcement contingencies. J. Exp. Anal. Behav. 31, 3–14.

Prigogine, I. and Stengers, I. (1984) Order Out of Chaos. Bantam Books, New York.

Ray, B.A. (1967) The course of acquisition of a line-tilt discrimination by rhesus monkeys. J. Exp. Anal. Behav. 13, 539–550.

Ray, B.A. and Sidman, M. (1970) Reinforcement schedules and stimulus control. In: W.N. Schoenfeld (Ed.), The Theory of Reinforcement Schedules. Appleton-Century-Crofts, New York, pp. 187–214.

Ray, R.D. and Brown, D.A. (1975) A systems approach to behavior. Psychol. Rec. 25, 459–478.

Ray, R.D. and Delprato, D.J. (1989) Behavioral systems analysis: methodological strategies and tactics. Behav. Sci. 34, 81–126.

Real, P.G. (1983) A time-series analysis of changeover performance on concurrent variable-interval schedules. Anim. Learn. Behav. 11, 255–265.

Real, P.G. and Dreyfus, L.R. (1985) Levels of aggregation: relative time allocation in concurrent-schedule performance. J. Exp. Anal. Behav. 43, 97–113.

Richter, C.P. (1927) Animal behavior and internal drives. Q. Rev. Biol. 2, 307–343.

Roper, T.J. (1978) Diversity and substitutability of adjunctive activities under fixed-interval schedules of food reinforcement. J. Exp. Anal. Behav. 30, 83–96.

Rumbaugh, D.M., Richardson, W.K., Washburn, D.A., Savage-Rumbaugh, E.S. and Hopkins, W.D. (1989) Rhesus monkeys (Macaca mulatta), video tasks, implications for stimulus-response spatial contiguity. J. Comp. Psychol. 103, 32–38.

Sackett, G.P. (Ed.) (1978) Observing Behavior, Vol. 2, Data Collection and Analysis Methods. University Park Press, Baltimore, MD.

240

Scott, G.K. and Platt, J.R. (1985) Model of response-reinforcer contiguity. J. Exp. Psychol.: Anim. Behav. Proc. 11, 152–171.

Shimp, C.P. (1967) The reinforcement of short interresponse times. J. Exp. Anal. Behav. 10, 425–434.

Shimp, C.P. (1969) Optimal behavior in free-operant experiments. Psychol. Rev. 76, 97–112.

Shimp, C.P. (1973) Sequential dependencies in free-responding. J. Exp. Anal. Behav. 19, 491–497.

Shimp, C.P. (1979) The local organization of behaviour: method and theory. In: M.D. Zeiler and P. Harzem (Eds.), Reinforcement and the Organization of Behaviour. Wiley & Sons, New York, pp. 261–298.

Shull, R.L. (1971) Sequential patterns in post-reinforcement pauses on fixed-interval schedules of reinforcement. J. Exp. Anal. Behav. 15, 221–231.

Sidman, M. (1960) Tactics of Scientific Research: Evaluating Scientific Data in Psychology. Basic Books, New York.

Silberberg, A. and Fantino, E. (1970) Choice, rate of reinforcement, and the changeover delay. J. Exp. Anal. Behav. 13, 187–197.

Silberberg, A., Hamilton, B., Ziriax, J.M. and Casey, J. (1978) The structure of choice. J. Exp. Psychol.: Anim. Behav. Proc. 4, 368–398.

Skinner, B.F. (1938) The Behavior of Organisms: an Experimental Analysis. Appleton-Century-Crofts, New York.

Skinner, B.F. (1950) Are theories of learning necessary? Psychol. Rev. 57, 193–216.

Skinner, B.F. (1953) Science and Human Behavior. MacMillan, New York.

Skinner, B.F. (1965) Stimulus generalization in an operant: a historical note. In: D.I. Mostofsky (Ed.), Stimulus Generalization. Stanford University Press, Stanford, pp. 193–209.

Spruijt, B.M. and Gispen, W.H. (1983) Prolonged animal observation by use of digitized videodisplays. Pharmacol. Biochem. Behav. 19, 765–769.

Spruijt, B.M. and Gispen, W.H. (1984) Behavioral sequences as an easily quantifiable parameter in experimental studies. Physiol. Behav. 32, 707–710.

Staddon, J.E.R. (1977) Schedule-induced behavior. In: W.K. Honig and J.E.R. Staddon (Eds.), Handbook of Operant Behavior. Prentice-Hall, Englewood Cliffs, NJ, pp. 125–152.

Staddon, J.E.R. and Simmelhag, V.L. (1971) The 'superstition' experiment: a reexamination of its implications for the principles of adaptive behavior. Psychol. Rev. 78, 3–43.

Steen, L.A. (1988) The science of patterns. Science 240, 611–616.

Stoddard, L.T. and Sidman, M. (1971) Stimulus control after intradimensional discrimination training. Psychol. Rep. 28, 147–157.

Suen, H.K. and Ary, D. (1989) Analyzing Quantitative Behavioral Observation Data. Erlbaum, Hillsdale, NJ.

Szechtman, H., Eilam, D., Teitelbaum, P. and Golani, I. (1988) A different look at measurement and interpretation of drug-induced stereotyped behavior. Psychobiol. 16, 164–173.

Tam, D.C., Ebner, T.J. and Knox, C.K. (1988) Conditional cross-interval correlation analysis with applications to simultaneously recorded cerebellar Purkinje neurons. J. Neurosci. Methods 23, 23–33.

Thompson, T. and Lubinski, D. (1986) Units of analysis and kinetic structure of behavioral repertoires. J. Exp. Anal. Behav. 46, 219–242.

Thompson, T. and Zeiler, M.D. (Eds.) (1986) Analysis and Integration of Behavioral Units. Erlbaum, Hillsdale, NJ.

Thorndike, E.L. (1911) Animal Intelligence. MacMillan, New York.

Tufte, E.R. (1983) The Visual Display of Quantitative Information. Graphics Press, Cheshire, CT.

Tukey, J.W. (1977) Exploratory Data Analysis. Addison-Wesley, Reading, MA.

Wainer, H. and Thissen, D. (1981) Graphical data analysis. Annu. Rev. Psychol. 32, 191–241.

Weiss, B. (1970) The fine structure of operant behavior during transition states. In: W.N. Schoenfeld (Ed.), The Theory of Reinforcement Schedules. Appleton-Century-Crofts, New York, pp. 277–311.

Weiss, B., Ziriax, J.M. and Newland, M.C. (1989) Serial properties of behavior and their chemical modification. Anim. Learn. Behav. 17, 83–93.

Wendt, G.R. (1936) An interpretation of inhibition of conditioned reflexes as competition between reaction systems. Psychol. Rev. 43, 258–281.

Wong, P.T. (1977) A behavioral field approach to instrumental learning in the rat: I. Partial reinforcement effects and sex differences. Anim. Learn. Behav. 5, 5–13.

Zeiler, M.D. (1986) Behavior units and optimality. In: T. Thompson and M.D. Zeiler (Eds.), Analysis and Integration of Behavioral Units. Erlbaum, Hillsdale, NJ, pp. 81–116.

Zener, K. (1937) The significance of behavior accompanying conditioned salivary secretion for theories of the conditioned response. Am. J. Psychol. 50, 384–403.

Zucker, M.H. (1969) Electronic Circuits for the Behavioral and Biomedical Sciences. W.H. Freeman and Co, San Francisco.

Experimental analysis of behavior, Part 2
Iversen and Lattal (eds.)
© *1991, Elsevier Science Publishers BV*

CHAPTER 7

Mathematical description of operant behavior: an introduction

RICHARD L. SHULL

Department of Psychology, The University of North Carolina at Greensboro, Greensboro, NC 27412,
U.S.A.

1. Introduction

Behavior analysts are interested in describing functional relations between classes of independent variables and classes of dependent variables. To be most useful such descriptions should be precise, succinct, and applicable to a wide range of particular cases. In psychology, including behavior analysis, most scientific descriptions are couched in a modified version of everyday language (e.g., English). Familiar-sounding terms are redefined and new terms are introduced to form a technical vocabulary. Such languages may be satisfactory for describing general trends. But they are clumsy for describing precise relationships.

The language of mathematics, in contrast, encourages descriptions that are precise, succinct and general. An equation, for example, describes precisely and succinctly how the terms are related to each other. The term on the left usually specifies the dependent variable (i.e., some property of behavior). The classes of independent variables are included among the terms on the right. The other terms on the right, and the organization of the right-hand terms in the equation, specify how the independent and dependent variables are related. What an equation can say precisely in a few lines might take several paragraphs to say in English.

Sometimes people speak of mathematical description as a *mathematical model*. An equation can be viewed as a model of some empirical phenomenon in the sense that it is a construction intended to resemble the phenomenon in certain important respects but not in all respects. The relevant aspects of the concrete empirical events should change in the same way as the corresponding terms of the equation.

An equation that provides a good description of the relevant aspects of the relation between the independent and dependent variables can aid prediction and control.

The effects of changing various independent variables can be explored quickly and easily in the model by changing the appropriate terms and solving the equation. The mathematical model (or mathematical description) will be useful to the extent that it does, in fact, predict well and efficiently over an appropriately wide range of circumstances.

2. Generating a mathematical model

If you are unfamiliar with mathematical description, the process of coming up with plausible equations to try can seem mysterious, and you may feel in awe of those who have been successful. But, in fact, the processes are not mysterious (Skinner, 1957, 1969; Marr, 1985, 1986; Langley et al., 1987). Historical and experimental evidence suggests that even the most spectacular achievements in mathematical description result from conventional problem-solving heuristics (Langley et al., 1987). Getting ideas about what classes of equations to try can come from analogies with other phenomena (i.e., metaphorical extension), as illustrated in Section 2.1, and from patterns revealed in plots of data, as illustrated in Section 2.2.

2.1. Metaphorical extension

A common strategy for generating ideas for mathematical models is to conceptualize the behavioral phenomenon as analogous to some other phenomenon – behavioral or even physical – for which effective mathematical descriptions already have been developed. Then, with appropriate adjustments and translations, the mathematical description can be applied to the new case. This is a form of metaphorical extension (cf. Langley et al., 1987; Skinner, 1957, 1989). Some examples are described below.

2.1.1. Example 1: Stimulus sampling theory
Under many learning procedures, the probability of a response increases as a function of trials. But the size of the increase progressively decreases with each successive trial. Prior to 1950 most mathematical models of learning (e.g., Hull, 1943) were expressed in the form of *deterministic functions*. Each value of the independent variable implied a particular value of the dependent variable. The obvious moment-to-moment variability in performance was attributed to the effect of additional uncontrolled variables.

With *stochastic* or *probabilistic* models, in contrast, each value of the independent variable can imply a frequency distribution of values of the dependent variable. Thus, variability is an intrinsic implication of the model rather than something treated as an additional effect.

A novel contribution of Estes (1950, 1959) was to conceptualize the learning process as analogous to some prototypic probabilistic process. First, Estes took learning to be the development of stimulus-response relations. Then, following Guthrie (1935) and others, Estes imagined that the stimulus was composed of a large number of independent elements. On any conditioning trial, only some subset of the total number of elements are effectively noticed. Of those, some elements already may have been conditioned to evoke the response while others have not. The ones that have not been conditioned are conditioned on that trial in an all-or-none fashion. The tendency to respond is assumed to be ordinally related to the number of noticed elements that have been conditioned.

This conception makes learning analogous to an urn problem of the following sort. Imagine an urn containing 100 white balls (analogous to the total number of elements comprising the stimulus). On each trial we randomly draw 10 balls (analogous to the noticed subset). We then mark each unmarked ball in our sample with an X (analogous to a conditioning effect), and put the balls back before the next trial. With each successive trial, progressively more of the balls in the urn will be marked so that, on average, the sample will contain fewer and fewer unmarked balls. More formally:

$$\Delta M_i = S (N - M_{i-1})$$

where ΔM_i indicates the expected number of new balls marked on any particular trial (i); S refers to the proportion of the total number of balls comprising a sample; N indicates the number of balls in the urn; and M_{i-1} indicates the total number of marked balls at the end of the previous conditioning trial. ΔM_i will get smaller and smaller on each successive trial.

The mathematical description of these sorts of urn problems had been well worked out, at least for prototypic cases (e.g., Feller, 1950). The real key, then, was in conceptualizing aspects of learning as analogous to the urn problem. To the extent that there are analogous aspects, the mathematical descriptions developed for the urn problem should provide an effective description of interesting properties of learning provided the terms are appropriately translated. The history of *stimulus sampling theory* (Estes, 1959) and its descendants (e.g., Rescorla and Wagner, 1972) demonstrates that it was indeed productive.

2.1.2. Example 2: Herrnstein's response-rate function
The development of stimulus sampling theory illustrates metaphorical extension from physical phenomena. Herrnstein's (1970, 1974) development of a function relating the rate of a response to its rate of reinforcement illustrates metaphorical extension from one behavioral phenomenon to another.

Two facts about behavior were relevant. One was the effect of rate of reinforcement on the emission rate of a single response. Suppose, as Skinner (1938) did, that reinforcement increased and nonreinforcement decreased the emission rate of a response. If so, the average response rate under stable conditions of intermittent reinforcement should be a blend of these two effects, with higher reinforcement rates changing the blend in favor of higher response rates.

Catania and Reynolds (1968) attempted to determine this function precisely by examining the rate of responding generated by extended exposure to each of a large number of variable-interval (VI) schedules of food reinforcement. The subjects were food-deprived pigeons. The results were that response rate increased as reinforcement rate increased, but the function was curved. It rose less and less steeply as reinforcement rate increased – that is, it was an increasing, negatively accelerated function (see Section 2.2).

The second relevant fact came from choice procedures where each response is reinforced on a different VI schedule (concurrent VI VI schedules; see Part 1, Ch. 6). Herrnstein (1961) and others (cf. Catania, 1966) discovered that a simple linear equation describes the relation between the proportion of responses and the proportion of reinforcers:

$$\frac{B_1}{B_1 + B_2} = \frac{R_1}{R_1 + R_2} \tag{1}$$

where B indicates responses; R indicates reinforcers; and the subscripts identify the particular alternative.

The question was whether these two facts about behavior – the curvilinear relation between response and reinforcement rates and the linear relation between response and reinforcer proportions in a choice procedure – were related. Several theorists (e.g., Bush and Mosteller, 1955; Estes, 1959) had tried to bridge choice and single response procedures by conceptualizing the single response procedure as analogous to a choice procedure but where the alternative responses are not measured directly. In this tradition, Herrnstein (1970) conceptualized the single response procedure, such as studied by Catania and Reynolds, as a concurrent schedule: the measured response plus all the other unmeasured responses (turning, grooming, exploring and so forth). Further, he imagined that these other responses are reinforced by unscheduled, perhaps intrinsic, reinforcers. Next, he assumed that the simple matching principle holds for choice, whether or not the responses and reinforcers are measured. These possibilities can be expressed formally. Assuming matching among all the responses and reinforcers:

$$\frac{B_1}{B_1 + B_2 + \ldots + B_N} = \frac{R_1}{R_1 + R_2 + \ldots + R_N}$$

or,

$$\frac{B_1}{\sum B_i} = \frac{R_1}{R_1 + R_o}$$

where R_o represents the rate of all other reinforcers and where responses and reinforcers from all sources are measured in the same units as the measured response and the scheduled reinforcer. Then to obtain the number of responses during the session time (response rate), we can simply multiply by the denominator on the left, giving:

$$B_1 = \frac{(\sum B_i) R_1}{R_1 + R_o}$$

Finally, Herrnstein (1974) assumed that the total amount of behavior is constant for a given session duration. Simply put, the subject is always doing something, even if sleeping, so that the total of all the 'somethings' per unit time does not change, only their distribution. If so, the equation can be rewritten, finally, as:

$$B_1 = \frac{k R_1}{R_1 + R_o} \tag{2}$$

where k represents the total rate of all behavior, expressed in units of the target response. Or, in other words, k represents the asymptotic rate of the target response in the limiting case where all the reinforcement is assigned to the target response. If the sum of all alternative reinforcement, R_o, is assumed to be constant, then Herrnstein's equation is a hyperbolic, which is a rising, negatively accelerated function. (The hyperbolic and other function types will be described more fully in Section 2.2.) In words, the equation says that response rate is an increasing, negatively accelerated function of its own reinforcement rate and a decreasing function of the rate of alternative reinforcement.

The hyperbolic function fit Catania and Reynolds' and a wide range of other data well, provided appropriate values were chosen for the two constants, k and R_o (deVilliers and Herrnstein, 1976; Davison and McCarthy, 1988). It also describes well some data obtained in applied settings (McDowell, 1982; Myerson and Hale, 1984; Bradshaw and Szabadi, 1988), and so applies with some generality.

A word of caution is in order, however. The fact that an equation of particular form describes a set of data well does not mean that the assumptions that gave rise to the equation are supported. It turns out, for example, that an equation of the same hyperbolic form as Herrnstein's can be derived from very different sets of assumptions (e.g., Catania, 1973; Staddon, 1977; Killeen, 1979; McDowell, 1980; and Equation 6). And the constants in the equation accordingly have different interpretations under these different derivations. As will be discussed below, the constants, which are derived from a data set, are really dependent variables even though they may be interpreted as representing the effects of unmeasured independent variables.

The point of these two examples (Estes and Herrnstein) is to emphasize that developing an effective mathematical description is neither a magical process nor a mechanical process of feeding a set of data into some curve-fitting routine and getting the 'correct' function out. Often the most important part is to conceptualize the phenomenon of interest in a way that reveals analogies with other phenomena for which mathematical descriptions have already been worked out. Then the derivation for the present case may be straightforward, even though the implications might turn out to be surprising.

There are many other examples within the operant tradition of this same sort of metaphorical extension including: McDowell's application of linear system theory from engineering (e.g., McDowell, 1987; McDowell and Wixted, 1988); applications of models developed for economic and regulatory systems (e.g., Baum, 1973, 1981; Lea, 1978; Staddon and Motheral, 1978; Rachlin et al., 1978; Timberlake, 1984; Collier et al., 1986; Hursh et al., 1988; Staddon and Ettinger, 1989); and applications derived from extensions of models of time-based probabilistic processes (e.g., Gibbon, 1979; Luce, 1986; Killeen and Fetterman, 1988; McGill, 1963). Most models within operant theory are static ones in the sense that they describe the asymptotic adjustment but not the time course of that adjustment. There are, however, many examples of dynamic and semi-dynamic models developed in other fields that might be applied by analogy (cf. Staddon, 1988, for a useful discussion of this class of models).

2.2. Familiar function forms in plots of data

Metaphorical extension, as just described, is one way to generate ideas about what equations to try. A second way, to be discussed in this section, is to plot a set of data and see whether the pattern suggests a familiar type of equation.

Sometimes the plot of points appears chaotic, perhaps indicating that the independent variable simply has no systematic effect on the aspect of behavior being measured or that influential variables are insufficiently controlled. But often an orderly relation can be discovered through further data exploration – i.e., through plotting the data different ways (cf. Tukey, 1977). For example, an orderly relation might emerge if the independent or dependent variables are reexpressed.

If the relation appears orderly, one may be able to see in the plot of data certain familiar trends that narrow the range of possibilities. Does the trend rise from left to right (a *positive* function) or fall (a *negative* function)? If the trend remains positive or negative, it is *monotonic* (i.e., one limbed). The normal curve, in contrast, is *bitonic* (i.e., two limbed). If a function (either positive or negative) becomes progressively less steep, going from left to right, then it is *negatively accelerated*. If it becomes progressively steeper, then it is *positively accelerated*.

The particular shape of any function will vary, depending on exactly how the X-axis and Y-axis variables are scaled, whether linear, logarithmic, and so forth. Which scaling is appropriate? Linear-scale expressions of the independent and dependent variables are most common. Such scales are linear transformations of common physical measurements. But it does not necessarily follow that such scaling is appropriate for behavioral relations. The familiar physical scales have evolved for effective description in physics. Different scales or complex transformations of conventional physical scales may yield simpler, more effective, and thus more natural descriptions of behavioral relations. Such descriptions are completely physical; but the scales are not the familiar ones from descriptions of physical phenomena (cf. Stevens, 1951; Gibson, 1966).

2.2.1. Obtaining data

The first step is to obtain enough data points to determine a functional relation between the independent and dependent variables over a sufficiently wide range. Although you may need to generate the critical data yourself, you may be able to find them in journal articles or book chapters. When procedures are similar across laboratories, data from different experiments and laboratories can be compared meaningfully. Data can be obtained from tabular presentations or from published graphs if you can enlarge them enough to read the values accurately (cf. Gibbon, 1977). You can prepare a transparency of the graph (e.g., by Xeroxing) that can be projected on a screen. Then adjust the size so that the scale values marked on the graph correspond to those on a standard grid that you have prepared. Next use the grid template to determine the values of the points from the projected image. The task goes quickly if one person reads the values and another records them.

2.2.2. Linear plots

Suppose the points are plotted on linear coordinates. If the points appear to scatter around a rising or falling straight line, the familiar linear form, $y = ax + b$, is immediately suggested. The a is the slope, or proportionality constant; it determines the steepness of the line. The b is the intercept constant; it indicates where the line will meet the Y-axis when the value of x is zero. If a is positive, the line will rise from left to right; if a is negative, the line will fall.

If, however, the trend of the points deviates systematically from a straight line, an equation other than a linear one is called for. There are an infinite number of such functions. But a relatively small number of monotonic functions are immediately suggested because they have been found effective for describing behavioral relations.

The upper-left panel of Fig. 1 shows several such functions plotted in linear coordinates. You can see how the direction and curvature differ depending on the type of function and on the values of the constants. Consider, for example, a *power function* of the form, $y = ax^b$ (Curves B and C in the top left panel). The exponent, b, determines the rate of acceleration in the function relating y to x. If b is greater than 1 (Curve B in Fig. 1), y is an increasing, positively accelerated function of x; if b is equal to 1, y is a linear function of x (zero intercept); and if b is less than 1 (Curve C in Fig. 1), y is an increasing, negatively accelerated function of x. Finally, a negative exponent is equivalent to raising the number to the appropriate power and then taking the reciprocal of the result. For example, x^{-2} is equivalent to $1/x^2$, which is a decreasing function.

For power functions, equal relative changes in the independent variable produce equal relative changes in the dependent variable. The power (i.e., b) sometimes is called the *sensitivity parameter* because its value determines what relative change in the dependent variable is produced by a given relative change in the independent variable. Power functions have proven useful for describing such things as the way stimulus and reinforcement differences between alternatives affect choice (e.g., Baum, 1974, 1979; Nevin, 1984; Davison and McCarthy, 1988; Logue, 1988; and Part 1, Ch. 6).

For the *exponential function* (Curves D and E in Fig. 1) the independent variable (*x*) operates as an exponent. If the exponent is positive (Curve D), *y* is an increasing, positively accelerated function of *x*. If the exponent is negative (Curve E), *y* is a decreasing, negatively accelerated function of *x*. Exponential functions have proven useful for describing certain growth and decay processes. For example, the negative exponential describes the discharge of an electrolytic capacitor, the distribution of interevent times generated by a random emitter, and the decay of radioactive substances. For the exponential, the amount gained or lost during a time interval of par-

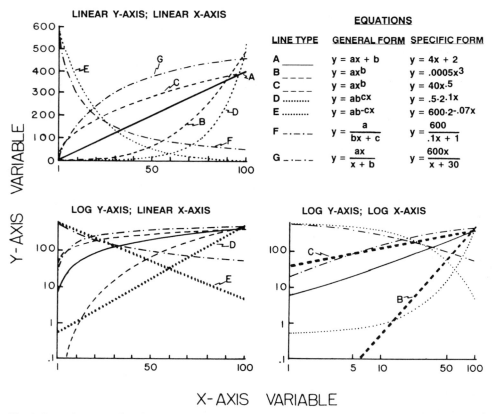

Fig. 1. Several common functions plotted in linear coordinates (top left panel), in semi-logarithmic coordinates (lower left panel), and in full logarithmic coordinates (lower right panel). The functions that are linear in each type of plot are shown by thickened lines. Curve A is a linear function; B and C are power functions; D and E are exponential; and F and G are hyperbolic.

ticular duration is a constant proportion of the amount at the beginning of the time interval. In the analysis of behavior the negative exponential has proven useful for describing such phenomena as the distribution of interresponse times (Blough, 1966; see Section 4.1.2), the decay of activity after the discontinuation of reinforcement (e.g., Killeen, 1975, 1979), and the deterioration of stimulus control as a function of the retention interval in delayed matching to sample (remembering) tasks (e.g., White and McKenzie, 1982; Watson and Blampied, 1989).

Herrnstein's equation relating response rate to reinforcement rate (Section 2.1.2) is a type of *hyperbolic function* where the X-axis variable appears both in the numerator and in the denominator (Curve G in Fig. 1). Here, y is an increasing, negatively accelerated function of x (see also deVilliers and Herrnstein, 1976, and McDowell and Wood, 1984). When the X-axis variable appears only in the denominator (Curve F in Fig. 1), y is a decreasing, negatively accelerated function of x. Hyperbolic functions like Curve F have proven useful for describing the effects of delayed reinforcement on choice (e.g., Rachlin and Green, 1972; Ainslie, 1975, 1989; Herrnstein, 1981; Mazur, 1987; and Section 4.4.1; see also Gibbon, 1977).

It should be apparent from Fig. 1 (top left) that several different kinds of equations produce trends that appear quite similar. The differences may appear mainly at the extremes. Nonetheless, it might be important to decide which one provides the better description because the equations might imply quite different kinds of controlling relationships. The decision might determine how we conceptualize the phenomenon we are studying and what other phenomena we relate it to. The question, then, is which function provides the best description of a set of data.

2.2.3. Logarithmic plots

Because it is easier to detect systematic deviations from a straight than from a curved line, it is often helpful to find a transformation that converts a curved function into a linear function. When the dependent and independent variables are reexpressed that way, the points should scatter unsystematically around a straight line if, indeed, the function provides an adequate description. Systematic deviations are likely to be apparent by eye. Two of the curved functions in Fig. 1 (the power function and the exponential function) have familiar and easy linear reexpressions involving logarithms.

A logarithm is the exponent that some base number (usually either 10 or e) must be raised to in order to equal the target number. Logarithms based on e ($e = 2.718...$) are called natural logarithms and are often abbreviated *ln* (e.g., on calculators); those based on 10 are called common logarithms and are often abbreviated *log*. Thus, for example, $\ln(x)$ would be read as the logarithm, base e, of the value specified by x. Although the numerical values of the two kinds of logarithms will differ, as long as one is consistent, it will not matter which type of logarithmic reexpression one uses. The logarithm of the base is 1.0; the logarithm of 1 is zero; the logarithm of a decimal is negative in sign; and the logarithm of 0 is undefined. Distances on the logarithmic scale correspond to ratios of the original numbers. To convert an equation to logarithmic form, exponents become multipliers and the logarithms of numbers that are multiplied in the original expression are added. For example, if $y = (10^2)$ (50), then $\log(y) = 2(\log(10)) + \log(50)$. For a power function of the form, $y = ax^b$:

$$\log(y) = b \log(x) + \log(a)$$

which is linear. In order to emphasize its linear form, it might be helpful to express this relation in a slightly different way: let $y' = \log(y)$, $a' = \log(a)$ and $x' = \log(x)$. Then for the power function:

$$y' = b\,x' + a'$$

Thus, the power function is linear when *both* the x and y variables have been converted to logarithms. And the slope in logarithmic coordinates is the exponent (b) in the power function (i.e., the sensitivity parameter).

The linearity of logarithmic reexpressions of power functions makes it relatively easy to see whether a power function provides a good description of the trend in a set of data. One can convert the X-axis and Y-axis values of each data point to its logarithm and then plot these logarithmic values. Alternatively, one can plot the original data values on double logarithmic graph paper – both axes scaled logarithmically – which is readily available with different numbers of logarithmic cycles. The logarithmic scaling on the graph paper is equivalent to transforming the coordinate values of the variables to their logarithms. Either way, if the trend of the points appears linear, a power-function description is suggested. The Generalized Matching Law (e.g., Baum, 1974; Davison and McCarthy, 1988; see also Part 1, Ch. 6) is a power function and is often expressed in its logarithmic form.

In the lower right panel of Fig. 1 both the X- and Y-axis values are scaled logarithmically (i.e., double logarithmic paper). The point is to show the shape of the various functions in double-logarithmic coordinates. Note that the power functions are linear, but the other function types are not. Thus, if the trend of the data is nonlinear in double logarithmic coordinates, another function type should be considered.

If the exponential function, $y = ae^{bx}$, is converted to its logarithmic form (base e), the e-term drops out because the logarithm of the base is 1.0, and so

$$\ln(y) = b\,x + \ln(a), \quad \text{or}$$
$$y' = b\,x + a'$$

Thus, the exponential function plots as a straight line when the Y-axis is scaled logarithmically and the X-axis is scaled linearly.

The lower left panel of Fig. 1 shows the several function types plotted in semi-logarithmic coordinates (logarithmic Y- axis, linear X-axis). Note that the exponential functions, but not the other functions, plot as straight lines.

It is important to recognize that many kinds of functions which are curved in linear coordinates are also curved in full-logarithmic and semi-logarithmic coordinates. In

Fig. 1, for example, the hyperbolic functions are linear in none of the plots. This fact may be useful for distinguishing among different functions. For example, it would be hard to distinguish a power function (power less than 1.0) from a hyperbolic function if the data were plotted in linear coordinates (e.g., compare Curves C versus G in the upper left plot). But the two functions appear different in the double logarithmic plot (lower right panel).

The best way to become familiar with these various patterns is to plot these kinds of functions with real or made-up data. If you would like a more extended treatment of the basic function types and of logarithmic and other reexpressions, Lewis' (1960) Quantitative Methods in Psychology would be a good place to start.

Fig. 2 illustrates the effects of logarithmic reexpressions on two sets of behavioral data. The data in the top row show for one pigeon the effect of the retention interval on a measure of discrimination in a delayed matching-to-sample task (Pigeon T5, easy discrimination, Experiment 2 in White and McKenzie, 1982); see also Part 1, Ch. 8. The data in the lower row show for one pigeon the effect of changing an aspect of the temporal distribution of reinforcers in the terminal link of a chain schedule (see Section 4.2.1) on the rate of initiating the terminal link (Pigeon 3819 in Shull et al., 1990); see also Part 1, Ch. 3. For the left-most panels in each row, the points are plotted in linear coordinates. For the middle column, the dependent variable is expressed in logarithmic units (i.e., $y' = \ln(y)$). And for the right-hand column both the independent and dependent variables are expressed in logarithmic units.

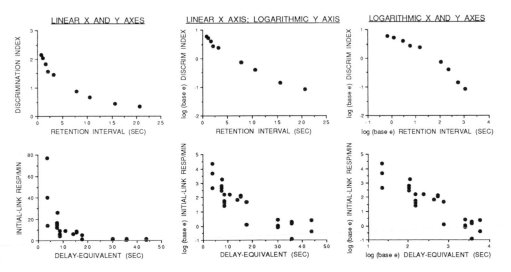

Fig. 2. Scatter plots showing the effects of logarithmic reexpression. The top row shows the values of a discrimination index from one pigeon (Pigeon T5) from Experiment 2, easy discrimination, reported by White and McKenzie (1982). The bottom row shows initial-link response rates from one pigeon (Pigeon 3819) trained under a chain schedule with FR 1 in the intial link and various numbers and delays of food reinforcers in the terminal link. (Adapted from Shull et al., 1990, with permission of the publisher.)

Again, the aim is to see if the trend in the data is linear in any of these plots because such linearity would indicate that a particular kind of function provides a good description of the trend. Conversely, systematic deviations from a straight-line trend would show that the function type that plots as a straight line does not provide a completely satisfactory description. A good way to detect curvature is to hold the graph horizontal to the ground at about chin level, with the right-hand end of the X-axis pointing toward your face. Then sight along the function. Holding the graph this way effectively shortens the X-axis relative to the Y-axis and exaggerates curvature.

Consider first the left-most panels in both rows (linear coordinates). Clearly, a linear function provides a poor description of the trends because the trends are bowed inward (i.e., decreasing, negatively accelerated). Consider next the data in the bottom row only. The trend is bowed inward in semi-logarithmic coordinates (middle panel) but is reasonably linear in full-logarithmic coordinates (right-hand panel). Thus, a negative power function, but not a negative exponential function, describes the trend well. Consider finally the data in the top row. Here the trend appears to deviate from a straight line in all three plots. Yet among the plots of points in the top row, the one in the middle (semi-logarithmic) appears most nearly linear, suggesting that a negative exponential offers the best description of the three.

There are different reasons for reexpressing data. The reason emphasized here is that reexpressions which produce a linear trend can help one decide how well a particular function type describes a given set of data. A different reason for reexpressing data is to make the data set better conform to the distributional requirements for interpreting certain statistical calculations and tests (e.g., they may equalize variances or make the distributions more nearly normal in form). Whether or not a certain reexpression will prove useful or appropriate will depend, in part, on the intended purpose of the reexpression.

Other functions, distributions, and mathematical techniques can become familiar and are readily suggested by certain kinds of patterns in the data sets to those who are experienced with them. Probability theory provides an especially rich source. Often there are conventional transformations to make evaluation easier.

2.3. Curve fitting

The next step is to fit the theoretical function to the set of data. Many text books are available on the topic of regression analysis and curve fitting (e.g., Mosteller and Tukey, 1977; Kleinbaum et al., 1988). The statistical issues can be complex and can have important implications for interpreting the results. Thus, consultation with a professional statistician is advisable.

2.3.1. Parameter estimation and interpretation
Normally a mathematical model is an equation with a term representing some aspect

of behavior on the left and a set of interrelated terms on the right. The terms on the right are of two sorts. Some of the terms refer to concrete, manipulable events (i.e., independent variables). Others are *curve-fitting parameters* (also called *curve-fitting constants* or *free parameters*).

The values of the independent and dependent variables are known from the procedure and data. But the values of the other terms are not known. Parameter estimation, or curve-fitting, procedures find the values that the curve-fitting parameters must have for the equation to fit the data as well as it can, according to some criterion of 'best fit' (e.g., Restle and Greeno, 1970). Since the values of the curve-fitting constants are extracted from the data, they are best regarded as *dependent variables*.

Usually the curve-fitting constants are given additional meaning outside their role in the equation. That is, the constants may be given a name that is meaningful within some broader, perhaps nonmathematical, theoretical conception. Sometimes those names seem to imply that the terms refer to genuine independent variables. For example, the lower right-hand term in Herrnstein's hyperbolic equation, R_o, is described as referring to other reinforcement, including unscheduled reinforcement, in the situation (see Equation 2 above). But, in fact, R_o is operationally defined very differently from how scheduled reinforcers are defined. The value of R_o is the result of a curve-fitting operation, not the result of measuring how frequently some event follows a response. Whether or not we wish to interpret that constant as analogous to rate of reinforcement (an independent variable) will depend on considerations apart from how well an equation of the particular form fits the data.

2.3.2. Linear regression and other techniques

The simplest and most familiar techique is fitting a straight line to a set of data by means of Pearson's product-moment method. This method gives the best fitting straight line based on the criterion of minimizing the sum of the squared deviations between the data points and the line. There are two curve-fitting constants, the slope and the intercept, that are determined from the data. The procedure can be applied to the original data or to the reexpressions intended to produce a linear form. Other techniques are available to fit functions to nonlinear functions. Sometimes these involve a sort of 'getting warm-getting cold' process, where the program tries different curve-fitting parameters, evaluates the fit, and then adjusts the parameters according to some rule to see if the fit is improved.

2.4. Means

2.4.1. Arithmetic, geometric and harmonic means

Average values (e.g., means) also can suggest the most useful forms of equations describing the relation between independent and dependent variables. Imagine a set of observations ordered along some scale. Think of the observations as equal weights placed at the appropriate places on a wooden ruler. The mean of that set is analogous to the balance point along the ruler. Now imagine that the ruler/scale is stretched at the low end and compressed at the high end. The weigths at the low end would be moved farther from and the weights at the high end would be moved closer to the original balance point, and so the balance point would shift leftward – toward lower values. More generally, the balance point, or the mean, depends on the scale along which the observations are ordered. The mean will be analogous to the balance point only if it is calculated based on numbers expressed in units appropriate to the scale.

For example, logarithmic reexpressions $(x' = \log(x))$ in effect stretch the low end and compress the high end of scales. Thus, the mean of the original numbers (i.e., the *arithmetic mean*) will be high relative to the balance point on the logarithmic scale. To find the balance point on the logarithmic scale, one would need to calculate the mean of the logarithmic reexpressions: convert each number to its logarithm, sum the logs, and divide by the number of observations. The anti-log of the mean of the logs is the *geometric mean* of the original set of numbers. For example, the geometric mean of 10 and 100 can be found by taking the anti-log of the mean of the logs: since the log of 10 is 1 and the log of 100 is 2, the mean of the logs is $0.5(1+2) = 1.5$, and so the geometric mean is the anti-log of 1.5 (i.e., 31.6). The *arithmetic mean*, in contrast, is $0.5(10+100) = 55$. Similarly, reciprocal reexpressions $(x' = 1/x)$ stretch the low end and compress the high end relative to the original scale. Thus, if the reciprocal reexpression is appropriate, then the mean of the reciprocals would be the appropriate description of the balance point. The reciprocal of the mean of the reciprocals is the *harmonic mean* of the original numbers (cf. Killeen, 1968). To calculate the harmonic mean of 10 and 100, first get the mean of the reciprocals: $0.5[(1/10)+(1/100)] = 0.5(0.1+0.01) = 0.055$. Then take the reciprocal of the mean of the reciprocals: $(1/0.055) = 18.2$.

The same logic would apply to any scale reexpression: convert the original numbers to units of the new scale, calculate the mean of these reexpressions, and finally convert the mean of the reexpressed values back to units of the original scale. This new mean will differ from the mean of the original numbers depending on the relation between the two scales.

Because the mean is a balance point, it is very sensitive to extreme values (i.e., to skew). Thus, if a distribution of data is skewed, the mean will be misleading if it is interpreted as representing the typical value (cf. Stevens, 1955). One kind of solution is to reexpress the data so that the distribution becomes more nearly symmetrical, and then calculate the mean based on the reexpressed set. Calculating means of ratio data illustrates this kind of problem and solution. Imagine a choice procedure where, let us assume, there really is no preference. Suppose for unknown reasons the subject distributes its responses between the left and right alternatives on a 2:1 ratio on one day and on a 1:2 ratio on the next. We can see first what happens if we calculate the arithmetic mean of these two ratios: $0.5(2+0.5) = 1.25$. That mean suggests, misleadingly, that choice favors the left alternative. The reason is that 2 is a greater linear distance from 1 than is 0.5 even though a 2:1 choice ratio seems intuitively equivalent to a 1:2 ratio. Equal distances on a logarithmic scale correspond to equal ratios on the original scale. Thus, the geometric mean seems appropriate for this problem: $0.5[\ln(2)+\ln(0.5)]=0.5[0.693+(-0.693)] = 0$; and the anti-log of 0 is 1. And so the geometric mean suggests, appropriately, that neither alternative is favored over the other.

As just described, if you know the original numbers and the scale-reexpression rule, you can calculate the balance point (mean) for the distribution of reexpressed values. And then you can covert that mean to the corresponding value in the original scale. But often the scale-reexpression rule is precisely what you are trying to discover rather than what you know in advance. It may be possible to discover the reexpression rule by, in effect, working backward from the mean value. Suppose you know the original-scale values of the events that comprise a distribution. And suppose also that you can determine the balance point of the distribution. Then you can determine what transformation rule, applied to the original set of numbers, will result in the known mean value. More formally, let M represent the balance point of a distribution comprised of some number (N) of values (X_i). And let f represent the reexpression rule. (For the geometric mean, for example, the f specifies a logarithmic reexpression; for the harmonic mean, the f specifies a reciprocal reexpression.) Then

$$f(M) = (1/N)(\Sigma f(X_i))$$

The analytic task, then, is to find the form of f that satisfies the equation. The experimental task is to discover the balance point of the set of values, which sometimes can be accomplished with choice procedures (see Section 4.4.1 and Part 1, Ch. 6). The basic strategy is to determine what fixed value along a dimension is functionally equivalent to a distribution of values. The equivalent fixed value is the balance point of the distribution. For example, one might give subjects (e.g., pigeons) a choice between two situations, one providing a constant delay to food and the other a set of variable delays of known duration. Then the constant delay is varied in order to discover the duration of the constant value that is equally preferred to the set of variable delays. Finally, one tries to determine what rule for reexpressing the delays comprising the variable set results in the observed balance point. Killeen (1968) used this strategy to determine the best power-function reexpression of a set of variable delay intervals.

2.4.2. Moving averages

Suppose the values of the independent variable change over time. Although earlier values of the independent variable probably have some effect on behavior, the most recently experienced values are likely to have the greatest impact. To describe the effect, then, we need some way of updating the average value of the independent variable that preferentially weights values based on their recency. Such calculations are called *moving averages* or *running means*. Killeen (1981) described the properties of several kinds of moving averages. One, the Exponentially Weighted Moving Average (EWMA), has wide applicability. For EWMA:

$$A_N = \beta X_N + (1-\beta) A_{N-1}$$

where A_N is the updated mean, A_{N-1} is the previous value of the mean, X_N is the new (i.e., most recent) value, and β is a weighting factor, ranging between 0 and 1.0. The value of β determines how much the most recent event affects the updated mean. If β is close to zero, the new event will have only a small effect on the updated mean because the term to the left of the plus sign will be near zero. But if β is close to 1.0, the term on the right of the plus sign will be near zero, and so the new event will have a large effect on the updated mean. Intermediate values of β imply intermediate effects of the recent events. One can use EWMA as a model and determine the value of β that results in the best description of the behavioral adjustment to changing values of the independent variable (see Killeen, 1981).

3. Evaluating a mathematical model

To determine how well a given equation describes the data, one can plot the equation through the set of points and see whether it represents the trend well. If deviations appear random, those deviations may reflect the effect of uncontrolled variables. If those deviations are small, the function gains support as providing a good description. If, however, the deviations are systematic, even if small, then the model is not describing some systematic effect of the independent variable, and so the model is flawed in some way. (Judgments about the seriousness of the flaw will depend on a variety of considerations including the available alternatives and the conceptual underpinnings of the model (e.g., see Section 3.3).)

Visual and computational techniques are available to assess both the size and the systematic nature of deviations from some function (e.g., Mosteller and Tukey, 1977; Tukey, 1977; Kleinbaum et al., 1988). Some techniques evaluate mainly the size; others evaluate the extent to which the deviations are systematic.

In determining whether or not the deviations are systematic, it helps if the function is linear because deviations from a straight line are easy to detect. Thus, if the function being considered has a simple linear transformation, it is useful to reexpress the variables in the way implied (see Section 2.2 above, and Tukey, 1977).

3.1. Goodness-of-fit criteria (e.g., percent variance accounted for)

The square of the Pearson correlation coefficient, r^2, indicates the proportion of the total variance accounted for by the best-fitting straight line. Other curve-fitting techniques provide analogous measures. Clearly, a model that accounts for only a small proportion of the variance is not likely to be very effective. But researchers sometimes report values of r^2 as if they were paramount for judging the model's adequacy. In fact there are many reasons to view proportion of variance accounted for as only one of a number of criteria.

First, the proportion of variance measure does not indicate whether the deviations are systematic or unsystematic. Fig. 3 illustrates the difference between these two kinds of deviations. The data in the top row of Fig. 3 are the same as those in the bottom row of Fig. 2. But in Fig. 3 the best fitting straight lines are drawn and the r^2 values indicated. Not surprisingly, the straight line accounts for a relatively small proportion of the variance in the linear plot (left-most panel). But the best fitting lines in both the middle and right-hand panels account for a fairly high proportion of the variance. Although the r^2 value is higher in the right-hand plot, supporting a power function over an exponential function, the difference between those r^2 values is too small to provide a firm basis for choosing one function over the other. But determining whether the deviations are systematic might help. One way to determine this is to plot the residuals, the difference between the obtained Y-value and the predicted Y-value derived from the best fitting function. Then these residuals are plotted over the X-axis values (or over the predicted Y-values) (e.g., Mosteller and Tukey, 1977; Tukey, 1977; Kleinbaum et al., 1988). If the deviations are unsystematic, then the residuals will scatter around a horizontal line. But if the deviations are systematic, then those residuals will vary in an orderly way. The residuals for the data in the top row are shown in the lower row of Fig. 3. These residual plots indicate that the deviations are indeed systematic for the linear and exponential functions (i.e., they are bitonic in form) but not for the power function. (Whether or not a power function

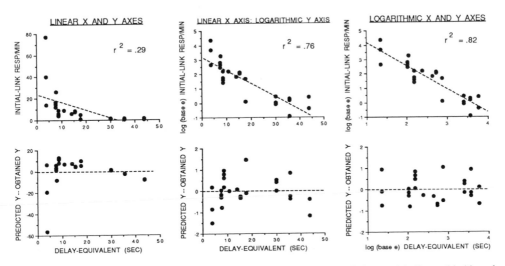

Fig. 3. *Top row*: Scatter plots from the bottom row of Fig. 2 with the best fitting straight lines added based on minimizing the squared deviations (Pearson product-moment). (Adapted from Shull et al., 1990, Pigeon 3819, with permission of the publisher.) *Bottom row*: The residuals plots.

is accepted as an adequate description would depend on additional considerations, as discussed in Section 3.3).

A second potential problem with 'blindly' accepting r^2 values to support a model is illustrated in the left-hand panel of Fig. 4. In this plot, eight of the nine points appear to scatter around a decreasing function. The remaining point, an *outlier*, falls on a positive function relative to the other eight. Regression analyses are based on relative variances, and so a single extreme point can dramatically affect the outcome. Here the single outlier results in a positive best fitting function which accounts for 75% of the variance in the set of data. Common sense, however, suggests that the extreme data point may not be comparable with the others and that we ought not take the results of the regression analysis at face value. Textbooks on regression analysis (e.g., Kleinbaum et al., 1988) discuss statistical tests to aid judgments about whether or not a given point should be considered an outlier.

For similar reasons, it is important to consider whether or not the independent variable is evenly distributed over the X-axis. An effective strategy usually is to sample a wide range of values of the independent variable but to concentrate values in the region where the function of interest is changing the most. In that region the various alternative functions are likely to be most different (see Fig. 1), and so it is important to determine the shape in that region as thoroughly as possible. Yet, if the majority of values are bunched at one end with a few others distributed toward the other end of the range, then the effects can be like that produced by an outlier: the few extreme points can have a disproportionately large effect on the regression analysis. One needs, then, to be especially sensitive to the possible effects of spacing on parameter estimates. The X-axis spacing can be a particular problem when the values of the independent variable are reexpressed. Suppose the experimenter selected values of an independent variable that were evenly spaced along a linear X-axis (e.g., 10, 20, 30, 40, 50 and 60). But if these values are converted to logarithms for the purpose, say, of fitting some function, then the values of the reexpressed independent variable will be spaced progressively closer together, moving left to right along the X-axis. (See Wetherington and Lucas, 1980, and McDowell, 1981, for a discussion of related issues in connection with fitting Herrnstein's equation to a set of data.)

A third problem is that the range of variables along the X-axis can have a profound effect on r^2 values. The scatter of points in the right-hand panel of Fig. 4 appears to follow a linearly decreasing trend (in double logarithmic coordinates). The data are the same as those in the upper right-hand panel of Fig. 3 (Pigeon 3819 in Shull et al., 1990). In fact, the best fitting straight line accounts for 82% of the variance in the full data set, suggesting a moderately good fit. But suppose the experiment had sampled the independent variable only over the range of values bracketed by the vertical lines (i.e., the closed points). If so, only a very weak trend would have been apparent based on the Pearson technique ($r^2 = 0.17$), and the conclusion about the adequacy of the equation for describing the data could have been quite different. Again, the value of r^2 depends on relative variance. So if the independent variable

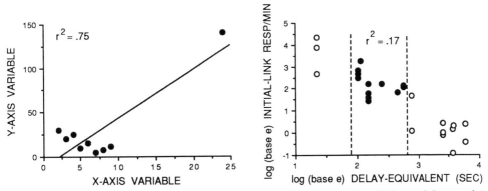

Fig. 4. *Left panel*: Scatter plot (made-up data) showing the effect of an outlier. *Right-panel*: Scatter plot showing the effect of restricted sampling along the X-axis. (Adapted from Shull et al., 1990, Pigeon 3819, with permission of the publisher.)

covers only a small range of values, it may contribute little to the variance in the data relative to 'noise' even if it exerts a relatively potent effect when a larger range is considered.

Finally, if the data set contains only two points, the best fitting straight line will account for 100% of the variance. Thus, to have a meaningful test, the data set has to contain substantially more data points than there are free parameters to estimate. Unfortunately, there is no simple, absolute guide as to how many data points are sufficient.

An equation that precisely describes a lot of data and that contains few free parameters is likely to be judged superior. And, in fact, quantitative formulas have been developed to compare models based on those three factors: the average size of the deviations from predicted values, the number of data points, and the number of free parameters (e.g., Akaike, 1974, as described by Davison and McCarthy, 1988, pp. 113–114). Although such formulas sometimes can be helpful, relying too heavily on them can be dangerous. The fact is that evaluating a model requires good judgement based on careful consideration of many factors (e.g., Baum, 1983).

3.2. Accuracy versus generality

A different kind of issue about the importance of variance accounted for should be considered. Should one aim primarily for the equation that most accurately describes the pattern of results in the particular set of data at hand? Consider again the full set of data points in the right-hand panel of Fig. 4. Although an equation could be found that would connect all the points, thus accounting for 100% of the variance in the data set, it would be a very complex one. In contrast, a linear equation provides a very simple description of the trend (in logarithmic coordinates). Yet the linear equation is inaccurate because no single straight line can connect all, or even most, of the points.

Which equation should we choose? The answer depends on how we weight the answers to the following questions: Which equation better describes other sets of data obtained under similar and different conditions? Which equation has the fewest free parameters? And for which equation do the parameters relate most clearly to manipulable variables and basic theoretical concepts? An equation generated with the sole criterion of providing the best fit to a particular set of data is unlikely to provide a general, integrative description.

Herrnstein's hyperbolic equation came to dominate the field not because its fit to Catania and Reynolds' (1968) data was demonstrably superior. A power function probably would have fit about as well. But the hyperbolic function was derived from an equation developed for other data sets (i.e., matching in concurrent schedules), and so its parameters made sense (see Section 2.1.2).

Estes (1959) discussed a related issue in connection with the development of stimulus sampling theory. He was concerned with describing data on the acquisition of barpressing in rats:

> Any number of simple mathematical functions can be fitted to the observed acquisition curves. ...we see the result of fitting a single empirical curve with two different mathematical functions. If we require only descriptive adequacy, then our choice of functions is clearly going to be quite arbitrary. If we are not willing to settle for an arbitrary choice, then some further reflection is in order.
>
> Why are we so reluctant to make an arbitrary choice of functions? Obviously because we are hoping eventually to achieve more than an accurate description of acquisition in one particular situation. We would like to arrive at a description which will hold for a variety of situations. And we would like to find that the parameters in our functions have theoretical significance, i.e., that their values reflect manipulations of variables in some reasonable way. These aspirations bring us up against a conservation law which has been recognized more or less explicitly since the time of John Locke to hold for all theoretical undertakings. Theories transform information; they do not create it. If we hope to get more out of our mathematical model than a description of a particular set of facts, then we will have to take a broader range of facts into account when formulating the model (pp. 389–390).

4. Examples of applications of mathematical description

4.1. Specification of the dependent variable

As Skinner (1935) noted, the search for the effective dimensions of responding (and of the environment) is an iterative process. The specifications are progressively modified until there is no further improvement in the orderliness of the relationship. Mathematical description can aid in this effort to specify the dependent variable better.

4.1.1. Response rate as composed of burst and pause modes
In operant conditioning experiments the experimenter usually measures responses as brief, discrete events that occur in time. Temporal distributions of responses sampled under different conditions or over different intervals of time under the same condition

can differ from each other along many different dimensions. One such dimension is the average rate of a response (number of response/time available to make the response). A critical question is whether average rate is the dimension of responding that is related most simply to significant classes of environmental variables.

Skinner (1950, 1953, 1957) described operant behavior as varying in tendency, or in its probability of occurrence. Intuitively, response tendency should vary as a function of such variables as reinforcement and nonreinforcement, the amount and frequency of the reinforcer, properties of the discriminative stimulus, and motivational variables. To determine these controlling relationships precisely, we need to measure some property of responding that varies in a straightforward way with these classes of variables. Average response rate sometimes shows the appropriate orderliness (e.g. Herrnstein, 1970), but often it does not (cf. discussion by Nevin, 1979, especially pp. 148–150; Shimp, 1975). This failure is troublesome.

Perhaps the problem is that response rate is not a unitary dimension. Suppose that different aspects of the temporal distribution of responses are controlled by different classes of environmental events. If so, the overall average response rate would be a complexly determined composite. It may be possible, however, to dissect out the components of the temporal distribution, thereby revealing more elementary relationships.

Suppose, for example, that responding occurs in bursts, where the time between responses within a burst is controlled by one set of variables and the time between bursts is controlled by another set (e.g., Gilbert, 1958; Blough, 1963; Premack, 1965; Williams, 1968; Pear and Rector, 1979; Nevin and Baum, 1980; Wearden, 1983). Assuming two different responding modes, the average rate of the response can be described as:

$$Total\ Resp\ Rate = \frac{Total\ Resp}{Total\ time} =$$

$$\frac{(Resp\ rate\ in\ burst) \times (Mean\ burst\ duration) \times (Number\ of\ bursts)}{Total\ time}$$

More formally:

$$B = \frac{P}{T} = \frac{FLN}{T} \tag{3}$$

where B refers to the total average rate of the response; P refers to the total number of responses; T refers to the total time that the response could occur; F refers to the average rate of the response during the bursts; L refers to the mean duration of the burst; and N refers to the number of times during the observation period that a burst was initiated. In words, the numerator in the right-hand expression says that the total number of responses is the product of the response rate during the burst, the average amount of time spent in the burst, and the number of times the burst was initiated.

We can consider, further, how to express the number of bursts. First, think of a cycle consisting of the time between bursts and the duration of the burst. The number of bursts (N) is the number of such cycles during the total session time (T). The mean time between the end of one burst and the start of the next is simply the reciprocal of the mean rate of burst initiations (i.e., $1/I$, where I refers to the rate of burst initiations). (The rate of burst initiations would be the number of bursts divided by the total time minus the time spent in the bursts.) For example, if the rate is three initiations per min, the average time between initiations is 20 s. Thus, the cycle time is $[(1/I) + L]$. And so the number of burst initiations is given by:

$$N = \frac{T}{\left(\dfrac{1}{I}\right) + L} \tag{4}$$

We can substitute the right-hand term in Equation 4 for N in Equation 3, which yields:

$$B = \frac{FL\left[\dfrac{T}{\left(\dfrac{1}{I}\right) + L}\right]}{T}$$

and which can further be reduced to:

$$B = \frac{FL}{\left(\dfrac{1}{I}\right) + L} \tag{5}$$

If the independent variable of interest changes only the rate of initiating bursts, without affecting the other components of the right-hand term, then the overall average response rate would change in the same direction. To appreciate this point, consider the denominator of Equation 5. As the rate of initiations (I) increases, $1/I$ decreases, and so B (the overall average response rate) will increase.

It may be worth emphasizing how the rate of initiating bursts should be calculated. A burst cannot be initiated during the time that it is occurring, only when it is not occurring. Thus, the rate of initiating bursts would be the number of bursts divided by the total time minus the time spent in the burst [i.e., $I = N/(T - (NL))$].

With some further rearranging, Equation 5 becomes:

$$B = \frac{FI}{I + (1/L)} \tag{6}$$

If the response rate during the burst (F) and the mean duration of the burst (L) were constant, then Equation 6 would be a hyperbolic function, of the general form, $y = kx/(x + c)$, where x and y are variables and k and c are constants.

Fig. 5 plots the average overall response rate as a function of the rate of burst initi-

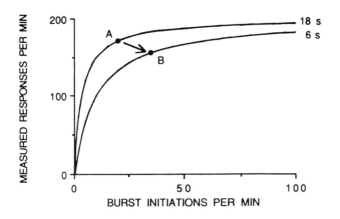

Fig. 5. The mean overall rate of the measured response (responses per min) plotted over the rate of burst initiations (initiations per min) based on Equation 6. The mean response rate during the burst was set at 200 per min. Each of the two curves assumes a different mean burst duration (6 or 18 s).

ations according to Equation 6. Two functions are shown, corresponding to two different mean burst durations ($L = 6$ s and $L = 18$ s). Note that the functions are negatively accelerated so that the average overall response rate becomes progressively insensitive to changes in the initiation rate as initiation rate increases. Further, this insensitivity becomes more pronounced with progressively longer burst durations. An implication is that a variable that might have a strong and systematic effect on the rate of initiations will have little or no effect on the average overall response rate except under conditions where response rate is very low.

Suppose, further, that the independent variable affected other components of the expression as well as the rate of initiating bursts. If so, then the relation between overall average response rate and the rate of initiations would be even more complex. In fact the two rates could change in opposite directions if the variable increased the rate of burst initiations but decreased either the response rate within a burst (F) or the average burst duration (L). Such an effect is illustrated in Fig. 5 by the arrow showing a shift from Point A to Point B.

The discussion to this point has been to show how average overall response rate can be described formally as a composite of separate properties. An analysis of this sort is most likely to be useful if the separate properties are related to different classes of controlling variables. That possibility can be expressed more formally. We begin with the general statement that each of the components of response rate identified in Equation 6 is some function of environmental variables (E), which can include natural selection in the evolutionary past. And so,

$$F = f_1 (E_1)$$
$$L = f_2 (E_2)$$
$$I = f_3 (E_3)$$

Substituting these into the equation for overall response rate (Equation 6) gives,

$$B = \frac{f_1(E_1) \times f_3(E_3)}{f_3(E_3) + \left(\dfrac{1}{f_2(E_2)}\right)} \tag{7}$$

Perhaps one or more of the components of overall response rate, such as burst-initiation rate, is simply and strongly related to classes of variables that we think should strongly affect response tendency in a fundamental way (e.g., rate or amount of reinforcement, deprivation, and variations of the discriminative stimulus). That is, $f_3(E_3)$ might be a simple one. But that simplicity will not show up in the overall measure of response rate if, in fact, overall response rate is composed of separately controlled components along the lines suggested here. The response rate within a burst, $f_1(E_1)$, might depend mainly on the differential reinforcement of response rate and on phylogenic variables.

The point of this discussion is not to advocate any particular representation of response rate but to illustrate an approach based on mathematical description. Such description can help one keep track of what the possibilities are, given certain assumptions about the possible composition of response rate. But they do not answer such difficult experimental questions as how to define and count 'bursts' (cf. Gilbert, 1958; Pear and Rector, 1979). An experimental analysis is needed to establish the utility of the description.

4.1.2. Latency and interresponse-time distributions

What do we mean when we say that operant behavior is emitted and that variables influence the probability of emission? One interpretation can be illustrated with an admittedly crude analogy. Imagine a pot of boiling oatmeal on a stove with a device above the pot that records 'spatters' from the bubbles. Certain variables, such as the heat level under the pot, will determine the rate of spattering. But the exact moment of a spatter is determined by events (e.g., convergence of particular molecules) that are not related in any one-to-one manner with the molar variables like heat level.

In this analogy the spatters correspond to operant responses (emitted) and the heat level corresponds to the classes of variables that affect the emission rate of operant behavior such as rate of reinforcement, deprivation level and characteristics of the discriminative stimulus. The example is intended to illustrate a system that has a probabilistic, or stochastic, output. Manipulable variables (e.g., heat level or rate of reinforcement) determine the average emission rate but not the moments of occurrence. A powerful descriptive language derived from probability theory has been developed for prototypic stochastic systems (McGill, 1963; Luce, 1986) and should apply to operant behavior if operant behavior is related stochastically to classes of environmental variables.

Of particular interest is the time elapsed from some event until a response occurs, that is, response *latencies*. If the time is measured from the end of one response unit until the beginning of the next, the latencies are called *interresponse latencies* or *interresponse times*. For the following discussion, it does not matter whether the latency is timed from the previous response or from some other event (e.g., from reinforcement). What is important is that the latencies vary in characteristic ways that may reveal the nature of the controlling relationships (cf. McGill, 1963; Fagen and Young, 1978; Luce, 1986; Clifton, 1987).

Suppose that the probability of a response is constant regardless of elapsed time since the start of the latency (e.g., $p = 0.2$ per bin, where bin refers to the time unit for recording latencies – i.e., the class interval). What should be the shape of the expected frequency distribution of latencies? Assume that we recorded the first 1000 latencies. The expected number of latencies that ended in the first bin would be the probability of a response during that bin (0.2) multiplied by the number of times the response could have occurred during that bin (1000): i.e., 0.2 (1000) = 200. The expected number of latencies ended in the second bin would likewise be the probability of a response during that bin (0.2) times the number of opportunities to respond during the second bin. But the number of opportunities would not be 1000, since any latency that ended during the first bin would have eliminated an opportunity to respond during the second bin. Thus, the number of opportunities would be (1000 – 200), or 800, and so the expected frequency in the second bin should be 0.2 (800) = 160. The expected frequency in the third bin would be calculated similarly: 0.2 (800 – 160) = 128. The theoretical calculations would proceed the same way if the constant probability per bin was 0.4 instead of 0.2 except that the values would, of course, be different.

The relative frequency distributions that would result from two different constant response probabilities (0.2 and 0.4) are shown in the upper left panel of Fig. 6. Relative frequencies are simply the expected number of latencies in a given bin divided by the total number of latencies. Even though the response probability is constant, the relative frequency function decreases continuously because there is a decreasing number of opportunities in each successive bin. Although the functions are similar in form, the function generated by the higher probability drops more sharply. Thus, both probability values produce a distribution of latencies, some long and some short. But a lower response probability generates relatively more long latencies.

The logic of these calculations can be generalized. There is an opportunity to respond in the ith bin only when the latency has not ended in an earlier bin. The probability that the latency has not ended in the first bin is $(1 - p)$, where p is the probability of a response during a bin and, for this example, is constant. Thus, the number of opportunities in the second bin is $N(1 - p)$, where N is the total number of latencies (N). Similarly, there is an opportunity to respond during the third bin only when the latency has not ended during either the first or the second bin. The chances of two nonoccurrences in a row is $(1 - p)(1 - p)$, and so the number of opportunities to respond during the third bin is $N(1 - p)(1 - p)$. More generally, the opportunities to respond during the ith bin, F_i, is:

$$F_i = N(1-p)^{i-1} \tag{8}$$

Then, the frequency in the ith bin, f_i, is:

$$f_i = N(1-p)^{i-1}p \tag{9}$$

which is a geometric decreasing progression; the frequency is a constant proportion of the opportunities remaining. (Relative frequencies and relative opportunities would be obtained by dividing through by N.) (Note that the opportunities value is represented by an upper case letter (F), while the frequency is represented by the same letter in lower case (f). This representation is commonly used to indicate that the two functions are tightly related. The opportunities function is a backward cumulative function of the frequency function.

We often are interested in determining how the probability of a response varies as a function of elapsed time during the latency, which can be determined from a logarithmic transformation of the opportunities function. Plots showing the logarithm of the opportunities as a function of elapsed time (not log-transformed) are called *log survivor functions* (cf. Luce, 1986).

When the response probability is constant, the opportunities function (Equation 8) is a geometric decreasing function, which is similar to a negative exponential (see Section 2.2). The logarithmic transformation of the opportunities function is

$$\log(F_i) = \log(1-p)\,(i-1) + \log(N) \tag{10}$$

Because the logarithm of a decimal is negative in sign, Equation 10 says that the log survivors decrease linearly as a function of elapsed time (i). This linearity should make some intuitive sense. A constant probability of responding (p) implies that a constant proportion of the remaining opportunities will be lost in each bin. Equal proportions, or ratios, correspond to equal distances on a logarithmic scale.

The key point is that if one plots the log survivor function based on real data, the slope will indicate how the response probability varies as a function of elapsed time since the start of the latency. If, for example, the log survivor function decreases linearly with elapsed time, then the probability of a response is constant. The steeper the slope, the higher the response probability. If, instead, the log survivor function curves downward (i.e., decreases at a positively accelerated rate), the probability of a response is increasing over elapsed time. Conversely, if the log survivor function decreases at a negatively accelerated rate, the probability of a response is decreasing.

A different kind of plot, one showing response probability as a function of time, is known as the *hazard function* (e.g., Luce, 1986) or the interresponse time per opportunity function (Anger, 1956). The hazard function shows response probability directly. In contrast, response probability is estimated from the slope of the log survivor function. But the log survivor function is useful because it can be plotted quickly.

The left two columns of Fig. 6 show from top to bottom, theoretical frequency

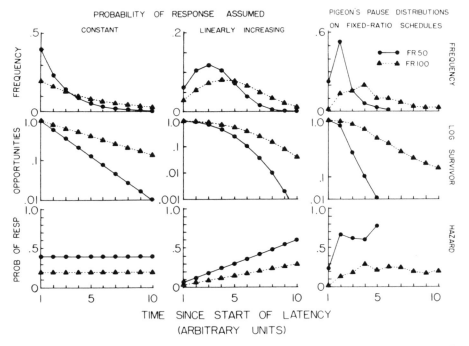

Fig. 6. Relative frequency distributions of response latencies (top row), log relative survivor functions (middle row), and hazard functions (bottom row) plotted over the class interval of elapsed time since the start of the latency. The graphs in the left and middle columns show data generated by assuming that response probability was constant (left) or increased linearly (middle) as a function of elapsed time. The graphs in the right column show response latencies (postreinforcement) from one pigeon studied under FR 50 and FR 100. (Adapted from Shull, 1979, with permission of the publisher.)

distributions, log survivor functions, and hazard functions based on different simple assumptions about response probability. In the far left column, the assumption was that response probability was constant over elapsed time (either 0.2 or 0.4). In the middle column the assumption was that the response probability increased linearly with elapsed time (two different linear functions). Note that the log survivor functions are linearly decreasing in the far left plot but are continuously curved downward in the middle plot. Also note that the frequency distributions in the middle column are bitonic instead of monotonic decreasing. The bitonicity is the product of a rising response probability and a declining number of opportunities.

For these illustrations, we worked backward compared to what is done in empirical research. Here, we asserted values for the response probability and then calculated the expected frequencies and opportunities. In actual research, we obtain the frequencies of latencies and from them estimate the response probabilities by dividing the frequency in each class interval by the opportunities.

We may illustrate these calculations by considering the response latencies generated by a pigeon under fixed-ratio (FR) schedules of food reinforcement. The FR value was 50 for a block of sessions and then 100 for another block. The latencies were timed from the completion of one FR 'run' until the start of the next. During each of the last 5 sessions of an FR value, the latencies were recorded in sequence on paper tape from which the frequency and opportunity distributions were constructed (5-s bins). The number of opportunities in a particular bin is the number of latencies as long or longer than the lower bound of the bin. Finally, the frequency per opportunity values were calculated by dividing the number of latencies ended in a bin by the number of opportunities to respond in that bin. These functions are shown in the right-hand panels of Fig. 6.

The log survivor functions appear roughly linear over much of their range after an initial period of curving downward. They indicate that the response probability is fairly constant after an initial rise. Furthermore, because the log survivor function is steeper under FR 50 than under FR 100, the response probability is higher under the smaller (more favorable) FR schedule. These variations in response probability can be seen more directly in the probability functions (the hazard functions).

The appearance of the log survivor functions for FR schedules is similar to that found with response-initiated fixed-interval (FI) schedules (e.g., chain FR 1 FI schedules) but is different from those found with FI schedules where the interval is timed from the last reinforcer delivery. Under FI schedules, the log survivor functions are continuously curved downward. These differences, which are not apparent in the frequency distributions of latencies, may suggest different temporal control relations under FR (and response-initiated FI) schedules versus under FI schedules (cf. Shull, 1979; Capehart et al., 1980).

With these sorts of plots, one can see the extent to which responding approximates a simple random emitter. As discussed earlier in this section, a simple random emitter implies a constant response probability (i.e., a horizontal hazard function and a linearly decreasing log survivor function). It is clear from the data in the right-hand column of Fig. 6, for example, that the response probability is not constant during the latency under FR schedules, although it may approach constancy after an initial rise.

Deviations from a simple random emitter can occur for a number of reasons (cf. McGill, 1963; Luce, 1986). For example, the measured response might be the end product of a chain of activities (e.g., Killeen and Fetterman, 1988). Each of the activities comprising the chain might have a constant probability of terminating. But if so, the probability of completing the whole chain will rise and then level off. Alternatively, the emission probability might be under discriminative control of elapsed time since the start of the latency. Or the temporal distribution of responses might be a composite of two or more different emission processes, such as discussed in Section 4.1.1. In such cases, there might be a sharp bend in the log survivor functions (cf. Clifton, 1987). For some prototypic cases of these types of processes the mathematical description has been worked out (cf. McGill, 1963; Fagen and Young, 1978; Luce, 1986; Clifton, 1987). It may be possible, therefore, to make inferences about the structure of responding and, perhaps, about the kinds of controlling relationships based on the match between actual latency distributions and the theoretical functions of interest. The treatment of these issues is, it must be noted, quite complex (cf. Luce, 1986 for a thorough discussion).

One additional point requires comment. In the discussion to this point, elapsed time was treated as divided into discrete class intervals. A parallel mathematical description is available for the limiting case where the class interval size is conceptualized as vanishingly small so that elapsed time can be represented as a continuous variable. There are analytical advantages to developing models based on continuous functions (e.g. the availability of the techniques of calculus), and one is likely to see descriptions expressed in that form (e.g., McGill, 1963; Killeen, 1975; Luce, 1986). For example, the analog of the geometric decreasing function would be:

$$f(t) = \lambda\, e^{-\lambda t}$$

where λ is a rate constant analogous to p in the geometric function; t is elapsed time analogous to i in the geometric function; and e is the base of the natural logarithms. In log form, $\ln(f(t)) = -\lambda t + \ln(\lambda)$, which is linear. (Recall that the e-term drops out because the log of the base is 1.) More complex functions describing probabilistic events in time usually have their discrete-interval counterparts that are harder to work with mathematically but that are often easier to appreciate conceptually. With some diligence, it is often possible, even for the mathematically unskilled, to construct some approximation to the discrete-interval analog.

4.2. Specification of the independent variable

A researcher manipulates concrete environmental events. The particular manipulations differ from each other along many different dimensions. Some of those dimensions may influence behavior whereas others may not. The task is to discover the dimensions that systematically affect behavior. More formally, we are seeking an effective specification of E (an environmental variable) in the general formula, $B = f(E)$. A few examples are described briefly.

4.2.1. The temporal distribution of reinforcers

A pigeon's choice between two stimulus situations depends on the temporal distribution of food reinforcers obtained in the two stimuli. But what exactly about the temporal distribution of reinforcers controls choice? One possible dimension is the amount of food reinforcement per time spent in the situation – that is, the arithmetic rate of food reinforcement, or $M_A = R/T$, where M_A refers to the arithmetic rate of reinforcement; R refers to the number of reinforcers obtained in a situation; and T refers to the time spent in the situation. But choice is not related consistently to (R/T) when the temporal distributions of reinforcement are varied systematically (e.g., McDiarmid and Rilling, 1965; Killeen, 1968; Mazur, 1986; Shull and Spear, 1987).

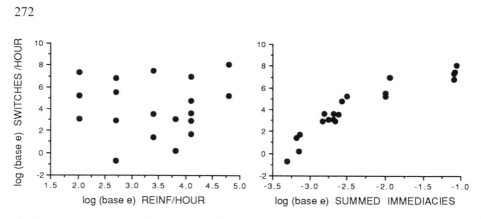

Fig. 7. Rate of switching to Stimulus B as a function of two ways of specifying the temporal distribution of food reinforcers in Stimulus B. (Adapted from Shull and Spear, 1987, Pigeon 3819, with permission of the publisher.)

In one study (Shull and Spear, 1987) pigeons could remain in one stimulus (Stimulus A) where they received food on a VI schedule or they could switch to another stimulus (Stimulus B). Over conditions, several aspects of the temporal distribution of reinforcers during Stimulus B were varied: the duration of this second situation, the number of food reinforcers delivered, and the delays to those food deliveries timed from the switch. The measure of responding was the rate of switching into the second situation. The left-hand panel of Fig. 7 shows, for one of the pigeons, the switching rate (logarithmic scale) plotted over the arithmetic rate of reinforcement in Stimulus B. The plot of points in that panel shows no apparent order. One might conclude either that the independent variable has no systematic effect or that uncontrolled variables mask any systematic effect. But the data in the right-hand panel of Fig. 7 suggest a different conclusion. Switching rate is plotted as a function of a different property of the temporal distribution of reinforcers, namely the sum of the immediacies, $\Sigma \, (1/D_i)$, where D_i indicates the delay to the ith (i.e., the first, the second, the third etc.) food reinforcer following the switch, where all delays are timed from the switch (McDiarmid and Rilling, 1965; Mazur, 1986; Shull et al., 1990). Switching rate appears to vary as an orderly function of the sum of the immediacies.

This example illustrates several points of relevance to a general consideration of mathematical description. First, behavior can appear unrelated to a set of concrete manipulations when those manipulations are described one way but can appear highly related to those same manipulations when those manipulations are described in a different way. Second, by specifying the dimensions (i.e., rate of reinforcement or sum of the immediacies) in quantitative terms, it was possible to order the experimental conditions along the X-axis in different ways and thus see which dimension had the most systematic effect on behavior. Third, one may be able to determine rather precisely what dimensions of the environment influence behavior without precisely specifying the function between that dimension and behavior. It may be sufficient to say merely that the dependent variable is an ordinal function of the independent variable dimension.

Other examples of using mathematical quantification to determine how best to specify the independent variable include: Fantino and Abarca's (1985) analyses of the temporal variables that influence choice in laboratory analogs of foraging; Killeen's (1968) work on finding the transformation rules for determining the conditioned reinforcement values produced by VI versus FI schedules of food reinforcement; Killeen's (1981) analysis of how best to describe the dimension of recency (see Section 2.4.2); and, efforts to determine how the relational property of the environment known as the *contingency* should be specified (cf. Gibbon et al., 1974; Gibbon and Balsam, 1981).

4.3. Reciprocal determinism (feedback functions)

In operant conditioning the variable that is assumed to influence responding inevitably depends on responding. The rate of the reinforcer, for example, is assumed to influence the rate of the response. But because the reinforcer is contingent on the response, the reinforcement rate depends to some degree on the response rate. Thus, the dependent variable affects the independent variable. Such reciprocal determinism may appear to prohibit an identification of simple controlling relations between behavior and the environment. That appearance is false, however (cf. Zuriff, 1985, pp. 108–110). There are mathematical techniques that can help disentangle the reciprocal controlling relationships.

Two functions are required. One, the *feedback function*, describes how the controlling aspect of the environment is altered by behavior. For example, a feedback function might describe how the reinforcement rate will depend upon the response rate. It is important to appreciate that the feedback function does not predict behavior. It is strictly a description of some aspect of the environment – a complex relational aspect, or a contingency (cf. Weingarten and Mechner, 1966). It describes the way the *environment* changes under certain conditions. The second function is the *behavior function*, which describes how some property of behavior is affected by the environmental variable. For example, it might describe how the rate of reinforcement is assumed to affect the rate of responding. That function cannot be determined empirically in the total absence of a dependency between rate of reinforcement and the rate of behavior. Nonetheless, conditions can be arranged that progressively weaken the feedback constraint. For example, response rate affects reinforcement rate much less under VI schedules than under variable-ratio (VR) schedules. Thus, VI schedules are commonly used in preparations intended to determine the behavior function for the effect of rate of reinforcement on the rate of behavior. Confidence in the behavior function depends on a variety of considerations including how well it fits the data as conditions more closely approximate the ideal (feedback free) situation, the validity of predictions about behavior in other situations, connections with other theoretical developments, and so forth. Once the feedback and behavior functions are specified (perhaps only as hypotheses to be tested), they can be combined to derive

274

equilibrium solutions. A simple illustration of this general approach follows (see also Baum, 1973, 1981; Nevin and Baum, 1980; Rachlin et al., 1981; McDowell and Wixted, 1988).

Under VR schedules, reinforcement is delivered when a specified number of responses has occurred. Thus, the faster the animal responds, the more quickly reinforcement occurs. Given a sufficiently long averaging interval, the reinforcement rate on VR schedules is proportional to the response rate, with the reinforcement-to-response ratio $(1/VR)$ determining the proportionality. That is:

$$R = \left(\frac{1}{C}\right) B \ (60) \tag{11}$$

where R is the reinforcement rate, B is the response rate, and C is the mean of the VR schedule (i.e., the mean response count per reinforcer). The 60 is simply a scaling factor due to the convention of expressing response rates in responses per min and reinforcement rates in reinforcers per h. Equation 11 is a feedback function. We may take Herrnstein's hyperbolic equation as an example of a behavior function (cf. McDowell and Wixted, 1988, for one of several alternatives). As presented earlier (Equation 2):

$$B = \frac{kR}{R + R_o}$$

Because the feedback function and the behavior function have the same two terms (B and R), they can be plotted in the same coordinates. Fig. 8 shows the feedback functions resulting from three different VR schedules. These are the three straight lines rising from the origin at the lower left. Also shown are two behavior functions based on the hyperbolic function with $k = 100$. The upper one is based on setting R_o

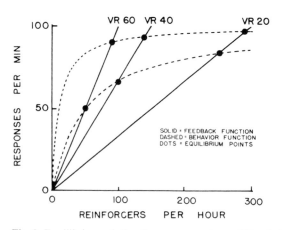

Fig. 8. Equilibrium solution for response rates on VR schedules.

equal to 10; the lower one is based on setting R_o equal to 50. The point where the feedback function intersects the behavior function is the *equilibrium point*. Thus, the response rate can be predicted, given the behavior function, by drawing a line horizontally from the intersection to the Y-axis. To appreciate why this is so, consider what would happen, say, for the VR 60 schedule if response rate were below the intersection point. That response rate generates a reinforcement rate (via the feedback function) that maintains a response rate specified by the behavior function. But because the behavior function is above the feedback function at that point, the response rate should tend to increase. When the response rate increases, the reinforcement rate will increase also, causing a shift to the right on the behavior function. Eventually, the response rate will generate a reinforcement rate that will generate exactly that same response rate again. That point is where the functions intersect. Response rates above the equilibrium point will adjust in a similar fashion except in the reverse direction.

The equilibrium points resulting from different VR sizes or from different behavior functions can be determined graphically, as just suggested (cf. McDowell and Wixted, 1988). It also may be possible to develop an equation for finding the equilibrium point. The goal is to generate an equation showing how response rate at equilibrium varies with, say, VR size. The key is to notice that at equilibrium the coordinate values of the two functions are equal. Thus, one writes both equations (the behavior equation and the feedback equation) in terms of reinforcement rate. Then one sets the two equations equal and solves for response rate. Visually, in terms of Fig. 8, you are moving along the X-axis until you reach the point where both functions have the same reinforcement rate – i.e., the point where they intersect. Then you go up to the intersection point and move left horizontally to get the response rate.

The feedback function (Equation 11) already is written in terms of reinforcement rate. The hyperbolic behavior function needs to be rewritten. With some rearranging of terms Equation 2 becomes:

$$R = \frac{B R_o}{k - B} \tag{12}$$

Now setting Equation 11 to Equation 12 gives:

$$\left(\frac{1}{C}\right) B (60) = \frac{B R_o}{k - B}$$

and solving for B, the response rate, produces

$$B = k - C R_o (1/60) \tag{13}$$

which is the equilibrium solution. By this solution, response rate should be a linearly decreasing function of the VR size. That implication can be seen visually in Fig. 8 since the VR schedules represented by the feedback functions comprise a linear progression. Read the Y-axis values corresponding to the intersections along a particular behavior function. Those Y-axis values will be spaced evenly, indicating a linear progression of response rates.

The point of this exercise is to show how, in principle, mathematical description can aid the analysis of controlling relations where the controlling variable (here reinforcement rate) depends, in turn, on the controlled variable (here the response rate). The discovery of feedback functions is straightforward conceptually but often difficult in practice. One needs to decide what environmental dimensions to represent in the equation. If, for example, one assumed that the average rate of reinforcement influenced responding, one would develop a feedback function that showed how rate of reinforcement depended on behavior under a given schedule. But if one assumed that some other dimension of reinforcement was important, then one would develop a feedback function that showed how that other dimension depended on behavior. For example, suppose that the temporal patterning of reinforcement, not just the average rate of reinforcement, was assumed to matter. Then the feedback function would need to describe how behavior affects the temporal patterning of reinforcers (cf. Nevin and Baum, 1980, for a related discussion). Regardless of the specific solution, the approach is to determine the equilibrium points based on the particular set of equations and then to see how well the data conform to those predictions.

4.4. Experimental tests based on nonobvious implications of mathematical models

Sometimes alternative models generate functions that are similar in shape despite being derived from very different conceptions of the process (see Fig. 1). It may be hard to decide among the models, then, unless one can find some set of circumstances where the different models imply clearly different outcomes. Mathematical description sometimes aids the discovery of such circumstances.

4.4.1. Example: indifference point analysis

Suppose, for example, that we are interested in describing the effect of reinforcement delay on responding. There is ample precedent for regarding the function as decreasing, negatively accelerated. Among the functions that have been proposed are the negative exponential and the reciprocal (or hyperbolic). Although they appear similar, they have different implications for understanding preference shifts between small immediate and large delayed reinforcers depending on the time of the choice (Ainslie, 1975, 1989). How should we test the adequacy of these two models? One approach would be to generate a set of data showing how response rate declined as a function of delay and then try to fit the two (or more) functions to that data set in order to see which one fits best. But the data might be too variable to discriminate between such similarly shaped functions.

An alternative strategy is to see if there are implications of the functions that can be exploited in an experimental test. Mazur's work (e.g., 1987) is exemplary. Imagine giving a pigeon the following choice: one response produces a certain amount of the reinforcer (A_1) after a particular delay (D_1). The other response produces a larger reinforcer amount (A_2) delivered after a different delay (D_2). If the delays are equal (i.e., if $D_1 = D_2$), then choice will favor the second alternative, which provides the larger reinforcer. But if D_2 were progressively lengthened, at some point the negative effects of the longer delay will balance the additional positive effect of the larger amount. That point is the *indifference point*.

   The predicted duration of D_2 at indifference depends on the function relating reinforcer effectiveness (V) to delay and amount. For each such function, one can show how the predicted duration of D_2 at indifference varies as a function of the duration of D_1 and the reinforcer amounts. These indifference functions are different enough for the different models to permit a clear experimental test. Table 1 shows the derivation for just two of the many possible function types. For the exponential function, the predicted duration of D_2 at indifference is a linear function of D_1, with slope of 1 and an intercept whose value depends on the magnitudes of the two reinforcers. For the reciprocal function, the predicted duration of D_2 at indifference is a linear function of D_1, with zero intercept and slope varying as a function of the ratio of the reinforcer amounts.

   The experimental task, then, would be to find the indifference points under different durations of a standard delay and under different reinforcer amounts for the alternatives. The quality of the data certainly should be sufficient to determine whether changing the reinforcer amounts alter the intercept or the slope of the indifference function (cf. Mazur, 1987).

TABLE 1
Derivation of indifference-point functions based on two different possible functions relating the effectiveness of a reinforcer to its delay. V = reinforcer effectiveness; A = reinforcer amount; D = reinforcer delay; b is a curve-fitting constant; the subscripts identify the choice alternative.

Negative exponential	Reciprocal
Reinforcer effectiveness function	
$V_1 = A_1 e^{-bD_1}; \quad V_2 = A_2 e^{-bD_2}$	$V_1 = \dfrac{A_1}{bD_1}; V_2 = \dfrac{A_2}{bD_2}$
At indifference, $V_1 = V_2$, and so	
$A_1 e^{-bD_1} = A_2 e^{-bD_2}$, and $\ln(A_1) - bD_1 = \ln(A_2) - bD_2$	$\dfrac{A_1}{bD_1} = \dfrac{A_2}{bD_2}$
Solving for D_2 as a function of D_1 by algebraic rearranging gives the indifference-point function:	
$D_2 = D_1 + \dfrac{\ln(A_2) - \ln(A_1)}{b}$	$D_2 = \dfrac{A_2}{A_1} D_1$

This example illustrates how implications of mathematical descriptions can suggest experimental procedures that magnify differences between models. The structure of the mathematical language permits those implications to be generated readily and unambiguously (cf. Gibbon and Church, 1981; Vaughan, 1981, for other examples).

5. Conclusion

It may appear that mathematical models explain phenomena in some special sense. But such a view is unnecessary. One view of science, often attributed to Mach, is that what science (or at least the best science) does is provide efficient descriptions of functional relations (cf. Skinner, 1957, 1969; Marr, 1985, 1986; Smith, 1986). From this view, there is no 'deeper' kind of explanation. Descriptions expressed in a mathematical language may be especially precise, general, and efficient, and so may be especially useful. But they are not fundamentally different from common language descriptions. The development of successful mathematical description, like the development of any kind of effective description, requires such things as noticing possible similarities among phenomena, careful experimental analyses and clear thinking.

Acknowledgements

Preparation of this chapter was supported by NSF Grant BNS-8519215 to UNCG. I am grateful to Peter Killeen for his helpful comments on an earlier draft.

References

Ainslie, G. (1975) Specious reward: a behavioral theory of impulsiveness and impulse control. Psychol. Bull. 82, 463–496.

Ainslie, G. (1989) Freud and picoeconomics. Behaviorism 17, 11–19.

Akaike, H. (1974) A new look at the statistical model identification. IEEE Trans. Auto. Control 19, 716–723.

Anger, D. (1956) The dependence of interresponse times upon the relative reinforcement of different interresponse times. J. Exp. Psychol. 52, 145–161.

Baum, W.M. (1973) The correlation-based law of effect. J. Exp. Anal. Behav. 20, 137–153.

Baum, W.M. (1974) On two types of deviation from the matching law: bias and undermatching. J. Exp. Anal. Behav. 22, 231–242.

Baum, W.M. (1979) Matching, undermatching, and overmatching in studies of choice. J. Exp. Anal. Behav. 32, 269–281.

Baum, W.M. (1981) Optimization and the matching law as accounts of instrumental behavior. J. Exp. Anal. Behav. 36, 387–403.

Baum, W.M. (1983) Matching, statistics, and common sense. J. Exp. Anal. Behav 39, 499–501.

Blough, D.S. (1963) Interresponse time as a function of continuous variables: a new method and some data. J. Exp. Anal. Behav. 6, 237–246.

Blough, D.S. (1966) The reinforcement of least-frequent interresponse times. J. Exp. Anal. Behav. 9, 581–591.

Bradshaw, C.M. and Szabadi, E. (1988) Quantitative analysis of human operant behavior. In: G. Davey and C. Cullen (Eds.), Human Operant Conditioning and Behavior Modification. Wiley & Sons, Chichester, UK, pp. 225–259.

Bush, R.R. and Mosteller, F.A. (1955) Stochastic Models for Learning. Wiley & Sons, New York.

Capehart, G.W., Eckerman, D.A., Guilkey, M. and Shull, R.L. (1980) A comparison of ratio and interval reinforcement schedules with comparable interreinforcement times. J. Exp. Anal. Behav. 34, 61–76.

Catania, A.C. (1966) Concurrent operants. In: W.K. Honig (Ed.), Operant Behavior: Areas of Research and Application. Appleton-Century-Crofts, New York, pp. 213–270.

Catania, A.C. (1973) Self-inhibiting effects of reinforcement. J. Exp. Anal. Behav. 19, 517–526.

Catania, A.C. and Reynolds, G.S. (1968) A quantitative analysis of the responding maintained by interval schedules of reinforcement. J. Exp. Anal. Behav. 11, 327–383.

Clifton, P.G. (1987) Analysis of feeding and drinking patterns. In: F.M. Toates and N.E. Rowland (Eds.), Feeding and Drinking. Elsevier, Amsterdam, pp. 19–35.

Collier, G.H., Johnson, D.F., Hill, W.L. and Kaufman, L.W. (1986) The economics of the law of effect. J. Exp. Anal. Behav. 46, 113–136.

Davison, M. and McCarthy, D. (1988) The Matching Law: a Research Review. Erlbaum, Hillsdale, NJ.

deVilliers, P. and Herrnstein, R.J. (1976) Toward a law of response strength. Psychol. Bull. 83, 1131–1153.

Estes, W.K. (1950) Toward a statistical theory of learning. Psychol. Rev. 57, 94–107.

Estes, W.K. (1959) The statistical approach to learning theory. In: S. Koch (Ed.), Psychology: a Study of a Science, Vol. 2: General Systematic Formulations, Learning and Special Processes. McGraw-Hill, New York, pp. 380–491.

Fagen, R.M. and Young, D.Y. (1978) Temporal patterns of behaviors: durations, intervals, latencies and sequences. In: P.W. Colgan (Ed.), Quantitative Ethology. Wiley & Sons, New York, pp. 79–114.

Fantino, E. and Abarca, N. (1985) Choice, optimal foraging and the delay-reduction hypothesis. Behav. Brain Sci. 8, 315–362.

Feller, W. (1950) An Introduction to Probability Theory and its Applications, Vol. 1. Wiley & Sons, New York.

Gibbon, J. (1977) Scalar expectancy theory and Weber's Law in animal timing. Psychol. Rev. 84, 279–325.

Gibbon, J. (1979) Timing the stimulus and response in aversive control. In: M.D. Zeiler and P. Harzem (Eds.), Advances in Analysis of Behaviour, Vol. 1, Reinforcement and the Organization of Behaviour. Wiley & Sons, Chichester, U.K., pp. 299–340.

Gibbon, J. and Balsam, P. (1981) Spreading association in time. In: C.M. Locurto, H.S. Terrace and J. Gibbon (Eds.), Autoshaping and Conditioning Theory. Academic Press, New York, pp. 219–253.

Gibbon, J., Berryman, R. and Thompson, R.L. (1974) Contingency spaces and measures in classical and instrumental conditioning. J. Exp. Anal. Behav. 21, 585–605.

Gibbon, J. and Church, R.M. (1981) Time left: linear versus logarithmic subjective time. J. Exp. Psychol.: Anim. Behav. Proc. 7, 87–107.

Gibson, J.J. (1966) The Senses Considered as Perceptual Systems. Houghton-Miflin, New York.

Gilbert, R.M. (1958) Fundamental dimensional properties of the operant. Psychol. Rev. 65, 272–282.

Guthrie, E.R. (1935) Psychology of Learning. Harper, New York.

Herrnstein, R.J. (1961) Relative and absolute strength of response as a function of frequency of reinforcement. J. Exp. Anal. Behav. 4, 267–272.

Herrnstein, R.J. (1970) On the law of effect. J. Exp. Anal. Behav. 13, 243–266.

Herrnstein, R.J. (1974) Formal properties of the matching law. J. Exp. Anal. Behav. 21, 159–164.

Herrnstein, R.J. (1981) Self control as response strength. In: C.M. Bradshaw, E. Szabadi and C. F. Lowe (Eds.), Quantification of Steady-State Operant Behavior. Elsevier, Amsterdam, pp. 3–20.

Hull, C.L. (1943) Principles of Behavior: an Introduction to Behavior Theory. Appleton-Century-Crofts, New York.

280

Hursh, S.R., Raslear, T.G., Shurtleff, D., Bauman, R. and Simmons, L. (1988) A cost-benefit analysis of demand for food. J. Exp. Anal. Behav. 50, 419–440.

Killeen, P. (1968) On the measurement of reinforcement frequency in the study of preference. J. Exp. Anal. Behav. 11, 263–269.

Killeen, P. (1975) On the temporal control of behavior. Psychol. Rev. 82, 89–115.

Killeen, P. (1979) Arousal: its genesis, modulation and extinction. In: M.D. Zeiler and P. Harzem (Eds.), Advances in Analysis of Behaviour, Vol. 1, Reinforcement and the Organization of Behaviour. Wiley & Sons, Chichester, U.K., pp. 31–78.

Killeen, P.R. (1981) Averaging theory. In: C.M. Bradshaw, E. Szabadi and C.F. Lowe (Eds.), Quantification of Steady-state Operant Behavior. Elsevier, Amsterdam, pp. 21–34.

Killeen, P.R. and Fetterman, J.G. (1988) A behavioral theory of timing. Psychol. Rev. 95, 274–293.

Kleinbaum, D.G., Kupper, L.L. and Muller, K.E. (1988) Applied Regression Analysis and Other Multivariable Methods. 2nd. Edn.. PWS-Kent, Boston.

Langley, P., Simon, H.A., Bradshaw, G.L. and Zytkow, J.M. (1987) Scientific Discovery: Computational Explorations of the Creative Processes. MIT Press, Cambridge, MA.

Lea, S.E.G. (1978) The psychology and economics of demand. Psychol. Bull. 85, 441–446.

Lewis, D. (1960) Quantitative Methods in Psychology. McGraw-Hill, New York.

Logue, A.W. (1988) Research on self-control: an integrating framework. Behav. Brain Sci. 11, 665–709.

Luce, R.D. (1986) Response Times: their Role in Inferring Elementary Mental Organization. Oxford University Press, New York.

Marr, M.J. (1985) 'Tis the gift to be simple: a retrospective appreciation of Mach's The Science of Mechanics. J. Exp. Anal. Behav. 44, 129–138.

Marr, M.J. (1986) Mathematics and verbal behavior. In: T. Thompson and M.D. Zeiler (Eds.), Analysis and Integration of Behavioral Units. Erlbaum, Hillsdale, NJ, pp. 161–183.

Mazur, J.E. (1986) Choice between single and multiple delayed reinforcers. J. Exp. Anal. Behav. 46, 67–77.

Mazur, J.E. (1987) An adjusting procedure for studying delayed reinforcement. In: M.L. Commons, J.E. Mazur, J.A. Nevin and H. Rachlin (Eds.), Quantitative Analyses of Behavior, Vol. 5, The Effect of Delay and of Intervening Events on Reinforcement Value. Erlbaum, Hillsdale, NJ, pp. 283–308.

McDiarmid, C.G. and Rilling, M.E. (1965) Reinforcement delay and reinforcement rate as determinants of schedule preference. Psychon. Sci. 2, 195–196.

McDowell, J.J. (1980) An analytic comparison of Herrnstein's equations and a multivariate rate equation. J. Exp. Anal. Behav. 33, 397–408.

McDowell, J.J. (1981) Wilkinson's method of estimating the parameters of Herrnstein's hyberbola. J. Exp. Anal. Behav. 35, 413–414.

McDowell, J.J. (1982) The importance of Herrnstein's mathematical statement of the law of effect for behavior therapy. Amer. Psychol. 37, 771–779.

McDowell, J.J. (1987) A mathematical theory of reinforcer value and its application to reinforcement delay in simple schedules. In: M.L. Commons, J.E. Mazur, J.A. Nevin and H. Rachlin (Eds.), Quantitative Analyses of Behavior, Vol. 5, The Effect of Delay and of Intervening Events on Reinforcement Value. Erlbaum, Hillsdale, NJ, pp. 77–105.

McDowell, J.J. and Wixted, J.T. (1988) The linear system theory's account of behavior maintained by variable-ratio schedules. J. Exp. Anal. Behav. 49, 143–169.

McDowell, J.J. and Wood, H.M. (1984) Confirmation of linear system theory prediction: changes in Herrnstein's k as a function of changes in reinforcer magnitude. J. Exp. Anal. Behav. 41, 183–192.

McGill, W.J. (1963) Stochastic latency mechanisms. In: R.D. Luce, R.R. Bush and E. Galanter (Eds.), Handbook of Mathematical Psychology, Vol. 1. Wiley & Sons, New York, pp. 309–360.

Mosteller, F. and Tukey, J.W. (1977) Data Analysis and Regression: a Second Course in Statistics. Addison-Wesley, Reading, MA.

Myerson, J. and Hale, S. (1984) Practical implications of the matching law. J. Appl. Behav.Anal. 17, 367–380.

Nevin, J.A. (1979) Reinforcement schedules and response strength. In: M.D. Zeiler and P. Harzem (Eds.), Advances in Analysis of Behaviour, Vol. 1, Reinforcement and the Organization of Behaviour. Wiley & Sons, Chichester, U.K., pp. 117–158.

Nevin, J.A. (1984) Quantitative analysis. J. Exp. Anal. Behav. 42, 421–434.

Nevin, J.A. and Baum, W.M. (1980) Feedback functions for variable-interval reinforcement. J.Exp. Anal. Behav. 34, 207–217.

Pear, J.J. and Rector, B.L. (1979) Constituents of response rate. J. Exp. Anal. Behav. 32, 341–362.

Premack, D. (1965) Reinforcement theory. In: D. Levine (Ed.), Nebraska Symposium on Motivation, Vol. 13. University of Nebraska Press, Lincoln, NE, pp. 123–180.

Rachlin, H., Battalio, R.C., Kagel, J.H. and Green, L. (1981) Maximization theory in behavioral psychology. Behav. Brain Sci. 4, 371–388.

Rachlin, H. and Green, L. (1972) Commitment, choice and self-control. J. Exp. Anal. Behav. 17, 15–22.

Rescorla, R.A. and Wagner, A.R. (1972) A theory of Pavlovian conditioning: variations in the effectiveness of reinforcement and nonreinforcement. In: A.H. Black and W.F. Prokasy (Eds.), Classical Conditioning II: Current Research and Theory. Appleton-Century-Crofts, New York, pp. 64–99.

Restle, F. and Greeno, J.G. (1970) Introduction to Mathematical Psychology. Addison-Wesley, Reading, MA.

Shimp, C.P. (1975) Perspectives on the behavioral unit: choice behavior in animals. In: W.K. Estes (Ed.), Handbook of Learning and Cognitive Processes, Vol. 2. Erlbaum, Hillsdale, NJ, pp. 225–268.

Shull, R.L. (1979) The postreinforcement pause: some implications for the correlational law of effect. In: M.D. Zeiler and P. Harzem (Eds.), Advances in Analysis of Behaviour, Vol. 1: Reinforcement and the Organization of Behaviour. Wiley & Sons, Chichester, U.K., pp. 193–221.

Shull, R.L., Mellon, R.C. and Sharp, J.A. (1990) Delay and number of food reinforcers: effects on choice and latencies. J. Exp. Anal. Behav. 53, 235–246.

Shull, R.L. and Spear, D.J. (1987) Detention time after reinforcement: effects due to delay of reinforcement? In: M.L. Commons, J.E. Mazur, J.A. Nevin and H. Rachlin (Eds.), Quantitative Analyses of Behavior, Vol. 5, The Effect of Delay and of Intervening Events on Reinforcement Value. Erlbaum, Hillsdale, NJ, pp. 187–204.

Skinner, B.F. (1935) The generic nature of the concepts of stimulus and response. J. Gen. Psychol. 12, 40–65.

Skinner, B.F. (1938) The Behavior of Organisms: an Experimental Analysis. Appleton-Century-Crofts, New York.

Skinner, B.F. (1950) Are theories of learning necessary? Psychol. Rev. 57, 193–216.

Skinner, B.F. (1953) Science and Human Behavior. MacMillan, New York.

Skinner, B.F. (1957) Verbal Behavior. Appleton-Century-Crofts, New York.

Skinner, B.F. (1969) Contingencies of Reinforcement: a Theoretical Analysis. Appleton-Century-Crofts, New York, pp. 133–171.

Skinner, B.F. (1989) The origins of cognitive thought. Am. Psychol. 44, 13–18.

Smith, L.D. (1986) Behaviorism and Logical Positivism: a Reassessment of the Alliance. Stanford University Press, Stanford, CA.

Staddon, J.E.R. (1977) On Herrnstein's equation and related forms. J. Exp. Anal. Behav. 28, 163–170.

Staddon, J.E.R. (1988) Quasi-dynamic choice models: melioration and ratio invariance. J. Exp. Anal. Behav. 19, 303–320.

Staddon, J.E.R. and Ettinger, R.H. (1989) Learning: an Introduction to the Principles of Adaptive Behavior. Harcourt, Brace, Jovanovich, Orlando, FL.

Staddon, J.E.R. and Motheral, S. (1978) On matching and maximizing in operant choice experiments. Psychol. Rev. 85, 436–444.

Stevens, S.S. (1951) Mathematics, measurement and psychophysics. In: S.S. Stevens (Ed.), Handbook of Experimental Psychology. Wiley & Sons, New York, NY, pp. 1–49.

Stevens, S.S. (1955) On the averaging of data. Science 121, 113–116.

Timberlake, W. (1984) Behavior regulation and learned performance: some misapprehensions and disagreements. J. Exp. Anal. Behav. 41, 355–375.

Tukey, J.W. (1977) Exploratory Data Analysis. Addison-Wesley, Reading, MA.

Vaughan, W. Jr. (1981) Melioration, matching and maximization. J. Exp. Anal. Behav. 36, 141–149.

Watson, J.E. and Blampied, N.M. (1989) Quantification of the effects of chlorpromazine on performance under delayed matching to sample in pigeons. J.Exp. Anal. Behav. 51, 317–328.

Wearden, J.H. (1983) Undermatching and overmatching as deviations from the matching law. J. Exp. Anal. Behav. 40, 333–340.

Weingarten, K. and Mechner, F. (1966) The contingency as an independent variable of social interaction. In: T. Verhave (Ed.), The Experimental Analysis of Behavior. Appleton-Century-Crofts, New York, pp. 447–459.

Wetherington, C.L. and Lucas, T.R. (1980) A note on fitting Herrnstein's equation. J. Exp. Anal. Behav. 34, 199–206.

White, K.G. and McKenzie, J. (1982) Delayed stimulus control: recall for single and relational stimuli. J. Exp. Anal. Behav. 38, 305–312.

Williams, D.R. (1968) The structure of response rate. J. Exp. Anal. Behav. 11, 251–258.

Zuriff, G.E. (1985) Behaviorism: a Conceptual Reconstruction. Columbia University Press, New York.

Iversen and Lattal (eds.) Experimental analysis of behavior
© *1991, Elsevier Science Publishers BV*

Glossary

A. CHARLES CATANIA

Department of Psychology, University of Maryland-Baltimore, Baltimore MD 21228, U.S.A.

Part of the evolution of the Experimental Analysis of Behavior is the progressive refinement of its terminology. This glossary provides definitions for some of that terminology. A glossary is adequate only to the extent that it reflects actual usage, and no glossary can provide definitions that will be undisputed by all or perhaps even by a majority of its users. Thus, any set of definitions must be treated as a preliminary guide to the basic classifications and concepts in the relevant literature rather than as an inflexible set of rules for usage. This glossary has been prepared in that spirit. It is a revision of a glossary that first appeared in a volume now out of print (Catania, 1968).

Like the earlier version, the present glossary attempts to acknowledge alternative definitions and to point out difficulties or potential ambiguities in existing usages. In some cases, one of several alternative definitions is emphasized when it appears logically dictated by the subject matter even though it does not represent the most common usage. Such definitions are presented with appropriate qualifications. In any case, sooner or later the reader must expect to encounter particular terms in the literature or even in this volume that are used in ways that disagree with the usages defined here.

It is worthwhile to recall that definitions are merely words that can substitute for other words, and the substitution is sometimes only an approximation. To the extent that the enterprise of framing or mastering a definition is primarily verbal, it cannot be counted on to establish the discriminations upon which the development and evolution of that verbal behavior was based. The student who has learned to define *reinforcement* may be able to offer a correct definition, but it does not follow that the student will then be able to discriminate reliably between actual instances of reinforcement and nonreinforcement in laboratory or real world settings.

Definition all too easily becomes rigid, and the temptation to legislate definitions must be resisted. Fixing definitions through rules of usage almost certainly entails greater risk than allowing definitions to be shaped by the practices of those who deal with the actual phenomena of behavior. Those who wish to propose or defend particular definitions or changes in definition are urged to do so on substantive grounds arising from the experimental and analytic issues at hand rather than on the basis of appeals to this or other glossaries as authorities.

With respect to range of coverage, it is also important to point out that glossaries are hardly ever exhaustive. Over time old terms are modified or dropped and new terms are added. This glossary covers much of the major terminology of the Experimental Analysis of Behavior both as it appears in this volume and as it has appeared in the closely related literature. It also includes some terminology from related areas of psychology, especially in cases in which behavior analysis has addressed issues in such areas experimentally (e.g., research on remembering). With some exceptions, however, it does not cover aspects of vocabulary consistent with everyday usage (e.g., technical terms that are nonetheless defined adequately in standard dictionaries), terms likely to be encountered in specialty areas or in other disciplines (e.g., drug classification in psychopharmacology), or terms defined in detail elsewhere in this volume (e.g., economic variables in behavioral ecology). For a review of other glossaries in behavior analysis, psychology and related disciplines, see Catania (1989); for a useful general dictionary of psychology, see Reber (1985). Some issues of usage are addressed in the journal The Behavior Analyst, in articles under the heading, 'On terms'.

The glossary does not attempt to cite sources of definitions or precedents in usage; to do so would be tantamount to citing the entire literature of the experimental analysis of behavior. In cross-references among definitions, *cf.* (as opposed to *see*) usually refers to elaborations or to useful contrasts or critical distinctions among related terms rather than to synonymous usages. Some matters of usage pertinent to the glossary as a whole are discussed under OPERATION.

References

Catania, A.C. (1968) Contemporary Research in Operant Behavior. Scott Foresman, Glenview, IL.
Catania, A.C. (1989) Speaking of behavior. J. Exp. Anal. Behav. 52, 193–196.
Reber, A.S. (1985) The Penguin Dictionary of Psychology. Viking Penguin, New York, NY.

* * *

A

Abstraction: discrimination based on a single property of stimuli, independent of other properties; therefore, generalization among all stimuli possessing that property (e.g., all red stimuli as opposed to specific red objects). *Cf. Concept formation, Stimulus.*

Acquisition: the process by which a new operant (occasionally, a new reflex relation) is added to an organism's repertory. The operant may be a discriminated operant, a topographically complex operant, or the performance controlled by a schedule (e.g., *see Higher-order schedule*); therefore, the term may refer to the change in performance caused by any change in contingencies. *Cf. Learning, Repertory.*

Adaptation: a diminution, produced by continued or repeated exposures, of the respondent behavior elicited by a stimulus or stimulus complex (e.g., the experimental chamber). *Cf. Potentiation.*

Additivity theory: a theory stating that responding within some setting is a summation of responses from two sources, typically one operant and one respondent (e.g., as when behavioral contrast is said to be based on the combination of operant responses maintained by reinforcers and autoshaped responses engendered by the differential correlation of reinforcers with discriminative stimuli).

Adjunctive behavior: responding that reliably accompanies some other response that has been produced or occasioned by a stimulus, especially when the stimulus is presented according to some temporally defined schedule. Some usages emphasize the stimulus rather than the responding it engenders. For example, temporally distributed presentations of food to a rat typically produce eating that is reliably followed by drinking. The drinking is called *adjunctive*, and is sometimes said to be *induced* by the schedule of food presentation.

Adjusting (adj) schedule: a schedule varying as a function of some property of performance. In one adjusting FR schedule, for example, the ratio increases or decreases by a specified number of responses depending on the duration of preceding post-reinforcement pauses; in adjusting avoidance, schedule parameters may change as a function of the frequency with which aversive stimuli occur.

Ad libitum (ad lib.) weight: *see Free-feeding weight.*

Advance procedure: a unidirectional changeover procedure that allows an organism to terminate one condition and advance to the next. In the most common application, in successive discrimination, a response is available that terminates an extinction trial and advances to the next reinforcement trial.

Adventitious chaining or reinforcement: *see Superstition.*

Aggression: a side effect of presenting aversive stimuli or removing positive reinforcers, which may generate responses that injure other organisms (e.g., biting) and/or increase that effectiveness with which opportunities for such responses serve as reinforcers.

Alternative (alt) schedule: a schedule in which a response is reinforced when either of two (or more) schedule requirements is satisfied. In alternative FR 10 FI 60-s, for example, the tenth response or the first response after 1 min, whichever occurs first, is reinforced, and both schedule requirements then start over.

Antecedent stimulus or event: a stimulus that precedes some event or contingency; typically, a discriminative stimulus in a three-term contingency.

Anxiety: *see Emotional behavior, Pre-aversive stimulus.*

Aperiodic reconditioning or reinforcement: a term, now uncommon, for VI reinforcement or, in some usages, VI and VR reinforcement.

Appetitive stimulus: usually, a positive reinforcer, especially one the efficacy of which is modifiable by deprivation.

Arbitrary matching: *see Matching to sample.*

Arithmetic schedule: a type of VI or VR schedule. *See Interval schedule.*

Arousal: a state of readiness for behaving, metaphorically extended from arousal in the colloquial sense of awakening.

Association: *see Contiguity.*

Asymmetrical stimuli: discriminative stimuli with different effects when correlated one way with differential contingencies (especially reinforcement and extinction) than when that correlation is reversed. *Cf. Feature-positive stimulus.*

G4

Asymptotic level: the level of responding approached in a maintained performance. *See Steady state.*

Attention: discriminative responding in which a functional relation between responding and some property of the discriminative stimulus has been demonstrated. An organism is said to *attend* to a stimulus or stimulus property when variation or elimination of that stimulus or stimulus property produces a change in behavior. For example, a pigeon that discriminates blue light from its absence is said to attend to color rather than brightness if variations in wavelength but not intensity produce changes in performance. *Cf. Discrimination, Functional stimulus, Observing response, Stimulus.*

Automaintenance: the maintenance of established autoshaped responding by the continuation of contingent stimulus-reinforcer relations. In *negative automaintenance*, the contingent stimulus-reinforcer relation operates on trials without responses, but the reinforcer is omitted on trials with responses. *See Autoshaping.*

Automated shaping: shaping conducted by a program that determines the criteria for differential reinforcement at successive stages of the procedure. *Cf. Percentile-reinforcement schedule, Shaping.*

Autopecking: pecking produced by an autoshaping procedure.

Autoshaping: a respondent procedure that generates skeletal responses. In the most common example, a pigeon's pecks on the key are engendered by contingent presentations of a key light and a feeder: a fixed key-light duration is followed by food, which is not presented at other times. In some procedures, pecks on the key, once they occur, produce food immediately rather than at the termination of the key light. Autoshaped pecks engendered by different stimuli (e.g., food or water) may share some topographical properties with reinforced pecking maintained by those stimuli as reinforcers. *Cf. Automaintenance.*

Aversive control: *see specific cases: Escape, Avoidance, Punishment, Pre-aversive stimulus.*

Aversive stimulus: a stimulus effective as a *negative reinforcer* or as a *punisher*, or that suppresses positively reinforced operant behavior in the presence of another stimulus that precedes it (*cf. Pre-aversive stimulus*). A stimulus with any one of these effects is likely also to have the others, but is not guaranteed to do so. *Cf. Noxious stimulus, Punishment, Reinforcement.*

Avoidance: the prevention of an aversive stimulus by a response. In *deletion* procedures, the response cancels the presentation of the aversive stimulus; in *postponement* procedures, the response only delays the presentation. In *discriminated, discrete-trials,* or *signalled avoidance*, an exteroceptive stimulus (sometimes called a *warning stimulus*) precedes the aversive stimulus; a response in the presence of this stimulus prevents the aversive stimulus on that trial. If no response occurs and the aversive stimulus therefore is presented, escape from the aversive stimulus typically depends on the same response that is effective for avoidance. In *continuous, free-operant,* or *Sidman avoidance*, no exteroceptive stimulus is arranged and, typically, there is no provision for escape. Each response postpones the aversive stimulus (usually, brief shock) for a fixed time period called the *response-shock (R-S) interval*; in the absence of responses, shocks are delivered regularly according to a *shock-shock (S-S) interval*. Discriminated avoidance has usually involved deletion and continuous avoidance postponement, but there is no necessary correlation between these two dimensions of avoidance procedures.

B

Background stimulus: *see Context.*

Backward chaining: *see Chain.*

Backward conditioning: respondent conditioning in which the CS follows rather than precedes the US. This procedure can be effective with aversive stimuli but is otherwise usually ineffective.

Bait-shyness: *see Taste aversion.*

Bar: lever. *See Operandum.*

Baseline: a stable and, usually, recoverable performance upon which effects of experimental variables can be assessed. For example, a drug effect may be expressed as the change produced in baseline response rate by a dosage of the drug. The term is also used occasionally to refer to the horizontal starting position (zero responses) of a cumulative-recorder pen. *Cf. Steady state.*

Behavior: anything an organism does. Although the definition may be too inclusive as it stands, it cannot easily be restricted further (e.g., to activity of muscles or glands). For example, a shift of attention need not involve eye movements but presumably qualifies as behavior.

Behavior can be measured in terms of time or in terms of event frequencies. In temporal measures, a time period is partitioned into periods during each of which the organism engages in a different class of behavior; so that time periods can be exhaustively categorized, one class is usually the class of other behavior or not responding. Given that the relative frequencies of the classes necessarily sum to one, such measures are consistent with the assumptions that the organism is always behaving, that it can engage in only one type of behavior at a time, and that the quantity of behavior is constant. In frequency measures, behavior can vary in quantity, without an upper limit. Such measures do not include implicit assumptions about whether or not responding should be treated as the absence of behavior or as a type of behavior. It is perhaps impossible to demonstrate that a quiescent organism is really doing nothing (it may be engaging in covert behavior), but it may be more useful to assume that the extent to which an organism behaves can vary, and therefore can approach zero, than to assume that the organism is necessarily always behaving. *See also specific cases: Covert behavior, Emotional Behavior, Species-specific behavior, Operant behavior, Overt behavior, Respondent behavior.*

Behavioral contrast: *see Contrast.*

Behavior analysis: breaking complex behavior down into its parts, especially its functional components rather than its topographies. The success of the analysis depends on whether the taxonomy of behavioral functions is adequate, and can be demonstrated by creating the complex behavior from its components in a behavior synthesis.

Bias: a systematic error in measurement. For example, if a device cannot record all responses when they follow each other rapidly, data recorded with the device will be biased in the direction of low rates of responding. For other usages, *see also Matching law, Preference.*

Blackout: a timeout arranged by turning out all lights.

Blocking: an attenuation of respondent conditioning with one stimulus that occurs because of prior conditioning with another. For example, if tone and bell together precede food after bell has been established as a CS, tone may remain ineffective as a CS even though it and bell have the same contingent relation to food. *Cf. Overshadowing.*

Break: an abrupt transition from responding to no responding (*cf. Ratio strain*); more generally, any abrupt transition from one pattern of responding to another.

Burst: a series of responses emitted at a high rate and bounded by lower-rate responding, especially when the series follows a stimulus (e.g., a burst after shock in avoidance).

C

Categories: *see specific cases: Abstraction, Concept formation, Equivalence class, Natural concept, Polymorphous stimulus class, Probabilistic stimulus class, Prototype.*

CER: conditioned emotional response. *See Pre-aversive stimulus.*

Chain: a sequence of discriminated operants such that responses in the presence of one stimulus are followed by other stimuli that reinforce these responses and set the occasion for subsequent ones (*see Chained schedule, Conditioned reinforcer, Discriminated operant*). Not all temporally integrated sequences are maintained through chaining, and those that are not must be distinguished from those that are. Parts of a chain are variously called *components, links* or *members.* Procedures that create chains often start with responses at the end of the sequence, closest to the reinforcer, and then work back (*backward chaining*) rather than with those at the beginning of the sequence, furthest from the reinforcer (*forward chaining*), because early responses in the latter procedure may be difficult to maintain while later responses are being established. When chained responses are topographically similar (e.g., successive FR responses or responses in successive components of a chained schedule), the chain is called *homogeneous*. When they are dissimilar (e.g., a sequence consisting of alley running, lever pressing, and moving to a feeder), the chain is called *heterogeneous*.

Chained (chain) schedule: a compound schedule in which a reinforcer is produced when the requirements of two or more successive component schedules, each operating in the presence of a different stimulus, have been completed. *Cf. Tandem schedule.*

Chamber: a space designed to minimize interference from stimuli (e.g., laboratory noises) irrelevant to experimental conditions, and including devices for recording behavior (*see Operandum*) and presenting stimuli. In typical chambers, stimulus sources include: mechanisms for delivering reinforcers (e.g., food dispensers variously called *magazines, hoppers* or *feeders*); discriminative-stimulus sources (e.g., speakers for presenting auditory stimuli; lamps or projectors for presenting visual stimuli); aversive-stimulus sources (e.g., *see Shock*); a houselight, which provides general illumination; feedback devices, which produce a distinctive stimulus such as a click after each response; and auditory sources that mask outside noises (often, a fan that provides masking noise along with ventilation).

Changeover: the behavior of switching from one response to another, as when a pigeon in a two-key chamber moves from pecking the left key to pecking the right key. *Cf. Concurrent operant.*

Changeover delay (COD): a feature sometimes incorporated into concurrent schedules to prevent sequences in which one response is closely followed by a reinforcer produced by a concurrent response. As typically arranged, the COD provides that no response can be reinforced within a specified time after a changeover has been completed (but CODs have occasionally been timed from other events, such as the last response before the initiation of a changeover).

Changeover-key procedure: *see Concurrent operants.*

Changeover-ratio (COR): a changeover contingency in which no response can be reinforced until some minimum number of responses has occurred since the last changeover. *Cf. Changeover delay.*

Choice: the emission of one of two or more alternative and, usually, incompatible responses. *Cf. Concurrent operant, Preference.*

Classical conditioning: *see Respondent conditioning.*

Clever Hans effect: a performance based on discriminative stimuli inadvertently provided by an experimenter. Clever Hans was a horse whose answers to arithmetic questions were controlled by irrelevant visual stimuli such as its trainer's facial expressions rather than by the numbers presented.

Clock: a device that records the passage of time; often used interchangeably with *timer*, which refers to a device that arranges events in time. Also, a stimulus correlated with the passage of time, such as a line projected on the pigeon's key that increases in length as time passes within an FI. *Cf. Counter.*

Closed economy: in operant contexts, the availability of appetitive stimuli only within the session, as reinforcers, with none provided independently of behavior on a supplementary basis outside of the session. *Cf. Open economy.*

COD: *see Changeover delay.*

Coding, coding response: an inferred variety of mediating behavior, as when humans remember visually presented letters on the basis not of geometric properties but rather of sound, perhaps as a result of saying or subvocally rehearsing them. Errors based on acoustic rather than visual similarity support the inference.

Cognition, cognitive processes: knowing, and the ways in which it takes place. Processes said to be cognitive are often varieties of behavior that need not be manifested as movements and therefore must be measured indirectly (e.g., doing mental arithmetic, shifting attention, imagining). *Cf. Behavior, Covert behavior.*

Collateral behavior: behavior that, like mediating behavior, appears in a consistent sequential relation to reinforced behavior while not itself instrumental in producing the reinforcer. The term does not necessarily imply that the behavior referred to mediates the reinforced behavior. *Cf. Mediating behavior.*

Complex schedule: *see Compound schedule.*

Component: one of the schedules, or the stimulus associated with it, in a compound schedule. The term is usually restricted to cases in which the individual schedules making up the compound schedule operate successively rather than simultaneously.

Comparison stimulus: *see Matching to sample.*

Compound schedule: a schedule in which two or more individual schedules are combined. The components may operate simultaneously or successively, and they may interact. In some usages, compound schedules, in which the components operate independently (e.g., concurrent or multiple schedules) are distinguished from *complex* schedules, in which the components interact (e.g., alternative or interlocking schedules). Because compound schedules that are designed for specific experimental purposes are often unnamed, an exhaustive list of such schedules is not feasible. For examples, see specific cases: *Adjusting, Alternative, Chained, Concurrent, Conjunctive, Interlocking, Mixed, Multiple, Percentile-reinforcement, Progressive* and *Tandem schedules.*

Concept formation: the formation of a discrimination based on a class of stimuli such that an organism generalizes among all stimuli within the class but discriminates these from those in other classes. This formulation plays much the same role in analyses of discriminative stimuli as the operant formulation plays in analyses of response classes. *Cf. Abstraction, Discrimination, Generalization, Stimulus.*

Concurrent chain schedules: concurrent schedules in which the reinforcers are themselves schedules that operate separately and in the presence of different stimuli. For example, equal and independent concurrent VI VI schedules may operate for a pigeon's pecks on two white keys; according to the VI schedules, left pecks produce an FI schedule operating on a blue key and right pecks produce an FR schedule operating on a yellow key. The concurrent VI VI schedules are called *initial links* and the separate schedules they produce are called *terminal links.* Preference for the conditions in the terminal links is given by relative response rates in the initial links. *Cf. Preference.*

Concurrent operants: two or more classes of alternative responses. Concurrent operants may be compatible (as when a rat simultaneously presses one lever with its left paw and another with its right) or incompatible (as when the pigeon, having only one beak, is limited to pecking only one of two keys at a time), as long as the organism has an opportunity to emit either or to change over from one to the other at any time. (Occasionally, responding and not responding are treated as concurrent operants; but see *Behavior*). Discriminated operants also may be concurrent if at any time the organism has an opportunity to produce the stimuli that occasion them. For example, in a *changeover-key procedure*, a pigeon changes the stimuli and their associated schedules on one key (the *main* key) by pecking a second key (the *changeover* key). In this case, two concurrent schedules operate on one key and changeovers are an explicit class of responses on the second key. *See also Changeover, Concurrent Schedules, Preference.*

Concurrent (conc) schedules: two or more schedules operating simultaneously and independently, each for a different response, as when separate VI schedules are arranged for a pigeon's pecks on each of two keys. In earlier usages, conjoint schedules were sometimes referred to as concurrent. *Cf. Conjoint schedules.*

Conditional: an often-preferred alternative to *conditioned.*

Conditional discrimination: a discrimination in which the reinforcement of responding in the presence of a given stimulus depends on, or is conditional upon, other stimuli. For example, matching-to-sample involves a conditional discrimination in the sense that whether a given comparison response is reinforced depends on the sample stimulus. Conditional-discrimination procedures involve four-term contingencies, in that they arrange stimuli in the presence of which different three-term contingencies operate.

Conditional probability: the probability of one event given some other event. For example: two responses, A and B, occur equally often, but A is followed by A three quarters of the time and by B one quarter of the time. In this case, the simple probability that a response will be A is $^1/_2$, whereas the conditional probability that it will be A given that the last one was A is $^3/_4$. *Cf. Probability; see Interresponse time for an additional example.*

Conditioned: *see Conditional.*

Conditioned aversive stimulus: a stimulus that has acquired its aversive properties because it has reliably accompanied another aversive stimulus. For example, in discriminated avoidance, the warning stimulus may become a conditioned aversive stimulus. *Cf. Avoidance, Pre-aversive stimulus.*

Conditioned emotional response (CER): *see Pre-aversive stimulus.*

Conditioned or conditional reflex: a reflex established by a contingent relation between stimuli (*see Conti-*

gency). One stimulus, originally neutral, sets the occasion for presenting a second stimulus, the *unconditioned stimulus* (US). A conditioned reflex is said to have been established when the neutral stimulus becomes a *conditioned stimulus* (CS), eliciting a response by virtue of its contingent relation to the US. This response, a *conditioned response* (CR), is often related to but is not necessarily the same as the *unconditioned response* (UR) elicited by the US. Responses elicited by the CS before conditioning (e.g., orienting responses) tend to disappear as conditioning progresses (*see Adaptation*). Stimuli effective as USs in respondent conditioning are often effective as positive or negative reinforcers in operant selection, and *reinforcement* is sometimes used in respondent vocabularies to refer to presentations of the US. The most typical respondent procedure, in which the CS is followed within no more than 5 s by the US, is ordinarily called *simultaneous conditioning* (this usage came about because the CR cannot be measured independently of the UR if the CS and US are simultaneous and, furthermore, strict simultaneity is actually less effective in conditioning than a brief delay between CS and US; thus, brief delays were incorporated into most so-called simultaneous conditioning procedures). *See also other specific cases: Backward conditioning, Delay conditioning, Higher-order conditioning, Temporal conditioning, Trace conditioning. Cf. Unconditioned reflex* and *Respondent*.

Conditioned or conditional reinforcer: a stimulus that functions as a reinforcer because of its contingent relation to another reinforcer. Such stimuli have also been called *secondary* reinforcers, but this designation is best reserved for cases in which the modifier specifies the number of stimuli separating the conditioned reinforcer from a primary reinforcer (e.g., a secondary reinforcer is followed directly by a primary reinforcer, a tertiary reinforcer is followed directly by a secondary reinforcer etc.). In some cases, convenience dictates the order assigned to a reinforcer. For example, a feeder operation may be referred to as a primary reinforcer even though the auditory and/or visual stimuli that accompany it are actually conditioned reinforcers that precede eating.

Conditioned or conditional response (CR) or stimulus (CS): *see Conditioned reflex*.

Conditioned suppression: *see Pre-aversive stimulus*.

Conditioning: *see Respondent conditioning*. The term still appears occasionally in conjunction with *operant*, but *operant conditioning* has become a less common usage.

Conflict: a situation involving any of the following: a single response produces both a reinforcer and a punisher (*approach-avoidance* conflict); two or more incompatible responses each produce a different reinforcer (*approach-approach* conflict); or, each of two or more incompatible responses terminates or avoids only one of two or more different aversive stimuli (*avoidance-avoidance* conflict).

Conjoint (conjt) schedules: two or more component schedules, usually involving different reinforcers, operating for a single response, as when lever presses are reinforced according to an FR schedule and simultaneously postpone shock according to an avoidance schedule. *Cf. Concurrent schedules*.

Conjugate reinforcement: reinforcement in which some property of an reinforcer varies systematically with some property of responding (e.g., as when the sharpness of focus of a reinforcing visual stimulus increases with the momentary rate of responding).

Conjunctive (conj) schedule: a schedule in which a response is reinforced when each of two (or more) schedule requirements is satisfied. In conj FR 10 FI 60-s, for example, a response is reinforced only after at least 9 other responses have been emitted and at least 1 min has elapsed since the last reinforcer.

Consequence: an event produced by some other event, especially, in operant accounts, an event produced by a response. It might include stimulus presentations or removals, changes in contingencies, or any other alterations of the environment. The term is particularly useful for referring to stimuli that do not have their status as reinforcers or punishers established (presenting such events contingent upon responding has sometimes been called *consequation*).

Constant-probability schedule: an RI or RR schedule, or an approximation to one. *See Interval schedule, Ratio schedule*.

Constraints on learning: *see Phylogenic constraints*.

Consummatory response: behavior occasioned by a reinforcer. The term originated with reinforcers that were actually consumed (e.g., food and water) but has been extended to other reinforcers, perhaps to a point of limited usefulness. For example, if the opportunity to run in a wheel is a reinforcer, wheel running is the consummatory response.

Context: the constant features of an experimental situation (e.g., the chamber within which an operant session occurs). Experimental contexts may acquire behavioral function, especially because they are embedded in the larger contexts that include the experimental session.

Contiguity: the juxtaposition of two or more events, especially in the case of their occurrence simultaneously or very closely together in time (e.g., the succession of a response and a reinforcer in a superstition procedure, or the pairing of CS and US in a respondent procedure). *Cf. Contingency.*

Contingency: in the operant case, the conditions under which a response may produce a consequence. In an FI, for example, the reinforcer may be said to be *contingent on* a response of a given force, topography, etc., as well as on the passage of a specified time. Studies of reinforcement schedules analyze contingencies and their effects (e.g., as when contingencies of reinforcement for various IRTs in interval and ratio schedules are compared). In this most general usage, contingencies describe any relation, whether completely specified by experimental operations or an incidental and perhaps fortuitous consequence of them. In a more specific sense, contingencies are the conditional probabilities that relate some events (e.g., responses) to others (e.g., stimulus presentations). The contingent relation that exists when responses produce reinforcers is defined by two conditional probabilities: the probability of the reinforcer given the response and its probability given no response. If both probabilities are not specified, contingent response-reinforcer relations cannot be distinguished from the incidental temporal *contiguities* that can result when responses and reinforcers occur independently over time. Response-reinforcer relations involve two terms, but they can be correlated with discriminative stimuli, thereby producing a *three-term contingency.* Conditional discriminations add a fourth term, and so on for other contingency relations of various orders of complexity.

The term *contingency* also applies to respondent cases, referring to the conditions under which some stimuli are followed by others. By analogy to the operant case, *stimulus-stimulus contingencies* expressed as conditional probabilities specify conditions more completely than descriptions in terms of pairings or temporal *contiguities,* distinguishing cases in which two stimuli always occur together from those in which they are frequently paired but also occur independently of each other; and stimuli correlated with stimulus-stimulus contingencies (sometimes called *occasion setters*) may enter into three-term or higher-order relations.

Contingency-governed or -shaped behavior: operant behavior. The terminology is ordinarily used to contrast responding that is not occasioned by verbal behavior with *rule-governed behavior*, behavior that is controlled by verbal antecedents (e.g., instructions).

Contingency space: any coordinate system within which contigencies expressed as conditional probabilities may be plotted.

Contingent stimulus: a stimulus the presentation of which depends on a response.

Continuous avoidance: *see Avoidance.*

Continuous repertoire: behavior that tracks continuous changes in some property of the environment, as when a driver steers a car so as to keep it in its lane.

Continuous reinforcement (CRF): reinforcement of every response within the limits of an operant class.

Contrafreeloading: see *Freeloading.*

Contrast or behavioral contrast: a change in the rate of one response that occurs when either the rate of a second response or the reinforcement rate produced by that response is changed in the opposite direction, where the reinforcement rate maintaining the first response remains constant. For example, the rate of reinforced responding in one multiple-schedule component typically increases if reinforcement is reduced or discontinued in the other component. The effect is most appropriately measured relative to a baseline performance in which responses in both components are maintained by the same reinforcement rate but has also been measured relative to rates in prior nonbaseline conditions. The term is usually restricted to responses in the presence of successive stimuli, as in multiple schedules, though similar phenomena occur within concurrent schedules. *Cf. Induction.*

Control: the systematic modification or maintenance of behavior by manipulating relevant conditions. The manipulation of conditions distinguishes control from *prediction* and *interpretation*. If control is not possible because relevant conditions are not manipulable, adequate information about relevant variables may make prediction possible (e.g., as in the history of astronomy before space flight). Interpretation usually occurs after the fact. Given an outcome, a plausible account of the relevant variables can be offered, but it may be difficult to determine its adequacy. Nevertheless, such an analysis is often expected or demanded of students of behavior (as when a psychologist is asked to explain in a court of law why a defendant acted in some way). In its most common behavior analytic usage, the term appears in conjunction with some variable that has a demonstrable effect on behavior (e.g., *schedule control, stimulus control*).

Coordinate: the value of a point plotted on a graph. In a two-dimensional system, the value plotted along the X-axis is called the *abscissa* and that plotted along the Y-axis is called the *ordinate*; the terms do not refer to the axes themselves.

COR: *see Changeover ratio.*

Correction procedure: the repetition or continuation of experimental conditions and/or stimuli after given responses or after their absence (especially, in a discrete-trial simultaneous discrimination, after errors). For example, stimuli on one trial may be repeated on the next if an error occurred or if, in a trial of limited duration, no response occurred. In a free-operant case, a multiple VI extinction schedule may be arranged so that each response during the extinction component delays the onset of the VI component. The term appropriately refers to any procedure that arranges continued or repeated opportunities for responses in alternative classes until a given response does (or does not) occur. Its colloquial origins imply procedures that eventually force an organism to emit a correct response (*cf. Error*), but the technical usage does not exclude procedures in which the alternative response classes cannot easily be categorized as correct responses and errors.

Correlated stimuli or reinforcers: *see Conjugate reinforcement.*

Correlation: *see Statistics.* The term is frequently extended to procedures, especially stimulus-control procedures (e.g., as when a schedule operating in the presence but not in the absence of a stimulus is said to be *correlated with* that stimulus), and *molar* analyses often rely on correlations between overall measures of behavior (e.g., correlations between response rates and reinforcement rates).

Cost: *see Response cost.*

Count (as procedure, versus time): *see Fixed consecutive number.*

Counter: a device that records how often some event occurs. *Counter* can also refer to a stimulus correlated with number of responses (e.g., a line projected on a pigeon key that increases in length with successive FR responses). *Cf. Clock.*

Covert behavior: behavior that is not observed or observable and is therefore only inferred. Alternatively, behavior inside an organism, but of such a sort or on such a small scale that it is not measurable or is measurable only with special equipment (e.g., thinking or counting to oneself, inferred from a human's verbal report, or muscle contractions too small to produce obvious movement).

CR: conditioned response. *See Conditioned reflex.*

CRF: *see Continuous reinforcement.*

Criterion for shaping (plural: criteria): *see Percentile-reinforcement schedule, Shaping.*

Critical period: the time during which a stimulus can become imprinted (*see Imprinting*). More generally, any time period to which the establishment of some behavioral process is limited.

CS: conditioned stimulus. *See Conditioned reflex.*

Cumulative record: a record in which total responses are plotted as a function of time, usually made by a marker or pen that moves a fixed distance with each response across a paper advancing at a constant speed. Thus, the faster the responding the steeper the slope of the record. Moment-to-moment changes in slope show the details of changing response rates over time. The largest changes in slope are produced by a given percentage change in rate when the combination of the paper speed and the step size made by each response is one in which typical response rates yield a slope of about 45°. A very steep or shallow slope changes only slightly even with large changes in rate; such records can sometimes best be read in foreshortening, by tilting the record and sighting along the line. Cumulative recorders typically include additional features: the pen can be reset to its starting position (sometimes called the *baseline*) after a full excursion across the paper or after some event; it can be briefly displaced downward or to one side, producing a pip, to indicate a reinforcer or other brief event; it can be held in its downward position, producing a displaced line, to indicate stimuli or other extended conditions; and an event pen at the bottom of the record can be used to indicate when other events occur. *Cf. Rate of responding.*

Cyclic schedule: any schedule with a repeating sequence of components.

D

Data; datum: any recorded information, usually in numerical form. *Data* is plural; *datum* is singular.

Defensive conditioning: respondent conditioning in which the US is an aversive or noxious stimulus.

Delay conditioning: respondent conditioning in which the CS is presented for some fixed, extended time period (in most usages, no less than 5 s) before the US is presented.

Delay of reinforcement: the time from a response to a subsequent reinforcer. Reinforcers usually lose effectiveness as delay increases, but properties of delay procedures complicate the determination of the delay-of-reinforcement function. In delay procedures that interpose a stimulus between the response and its delayed reinforcer (*signalled delay of reinforcement*), the stimulus will probably function as an immediate conditioned reinforcer. In procedures that interpose no stimulus, either the delay is extended by additional responses, thereby limiting response rate because a reinforcer will be delivered only after a pause equal to the delay interval, or the delay is unaffected by additional responses, thereby allowing the delay to be effectively reduced to the shorter time between those responses and the reinforcer at the end of the delay. Delayed reinforcement presumably operates ubiquitously in schedules. In an FR, for example, all responses preceding the reinforced response are also in a sense reinforced, because each is eventually followed by the reinforcer, albeit with some delay.

Delayed matching-to-sample: *see Matching-to-sample* and *Delayed Response.*

Delayed response: a discriminative response that occurs some time after the removal of a discriminative stimulus. For example, the sample in a matching-to-sample procedure may be turned off for some specified time before the comparison stimuli are presented. Thus, the matching response is delayed, and accuracy may vary as a function of the delay interval. The term may also refer to a discrete-trial equivalent of spaced responding (*see Differential-reinforcement schedules, Trial*), in which a response is reinforced only if it occurs after some fixed time has elapsed since the onset of a stimulus.

Deletion: *see Avoidance.*

Density: a synonym for rate, as in reinforcement density or shock density. *Cf. Rate of reinforcement.*

Dependency: roughly, a contingency completely specified by the experimenter or with a conditional probability very close to 1.0. *Cf. Contingency.*

Deprivation: an establishing operation, the reduction in the availability of a reinforcer, that increases the effectiveness of the reinforcer. With food reinforcers, two criteria for levels of deprivation have been a fixed percentage of free-feeding body weight or a fixed period of deprivation after free feeding. Deprivation is also effective for such other reinforcers as a rat's opportunity to run in a running wheel, and may be a necessary condition for making any positive reinforcer effective.

Descriptive operant: *see Operant.*

Differential conditioning: usually, establishing a discrimination in respondent conditioning. *See Respondent discrimination.*

Differential reinforcement: reinforcement of some responses but not others, depending on the intensive, temporal, topographical, or other properties of the response (including the stimuli in the presence of which they are emitted; *cf. Discriminated operant*); thus, an operation that may define an operant class (*cf. Operant*). When responding has come under the control of differential reinforcement, so that the proportion of responses falling within the limits of the operant class increases, responding is said to be *differentiated*. *Cf. Induction.*

Differential-reinforcement schedules: schedules in which reinforcers depend on the temporal spacing of responses; contingencies have been based on preceding interresponse times (IRTs), response rates during a preceding time period, or periods of no responding either preceded by a response or without a required preceding response. Terms for the first two types have often been used interchangeably, so that schedule vocabularies sometime fail to distinguish between them.

In *differential-reinforcement-of-long-interresponse-times, differential-reinforcement-of-low-rate (DRL), IRT > t*, or *spaced-response* schedules, a response is reinforced only if at least a specified time period has elapsed since the last response. In the alternative and less common method based on rates rather than IRTs, a response is reinforced only if fewer than a specified number of responses was emitted during a preceding time period. Such schedules can also be arranged in discrete trials, when a response is reinforced only if it follows the onset of a stimulus by more than a specified time period (e.g., a *differential-reinforcement-of-long-latencies schedule; cf. Delayed response*).

In *differential-reinforcement-of-high-rate (DRH)* or *IRT < t* schedules, a response is reinforced if at least a specified number of responses was emitted during a preceding time period. In this case, the alternative but less common method is scheduling based on IRTs rather than rates, because reinforcing single short IRTs tends to produce short IRTs separated by frequent pauses rather than sustained high rates of responding.

In *paced-response* or *differential-reinforcement-of-pacing (DRP)* schedules, a response is reinforced if the time since the last response falls within specified limits (e.g., an IRT of at least 5 but no more than 10 s) or if the number of responses emitted during a preceding interval of time falls within specified limits (e.g., at least 10 but no more than 15 responses during the preceding 5 s). When the schedule is based on IRTs rather than rates, it is sometimes referred to as *DRL with limited hold (see Limited hold)*. In addition, the term *pacing* has also been applied to schedules in which responding is paced by a stimulus (e.g., a stimulus is presented every 3 s and is terminated by the first response, and the response is reinforced according to some schedule).

Another type of differential-reinforcement schedule arranges delayed reinforcement after responses: a reinforcer is delivered if a response occurs and is then followed by a specified period of no responding (*see Delay of reinforcement*). Still another does not require a response: a reinforcer is delivered after a specified period of no responding. This schedule has been variously called *differential-reinforcement-of-zero-behavior, differential-reinforcement-of-other-behavior,* and *differential-reinforcement-of-pausing* (usually abbreviated *DRO*, but occasionally *DRP; cf. Behavior*). *See also Interresponse time* and *Rate of responding*.

The terminology has also been applied to schedules differentially reinforcing responses in given classes rather than temporal properties, as in *differential-reinforcement-of-alternative-response (DRA)* and *differential-reinforcement-of-incompatible-response (DRI)* schedules.

Differentiation: *see Differential reinforcement.*

Discrete trials: *see Trial.*

Discriminated operant: an operant defined in terms of the stimuli in the presence of which it occurs as well as its environmental effect. In this case, the operant is defined by the relations among three events (sometimes referred to as the *three-term contingency*): a stimulus in the presence of which a response may be followed by consequences. In one sense, the stimulus sets the occasion on which the response may be reinforced; in another, the presence of the stimulus defines one of the properties of the operant class and therefore sets the occasion for the response. In either usage, the joint dependence of the response on both stimulus and reinforcer distinguishes the relation from that of a reflex. *See also Discrimination, Operant.*

Discrimination: any difference in responding in the presence of different stimuli; in a more restricted usage, a difference resulting from differential consequences of responding in the presence of different stimuli. *See also Abstraction, Discriminated operant, Generalization, Respondent discrimination, Simultaneous discrimination, Stimulus, Successive discrimination.* Usually the organism is said to discriminate among relevant stimuli. In some cases, however, it may be useful to speak of responses as discriminating (e.g., if response rate varies with color whereas response location varies with form, rate might be said to discriminate color while location might be said to discriminate form). Further, when discriminated responding is produced by differential contingencies in the presence of different stimuli, it is appropriate to say that the stimuli are discriminated, but it is not appropriate to say that the contingencies are discriminated.

Discriminative stimulus: any stimulus having a discriminative function; according to an alternative usage, a stimulus correlated with reinforcement, when a second stimulus is correlated with extinction. The latter usage has become less common because it cannot be applied easily to stimuli correlated with different reinforcement schedules (e.g., multiple FI FR). The abbreviations of the stimuli in a reinforcement-extinction discrimination as, respectively, S^D ('S-dee': discriminative stimulus) and S^Δ ('S-delta': absence of discriminative stimulus) evolved from the second usage, but these abbreviations have lost ground to $S+$ (positive stimulus) and $S-$ (negative stimulus). Strictly, S^0 ('S-zero') is more appropriate for the absence of reinforcement, but $S-$ is typographically more convenient.

Displacement activity: an ethological term referring to a response (*see Fixed action pattern*) occurring not in the presence of the stimulus that usually produces it (*see Releaser*), but rather in the presence of one that usually produces some other response (*cf. Vacuum activity*). Both displacement activity and vacuum activity depend on deprivation of opportunities to complete the fixed action pattern, but displacement activity is likely to be observed at lower levels of deprivation than vacuum activity.

Distribution: a classification of events according to location along some continuum. For example, a distribution of IRTs classifies them into several temporal categories (e.g., less than 1 s, 1 but less than 2 s, 2 but less than 3 s, and 3 or more s). *Frequency distributions* show the number of events in each category; *relative frequency distributions* show the events in each category as a proportion of the total. Each category is called a *class interval* (sometimes, a *bin*) and class intervals are ordinarily of equal size (or *bandwidth*). Distributions often include a category for all events falling beyond some point on the continuum (e.g., in the above example, 3 or more s) so that a category exists for any event no matter how extreme its value. *Cf. Interresponse time, Statistics.*

DMTS: delayed matching-to-sample. *See Delayed response* and *Matching-to-sample.*

Dosage; dose; dose-response or dose-effect curve: a *dosage* is the administration of a drug; *a dose* is the amount administered. Drugs are stimuli with unique routes of administration, and they typically produce different effects at some doses than at others. *Dose-response curves* describe the effects of drugs as a function of dose. Drug A is said to be more *potent* than Drug B if a smaller dose of A is needed to produce the same drug effect as A. Dose-effect functions are obtained through administering different doses at different times, or through *cumulative dosing*, when increments to a dose are administered over time within single sessions.

DRH: differential reinforcement of high rate. *See Differential-reinforcement schedules.*

Drinkometer: a device that measures licking. When the organism's tongue contacts the water spout, an electrical circuit between the water-delivery mechanism and the floor and/or walls of the chamber closes, permitting a current flow too weak to affect behavior but sufficient for recording. In some procedures with rats, such licking is reliably accompanied by drinking and thus the drinkometer can be used indirectly to record water intake.

Drive operation: *see Establishing operation.*

DRL: differential reinforcement of long interresponse times or low rate. *See Differential-reinforcement schedules.*

DRO: differential reinforcement of zero behavior or other behavior. *See Differential-reinforcement schedules.*

DRP: differential reinforcement of paced responding or pacing; also, differential reinforcement of pauses. *See Differential-reinforcement schedules.*

Duration of response: the time from the beginning to the end of a response (sometimes called *holding time*). Analyses of this property of responding depend heavily on procedural details. For example, if a reinforcer is delivered when a lever is pressed, response duration will be short because the reinforcer occasions quick release, but if it is delivered upon lever release, then each member of the chain (press, hold, release) may be differently affected by the contingencies.

Duration of stimulus: *see Temporal discrimination.*

Dwell time: *see Interresponse time.*

E

Electric shock: *see Shock.*

Elicitation: the reliable production of a response by a stimulus in unconditioned or conditioned reflexes. *Cf. Respondent behavior.*

Emergent relation: conditional stimulus control that emerges as a by-product of other stimulus-control relations rather than through differential reinforcement. For example, if arbitrary matching has been arranged for pairs AB and BC (where the first letter of each pair corresponds to the sample and the second to the matching comparison) and testing shows that the transitive relation AC has also been established, then this relation is said to be emergent. *Cf. Equivalence class.*

Emission: the occurrence of operant behavior. A response that occurs without an eliciting stimulus is said to be *emitted.* The term applies to responding occasioned by a discriminative stimulus as well as to undiscriminated responding. *Cf. Operant behavior.*

Emotional behavior: correlated changes in a variety of different response classes as a result of environmental events. For example, a pre-aversive stimulus that simultaneously alters heart rate, respiration, blood pressure, defecation and urination, and operant behavior maintained by reinforcement may be said to produce emotional behavior. Because this and related terms evolved from an imprecise colloquial vocabulary, it is impossible to define specific types of emotional behavior unambiguously in terms of the response classes involved. Types of emotional behavior may be defined more consistently in terms of the operations that produce them: e.g., *fear, anxiety* or, with another organism present, *anger*, produced by primary or conditioned aversive stimuli; *relief*, produced by the termination of aversive stimuli; *joy* or *hope*, produced by primary or conditioned reinforcers; and *sorrow* produced by the termination of reinforcers. Different observers are likely to disagree on definining characteristics of the various cases (e.g., stimulus magnitudes, the direction of change in different responses etc.), and the terms have not acquired technical usages within the analysis of behavior. *Cf. Aggression, Frustration, Pre-aversive stimulus.*

Equivalence class: a stimulus class (usually established through conditional discrimination in matching-to-sample) that includes all possible emergent relations among its members. Equivalence may be derived from the logical relations of reflexivity, symmetry and transitivity. *Reflexivity* refers to the matching of a sample to itself, sometimes called identity matching (AA, BB, CC; in these examples, each letter pair represents a sample and its matching comparison stimulus). *Symmetry* refers to the reversibility of the relation (if AB, then BA). *Transitivity* refers to the transfer of function through shared membership (if AB and BC, then AC). If these properties are characteristics of an organism's matching-to-sample performance, then establishing AB and BC may also produce AC, BA, CA and CB as *emergent* relations (reflexivity provides the three other possible relations, AA, BB and CC). Given AB and BC as antecedents, for example, the CA relation implies both symmetry and transitivity. The emergence of all possible stimulus relations after only AB and BC are established through contingencies is the criterion for calling the three stimuli members of an equivalence class. The class can be extended by establishing new stimulus relations (e.g., if CD is established, then AD, DA, BD, DB and DC may be created as emergent relations). Stimuli that are members of an equivalence class are likely also to be *functionally equivalent.* It remains to be seen whether the logical properties of these classes are fully consistent with their behavioral ones. *Cf. Equivalence relation.*

Equivalence relation: a term with various usages, including functional equivalence (the relation between stimuli that have become members of a *functional class*) as well as the mathematical relations that define an *equivalence class* (especially the CA relation). The terminology of equivalence relations has often been interchanged with that of equivalence classes, but the class and relation terminologies should be distinguished because functionally equivalent stimuli are not necessarily members of an equivalence class. *Cf. Equivalence class.*

Error: in a simultaneous discrimination, a response to a stimulus not correlated with reinforcement; in a successive discrimination, a response in the presence of a stimulus correlated with extinction. Because of its colloquial origins, the term often assumes an evaluative as well as a descriptive function. *Cf. Correction procedure.*

Escape: the termination of an aversive stimulus by a response. A reduction in the magnitude of an aversive stimulus by a response is sometimes called partial or fractional escape. *Cf. Reinforcement.*

Establishing operation: any operation that changes the effectiveness of a stimulus as a reinforcer or punisher: deprivation, satiation, procedures that establish formerly neutral stimuli as conditioned reinforcers or as conditioned aversive stimuli, and stimulus presentations that change the reinforcing or punishing status of other stimuli (e.g., as when an already available screwdriver becomes a reinforcer in the presence of a screw that needs tightening). Establishing operations are sometimes said to produce motivational or drive states within the organism.

Estes-Skinner procedure: *see Pre-aversive stimulus.*

Ethology: an area of biology concerned with the analysis of the behavior patterns that evolve in natural habitats, either in species or in individual organisms, with particular emphasis on those patterns that do not depend on, or are not known to depend on, prior operant selection or respondent conditioning. *Cf. Fixed action pattern, Species-specific behavior* and *Releaser.*

Event recorder: a device that produces one or more time lines along which the timing of events is recorded (e.g., by displacement of a marker or pen that draws a line at a constant rate).

Evocation: the production of a response. A response is sometimes said to be *evoked* if it is unclear whether it is emitted or elicited.

Excitation: roughly, the production of behavior or the variables that produce it, used especially in contrast with *inhibition.*

Expectancy: a colloquial term referring to behavior that precedes a predictable event. Expectancy depends on a history with respect to that event (it cannot depend on an event that has not yet occurred).

Exteroceptive stimulus: any stimulus presented at or outside of the organism's skin. *Cf. Interoceptive stimulus.*

Extinction: in operant behavior, discontinuing the reinforcement of a response (or the reduction in responding that follows this operation). In negative reinforcement (escape and avoidance), extinction has often referred to the discontinuation of aversive stimuli, although the more appropriate application of the term is to discontinuing the consequences of responding: aversive stimuli are presented, but responses no longer prevent them. The discontinuation of punishment (*see Recovery*) is rarely referred to as a variety of extinction. In respondent conditioning, extinction is presenting the CS without, or no longer in a contingent relation to, the US (or the diminution in conditioned responding that follows this operation).

Extinction gradient: a gradient obtained after extinction, when the extinction stimulus is represented on the continuum along which the gradient is determined. In one type, responding is reinforced in the presence of several stimuli along the continuum and then extinguished in the presence of one of them. In another, reinforcement is correlated with stimulus 1 and extinction with stimulus 2, but only stimulus 2 is represented on the continuum along which the gradient is determined (e.g., stimulus 1 is a form and stimulus 2 is a color, and the gradient is determined along the wavelength continuum). *Cf. Inhibitory gradient.*

Extrinsic reinforcer: a reinforcer that has an arbitrary relation to the responses that produce it (as when a musician plays for money rather than because the playing produces music). The term has also been applied to stimuli presumed to function as a reinforcers because their function has been instructed (as when children are told that it is important to earn good grades); despite their label, such stimuli are often ineffective as reinforcers. *Cf. Intrinsic reinforcer.*

F

Facilitation: *see Potentiation.*

Fading: a procedure for transferring control of responding from one stimulus or set of stimuli to another by gradually removing one while the other is gradually introduced. Stimuli may be faded in or out. For example, once a discrimination based on color has been established (e.g., on a pigeon's key), it may be transferred to line orientation by maintaining differential reinforcement while the colors are gradually reduced in intensity and the lines are increased. The term *stimulus shaping* has sometimes been applied to fading procedures that vary the form of a visual stimulus, but that terminology is based on topographical rather than functional properties of stimuli.

In a less common usage, fading may refer to eliminating stimulus control without disrupting performance during the transition. For example, a pigeon's key pecking may be established by taping a grain to the key and then maintained by replacing the grain with a spot that is gradually reduced in size until it is completely eliminated (sometimes called *baiting* the key or lever). The procedure is usually effective for key pecks, but it may occasionally establish an inefficient topography that persists through later conditions: *cf. Shaping*.

FCN: *see Fixed consecutive number*.

Feature-positive stimulus: in a successive discrimination between one stimulus correlated with reinforcement and another correlated with extinction, a stimulus property present only during reinforcement components (e.g., as when, in a discrete-trial procedure with pigeons, a star appears on a green key during reinforcement trials but the green key appears alone during extinction trials). Stimulus control is more easily established when such stimuli are correlated with reinforcement (*feature positive*) than when they are correlated with extinction (*feature negative*). *Cf. Sign-tracking*.

Feedback: roughly, a stimulus or stimulus property correlated with or produced by the organism's own behavior. The stimulus may in turn change the behavior, which again changes the stimulus, and so on. The mathematical relation between the behavior and the stimulus is called a *feedback function*.

FI: fixed interval. *See Interval schedule*.

Fixed action pattern: an ethological term for a sequence of responses, usually but not necessarily produced by a releaser, the consistent patterning of which cannot be attributed to the operation of an operant chain. Fixed action patterns are sometimes preceded by responses, presumably operant, that produce the appropriate releasers. When the stimuli that elicit or set the occasion for a fixed action pattern are absent, their presentation, and thereby an opportunity to engage in the fixed action pattern, may serve as a reinforcer. *Cf. Releaser, Displacement activity* and *Vacuum activity*.

Fixed consecutive number (FCN): a two-operandum trial procedure in which trials are initiated by responses on one operandum and are terminated by a changeover to the other, and in which the changeover is reinforced if at least a minimum number of responses preceded it (e.g., as when a pigeon's left-key peck is reinforced only if at least 10 right-key pecks had occurred before the changeover to the left key).

Fixed-interval schedule: *see Interval schedule*.

Fixed-ratio schedule: *see Ratio schedule*.

Fixed-time schedule: *see Time schedule*.

Foraging: searching for food. Foraging in natural habitats has been treated as a chain that includes search, prey identification, procurement of prey, and handling and/or consumption of prey, with performances in concurrent or concurrent chain schedules sometimes treated as analogs of parts of this chain. For example, the foraging patterns according to which organisms switch from partially depleted patches of food to fresh ones can be characterized in terms of strategies examined within concurrent performances, such as *matching, momentary maximizing* and *optimizing*.

Forced choice: *see Free choice*.

Force of response: typically measured in Newtons. Differential reinforcement of force is implicit in the design of most operanda (e.g., a pigeon's peck must be of some minimum force, sometimes called *threshold force*, to operate the key). The maximum force produced during a response is called *peak force*. By physical definition, an organism exerting force on an operandum but not moving it is not doing work (work equals force times distance). For this reason, one index of response effort is based not on work but on the *time-integral of force*, an integration over time of the forces exerted during a response.

Forward chaining: *see Chain*.

FR: fixed ratio. *See Ratio schedule*.

Fractional escape: *see Escape*.

Free choice: the availability of two or more concurrent operants even if one is consistently chosen over the other. The term is best restricted to cases in which each class is maintained by reinforcement but has been extended to response classes correlated with extinction. With only one operant available, the choice is said to be *forced* (as when one of the two arms in a T-maze is blocked).

Free-feeding weight: the stable weight maintained by a mature organism with unlimited access to food and water. A percentage of this weight (e.g., 80%) may serve as a criterion for a level of deprivation.

Free food: *see Response-independent reinforcer.*

Freeloading: accepting response-independent reinforcers when both response-dependent and response-independent reinforcers are available. If instead the organism responds and produces the response-dependent reinforcers, the performance is called *contrafreeloading.*

Free operant: *see Operant.*

Free reinforcer: *see Response-independent reinforcer.*

Frequency of reinforcement: total reinforcers, over a fixed time period, over an experimental session of variable duration, over a fixed number of responses, or, in a trial procedure, over a fixed number of trials. With respect to reinforcement, frequency is most commonly used as a synonym of rate; the usage for responding is more likely to be variable. *Cf. Frequency of responding* and *Rate of reinforcement.*

Frequency of responding: total responses, over a fixed time period, over an experimental session of variable duration, or, in a trial procedure, over a fixed number of trials. *Cf. Frequency of reinforcement* and *Rate of responding.*

Frustration: any operation that reduces an organism's opportunities to emit highly probable responses (or the consequences of such operations, especially emotional behavior, aggression or escape from correlated stimuli). The term is most commonly applied to extinction, which eliminates an organism's opportunity to eat. Thus, in referring to the behavioral consequences of an operation, the term is a label for some side effects of extinction.

FT: fixed time. *See Time schedule.*

Functional analysis: an analysis in terms of behavioral functions, i.e., what effects responses have; alternatively, an analysis in terms of functional relations (e.g., the production of pupillary constriction by light might be discussed as a pupillary reflex, but a functional analysis would instead deal with the phenomenon as a transition from one point to another on a continuous mathematical function relating pupillary diameter to light intensity).

Functional class: a class the members of which have common behavioral functions, either produced by similar histories or acquired through emergent relations. If two stimuli are members of a functional class, then the behavior occasioned by one will also be occasioned by the other; such stimuli are sometimes said to be *functionally equivalent. Cf. Equivalence class,* and *see also Equivalence relation, Operant* and *Stimulus.*

Functional operant: *see Operant.*

Functional relation: a mathematical function appealed to by a functional analysis. *See Functional analysis.*

Functional stimulus: those properties of a stimulus that control behavior. The term is usually used in contrast to *nominal stimulus.* For example, if a pigeon attends to the color but not the form of a green circle, then the functional stimulus is simply green even though the nominal stimulus is a green circle.

Fuzzy set: *see Probabilistic stimulus class.*

G

Generalization: the spread of the effects of reinforcement (or other operations such as extinction or punishment) in the presence of one stimulus to other stimuli differing from the original stimulus along one or more dimensions. To the extent that responding is similar in the presence of two different stimuli, the organism is said to generalize between them (or the stimuli are said to be generalized). If responding is identical in the presence the different stimuli, generalization between them is said to be complete. (This outcome may also be referred to as the absence of discrimination between the stimuli or as the organism's failure to attend to the dimension or dimensions along which they differ.) *Cf. Attention, Discrimination, Gradient, Induction* and *Stimulus.*

Generalization gradient: a gradient obtained after reinforcement correlated with a single stimulus (occasionally, in studies of the summation of gradients, two or more stimuli), when no discrimination has been established between this and other stimuli on the continuum along which the gradient is determined.

Generalized matching law: *see Matching law.*

Generalized reinforcer: a conditioned reinforcer based on several different primary reinforcers. Its effectiveness depends less on the establishing operations appropriate to any one primary reinforcer than does that of conditioned reinforcers based on only a single primary reinforcer. Money is often offered as an example of a generalized reinforcer of human behavior.

Geometric schedule: a type of VI or VR schedule. *See Interval schedule.*

Go-no go discrimination: usually, a discrete-trials successive discrimination with reinforcement in the presence of one stimulus (*go*) and extinction in presence of the other (*no go*).

Gradient: a measure of responding in the presence of different stimuli as a function of their location along a continuum (*cf. Stimulus*). Gradients are ordinarily determined by presenting the stimuli successively but in irregular order during extinction. The slope or steepness of a gradient is determined by how much change in responding occurs from one point on the continuum to another; the larger the change, the steeper the gradient. The case in which responding does not change is usually called a *flat* gradient, although it may also be called the absence of a gradient. *See specific cases: Extinction gradient, Generalization gradient, Inhibitory gradient, Post-discrimination gradient.*

Grain: a reinforcer effective with food-deprived pigeons; also a characteristic of cumulative records (*see Rate of responding*).

H

Habituation: *see Adaptation.*

Helplessness, learned: *see Learned helplessness.*

Herrnstein equation: *see Matching law.*

Higher-order class of behavior: a class that includes within it other classes that can themselves function as operant classes, as when generalized imitation established as a higher-order class includes all the component imitations that could have been established separately. Higher-order classes may be a source of novel behavior (e.g., as in the generalized imitation of some behavior that the imitator had not seen before). They also have the property that contingencies may operate differently on the higher-order class than on the classes that are its components. For example, if all instances are reinforced except imitations within one component class (e.g., jumping whenever the model jumps), that class will change with the higher-order class rather than with the contingencies arranged for it (i.e., imitations of jumping will not extinguish, even though no longer reinforced). Control by the contingencies arranged for the higher-order class rather than for component classes defines higher-order classes. The component classes are therefore sometimes said to be *insensitive* to the contingencies arranged for them. A higher-order class is sometimes called a *generalized* class, in that contingencies arranged for some component classes within it generalize to all the others. Generalized matching and rule-governed behavior are examples of higher-order classes.

Higher-order conditioning: respondent conditioning in which the stimulus that functions as the US in establishing one conditioned reflex is itself the CS of another.

Higher-order schedule: a schedule that reinforces a complex operant consisting of completion of a schedule requirement. For example, with FR 10 reinforced according to an FI schedule, every tenth response that occurs at least 50 s after the last reinforcer will be reinforced. In this example, FR 10 is the first-order schedule and FI 50-s the second-order schedule. Such schedules often include a stimulus presented upon each completion of the first-order schedule, (e.g., adding a brief flash of light after every tenth response to the above example). The notation for such schedules includes the first-order schedule and the stimulus it produces in parentheses: FI 50-s (FR 10: stimulus). A *percentage-reinforcement* schedule is a higher-order schedule in which the second-order schedule is a VR.

History: the conditions an organism has been exposed to and its performances under them; often an abbreviation for *experimental history*, simply because experimental organisms are rarely observed continuously from birth (or hatching). History is particularly important when some conditions have had irreversible or only slowly reversible effects.

HL: houselight. *See Chamber.*

Houselight: *see Chamber.*

I

Identity matching: *see Matching-to-sample.*

Imitation: behavior that duplicates some properties of the behavior of a model. Imitation need not involve the matching of stimulus features (e.g., when one child imitates the raised hand of another, the felt position of the child's own limb has different stimulus dimensions than the seen position of the other child's). *Cf. Higher-order class of behavior.*

Imprinted stimulus: a stimulus that, by virtue of its presentation during some period in the lifetime of an organism, has become effective as a reinforcer. Imprinting is noted primarily in some bird species (e.g., ducks), and occurs within a few days of hatching.

Impulsivity: *see Self-control.*

Incentive: discriminative effects of reinforcing stimuli (e.g., the smell of food may make responses reinforced by food more likely).

Incidental chaining or reinforcement: *see Superstition.*

Index of curvature: *see Rate of responding.*

Induction: the spread of the effects of reinforcement to responses outside the limits of an operant class (sometimes also called *response generalization*). This phenomenon is essential to shaping because through it responses more closely approximating some final form may be emitted and therefore reinforced (e.g., reinforcement of a 10-N key peck may be followed by the first instance of a 15-N peck; *cf. Shaping*). With discriminated operants, induction may refer to the spread of the effects of reinforcement to stimuli other than those defining the operant class (e.g., as when, after extinction in the presence of green and red, reinstating reinforcement in the presence of green produces not only responding during green but also a transient increase in responding during red; *cf. Generalization*).

Information: strictly, the reduction in uncertainly provided by a stimulus, usually quantified in *bits*, the number of binary decisions needed to specify the stimulus. One bit specifies 2 alternatives, two bits 4, three bits 8, and so on in increasing powers of 2. The term is often used in a colloquial rather than a technical sense, however (as in common applications of the phrase *information processing*).

Informative stimulus: a discriminative stimulus, though not necessarily a conditioned reinforcer. For example, a stimulus correlated with differential punishment that is superimposed on on-going reinforced behavior is informative, but its onset does not ordinarily reinforce observing responses.

Inhibition: a process inferred from a response decrement. The term, extended to behavior by analogy to usage in physiology, is appropriate only when it can be demonstrated that the decrement is produced by an increment in something else. For example, if reinforcing one response reduces the rate of another, the reinforcement may be said to inhibit the second response. The term is sometimes extended to accounts of the process of extinction, in part because extinction may be accompanied by increments in other responding (e.g., behavior characterized as emotional). Such accounts are often unsupported by demonstrations that the increments produce the extinction decrement rather than simply accompany it, and when they do not distinguish between conditions that reduce responding and those that fail to maintain it they may be misleading.

Inhibitory gradient: an extinction gradient in which responding increases along the stimulus continuum as the distance from a stimulus previously correlated with extinction increases. This is taken to indicate that the extinction stimulus controls a low or zero rate of responding rather than fails to maintain responding. *Cf. Extinction gradient, Inhibition.*

Inhomogeneous data: data derived from more than one type of performance and that, when summarized statistically, may misrepresent the performances from which they were derived (e.g., if an avoidance schedule produces both a moderate response rate and bursts of high-rate responding after shock, the average rate will not represent either of the two contributions to overall rate).

Initial links: *see Concurrent chain schedules.*

Innate behavior: *see Species-specific behavior.*

Insensitivity to contingencies. *see Higher-order class of behavior.*

Instinctive behavior: *see Species-specific behavior.*

Instructional stimulus, instructions: typically, in nonverbal settings, a conditional discriminative stimulus (though a simple discriminative stimulus may sometimes also be said to have instructional functions); a rule (*cf. Rule-governed behavior*).

Instrumental behavior: *see Operant behavior.*

Interdependent schedules: schedules in which the operation of one depends of some property of the other (e.g., in one version of interdependent concurrent VI VI schedules, each VI can arrange setups only during runs of responding on the other).

Interdimensional: between or across dimensions.

Interim behavior: varying responding that occurs, usually early or midway rather than late within interstimulus intervals, in superstition procedures or temporal conditioning. *Cf. Superstition* and *Terminal behavior.*

Interlocking schedule: a schedule in which time, number, and/or IRT requirements vary together according to some function. For example, in one schedule with interlocking interval and ratio requirements, the number of responses that will produce a reinforcer decreases linearly as time passes since the last reinforcer.

Intermittent reinforcement: reinforcing some but not all responses or, in other words, reinforcing according to any schedule except continuous reinforcement or extinction. *See Specific schedules.*

Interoceptive stimulus: a stimulus inside the organism. The stimulus may be presented from outside, as when an experimenter passes electric current through an area of the brain, or it may be produced by the organism itself, as when responses produce proprioceptive stimulation on the basis of which the organism may discriminate among different movements. In the case of self-produced stimulation, however, the stimuli and their discriminative functions are usually inferred rather than demonstrated.

Interpretation: *see Control.*

Interresponse time (IRT): the time between two responses or, more strictly, from the beginning of one response to the beginning of the next. The time from a reinforcer to the next response is a latency and not an IRT, even if the reinforcer is response-produced. Reinforcing a response that ends an IRT is said to reinforce that IRT. An *IRT distribution* summarizes the temporal spacing of the responses making up a response rate (though it does not show sequential patterning). In assessing probabilities of different classes of IRTs, calculating proportions of IRTs falling into an IRT class may be misleading because short IRTs reduce the organism's opportunity to emit responses at the end of longer ones. For this reason, conditional probabilities, *IRTs per opportunity (IRTs/Op)*, are often calculated: the probability of IRTs in a class interval, given that sufficient time had elapsed since the last response to permit an IRT to end in that class interval. For example, if 80 of 100 IRTs were less than 1 s, 10 were 1 but less than 2 s, and the remaining 10 were 2 or more s, then the organism had only 20 opportunities to complete the 10 IRTs of 1 but less than 2 s and the conditional probability for this class interval was 0.5 (10/20). Another measure, *dwell time*, takes into account the different proportions of time taken up by different IRTs. For example, if 100 s included 10 5-s IRTs and a single 50-s IRT, the same dwell time, 50 s was spent engaging in each IRT class. *Cf. Conditional probability, Rate of responding, Differential-reinforcement schedules.*

Interresponse times per opportunity (IRTs/Op): *see Interresponse time.*

Intertrial interval (ITI): *see Trial.*

Interval schedule: a schedule in which some minimum time must elapse before a response is reinforced.

The time is measured from some event, typically the onset of a stimulus or the end of the last reinforcer, and excluding responses in the reinforced class. In an alternate method of scheduling, each interval is timed from the end of the last interval, and its start cannot be delayed by the time to the reinforced response after the end of the last interval. In *fixed-interval* (FI) schedules, the time that must elapse before a response can be reinforced is constant from one interval to the next; performance is characterized by a pause after the reinforcer followed by a gradual or an abrupt transition to a moderate rate of responding (*cf. Rate of responding*). In *variable-interval* (VI) schedules, the time varies from one reinforcer to the next; compared with FI schedules, the rate of responding is relatively constant between reinforcers. Interval schedules are usually identified by average interval (e.g., FI 60-s and VI 60-s arrange one reinforcer per min). Historically, VI schedules have been based on successive intervals selected in irregular order from a set of intervals (perhaps described by a mathematical progression: e.g., *arithmetic* VI schedules, derived from progressions with terms differing by an additive constant, such as 10, 20, 30, 40 s etc.; *geometric* VI schedules, derived from progressions in which they differ by a multiplicative constant, such as 5, 10, 20, 40 s etc.; and so on). Current practice, however, favors schedules in which reinforcement probability does not vary with time since the start of the interval (where probability is measured by *reinforcers per opportunity* or *Rf/Op*: the probability that a response will be reinforced at a given time in an interval, given that that time in the interval has been reached). Such conditions are met by a type of VI schedule called *random interval (RI)*, which arranges a setup (makes the next response eligible to produce a reinforcer) with a fixed probability at the end of a recycling time interval. In RI schedules, the average interval equals the recycling time interval divided by the probability (for example, arranging setups once per second with a probability of 0.02 produces an RI 50-s schedule). In one arrangement, the schedule stops operating after a setup until the scheduled reinforcer has been produced, and time elapsed between the setup and the reinforced response may make the obtained reinforcement rate lower than the one that has been scheduled; in another, the schedule continues to operate and successive setups accumulate, so that obtained and scheduled reinforcement rates remain equal as long as some responding is maintained by the schedule.

Intradimensional: within a dimension.

Intrinsic reinforcer: a reinforcer that is naturally related to the responses that produce it (as when a musician plays not for money but because the playing produces music). *Cf. Extrinsic reinforcer.*

IRT: *see Interresponse time.*

IRT schedules: IRT < *t*, IRT > *t*. See *Differential-reinforcement schedules.*

IRTs/Op: interresponse times per opportunity. *See Interresponse time.*

ITI: intertrial interval. *See Trial.*

J

Jumping stand (also Lashley jumping stand): an apparatus used in early studies of simultaneous discrimination. A rat is forced to jump from a platform to one of two doors on which different stimuli are displayed. One door is unlocked, and by jumping to it the rat gains access to a reinforcer located behind it. If the rat jumps to the other door, which is locked, it falls into a net below the doors.

K

Key: *see Operandum*

Kinesthetic stimulus: *see Proprioceptive stimulus.*

L

Latency: the time from an event, usually the onset of a stimulus, to a response.

Latent learning: *see Learning.*

Law of effect: the classic statement of the principle of reinforcement and, in one version, of punishment. Reinforcers and punishers were referred to as satisfying and annoying states of affairs that an organism tended respectively to maintain or renew, and to put an end to or avoid.

Learned helplessness: a retardation in the acquisition of escape or avoidance responding produced by a history in which responding in the presence of the relevant aversive stimuli has had no consequences.

Learning: roughly, acquisition, or the process by which behavior is added to an organism's repertoire; a relatively permanent change in behavior. The term has been used in many different ways in both technical and colloquial vocabularies and thus may be of limited usefulness. The decision about whether learning has occurred and what has been learned sometimes depends on what is accessible to the experimenter. The phenomenon called latent learning provides an example. A rat is allowed to explore a maze, and the consequences of this exploration are assessed when food reinforcers are later made available at the end of the rat's run through the maze. Latent learning is said to have occurred if the rat then negotiates the maze more rapidly and/or with fewer entries into blind alleys than if it had not been allowed to explore. The difficulty is that exploring the maze involves other contingencies (e.g., some parts of the maze may appear as novel stimuli, entry into blind allies may involve physical constraint, and removal from the maze may be followed by reinforcers). These contingencies act on behavior but are less accessible than those involving the food reinforcers. *Cf. Acquisition* and *Performance.*

Learning set or learning-to-learn: a case of transfer in which, on the basis of similar relations among stimuli in a sequence of discrimination problems, accuracy in later problems improves more rapidly over trials than in the earlier problems (perhaps to the point at which correct responses occur on the first presentations of a new problem). Cf. *Concept formation, Transfer.*

Lever: *see Operandum.*

LH: *see Limited hold.*

Limited hold (LH): termination of the scheduled availability of a reinforcer if the response to be reinforced does not occur within a specified time. For example, in an FI 100-s schedule with a 10-s limited hold, the first response that occurs between 100 and 110 s after the start of the interval is reinforced, but if no response occurs within that time period the interval is discontinued and a new condition begins (e.g., a new interval or a change in stimuli).

Limits on learning: *see Phylogenic constraints.*

Link: a response in a chain or a component in a chained schedule.

Local rate: *see Rate of responding.*

Long-term memory (LTM): *see Remembering.*

LTM: long-term memory. *See Remembering.*

M

Main key: *see Concurrent operants.*

Maintenance: continuation of the experimental conditions that generated a performance. The analysis of maintained performances, as a subject matter, is different from but not incompatible with that of acquisition. For example, many experiments concerned with effects of different schedule parameters on performance do not really begin until acquisition has been completed. *Cf. Steady-state.*

Manipulandum: *see Operandum.*

Matching: in performance involving concurrent operants, distributing responses so that the relative response rate of each roughly matches its relative reinforcement rate. *See Matching law and cf. Maximizing, Melioration* and *Optimizing.*

Matching law: a quantitative formulation stating that the relative rates of different responses tend to equal the relative reinforcement rates produced by those responses. The *generalized matching law* summarizes this relation in the form of an equation in which relative response rate equals a constant times relative reinforcement rate raised to a power. The constant takes into account units of measurement and includes *bias* (e.g., one response might call for a larger constant than another that is more effortful); the performance is described as *undermatching* when the exponent (the power to which the function is raised) is less than 1 and *overmatching* when it is greater than 1.

Matching-to-sample: a simultaneous conditional discrimination procedure, or the performance maintained by such a procedure. As it is typically arranged for pigeons, a *sample* stimulus is presented on the middle key of three keys. A peck on it turns on *comparison* stimuli on the two side keys (*see Observing response and Sample-specific behavior*). A peck on the matching side key is reinforced (perhaps according to some schedule); a peck on the other side key may produce a timeout or invoke a *correction procedure*. When the criterion for matching is physical correspondence (e.g., as when a pigeon must peck a green comparison given a green sample and a red comparison given a red one), the procedure is sometimes called *identity matching*, though accurate matching may be based on other features than the identity relation, such as stimulus configurations. When the matching is based on arbitrary sample-comparison relations (e.g., as when a pigeon must peck a circle given a green sample and a triangle given a red one), the procedure is sometimes called *arbitrary matching (symbolic matching,* an alternative terminology, has the disadvantage of suggesting that the sample and comparison stimuli have additional stimulus functions besides those in the matching-to-sample procedure). *Cf. Conditional discrimination, Delayed response, Oddity.*

Maximizing: given two or more responses, emitting the one with the higher probability of reinforcement. If reinforcement probabilities change from moment to moment and responding follows the one currently highest, the maximizing is said to be *momentary maximizing*. *Cf. Matching* and *Optimizing*, and note that matching requires a population of responses whereas maximizing can occur with a single response.

Maze: an apparatus through which an organism locomotes, usually from a start box to a goal box that contains some reinforcer such as food, and often including alternative paths that divide at *choice-points* and some of which end in a *blind alley* or *cul-de-sac*. Mazes come in a variety of configurations, including T mazes or Y mazes with a single choice point, mazes with a single sequence of choices between blind alleys and a continuing path, and radial mazes with paths arranged like the spokes of a wheel. *Cf. Learning.*

Mediating behavior: behavior that occurs in a consistent temporal or sequential relation to reinforced behavior and that, although reinforcers are not explicitly arranged for it, can be shown to be maintained because reinforcers are more likely when it occurs. For example, a stereotyped pattern of drinking is said to mediate spaced responding if, when the pattern is maintained, the next response is more likely to be late enough after the last response that it will be reinforced; or, two different postures held after one or another sample stimulus are said to mediate delayed matching-to-sample if a correct matching response is more likely when the organism has held the posture since the sample was presented (e.g., the organism leans to the right after a red but not a green sample and subsequently is more likely to respond to red rather than green if still leaning to the right). *Cf. Collateral behavior, Superstition.*

Melioration: allocating time to two or more response classes so all local reinforcement rates are equal. For example, assume a pigeon whose pecks in a changeover-key procedure are maintained by concurrent VI 20-s VI 60-s schedules. In an hour, the former will provide about 180 reinforcers and the latter about 60, but if the pigeon allocates 45 min to the VI 20-s schedule and 15 min to the VI 60-s schedule both local reinforcement rates will equal about 4 per min (180 in 45 min and 60 in 15 min). *Cf. Matching, Maximizing* and *Optimizing.*

Memory: *see Remembering.*

Metastability: *see Stability.*

Metathetic stimuli: *see Stimulus continuum.*

Microanalysis: *see Molar and molecular analyses.*

Misbehavior: a nontechnical term sometimes used to refer to the intrusion into on-going operant behavior of behavior with phylogenic origins. For example, if food is used with raccoons to reinforce their deposit into a container of objects they have picked up, they may begin to rub the objects together instead of releasing them into the container. Raccoons ordinarily rub and wash their food before eating it. To the extent that rubbing the food is sometimes more probable than eating it, the phenomenon simply demonstrates the relativity of reinforcers (*see Reinforcement*). Under appropriate conditions, the opportunity for rubbing may reinforce other responses, perhaps including eating. Intrusions also occur in the opposite direction (e.g., as when food-reinforced behavior intrudes into a fixed action pattern), but they are rarely referred to as misbehavior.

Mixed (mix) schedule: a compound schedule in which two or more component schedules operate in alternation, all in the presence of the same stimulus (*cf. Multiple schedule*). Occasionally, a VI or VR schedule with a limited number of schedule values is referred to as a mixed schedule (e.g., in describing a VR schedule arranged by randomly alternating between FR 10 and FR 20 as mixed FR 10 FR 20).

Molar and molecular analyses: analyses distinguished on the basis of the level of detail in the data they consider. A molar analysis generally considers overall measures such as average response rates over sessions, whereas a molecular analysis breaks such measures down into components such as the distribution of IRTs that makes up a particular response rate. Because many levels of analysis are possible, either molar or molecular is sometimes defined relative to the other. Both, however, rely on data sampled over some period of time, and are therefore to be distinguished from *microanalysis*, which proceeds at the level of individual stimuli and responses.

Momentary maximizing: *see Maximizing.*

Motivation: *see Establishing operation.*

Movement: *cf. Behavior.*

Multiple causation of behavior: the determination of behavior by two or more variables acting at the same time. Behavior is always controlled by multiple variables, although some may be more important than others. Behavior analysis involves procedures that allow the multiple factors controlling behavior to be examined one at a time.

Multiple (mult) schedule: a compound schedule in which two or more component schedules operate in alternation, each in the presence of a different stimulus. Alternation of the component schedules is typically arranged after reinforcers or after fixed or variable periods of time. *Cf. Mixed schedule.*

N

N: *see Newton.*

Natural concept: a class of discriminative stimuli established through presentations of complex natural stimuli (e.g., as when a pigeon discriminates between pictures with and pictures without trees in them). *Cf. Probabilistic stimulus class.*

Natural reinforcer: sometimes used in place of *primary reinforcer* or *extrinsic reinforcer*. The relativity of reinforcers limits the usefulness of this term: *cf. Reinforcement.*

Negative automaintenance: *see Automaintenance.*

Negative reinforcement: *see Reinforcement.*

Negative stimulus: *see Discriminative stimulus.*

Newton (N): a measure of force, often used to specify the minimum force required by an operandum such as a pigeon key or rat lever. One Newton is equivalent to the force exerted by a weight of 100 grams.

Nominal stimulus: *see Functional stimulus.*

Novel behavior and novel stimuli: new behavior and new stimuli. The problem with these terms is that what is novel to the experimenter may not be novel to the organism, and vice versa.

Noxious stimulus: often used as a synonym for aversive stimulus, but more strictly defined as a stimulus that affects pain receptors or produces tissue damage. In this strict sense, the term is useful for referring to an extensive class of stimuli without specifying the behavioral consequences of the stimuli.

O

Observational learning: learning based on observing the responding of another organism (and/or its consequences). Observational learning need not involve imitation (e.g., organisms may come to avoid aversive stimuli upon seeing what happens when other organisms produce them).

Observing response: a response that produces or clarifies a discriminative stimulus and that may be maintained by the effectiveness of that stimulus as a conditioned reinforcer. Observing responses are sometimes only inferred (as when a pigeon's head movements are assumed to bring a visual stimulus into view or better focus), but conditions may be arranged to control them. For example, in matching-to-sample the pigeon may be more likely to observe the sample if a peck on the sample key is required. In a more explicit arrangement, pigeon's pecks on one key may produce the stimuli correlated with the components of a multiple schedule on a second key.

Occasion: an opportunity for a response or some other event, or the circumstances under which a contingency operates, as when a discriminative stimulus *sets the occasion* on which a response has some consequence. The term is sometimes used as a verb, as when a stimulus is said to *occasion* a response (especially in distinguishing between responses emitted in the presence of discriminative stimuli and cases in which stimuli elicit responses in a reflex relation).

Occasion setter: *see Contingency.*

Oddity procedure: a conditional discrimination procedure in which only one of three or more stimuli differs from the others in some property (e.g., color) and responses to the odd stimulus are reinforced. Versions of matching-to-sample in which responses to the comparison stimulus that does not match the sample are reinforced (mismatching) also qualify as oddity procedures. *Cf. Matching-to-sample.*

Omission training: a discrete trials equivalent of differential reinforcement of zero behavior (*see Differential-reinforcement schedules*): a reinforcer is delivered only if no response has occurred in a trial or within a given time period. It is formally analogous to avoidance, with reinforcers substituted for aversive stimuli.

Ontogeny: the development or life history of an individual organism. *Cf. Phylogeny.*

Open economy: in operant contexts, the availability of appetitive stimuli not only as reinforcers within the session but also, independently of behavior, on a supplementary basis outside of the session (as when food is provided after a session of food-reinforced responding to maintain the organism at a standard percentage of free-feeding weight). *Cf. Closed economy.*

Operandum: any device that may be operated by an organism and that defines an operant class in terms of an environmental effect (*descriptive operant: see Operant*). Many operanda consist of switches operated either directly or indirectly (e.g., as in rats' lever presses and pigeons' key pecks). Operanda also may define operants involving locomotion, as when a rat operates a switch by stepping off a platform. In the broadest sense, any apparatus by means of which behavior is recorded is an operandum. For example, an experimenter may record a rat's alley running by noting the time at which the rat crosses different lines on the alley floor. To the extent that the rat's running has consistent effects on the experimenter, who then records and reinforces running accordingly, the alley-experimenter combination is an operandum. The term, however, would be less likely to be used than if the experimenter were replaced by photocells, which would more reliably record the rat's movement through the alley. Operandum replaces an earlier term, *manipulandum*, which suggested a device that is handled. For other examples of operanda, *see Drinkometer, Jumping stand* and *Wheel running.*

Operant: a class of responses. Responses are assigned to classes because no two instances can be exactly the same. Special cases include the *free operant*, in which the class is such that completing one response leaves the organism in a position to emit the next, and the *discrete operant* or constrained operant (see *Trial*). A distinction is sometimes made between defining the class descriptively (*descriptive operant*) and defining it functionally (*functional operant*).

For the purposes of measuring responses, the class is usually defined descriptively, in terms of its environmental effect (e.g., a lever press defined in terms of operating a switch; *see Operandum*). To count as a member of an operant, a response must have a certain force, topography, and so on; an additional defining property may be the stimuli in the presence of which the response occurs (*see Discriminated operant*). The environmental effect that defines an operant in this usage may be different from the scheduled consequences of responses in the class (e.g., in a schedule, every response in the class does not necessarily produce a reinforcer).

In the functional usage, an operant is defined as a class that is modifiable by the consequences of responses in it. The class is defined not by consequences alone but rather by the relation between consequences and subsequent responding. According to this functional definition, a class of responses is not an operant until its modifiability has been demonstrated (e.g., a pigeon's key pecking can be said to be an operant only when consequences have been shown to modify it). Whether certain classes of responses can be established as operants in this functional sense or whether some are more easily established or modified than others have been recurrent themes in the history of learning theories. For example, the issue of place learning versus response learning was concerned with whether a rat in a maze is more likely to learn a sequence of particular skeletal responses (right turns or left turns) or a sequence of responses under the control of stimuli outside the maze (east turns or west turns); it turned out that the outcome can be made to go one way or the other depending on the availability of stimuli outside the maze.

In many cases, operants defined descriptively and those defined functionally include roughly the same responses. If they do not, it may be appropriate either to change the method of measurement or to search for variables that might limit the modifiability of the class. *See also Operant behavior*.

Operant behavior: behavior the properties of which can be modified by its consequences. This class of behavior has also been called *instrumental*, and often corresponds closely to behavior colloquially referred to as voluntary or purposive. Operant behavior is typically said to be *emitted*, because it is primarily controlled by consequences rather than by eliciting stimuli (*cf. Respondent, Respondent Behavior*). Few responses, however, are either exclusively emitted or exclusively elicited. The probability of many emitted responses (e.g., a pigeon's pecks) may be raised by presenting certain stimuli (e.g., lights or spots on the pigeon's key), although the production of responses by these stimuli is not as reliable as in the reflex relation; and many elicited responses may occur in the absence of the typical eliciting stimulus (e.g., as in spontaneous salivation). Operant and respondent classes are therefore probably best regarded as extremes on a continuum along which the probability varies that a response will be produced by a stimulus. *See also Operant*.

Operant selection: the modification of operant behavior by its consequences (*see especially Diferential reinforcement* and *Shaping*). This type of selection was once called operant or instrumental conditioning. Those who work in this research area are sometimes called *behavior analysts* or *experimental analysts of behavior*.

Operant level: the baseline level of an operant, or the rate at which responses occur before they have been reinforced.

Operation: any experimental procedure or condition: e.g., presenting a stimulus, reinforcing a response, arranging a schedule, etc. The behavioral vocabulary often fails to provide separate terms for operations and for their behavioral consequences, processes. For example, 'a response was reinforced' may mean that the response produced a reinforcer or that the response increased in rate as a result of producing a reinforcer. The correct reading is ordinarily given by context. This dual usage is common to a number of fundamental terms: e.g., conditioning, extinction, punishment. In this glossary, the process definitions of such terms are usually indicated parenthetically. Ambiguity can be avoided by restricting the usage of such terms to operations and describing the consequences directly in terms of changes in responding (e.g., 'A response was reinforced and as a result its rate increased').

Optimizing: responding so as to produce the maximum possible reinforcers over some extended time period rather than from moment to moment, especially within concurrent or concurrent chain schedules. Contingencies can be designed under which optimizing requires a performance different from *matching, melioration* or *momentary maximizing*.

Orienting response: in operant behavior, a response that puts an organism in a position to emit other responses or that allows it to attend to a discriminative stimulus (*cf. Observing response*). In respondent behavior, a response elicited by the initial presentations of a stimulus (e.g., the first few times a bell is sounded or the first few times its sound is paired with food, a dog may prick up its ears and/or turn its head toward the bell: *cf. Conditioned reflex*).

Overall rate: *see Rate of responding.*

Overmatching: *see Matching law.*

Overshadowing: an attenuation of respondent conditioning with one stimulus caused by the presence of another stimulus. For example, if soft tone and loud bell together precede food, tone may remain ineffective as a CS even though it and bell have the same contingent relation to food. *Cf. Blocking.*

Overt behavior: behavior that is observed or observable, or that affects the organism's environment. *Cf. Covert behavior.*

P

Paced response; pacing: *see Differential reinforcement schedules.*

Pairing: *see Contiguity and cf. Contingency.*

Paradigm: a symbolic representation of relations. For example, a three-term contingency in which a response (R) produces a reinforcer (Rf) in the presence of a discriminative stimulus (S^D) might be written as: S^D:R$\rightarrow$Rf. The term *paradigm* is often incorrectly used as a synonym for procedure.

Parameter: a variable held constant while some other variable changes. When different values of a parameter are examined, the parameter distinguishes different functions within a family of functions. For example, a graph of avoidance behavior can show rate of avoidance responding either as a function of RS interval with SS interval as a parameter or as a function of SS interval with RS interval as a parameter.

Partial reinforcement: *see Intermittent reinforcement.*

Passive avoidance: a misnomer for punishment. To avoid passively is not to respond when responding has been punished. For example, a rat is placed on a platform above an electrified grid. Its failure to step down onto the grid has been called passive avoidance, in the sense that in doing so it is not shocked. But it may be misleading to define contingencies in terms of the absence of responses (cf. *Behavior*), and in this instance it is more appropriate to say that the stepping down is punished by shock.

Pause: a period of no responding not necessarily bounded by responses. *Cf. Interresponse time, Latency, Rate of responding.*

Pavlovian conditioning: *see Respondent conditioning.*

Peak force: *see Force of response.*

Peak procedure: omitting some proportion of the reinforcers arranged by an FI schedule and thereby allowing responding to continue for some time after the usual end of the interval. Response rate typically passes through some maximum and then decreases over time (the increasing and then decreasing rates are sometimes treated as the two sides of a temporal generalization gradient: cf. *Temporal discrimination*). The peak, the time at which response rate reaches its maximum, is one of several features of performance that can be measured in this procedure (e.g., variability of the peak over intervals).

Peak shift: *see Post-discrimination gradient.*

Percentage reinforcement: the omission of a fixed proportion of the reinforcers arranged by a schedule. For example, in an FR 100 schedule with 50% reinforcement, only half of the completed ratios end with a reinforcer. A stimulus (e.g., a brief tone) is often substituted for the omitted reinforcer; without a substituted stimulus, the above schedule is equivalent to a VR 200 schedule in which the constituent ratios are all multiples of 100 responses. *Cf. Higher order schedule.*

Percentile-reinforcement schedule: a schedule in which the eligibility of a response to produce a reinforcer depends on its location within a response distribution. For example, a schedule for long IRTs might reinforce any IRT in the top 25% of an IRT distribution taken over the last 100 responses. The schedule must specify both the percentile criterion for reinforcement and the source of the reference response distribution. Because its criteria for differential reinforcement are relative rather than absolute, it operates consistently over a range of changes in performance and therefore allows the automated shaping of response properties.

Performance: behavior, usually over an extended time period. Performance, a subject matter in itself, has often been treated instead as an index of something else (e.g., learning, motivational states). *Cf. Acquisition, Learning, Maintenance.*

Periodic reconditioning or reinforcement: a term, now rare, for FI reinforcement or, in some usages, FI and FR reinforcement.

Phenomenon (plural: phenomena): an event; something that happens.

Phylogenic constraints: limitations on learning or differential capacities for learning that depend on phylogenic selection, including properties of the behavior classes that can be established and limits on the contingencies that can modify behavior (e.g., it may be impossible to shape alternating as opposed to synchronized wing flapping in newly hatched birds). The terminology is not usually invoked when the limitations involve obvious anatomical features (e.g., hardly anyone expects rats to learn to fly). *See Taste aversion,* for an example, and *cf. Preparedness.*

Phylogeny: the development or evolutionary history of a species. *Cf. Ontogeny.*

Place learning versus response learning: *see Operant.*

Polydipsia: the schedule-induced enhancement of water intake. *See Adjunctive behavior.*

Polymorphous stimulus class: a probabilistic stimulus class in which each member includes a subset of exactly N of M distinguishing features (e.g., as when a stimulus is a member of a class by virtue of containing exactly 2 of 3 critical features). In such cases, any feature may also appear in stimuli that are outside the class.

Positive reinforcement: *see Reinforcement.*

Positive stimulus: *see Discriminative stimulus.*

Post-discrimination gradient: a gradient obtained after establishing a discrimination between a stimulus correlated with reinforcement and one correlated with extinction (occasionally, between two stimuli correlated with different reinforcement schedules), usually with both stimuli represented on the continuum along which the gradient is determined. It often includes a *peak shift,* a displacement of the point of maximum responding to one side of the reinforcement stimulus in a direction away from the extinction stimulus.

Postponement: *see Avoidance.*

Post-reinforcement pause: the period of no responding following a reinforcer, especially in an FR or an FI. In an FR, the pause may be measured as the time to some response other than the first (e.g., the fifth response in FR 100), because the first few responses are sometimes followed by more pausing before responding continues at the roughly constant rate that terminates with the next reinforcer.

Potency (of drug): *see Dose.*

Potentiation: an increase, produced by continued or repeated exposures, in the respondent behavior elicited by a stimulus (especially, an aversive stimulus). *Cf. Adaptation.*

Pre-aversive stimulus: a stimulus that reliably precedes an aversive stimulus and that thus may be a conditioned aversive stimulus. The presence of such a stimulus may reduce the responding maintained by positive reinforcers, an effect variously called *anxiety, conditioned emotional response (CER),* or *conditioned suppression.* In some contexts, the stimulus may increase responding, as when it is presented during avoidance responding or during positively reinforced responding after a history of avoidance responding. This effect has been called *conditioned acceleration* or *conditioned facilitation.*

Prediction: *see Control.*

Predictive stimulus: a discriminative stimulus. A stimulus predicts an event if the probability of the event given the stimulus is greater than that without the stimulus.

Preference: the probability of one of two or more alternative responses, derived from the relative frequencies of the responses over an extended sequence of choices. The term is not applicable to cases in which the different probabilities of each response can be attributed to the different schedules according to which each response produces its consequences. Preferences quantify the relative effectiveness of different consequences as reinforcers (*cf. Reinforcement*); when each response produces a different consequence, the organism is said to prefer the consequence produced by the response that is most probable. If different probabilities of two or more responses cannot be accounted for, as when they occur despite identical consequences and schedules for each response, the preference is sometimes called a *bias*. *Cf. Choice, Concurrent chain schedules, Concurrent operants*.

Premack principle: the relativity of reinforcers and punishers. *See Reinforcement*.

Preparedness: a capacity, presumably of phylogenic origin, to learn some response-stimulus or stimulus-stimulus contingencies more readily than others. For example, organisms may be predisposed to learn relations between tastes and gastrointestinal consequences but not those between lights or sounds and such consequences. *See Taste aversion*.

Primary reinforcer: a reinforcer the effectiveness of which does not depend on its contingent relation to another reinforcer. *Cf. Conditioned reinforcer*.

Priming: presenting a stimulus that occasions responding that continues after the stimulus is removed. Priming functions have also been attributed to responses (e.g., in the statement that FR responding is primed by the response that terminates the post-reinforcement pause), on the assumption that a response may produce proprioceptive stimuli that occasion continued responding.

Probabilistic stimulus class: a stimulus class in which each member contains some subset of features but none is common to all members. The number of features in the subset may vary from one class member to another (*cf. Polymorphous stimulus class*). Such classes, sometimes called *fuzzy sets*, do not have well-defined boundaries, though class members may have family resemblances. Examples include *natural concepts* and classes defined by reference to a *prototype*.

Probability: in experimental analyses, a proportion or relative frequency, either scheduled or derived from data. The probability of an event is given by the number of times it occurs divided by the opportunities for it (the number of occasions on which it is possible). For example, if a stimulus is presented on 50 occasions and on 40 of these a response occurs, response probability in the presence of that stimulus is 0.8 (40/50). Response probability can be measured with respect to its relative frequency in the presence of a stimulus (as in the above example), within successive short periods of time, or relative to other responses. *See also Conditional probability*.

Probe: a condition or stimulus introduced into a maintained performance to clarify the variables controlling it (*e.g.*, the extent to which an occasional brief stimulus correlated with reinforcement of an alternative response interrupts FR responding may be used to analyze the chaining of FR responses).

Procedure: An experimental arrangement or operation. *Cf. Paradigm*.

Process: the changes in behavior produced by an experimental operation. *See Operation*.

Processing: whatever goes on within an organism between the presentation of a stimulus and subsequent responding. *Cf. Cognitive processes*.

Productivity: the generation of novel behavior through the recombination and reorganization of existing response classes.

Programming: arranging experimental conditions such as reinforcement schedules. In some usages, *programming* is restricted to arranging progressive changes in conditions (as in shaping or the transfer of stimulus control through fading) and is therefore distinguished from *scheduling*, arranging maintained conditions.

Progressive schedule: a schedule in which requirements change in an orderly fashion with each reinforcer (e.g., in one progressive ratio schedule, the ratio increases by 5 responses after each reinforcer). The schedule may or may not include a provision for allowing the organism to reset the requirement to its initial value (e.g., by responding on a second operandum).

Proprioceptive stimulus: an interoceptive stimulus produced by the effects of movement on receptors in muscles, tendons or joints.

Prospective memory: *see Remembering*.

Prothetic stimuli: *see Stimulus continuum*.

Prototype: a typical member of a probabilistic class, described by a weighted average of all features of all members of the class. For example, feathers will be weighted more heavily than webbed feet among birds because more have feathers than have webbed feet. Thus, a robin is more prototypical than a duck because it shares more features with other birds than does a duck. *Cf. Probabilistic stimulus class.*

Pseudo-conditioning: the elicitation of responding by one stimulus as a result of its presentation in the same context as another, even though neither had been presented in a contingent relation to the other. *See Sensitization* for an example.

Pseudo-reflex: a discriminated operant; a relation between a discriminative stimulus and a response that, because of its superficial similarity to a reflex, may be confused with a respondent relation. For example, if a warning stimulus is always rapidly followed by an avoidance response, the avoidance response may appear to be elicited by the warning stimulus. This stimulus-response relation, however, is established and maintained through consequences and the terminology of operant behavior is required. *See Discriminated operant.*

Pseudo-trial: a time period corresponding to that of a trial but within which no trial stimuli are presented. Pseudo-trials are used to assess response probability in the absence of the trial stimuli over time periods corresponding to those of trials.

Psychophysics: an area of psychology that evolved out of the philosophical concern with the relation between the mind and the body. Psychophysics relates the behavioral properties of stimuli to their properties as defined in physical terms. Studies of *detection* or discrimination examine *absolute thresholds*, or minimum effective differences between stimuli along some continuum (*see also Signal detection analysis*). Studies of scaling relate the effects of changes in the properties of one stimulus to those of changes in the properties of another (e.g., if responding is controlled by the intensity of either an auditory or a visual stimulus, determining how much one must be increased to equal the effect of doubling the other).

Punisher: *see Punishment.*

Punishment: the response-produced presentation of positive punishers or termination of negative punishers (or, the decrement or suppression of responding that results from this operation). The terminology closely parallels that of reinforcement. *Punishers* are stimuli (e.g., shock), *punishment* is an operation (or process), and responses rather than organisms are said to be punished. The classic definition of punishers is indirect, in terms of reinforcers; a stimulus is a positive punisher if it has been shown to be a negative reinforcer, or a negative punisher if it has been shown to be a positive reinforcer. Such correspondences undoubtedly exist but are seldom confirmed experimentally. Shock may serve as a positive punisher or as a negative reinforcer depending on whether it is produced or terminated by a response; on the other hand, some shock levels or some comparisons of schedules of positive punishment and negative reinforcement may show one operation to be effective when the other is not. For this reason, punishers are best defined independently of reinforcers: a stimulus is a *positive punisher* if its presentation reduces the likelihood of responses that produce it, or a *negative punisher* if its removal reduces the likelihood of responses that terminate it. Like reinforcers, however, punishers may be defined independently of their behavioral consequences. The probabilities of two responses can be assessed by forcing the organism to choose between engaging in one or the other. If a more probable response (e.g., a lever press) produces a stimulus that forces the organism to engage in a less probable response (e.g., behavior elicited by shock), then the stimulus will punish the more probable response and is called a *positive punisher*. If a less probable response (e.g., lever pressing) terminates or postpones a stimulus that occasions a more probable response (e.g., eating), then the termination or postponement will punish the less probable response and the stimulus is called a *negative punisher*. These definitions parallel the definitions of reinforcers; punishers are equivalent except for the difference in sign. The definitions take into account the *relativity of punishers*, in that the effectiveness of a punisher depends on the response that is punished, and they define punishment directly rather than in terms of another process. *Cf. Aversive stimulus, reinforcement.*

Q

Quarter-life: *see Rate of responding.*

R

R, r: usually, response.

Radial maze: *see Maze.*

Random control: a procedure for presenting two stimuli randomly in time, as a baseline against which to compare the effects of stimulus-stimulus contingencies. The random presentations are usually arranged in the context of a sequence of pseudo-trials and therefore typically include incidental stimulus-stimulus contiguities as well as presentations of each stimulus alone.

Random-interval schedule: *see Interval schedule.*

Randomness: Variability generated by a process that produces successive events that are completely independent of one another, in the sense that none can be predicted from any of the others. Randomness is a property of a distribution of events (or the process that generates the distribution); no single event can be random.

Random-ratio schedule: *see Ratio schedule.*

Rate convergence: a rate dependency in which the changed response rates converge on some common value (e.g., as when a stimulus increases a low rate or decreases a high rate to the same intermediate rate).

Rate dependency: changes in the magnitude and perhaps direction of effect of a variable that depend on baseline response rate, especially in reference to drug effects (e.g., as when some drug dose increases low response rates but decreases high ones).

Rate of reinforcement: reinforcers per unit time; sometimes used in preference to reinforcement frequency because frequency occasionally refers not to reinforcers per unit time but rather to reinforcers per response, per session or per trial.

Rate of responding: responses per unit time. Several types have been distinguished: *overall* or *average rate,* determined over a substantial time such as an experimental session; *local, momentary* or *moment-to-moment* rate, determined over a short time, particularly when it is relatively constant throughout that time; *running* rate, roughly equivalent to local rate, but sometimes with the provision that it is determined over a time bounded by pauses; and *terminal rate,* determined over a short time just before a reinforcer, especially in an FI. Criteria for distinguishing segments of performance, such as the response sequence over which a running rate is determined, may be based on informal criteria such as visual inspection, but such limits can be defined more explicitly (e.g., a period of no responding may be treated as a pause only if it is more than 5 s long).

Other terms distinguish different changes in rate: *acceleration* or *positive acceleration* is a gradual increase in rate, appearing as concave-upward curvature on a cumulative record; *deceleration* or *negative acceleration* is a gradual decrease in rate, appearing as concave-downward curvature; cyclic changes are repeated increases and decreases, each completed over a roughly constant time period; and compensation is a low rate immediately following an unusually high rate, or a high rate immediately following an unusually low one. The acceleration typically produced by an FI schedule is often called a *scallop,* especially in reference to its appearance in a cumulative record. The term has been extended to accelerations produced by other schedules but is ordinarily restricted to periods of acceleration bounded by some event, such as a reinforcer. The curvature in an FI has been measured in terms of *quarter-life* (the time to complete one quarter of the responses within an interval) and *index of curvature* (a statistic based on the number of responses in successive fractions of an interval). Moment-to-moment changes in rate are often described in terms of *grain* (e.g., a relatively constant rate is said to have a finer grain than one that rapidly fluctuates), again especially in reference to the appearance of a cumulative record. *Cf. Cumulative record* and *Interresponse time.*

Ratio schedule: a schedule in which the last of a specified number of responses is reinforced. In a *fixed-ratio (FR)* schedule, the number is constant from one reinforcer to the next; performance is characterized by pauses after the reinforcer followed by a relatively high and constant response rate. In a *variable-ratio (VR)* schedule, the number of response varies from one reinforcer to the next; relative to FR schedules, the post-reinforcement pause is ordinarily reduced or eliminated. A VR schedule is usually identified in terms of the average ratio, the average responses per reinforcer. In the variety of VR schedule called *random ratio (RR)*, the ratio specifies the probability with which a response will be reinforced. For example, in RR 20 that probability is 0.05 (1/20) and is independent of the number of responses emitted since the last reinforcer. In some VR schedules, successive ratios are selected in irregular order from a set of ratios described by a mathematical progression, analogous to those used in VI schedules (*see Interval schedule*).

Ratio strain: the appearance of pauses in FR or VR responding at times other than after a reinforcer (*cf. Post-reinforcement pause*); a result of large ratio size and/or low reinforcement frequency.

Reaction time: usually equivalent to latency.

Recovery: return to an earlier level of responding after responding has been reduced by an operation such as extinction or punishment. This vocabulary does not distinguish between recovery during maintained conditions and recovery after the conditions have been discontinued. For example, *recovery during punishment* refers to a return of responding toward pre-punishment levels while punishment continues, whereas *recovery after punishment* refers to the return toward pre-punishment levels after punishment is discontinued.

Reflex: *see Unconditioned reflex, Conditioned reflex.*

Reflex reserve: a theory, formulated before the operant-respondent distinction was made explicit, stating that each reinforcer generates a reserve of responses depleted as responses are emitted and, to some extent, with time. The reserve was measured by an extinction ratio (responses in extinction divided by reinforced responses).

Reflexive relation or reflexivity: the identity relation. *See Equivalence class.*

Regression: the reappearance of previously extinguished behavior during the extinction of more recently reinforced behavior (sometimes referred to as *extinction-induced resurgence*).

Regular reinforcement: *see Continuous reinforcement.*

Rehearsal: *see Remembering.*

Reinforcer: *see Reinforcement.*

Reinforcement: the response-produced presentation of positive reinforcers or termination of negative reinforcers (or the increase or maintenance of responding resulting from this operation). *Reinforcers* are stimuli (e.g., food); *reinforcement* is an operation (e.g., the presentation of food) or a process. The operation is said to reinforce responses, not organisms (organisms are sometimes said to be *rewarded*, but this term often implies other effects of stimuli than reinforcing effects). In the classic definition of reinforcers, as stimuli that produce increments in responding (and, in some usages, as unconditioned stimuli in respondent conditioning), the apparent circularity of definition was resolved by observing that a stimulus that serves as reinforcer with one organism of a species or in one situation is ordinarily effective, given appropriate establishing operations, with other organisms of the species or in other situations. Thus, the definition states that a stimulus that has been effective as a reinforcer is likely to continue to be effective.

A stimulus is a *positive reinforcer* if its presentation increases the likelihood of responses that produce it, or a *negative reinforcer* if its removal increases the likelihood of responses that terminate or postpone it. The most important basis for distinguishing between positive and negative reinforcement is whether the reinforcer produces responses after the to-be-reinforced responding and therefore does not interfere with it, or before the to-be-reinforced responding and therefore does interfere (e.g., the reinforcement by heat of a rat's lever presses in the cold is more likely to be called negative reinforcement by removal of cold than positive reinforcement by presentation of heat because cold produces huddling, shivering or other behavior that may compete with lever pressing).

A formulation that defines reinforcers independently of their behavioral consequences states that the effectiveness of a stimulus as a reinforcer is based on the relative probabilities of the responses that it occasions and the responses to be reinforced. These probabilities can be assessed by allowing the organism to choose between engaging in one or the other and they can be altered by limiting the organism's opportunities to engage in one or the other response (*response deprivation: cf. Establishing operation*). If a less probable response (e.g., a lever press) produces a stimulus that occasions a more probable response (e.g., eating), then the stimulus will reinforce the less probable response and is called a *positive reinforcer*. If the organism is more likely to terminate or postpone a stimulus that produces one response (e.g., behavior elicited by shock) than to engage in some other response (e.g., a lever press), then the termination or postponement will reinforce the other response and the stimulus is called a *negative reinforcer*. These definitions take into account the *relativity of reinforcers*, in that the effectiveness of a reinforcer depends on the response that is reinforced. The reinforcement relation is reversible (e.g., if water deprivation makes drinking more probable than wheel running, the opportunity to drink will reinforce running, but if limited access to the wheel makes running more probable than drinking, the opportunity to run will reinforce drinking). *Cf. Operant, Punishment.*

Relational discrimination or learning: discrimination based on relational rather than absolute properties of stimuli (e.g., to the left of or to the right of, same or different, greater than or less than; *see also Matching-to-sample*).

Relative rate: the rate of one event (especially a response or a reinforcer) as a proportion of the summed rates of that and other events. For example, given the rate of A and that of B, the relative rate is A is usually calculated as A divided by the sum of A and B.

Relativity (of reinforcers): *see Reinforcement.*

Releaser: an ethological term for a stimulus that elicits a stereotyped pattern of behavior (*cf. Fixed action pattern*). Releasers are often USs provided by the behavior or the physical features of another organism. In some usages, releasers have some of the properties of discriminative stimuli that occasion operant behavior. The comparison is complicated because the functions of releasers are typically analyzed differently from those of CSs, USs, and discriminative stimuli. For example, releasers are usually presented for extended time periods and may vary during those times (particularly when they depend on the behavior of another organism), whereas CSs and USs are more often presented briefly, in discrete trials. An artificial releaser that is more likely to produce a fixed action pattern than its natural counterpart is called a *supernormal* stimulus. *Cf. Displacement activity, Respondent behavior, Vacuum activity.*

Remembering: a response occasioned by a stimulus that is no longer present, perhaps directly or perhaps through the mediation of some other behavior with respect to that stimulus (*cf. Mediating behavior*). The time between the stimulus and the later response is sometimes called a *delay* or *retention* interval. Much of the vocabulary of remembering originates in verbal memory experiments with humans, and remembering is often discussed in terms of a metaphor of storage and retrieval, where *storage* refers to what the organism does when the stimulus is presented and *retrieval* refers to what it does at the end of the retention interval. Retrieval is typically occasioned by a discriminative stimulus that sets the occasion for it (e.g., in delayed matching-to-sample, by presentation of the comparison stimuli). Behavior relevant to the stimulus that occurs between storage and retrieval has been called *rehearsal* (*cf. Delayed response, Mediating behavior*). Types of remembering include *short-term memory (STM)* and *long-term memory (LTM)*. Short-term memory is remembering based on a single presentation of items (therefore precluding rehearsal); it is of short duration (e.g., 10 to 20 s) and limited to roughly 5 to 9 items (historically, the span of immediate memory). Long-term memory occurs after rehearsal and/or multiple presentations of items and is therefore of unlimited duration and capacity. Remembering has also been classified in terms of what is remembered. Examples of such classes of remembering include: *procedural memory* (remembering operations or ways of doing things), often contrasted with *declarative memory* (remembering facts); *episodic memory* (remembering specific events in one's life); *semantic memory* (remembering one's language); *spatial memory* (remembering paths and things located on them); and *retrospective memory* (remembering past events), often contrasted with *prospective memory* (remembering things one has to do in the future).

Remote extinction: extinction of an earlier response in a chain when a later response is no longer reinforced.

Repeated acquisition: a procedure that examines acquisition as steady-state performance. For example, assume a monkey must emit a sequence of presses on four levers to produce a reinforcer and that the required sequence changes from one session to the next. After many sessions, the monkey has had sufficient contact with correction procedures, trial organization and other experimental details that all it has to learn within a session is the new sequence of presses. The repeated acquisition of new sequences may then be used as a baseline for studying how acquisition is affected by different variables (e.g., drugs). The consistent way the monkey comes to master each new sequence in steady-state performance is a higher-order class of behavior and may be called a *strategy*. *Cf. Learning set.*

Repertoire (also repertory): the behavior that an organism is capable of emitting, in the sense that the behavior exists at a nonzero operant level, has been shaped, or, if it has been extinguished, may be rapidly reinstated. The organism need not be engaging in the behavior for it to be in its repertoire. For example, a pigeon that has matched to sample is said to have matching-to-sample behavior in its repertoire even when not in the experimental chamber. A repertoire may be said to consist of a hierarchy, to the extent that some responses in it are more likely than others, and operant procedures may be said to modify the relative positions of different responses in this hierarchy.

Representation: a transformation of stimuli occurring either when an organism responds to them or later (e.g., in remembering). In some accounts they are copies, but it is implausible to assume that seeing involves making copies of the world or that organisms store them. In other accounts representations have arbitrary relations to stimuli, as when a visually presented letter is represented by its sound. Such representations are more like recipes than like copies. They usually have the dimensions of behavior and therefore can be readily incorporated into behavioral treatments. *Cf. Coding, Remembering.*

Resistance to change: *see Strength.*

Resistance to extinction: the responses emitted, the time elapsed, or the number of trials from the beginning of extinction to the point at which the performance has met some criterion (e.g., the number of responses emitted before 10 min have elapsed without a response). The measure used must be specified, because a given contingency or schedule may produce more resistance to extinction than another according to one measure but less according to a different one.

Respondent: a class of responses defined in terms of stimuli that reliably produce them. For example, salivation elicited by food in the mouth is a member of one respondent class; salivation elicited by a CS is a member of another. Spontaneous salivation, in the absence of identifiable stimuli, is not strictly a member of a respondent class, although it is sometimes loosely referred to as such. *Cf. Operant.*

Respondent behavior: behavior elicited by stimuli (*cf. Respondent, Unconditioned reflex, Conditioned reflex*). Respondent behavior was once considered primarily autonomic (e.g., responses of glands and smooth muscles), but the reflex relation defines respondent behavior regardless of the character of the response. Thus, skeletal responses may have respondent characteristics (*see Autoshaping; cf. Operant behavior*).

Respondent conditioning: the modification of respondent behavior by stimulus-stimulus contingencies, also referred to as *classical conditioning* or *Pavlovian conditioning. Cf Conditioned reflex.*

Respondent discrimination: classically, differential conditioning, respondent conditioning in which one stimulus is followed by the US but a second is not (e.g., food in the mouth follows bell but not tone). Discrimination has occurred when the CR is elicited by the first stimulus but not the second. The term does not refer to respondent conditioning in general, even though such conditioning entails discrimination between the presence and absence of stimuli.

Response: a unit of behavior, a discrete and usually recurring segment of behavior. *Cf. Operant, Respondent* and *Strength; see also specific properties: Duration of response, Force of response, Topography of response* and *Rate of responding.*

Response competition: the reduction of one response by the time and/or effort involved in concurrent responding. The terminology distinguishes reductions directly caused by concurrent responding from those caused by the reinforcers produced by concurrent responding. *Cf. Inhibition.*

Response cost: any property of responding or consequence of responding that may reduce or punish it. Examples include increases in response effort or force and response-contingent loss or reduction of reinforcers (especially, with humans, point loss superimposed on responding maintained by points; in such cases, however, the effectiveness of points as reinforcers is often assumed rather than confirmed experimentally).

Response deprivation: *see Establishing operation* and *Reinforcement.*

Response generalization: an alternative term for *induction.*

Response-independent reinforcer: the delivery of a reinforcer without reference to the organism's behavior. *See Time schedule.*

Response induction: *see Induction.*

Response rate: *see Rate of responding.*

Response strength: *see Strength.*

Resurgence: *see Regression.*

Retrieval: *see Remembering.*

Retrospective memory: *see Remembering.*

Reversible effects: changes in performances that are eliminated, either immediately or over some time period, when the operations that produced them are discontinued. For example, if responding returns to earlier levels after punishment is discontinued, the punishment effect is said to be reversible. Effects that are not completely eliminated are sometimes said to be partially reversible.

Reward: *see Reinforcement.*

Rf: reinforcement or reinforcer. *See Reinforcement.*

Rf/Op: reinforcers per opportunity. *See Interval schedule.*

RI: random interval. *See Interval schedule.*

RR: random ratio. *See Ratio schedule.*

R-S interval: response-shock interval. *See Avoidance.*

Rule-governed behavior: behavior controlled by verbal antecedents. *Cf. Contingency-governed behavior.*

Run: a sequence of responses, bounded by pauses or by some event (e.g., an FR run is the sequence of responses within a single ratio).

Running rate: *see Rate of responding.*

S

S, s: usually, stimulus; also, seconds.

S+, S^D ('S-dee'): positive or discriminative stimulus; **S−, S^Δ ('S-delta'):** negative stimulus. *See Discriminative stimulus.*

Sample-specific behavior: in matching-to-sample, differential responding to each sample stimulus, usually established experimentally to ensure sample-stimulus control. For example, pigeon matching-to-sample may be arranged with a fixed-duration sample after which a sample-key peck turns on the comparison stimuli only if some differential criterion for sample-key pecking is met (e.g., more than 5 pecks given a green sample or fewer than 4 given a red sample); the trial is terminated without comparison stimuli if sample-key responding does not meet the criterion. Although sample-specific responding may guarantee attention to the sample stimuli, it does not necessarily do so for the sample-comparison relation.

Sample stimulus: *see Matching-to-sample.*

Satiation: an establishing operation, the continued presentation or availability of a reinforcer, that reduces its effectiveness as a reinforcer (or, as a process, the reduction in effectiveness produced by this operation). Satiation may be arranged independently of responses, or in the course of reinforcement, while the reinforcer is produced by responses. One criterion for a satiation level with food reinforcers is prefeeding, presenting a fixed amount of food or a fixed duration of food availability before a session. *Cf. Deprivation.*

Scallop: *see Rate of responding.*

Schedule: a specification of the criteria by which responses become eligible to produce reinforcers. The term has also been extended to other operations (e.g., schedules of escape, avoidance or punishment). See specific cases: *Compound schedule, Differential-reinforcement schedule, Higher-order schedule, Interval schedule, Limited hold, Ratio schedule, Time schedule.*

Schedule control: *see Control.*

Schedule-induced behavior: *see Adjunctive behavior.*

Secondary reinforcer: *see Conditioned reinforcer.*

Second-order: *see Higher-order.*

Selection by consequences: operant selection or the ontogenic analog of phylogenic or Darwinian selection, expressed as an abbreviated form of *the selection of behavior by its consequences.* In a more general sense, all varieties of selection involve consequences (e.g., the evolution of the eye depends on the consequences of more finely differentiated seeing). Phylogenic selection operates on populations of organisms over evolutionary time whereas operant selection operates on populations of responses within the lifetime of an individual organism. In cultural selection, a third kind of selection, behavior that occurs within the members of a group is selected by the success with which it is passed from one individual to another (examples include imitated behavior and verbal behavior).,

Selective reinforcement: *see Differential reinforcement.*

Self-control: a term derived from the colloquial vocabulary that applies to cases in which a relatively immediate small reinforcer is deferred in favor of a later large reinforcer or in favor of avoiding a later large aversive event, or in which a relatively immediate small aversive event is accepted when the acceptance leads to a later large reinforcer or avoids a later large aversive event. Examples include deferring a small purchase to save for a large one, refusing a drink to avoid a hangover, exercising to perform well in a later athletic event, and undergoing preventive dental procedures. The opposite of self-control is called *impulsiveness* or *impulsivity.*

Self-reinforcement: a misnomer for an organism's delivery of a reinforcer to itself based on its own behavior. The implication of reinforcers arranged for organisms rather than responses is only part of the problem. In so-called self-reinforcement, the contingencies and establishing operations that affect the behavior that is purportedly reinforced cannot be separated from those that affect the behavior of self-reinforcing itself. But the organism that appears to self-reinforce must be able to discriminate behavior that qualifies for the reinforcer from behavior that does not. Thus, such behavior is more appropriately described as an example of the organism's discrimination of properties of its own behavior.

Sensitivity: in most behavioral usages, a measure of threshold, i.e., the organism's capacity to respond differentially to different stimuli or conditions. *Cf. Psychophysics.*

Sensitivity to contingencies: *see Higher-order class of behavior.*

Sensitization: the lowering of a threshold, as when prior delivery of an aversive stimulus lowers the intensity at which a noise elicits a startle response.

Sensory preconditioning: in respondent conditioning, a type of higher-order conditioning in which a contingent relation between two stimuli precedes making one of them a CS. Sensory preconditioning is said to have occurred if the other stimulus elicits the CR solely by virtue of its relation to the first stimulus. Preconditioning procedures have also been extended to operant cases. For example, correlating response-independent reinforcers with one stimulus that is later to signal reinforcement but not with a second that is later to signal extinction sometimes facilitates the subsequent establishment of an operant discrimination between the two stimuli.

Sensory superstition: *see Superstition.*

Sequential dependencies: conditional probabilities of successive events (e.g., given concurrent responses A and B, the probabilities of A followed by A, A followed by B, B followed by A, and B followed by B).

Set: loosely, a disposition to respond. The term may refer to stereotyped patterns of operant behavior (especially under stimulus control) or to effects of the conditional stimuli of a conditional discrimination. A common use of the term is provided by instructions at the start of an experiment, often said to produce in human subjects a set to attend to particular features of the subsequent experimental situation. *Cf. Attention, Conditional discrimination.*

Setup: in reinforcement schedules (especially interval schedules), an arrangement that makes a response eligible to produce a reinforcer.

Shaping: gradually modifying some property of responding (often but not necessarily topography) by differentially reinforcing successive approximations to an operant class that is to be established. Shaping is used to produce responses that, because of low operant levels and/or complexity, might not otherwise be emitted or might be emitted only after a considerable time. The variability of responses after one response has been reinforced usually provides an opportunity to reinforce a response that still more closely approximates the criteria that define the to-be-established operant class. Shaping is therefore a variety of operant selection. *Cf. Induction; see Fading* for another method of producing the initial response in an operant class.

Shock: a stimulus often used as an aversive stimulus. One method for delivering electric shock is through a grid floor, a series of parallel rods on which the organism stands and sufficiently spaced that feces or urine cannot short-circuit them. The electrical polarity of the rods is scrambled several times a second so that the organism cannot escape by standing only on rods with the same polarity. Level of shock is typically varied by changing current (milliamperes). The organism's resistance (or, for alternating current, impedance) is relatively constant over short time periods but may change with continued shock deliveries (*cf. Potentiation*). A further complication is that shock level may be altered by the organism's behavior (e.g., by changing contact with the shock source as, with rats, through either a furred or an unfurred area of the skin). Some shock sources include a provision for holding current constant when such changes occur.

Short-term memory (STM): *see Remembering.*

Side effect: any effect that accompanies the main effect with which an experimenter is concerned. The distinction is often arbitrary, because no stimulus has a single effect. For example, a researcher interested in extinction-induced aggression may regard the decrease in previously reinforced responding during extinction as a side effect, whereas another interested in operant extinction may regard the aggression as the side effect. *Cf. Multiple causation.*

Sidman avoidance: *see Avoidance.*

Sign-tracking: responding directed toward some feature of a stimulus correlated with reinforcement. *Cf. Feature-positive stimulus.*

Signal: roughly, a discriminative stimulus or an occasion-setting stimulus, i.e., a stimulus that sets the occasion on which some contingency operates or on which some other stimulus may be presented.

Signal detection analysis: an analysis of stimulus detectability in terms of the conditional probabilities of a response given the presentation of a signal in noise or of noise alone. A response to a signal in noise is called a *correct detection* or a *hit*, and a response to noise alone is called a *false alarm*; the absence of a response given a signal in noise is called a *miss*, and to noise alone is called a *correct rejection*. These measures change differently with changes in signal intensity than with changes in contingencies for responding or non-responding, and therefore allow the effects of stimulus variables on detectability to be separated from those of contingencies.

Signalled avoidance: *see Avoidance.*

Signalled delay of reinforcement: *see Delay of reinforcement.*

Signalled reinforcement: presenting a stimulus when a response becomes eligible to produce a reinforcer (e.g., as when, in a *signalled VI schedule* operating for a pigeon's pecks, the key is lit only when a setup is arranged at the end of an interval).

Simultaneous discrimination: a discrimination in which two or more discriminative stimuli are presented at the same time rather than successively (e.g., *see Jumping stand*) and which therefore involves two or more alternative responses. The locations of the stimuli are ordinarily at or close to those of the alternative responses (e.g., stimuli on each of two pigeon keys), and the organism is said to respond to one or the other stimulus. *Cf. Successive discrimination.*

Skinner box: a term not in current usage. *See Chamber.*

Spaced responding; spaced-response schedule: *see Differential-reinforcement schedules.*

Species-specific behavior: behavior observed in all or almost all members of a given species (of only one or of both sexes, and perhaps only over a limited time in each organism's life). In different usages, it may include: emitted behavior prior to its selection by consequences; unconditioned respondent behavior; stereotyped operant behavior, produced in a fairly consistent environment by primary reinforcers the effectiveness of which is specific to a species; and conditioned reflexes that depend on unconditioned reflexes specific to a species and that operate in a fairly consistent environment. See also specific examples: *Dis-*

placement activity, Fixed action pattern, Releaser, Vacuum activity.

Species-specific defense reaction (SSDR): avoidance or escape responding with a phylogenic origin. Such behavior presumably evolved because natural environments do not allow organisms to learn certain types of avoidance or escape responses. For example, a mouse that fails to avoid a predatory cat on its first encounter will probably never have another opportunity to do so.

Spontaneous recovery: in operant or respondent extinction, an increment in responding at the beginning of one experimental session of extinction, relative to the level of responding at the end of the preceding session. *Cf. Warm-up.*

Spurious chaining or reinforcement: *see Superstition.*

SSDR: *see Species-specific defense reaction.*

S-S interval: shock-shock interval. *See Avoidance.*

Stability: session-to-session variability in performance (the lower the variability, the more stable the performance). A performance that can shift from one to another of two or more steady-state baselines maintained by the same conditions is said to be *metastable. Cf. Steady-state.*

State-dependent learning: learning that is most likely to be demonstrated when the organism is in the same context as that in which the learning originally took place. The term is often reserved for learning under specific physiological conditions such as drug states. For example, an organism that has learned a discrimination while drunk may be more likely to perform accurately when again under the influence of alcohol than when sober.

Statistics: quantitative methods for summarizing data (descriptive statistics) or evaluating data (statistical inference). Descriptive statistics include measures of *central tendency* or average value (e.g., mean, median and mode); measures of *variability* or dispersion, or the spread of successive measures around an average value (e.g., range, standard deviation, variance); measures of *regression*, or the relation between two variables (e.g., the function best describing how two measures of responding vary together); and measures of *correlation*, or how well one variable predicts the value of another (e.g., the correlation coefficient, which is positive when two variables vary directly and negative when they vary inversely and the absolute value of which ranges from 1.0 when one variable is perfectly predicted by the other to zero when one variable is completely independent of changes in the other). *See also Distribution, Probability.*

Statistical inference estimates whether an experimental outcome is likely to have been produced by experimental operations or is better regarded as having occurred by chance. It ordinarily proceeds by comparing an experimental outcome with a theoretical distribution of possible outcomes (e.g., normal, chi-square, or, in analyses of variance, F) based on the assumption that the outcome depended on chance. If the comparison shows that the outcome was highly unlikely on this basis (e.g., probability less than 0.05), the outcome is said to be *statistically significant.* Statistical significance need not be related to substantive significance.

Steady state: performance maintained by a set of conditions after systematic session-to-session changes have become negligible with continued exposure to the conditions. For example, when the overall rate and pattern of responding within successive FIs does not vary systematically over sessions, the FI performance may be said to have reached a steady state. Steady-state performance is a preferred baseline for analyzing the effects of experimental variables (e.g., if a baseline is unstable, it might be impossible to assess where it would have been if the variable had not been introduced). The decision as to when a performance has reached a steady state necessarily depends on the criteria for stating that systematic changes have become negligible. Such criteria have ranged from informal observations to stringent quantitative assessments.

Stereotyped response: a response with properties (especially topography) that are relatively invariant over successive occurrences.

Stimulus (plural: stimuli): any physical event, combination of events, or relation among events. The vocabulary of stimuli classifies aspects of the environment in much the same way that the vocabulary of responses classifies aspects of behavior. The term refers to an instance of a class of events. Like responses, stimuli may be described in terms of physical properties or behavioral properties, and, again like responses, they may be defined in terms of descriptive classes or functional classes (*cf. Operant*). Differentiated usages in the vocabulary of stimuli are not as well established as those in the vocabulary of responses. The term may therefore refer to any of the following: specific instances of physical events (e.g., the sound of a bell), or combinations of events, sometimes also referred to as *compound stimuli* or *stimulus complexes* (e.g., feeder operations, with accompanying auditory and visual components), or the absence of events (e.g., a blackout as a stimulus), or a relation among events (e.g., the matching relation as a stimulus in a matching-to-sample problem); specific physical properties of events (e.g., green referred to as a stimulus even though it is only one of several properties of a light that has been presented); classes defined by physical properties (e.g., a stimulus class consisting of all lights within certain limits of intensity and wavelength, specifying the stimuli presented during an experiment); and classes defined in terms of behavioral functions (e.g., classes of effective discriminative stimuli or classes of stimuli effective as reinforcers or punishers).

When *stimulus* is used descriptively, the *continua* or dimensions along which stimuli vary (e.g., intensity, wavelength or frequency, spatial extent, duration) may be discussed in at least two distinct ways: a change in some stimulus property is said to produce a change in the stimulus, or it is said to change one stimulus to another. The usage is typically determined by convenience of exposition rather than convention (e.g., 'the light was changed from green to blue' is equivalent to 'the green light was replaced by blue').

When *stimulus* is used functionally, an event is not a stimulus unless it has been shown to exert control over behavior. In this sense, the definition becomes a behavioral problem: it depends on the limits within which different events or their properties can become effective in controlling behavior (*cf. Psychophysics*). Furthermore, functional classes can often be characterized verbally even though their limits cannot be specified adequately in physical terms (e.g., red stimuli do not necessarily include wavelengths in the red region of the spectrum; consider also smiles, frowns, and other facial expressions as stimuli). Thus, functional classes may be more fundamental than descriptive classes. To the extent that the scientific practices of the behavior analyst must be determined by behavior acting as a stimulus, this seems fitting. *See also Abstraction, Concept formation, Discrimination, Generalization.*

Stimulus continuum (Plural: continua): a stimulus dimension. Stimulus continua that vary along an intensive dimension (e.g., brightness, loudness) are called *prothetic*; those that vary along a non-intensive dimension (e.g., color, pitch) are called *metathetic*. *See also Stimulus.*

Stimulus control: the discriminative control of behavior (including control in respondent discrimination). *See Control, Discrimination, Generalization, Stimulus.*

Stimulus generalization: *see Generalization.*

Stimulus-sampling theory: a mathematical model of learning that deals with learning in terms of the probabilities with which different stimuli or stimulus properties come to control responding.

Stimulus shaping: *see Fading.*

Stimulus substitution: an account stating that when the CS in respondent conditioning elicits a CR it has become a substitute for the US. But a CR is not simply a UR now elicited by a new stimulus. One problem with this account is that CRs typically differ from URs in various ways (e.g., chemical composition may distinguish the salivation elicited by a CS from that elicited by a US).

STM: short-term memory. *See Remembering.*

Storage: *see Remembering.*

Strain: *see Ratio strain.*

Strategy: a higher-order discriminated operant characterized by relations among different stimuli, responses and/or consequences across trials and/or conditions rather than by specific stimulus or response properties within trials and/or conditions. Different strategies may be appropriate to different settings. For example, if the availability of reinforcers for a rat's lever presses alternates between two levers, a *win-shift lose-stay* strategy (change levers after each reinforcer) will be effective, but a *win-stay lose-shift* strategy will not.

Strength: as a property of behavior, the resistance of behavior to change (e.g., resistance to extinction, to disruption by added stimuli, and/or to effects of reinforcing alternative responses). The term has also been used, in place of specific measures, to describe the general state of a response or reflex, on the assumption that the different measures vary together and reflect an underlying disposition to respond. For example, if response latency decreases while magnitude, duration, and resistance to extinction increase, response strength is said to have increased. With operants, measures such as rate, latency, force, and duration have been used as indices of strength, but each is independently modifiable by differential reinforcement. For brevity without sacrificing generality, processes that might otherwise be described in terms of each of several different measures (especially rate, latency and probability of response) are often described simply as increments or decrements in responding.

Substitution: *see Stimulus substitution.*

Successive discrimination: a discrimination in which two or more discriminative stimuli are presented one at a time rather than simultaneously and which therefore usually involves only a single response (e.g., as in a multiple schedule). In the most accurate usage, the organism is said to respond *in the presence of* each stimulus, but this usage is often abbreviated to responding *in, during,* or *to* each. *Cf. Simultaneous discrimination.*

Supernormal stimulus: *see Releaser.*

Superstition: the modification or maintenance of behavior resulting from *accidental* (also *adventitious, incidental* or *spurious*) relations between responses and reinforcers, as opposed to those that are either explicitly or implicitly arranged (*cf. Contingency*). Classes of superstitions include: simple superstitions, in which responses are maintained, usually unstably, by reinforcers delivered independently of behavior; *topographical* superstitions, in which reinforcers produce and maintain a response topography that varies over a much narrower range than that specified by the limits of the operant class; *concurrent* superstitions, in which one response is maintained by reinforcers produced by a second response (but *cf. Collateral behavior, Mediating behavior*); and *sensory* superstitions, in which identical schedules of reinforcement in the presence of different stimuli produce different performances in the presence of each stimulus. Interpretations in terms of superstitious behavior must be drawn with caution, because it is inevitably variable either within or across organisms, and because performances that superficially appear to be superstitious can sometimes be shown to depend instead on subtle contingencies. Many human superstitions depend on rule-governed behavior rather than or in addition to accidental contingencies (e.g., to be superstitious about breaking mirrors, one does not need first to have seven years of bad luck after doing so).

Suppression: a reduction in responding directly or indirectly produced by an aversive stimulus (e.g., by punishment or by the presentation of a pre-aversive stimulus). The term is sometimes extended to any reduction of responding by a stimulus (e.g., an extinction stimulus), but such usages are not always accompanied by a demonstration that the stimulus in fact reduced responding as opposed to having simply failed to maintain responding. *Cf. Inhibition.*

Symbolic behavior: behavior the function of which has transferred from one stimulus to another by virtue of the membership of both stimuli in an *equivalence class.*

Symbolic matching: *see Matching-to-sample.*

Symmetrical relation or symmetry: *see Equivalence class.*

T

T, t: usually, time.

T^D ('T-dee'); T^Δ ('T-delta'): two variables in the T-tau system, a systemization of reinforcement schedules. They are, respectively, a time period during which the first response is reinforced with some probability and a time period during which no response is reinforced (or is reinforced with a lower probability). These time periods alternate regularly in repeating cycles, usually without correlated discriminative stimuli; the cycle duration, T, equals their sum. Various schedules can be generated by combining these and other system parameters (e.g., very short cycles produce RR schedules whereas long cycles produce schedules functionally equivalent to FI schedules).

Tandem (tand) schedule: a compound schedule in which the reinforcer depends on completing in succession the requirements of two or more component schedules all of which operate in the presence of a single stimulus. Thus, a tandem schedule is equivalent to a chained schedule without different stimuli correlated with each component.

Taste aversion: rejection of substances with a given taste after their ingestion has been followed some time later by gastrointestinal distress or nausea (e.g., as produced by X-irradiation). It might be interpreted as a variety of operant behavior (punishment of ingestion of substances with this taste) or as an instance of respondent conditioning (where gastrointestinal distress is the US and the taste becomes a CS). In either case, its special characteristic is the long delay (sometimes several hours) between the taste and its aftermath. The procedure is ineffective over such delays if other stimuli such as sounds or lights are substituted for taste. For this reason, taste aversion is often cited as an example of *preparedness* in learning.

Temporal conditioning: respondent conditioning in which a US is presented at regular intervals (e.g., every 10 min). Conditioning is said to have occurred when the CR tends to occur shortly before each US. In this case, the passage of time, as a stimulus property, comes to serve as a CS. *Cf. Superstition, Temporal discrimination.*

Temporal discrimination: discrimination based on temporal properties of stimuli (i.e., stimulus duration), often appealed to in accounts of spaced responding. For example, if a response at 10 s since the last response is more likely to be emitted than one at 5 s, the two durations may be said to be discriminated (*cf. Interresponse time*). When changes in contingencies alter response rate, the temporal spacing of responses necessarily changes also. Thus, it is preferable to study temporal discrimination directly, as by reinforcing one response after one stimulus duration and a second after another. Unique features of duration as a discriminable property of stimuli enter into temporal discrimination procedures: for example, a duration is not determined until time has passed and a discriminative response therefore cannot occur in its presence; and durations cannot be changed discontinuously in time, unlike other stimulus properties such as intensity.

Temporal integration: control of behavior by the distribution of events in time. Behavior may be affected by separate events extended over some time, and recent events may weigh more heavily than those further in the past. The way in which the events combine to affect current behavior is called temporal integration. When events are sufficiently removed in time that they no longer contribute, they are said to be beyond the organism's *time horizon.*

Terminal behavior: stereotyped behavior that reliably occurs late in interstimulus intervals in superstition procedures or temporal conditioning. It is usually related topographically to the behavior engendered by the reinforcer or the CS (e.g., with pigeons, pecking given food presentations). *Cf. Interim behavior* and *Superstition.*

Terminal link: *see Concurrent chain schedules.*

Terminal rate: *see Rate of responding.*

Three-term contingency: *see Contingency.*

Threshold: *see Force of response* or *Psychophysics.*

Time horizon: *see Temporal integration.*

Timeout (TO): a period of non-reinforcement arranged either by extinction in the presence of a stimulus or by removal of an opportunity to respond (e.g., with pigeons, which only rarely peck keys in darkness, by turning off all lights in the chamber). The term is occasionally extended to other cases (e.g., *timeout from avoidance,* during which no shocks are delivered) and is therefore more precisely specified as *timeout from positive reinforcement.*

Time schedule: a schedule of response-independent reinforcer deliveries. Barring this difference in contingencies, time schedules are classified like interval schedules. In *fixed-time (FT)* schedules, the time between reinforcers is constant (*cf. Temporal conditioning*); in *variable-time (VT)* schedules, it varies from one delivery to the next. A *random-time (RT)* schedule arranges a constant probability of reinforcer delivery at the end of recycling constant time periods. *Cf. Interval schedule.*

Timer: *see Clock.*

Timing behavior: *see Mediating behavior, Temporal discrimination.*

Titration schedule: a schedule in which one response changes a variable in one direction and either a second response or nonoccurrence of the first changes it in the opposite direction. For example, one response may increase stimulus intensity while another decreases it, or each response may produce an increment while each 5-s period of no responding produces a decrement.

TO: *see Timeout.*

Token reinforcer: a conditioned reinforcer (e.g., a coin) that the organism may accumulate and later exchange for other reinforcers.

Topographical drift: gradual changes over time in the topography of responses maintained by a superstition procedure.

Topographical tagging: the identification of different functional properties of responding by correlating each with a different topography, especially a different spatial location. For example, shock avoidance in rats often consists of moderate rates of lever pressing interrupted by occasional high-rate bursts after shock. If an escape lever is added, so that presses on the original lever continue to avoid shock but the rat can terminate shock once it is delivered only by pressing the escape lever, the high-rate bursts move to that lever. Thus, the moderate rates that continue on the original lever are tagged by their location as depending on the avoidance contingency whereas the high-rate bursts are tagged as depending on shock deliveries and the escape contingency.

Topography of response: spatial configuration or form (e.g., how an organism operates an operandum or moves from one place to another), sometimes also specifying location (e.g., the place on a key the pigeon's beak strikes). Topographies can be complex, and are therefore more often described verbally than quantitatively (e.g., specifying the limb with which a rat presses a lever).

Trace conditioning: respondent conditioning in which a brief presentation of the CS is followed, after some fixed, extended time period (according to general usage, no less than 5 s), by the US. *Cf. Temporal conditioning.*

Transfer: substituting one set of discriminative stimuli for another (or, as a process, maintaining at least partial stimulus control after such a substitution). For example, a discrimination based on size of circles might be changed to one based on size of squares. If initial performance with squares is more accurate than it would have been had the organism never performed with circles, stimulus control is said to have transferred; if the performance with squares equals that with circles, transfer is said to be complete. Transfer may be based on common properties of two sets of stimuli (e.g., size in the above example) or on similar correlations of the two sets of stimuli with differential contingencies. *Cf. Fading; see also Generalization, Transposition.*

Transitive relation or transitivity: *see Equivalence class.*

Transposition: in transfer experiments, a reversal of stimulus function depending on control by relations among stimuli on a continuum rather than by their absolute values. For example, a rat learns to choose the larger of two circles and the smaller circle is then replaced by a new one larger than either of the others. Transposition with respect to size is shown if the rat chooses the new larger circle rather than the circle, now smaller, it had previously chosen.

Trial: a discrete time period, usually stimulus-correlated, during which an organism has an opportunity to respond (sometimes restricted to cases in which a single response terminates the trial). Trials are separated by intertrial intervals that may consist of any of the following: a stimulus condition (e.g., blackout); removal of the operandum (or operanda); or removal of the organism from the chamber (especially when the organism, after emitting a response such as running an alley, is no longer in a position to respond again). Trials distinguish discrete-operant procedures from free-operant procedures. *Cf. Operant* and *Pseudo-trial.*

Two-factor theory: in general, any behavioral theory involving the interaction of operant and respondent processes; more specifically, an avoidance theory stating that avoidance responses are operants reinforced by termination of conditioned aversive stimuli established through a respondent process.

U

Unconditioned (or unconditional) reflex: a relation between a stimulus and a response that does not depend on prior conditioning. A reflex is the reliable production of response by a stimulus. The stimulus is an unconditioned stimulus (US) and the response an unconditioned response (UR). The stimulus is said to elicit the response. Examples of unconditioned reflexes are the salivary reflex (salivation elicited by food or acid in the mouth) and the patellar reflex (a knee jerk elicited by a blow on the patellar tendon). In each case, the elicitation of the response by the stimulus, not the response alone or the stimulus alone, defines the reflex. *Cf. Respondent.*

Unconditioned or unconditional response (UR) or stimulus (US): *see Unconditioned reflex.*

Undermatching: *see Matching law.*

UR: unconditioned response. *See Unconditioned reflex.*

US: unconditioned stimulus. *See Unconditioned reflex.*

V

Vacuum activity: an ethological term that refers to responding (*see Fixed action pattern*) that occurs in the absence of the stimulus (*see Releaser*) that ordinarily produces it. *Cf. Displacement activity.*

Value: with respect to stimuli, the effectiveness of a reinforcer (a punisher may be said to have negative value).

Variability: *see Statistics.* The variability of behavior is the raw material upon which selection operates. It is also a property of responding for which contingencies can be arranged, but no single response can have variability because variability can only be a property of a population of responses.

Variable-interval schedule: *see Interval schedule.*

Variable-ratio schedule: *see Ratio schedule.*

Variable-time schedule: *see Time schedule.*

VI: variable interval. *See Interval schedule.*

Vicarious learning: *see Observational learning.*

VR: variable ratio. *See Ratio schedule.*

VT: variable time. *See Time schedule.*

W

Warm-up: a low or zero response rate at the start of a session followed by an increase to the rate maintained later, especially in avoidance performances. In avoidance, the warm-up often can be eliminated by delivering several aversive stimuli just before the session. The opposite of warm-up, a relatively high rate that decreases to that maintained thereafter, is common early in sessions of positive reinforcement. The logical description, *cool-down*, has not been applied to it, perhaps because the change is in the same direction as that produced by satiation.

Warning stimulus: a stimulus that precedes an avoidable aversive stimulus. *See Avoidance.*

WGTA: Wisconsin General Testing Apparatus, an apparatus for studying primate simultaneous discriminations.

Wheel running: sometimes taken as an index of level of activity, especially in rats. The organism runs inside the wheel, which usually turns in only one direction to simplify recording of revolutions or distance run. Wheel running has a high baseline level and is relatively continuous compared to such discrete responses as lever presses.

Win-shift lose-stay (or win-stay lose-shift): *see Strategy.*

G44

Yoking: connecting chambers so that the performance of an organism in one determines the stimuli and/or schedules for an organism in the other (e.g., equating VR and VI reinforcement rates by letting the times between reinforcers in one organism's VR performance determine the intervals of another organism's VI schedule). In within-organism yoking, an experimental condition is yoked to some property of the organism's own performance in an earlier condition.

Conclusions from yoking must be cautiously drawn. For example, assume two types of rats equally distributed among groups in a yoking experiment on the role of avoidance in shock-induced ulcers. Sensitive types are prone to ulcers when shocked; they also respond rapidly at low shock levels receiving few shocks, but sporadically at higher levels receiving many shocks. Insensitive types are resistant to ulcers when shocked; they also respond slowly at low shock levels receiving many shocks, but rapidly at higher levels receiving few shocks. For each shock received by an avoidance rat, an unavoidable shock is delivered to its yoked partner. At low shock levels, only yoked rats develop ulcers (only insensitive avoidance rats respond slowly and receive frequent shock; they do not develop ulcers, but all their yoked partners also receive frequent shock and half of those are sensitive). At higher levels, more avoidance rats develop ulcers than their yoked partners (sensitive avoidance rats respond sporadically, thereby receiving frequent shock and developing ulcers; all their yoked partners also receive frequent shock but only half of those are sensitive and develop ulcers). Thus, a yoking experiment done at one shock level would yield a different conclusion about avoidance and shock-induced ulcers than one done at the other.

Appendix

Guidelines for Ethical Conduct in the Care and Use of Animals*
American Psychological Association

Psychology encompasses a broad range of areas of research and applied endeavors. Important parts of these endeavors are teaching and research on the behavior of nonhuman animals, which contribute to the understanding of basic principles underlying behavior and to advancing the welfare of both human and nonhuman animals. Clearly, psychologists should conduct their teaching and research in a manner consonant with relevant laws and regulations. In addition, the conscience of the individual psychologist critically contributes to establishing and implementing the humane use of animals. Ethical concerns mandate that psychologists should weigh the probable costs and benefits of prodecures involving animals.

The following Guidelines were developed by the American Psychological Association for use by psychologists working with non-human animals (vertebrates). They are based upon and are in conformity with Principle 10, 'Care and Use of Animals' of the *Ethical Principles of Psychologists* of APA:

An investigator of animal behavior strives to advance understanding of basic behavioral principles and/or to contribute to the improvement of human health and welfare. In seeking these ends, the in-

vestigator ensures the welfare of animals and treats them humanely. Laws and regulations notwithstanding, an animal's immediate protection depends upon the scientist's own conscience.

These Guidelines are incorporated by reference in the *Ethical Principles of Psychologists* of APA. Individuals publishing in APA journals shall attest to the fact that animal research was conducted in accordance with these Guidelines.

I. General

A. In the ordinary course of events, the acquisition, care, housing, use, and disposition of animals should be in compliance with relevant federal, state, local, and institutional laws and regulations and with international conventions to which the United States is a party. In accordance with Principle 3 (d) of the *Ethical Principles of Psychologists* of APA, when federal, state, provincial, organizational, or institutional laws, regulations, or practices are in conflict with Association Guidelines, psychologists should make known their commitment to Association Guidelines and, whenever possible, work toward resolution of the conflict.

B. Psychologists and students working with animals should be familiar with these Guidelines, which should be conspicuously posted in every laboratory, teaching facility, or other setting in which animals are maintained and used by psychologists and their students.

C. Violations of these Guidelines should be reported to the facility supervisor whose name is appended at the end of this document. If not resolved at the local level, allegations of violations of these Guidelines should be referred to the APA Committee on Ethics, which is empowered to impose sanctions. No psychologist should take action of any kind against individuals making, in good faith, a report of a violation of these Guidelines.

D. Individuals with questions concerning these Guidelines should consult with the Committee on Animal Research and Experimentation.

E. Psychologists are strongly encouraged to become familiar with the ethical principles of animal research. To facilitate this, the Committee on Animal Research and Experimentation will maintain a list of appropriate references.

II. Personnel

A. A supervisor, experienced in the care and use of laboratory animals, should closely monitor the health, comfort, and humane treatment of all animals within the particular facility.

B. Psychologists should ensure that personnel involved in their research with animals be familiar with these Guidelines.

C. It is the responsibility of the supervisor of the facility to ensure that records of the accession, utilization, and disposition of animals are maintained.

D. A veterinarian should be available for consultation regarding: housing, nutrition, animal-care procedures, health, and medical attention. The veterinarian should conduct inspections of the facility at least twice a year.

E. Psychologists should ensure that all individuals who use animals under their supervision receive explicit instruction in experimental methods and in the care, maintenance, and handling of the species being studied. Responsibilities and activities of all individuals dealing with animals should be consistent with their respective competencies, training, and experience in either the laboratory or the field setting.

F. It is the responsibility of the psychologist to ensure that appropriate records are kept of procedures with animals.

G. It is the responsibility of the psychologist to be cognizant of all federal, state, local, and institutional laws and regulations pertaining to the acquisition, care, use, and disposal of animals. Psychologists should also be fully familiar with the *NIH Guide for the Care and Use of Laboratory Animals.*

III. Facilities

A. The facilities housing animals should be designed to conform to specifications in the *NIH Guide for the Care and Use of Laboratory Animals.*

B. Psychologists are encouraged to work toward upgrading the facilities in which their animals are housed.

C. Procedures carried out on animals are to be reviewed by a local institutional animal care and use committee to ensure that the procedures are appropriate and humane. The committee should have representation from within the institution and from the local community. If no representative from the local community is willing to serve, there should be at least one representative on the committee from a non-science department. In the event that it is not possible to constitute an appropriate local institutional animal care and use committee, psychologists should submit their proposals to the corresponding committee of a cooperative institution.

IV. Acquisition of Animals

A. When appropriate, animals intended for use in the laboratory should be bred for that purpose.

B. Animals not bred in the psychologist's facility are to be acquired lawfully. The U.S. Department of Agriculture (USDA) may be consulted for information regarding suppliers.

C. Psychologists should make every effort to ensure that those responsible for transporting the animals to the facility provide adequate food, water, ventilation, and space, and impose no unnecessary stress upon the animals.

D. Animals taken from the wild should be trapped in a humane manner.

E. Endangered species or taxa should be utilized only with full attention to required permits and ethical concerns. Information can be obtained from the Office of Endangered Species, U.S. Department of the Interior, Fish and Wildlife Service, Washington, D.C., 20240. Similar caution should be used in work with threatened species or taxa.

V. Care and Housing of Animals

Responsibility for the conditions under which animals are kept, both within and outside of the context of active experimentation or teaching, rests jointly upon the psychologist and those individuals appointed by the institution to administer animal care. Animals should be provided with humane care and healthful conditions during their stay in the facility. Psychologists are encouraged to consider enriching the environments of their laboratory animals, where appropriate.

VI. Justification of the Research

A. Research should be undertaken with a clear scientific purpose. There should be a reasonable expectation that the research will a) increase knowledge of the processes underlying the evolution, development, maintenance, alteration, control, or biological significance of behavior, b) increase understanding of the species under study, or c) provide results that benefit the health or welfare of humans or other animals.

B. The scientific purpose of the research should be of sufficient potential significance as to outweigh any harm or distress to the animals used. In this regard, psychologists should act on the assumption that procedures that would produce pain in humans will also do so in other animals.

C. The psychologist should always consider the possibility of using alternatives to animals in research and should be familiar with the appropriate literature.

D. Research on animals may not be conducted until the protocol has been reviewed by the institutional animal care and use committee to ensure that the procedures are appropriate and humane.

E. The psychologist should monitor the research and the animals' welfare throughout the course of an investigation to ensure continued justification for the research.

VII. Experimental Design

Humane considerations should constitute one of the major sets of factors that enter into the design of research. Two particularly relevant considerations should be noted:

1. The species chosen for study should be well-suited to answer the question(s) posed. When the research paradigm permits a choice among species, the psychologist should employ that species which appears likely to suffer least.

2. The number of animals utilized in a study should be sufficient to provide a clear answer to the question(s) posed. Care should be exercised to use the minimum number of animals consistent with sound experimental design, especially where the procedures might cause pain or discomfort to the animals.

VIII. Experimental Procedures

Humane consideration for the well-being of the animal should be incorporated into the design and conduct of all procedures involving animals. *The conduct of all procedures is governed by Guideline VI.*

A. Procedures which involve no pain or distress to the animal, or in which the animal is anesthetized and insensitive to pain throughout the procedure and is euthanized before regaining consciousness, are generally acceptable.

B. Procedures involving more than momentary or slight pain not relieved by medication or other acceptable methods should be undertaken only when the objectives of the research cannot be achieved by other methods.

C. Procedures involving severe distress or pain that is not alleviated require strong justification. An animal observed to be in a state of severe distress or chronic pain that cannot be alleviated and that is not essential to the purposes of the research, should be euthanized immediately.

D. When aversive or appetitive procedures appear to be equivalent for the purposes of the research, then appetitive procedures should be used. When using aversive stimuli, psychologists should adjust the parameters of stimulation to levels that appear minimal, though compatible with the aims of the research. Psychologists are encouraged to test painful stimuli on themselves whenever reasonable. Whenever consistent with the goals of the research, consideration should be given to providing the animal with control of painful stimulation.

E. Procedures involving extensive food or water deprivation should be used only when minimal deprivation procedures are inappropriate to the design and purpose of the research.

F. Prolonged physical restraint should be used only if less stressful procedures are inadequate to the purposes of the study. Convenience to the psychologist is not a justification for prolonged restraint.

G. Procedures that entail extreme environmental conditions, such as high or low temperatures, high humidity, modified atmospheric pressure, etc. should be undertaken only with particularly strong justification.

H. Studies entailing experimentally-induced prey killing or intensive aggressive interactions among animals should be fully justified and conducted in a manner that minimizes the extent and duration of pain.

I. Procedures entailing the deliberate infliction of trauma should be restricted and used only with very strong justification. Whenever possible, without defeating the goals of the research, animals used in such research should be anesthetized.

J. Procedures involving the use of paralytic agents without reduction in pain sensation require particular prudence and humane concern. Utilization of muscle relaxants or paralytics alone during surgery, without general anesthesia, is unacceptable and shall not be used.

K. Surgical procedures, because of their intrusive nature, require close supervision and attention to humane considerations by the psychologist.

   1. All surgical procedures and anesthetization should be conducted under the direct supervision of a scientist who is competent in the use of the procedure.

   2. If the surgical procedure is likely to cause greater discomfort than that attending anesthetization, and unless there is specific justification for acting otherwise, animals should be maintained under anesthesia until the procedure is ended.

   3. Sound post-operative monitoring and care should be provided to minimize discomfort and to prevent infection and other untoward consequences of the procedure.

   4. As a general rule, animals should not be subjected to successive surgical procedures unless these are required by the nature of the research, the nature of the surgery, or for the well-being of the animal. However, there may be occasions when it is preferable to carry out more than one procedure on a few animals rather than to carry out a single procedure on many animals. For instance, there may be experimental protocols where it would be appropriate to carry out acute terminal surgical procedures on animals scheduled for euthanasia as part of another protocol rather than to utilize additional animals.

IX. Field Research

A. Psychologists conducting field research should disturb their populations as little as possible. Every effort should be made to minimize potential harmful effects of the study on the population and on other plant and animal species in the area.

B. Research conducted in populated areas should be done with respect for the property and privacy of the inhabitants of the area.

C. Particular justification is required for the study of endangered species. Such research should not be conducted unless all requisite permits are obtained.

X. Educational Use of Animals

A. For educational purposes, as for research purposes, consideration should always be given to the possibility of using non-animal alternatives. When animals are used solely for educational rather than research purposes, the consideration of possible benefits accruing from their use vs. the cost in terms of animal distress should take into account the fact that some procedures which can be justified for research purposes cannot be justified for educational purposes. Similarly, certain procedures, appropriate in advanced courses, may not be appropriate in introductory courses.

B. Classroom demonstrations involving animals should be used only when instructional objectives cannot effectively be achieved through the use of videotapes, films, or other alternatives. Careful consideration should be given to the question of whether the type of demonstration is warranted by the anticipated instructional gains.

C. Animals should be used for educational purposes only after review by a departmental committee or by the local institutional animal care and use committee.

D. Psychologists are encouraged to include instruction and discussion of the ethics and values of animal research in courses, both introductory and advanced, which involve or discuss the use of animals.

E. Student projects involving pain or distress to animals should be undertaken judiciously and only when the training objectives cannot be achieved in any other way.

F. Demonstrations of scientific knowledge in such contexts as exhibits, conferences, or seminars do not justify the use of painful procedures or surgical interventions. Audiovisual alternatives should be considered.

XI. Disposition of Animals

A. When the use of an animal is no longer required by an experimental protocol or procedure, alternatives to euthanasia should be considered.

1. Animals may be distributed to colleagues who can utilize them. Care should be taken that such an action does not expose the animal to excessive surgical or other invasive or painful procedures. The psychologist transferring animals should be assured that the proposed use by the recipient colleague has the approval of, or will be evaluated by, the appropriate institutional animal care and use committee and that humane treatment will be continued.

2. It may sometimes be feasible to return wild-trapped animals to the field. This should be done only when there is reasonable assurance that such release will not detrimentally affect the fauna and environment of the area and when the ability of the animal to survive in nature is not impaired. Unless conservation efforts dictate otherwise, release should normally occur within the same area from which animals were originally trapped. Animals reared in the laboratory generally should not be released because, in most cases, they cannot survive or they may survive but disrupt the natural ecology.

B. When euthanasia appears to be the appropriate alternative, either as a requirement of the research, or because it constitutes the most humane form of disposition of an animal at the conclusion of the research:

1. Euthanasia shall be accomplished in a humane manner, appropriate for the species, under anesthesia, or in such a way as to ensure immediate death, and in accordance with procedures approved by the institutional animal care and use committee.

2. No animal shall be discarded until its death is verified.

3. Disposal of euthanized animals should be accomplished in a manner that is in accord with all relevant legislation, consistent with health, environmental, and aesthetic concerns, and approved by the institutional animal care and use committee.

Index

1: Refers to Part 1; **2:** Refers to Part 2